Life's too short
for ordinary.
That's why we've
spent 25 years
finding, visiting and
choosing brilliant
places to stay.

For people who
love special.

First edition
Copyright © 2019 Alastair Sawday
Publishing Co. Ltd
Published in 2019
ISBN-13: 978-1-906136-81-9

Alastair Sawday Publishing Co. Ltd,
Merchants House, Wapping Road,
Bristol BS1 4RW, UK
Tel: +44 (0)117 204 7810
Email: info@sawdays.co.uk
Web: www.sawdays.co.uk

Series Editor Alastair Sawday
Editorial Patrick Henry, Agnès Perkin,
Nicky de Bouille
Coordinators Lillie Mitchell, Sarah Barratt
Writing Claire Baranowski, Becca Bill,
Jo Boissevain, Ann Cooke-Yarborough,
Nicola Crosse, Carmen McCormack,
Sue Nottingham, Honor Peters,
Annie Shillito, Wendy Ogden
Inspections Connie Barney, Peter and
Carolyn Bear, Lillian Bell, June Bibby,
Ann Cooke-Yarborough, Pippa Curtis,
Nicky de Bouille, Georgina Gabriel,
Diana Harris-Sawday, Patrick Henry,
Nicky Hilyer, Suzie Immediato,
Roslyn Innocent, Rosie Jackson,
Sarah Jones, Agnès Perkin,
Patricia Shears, Dana Silk,
Amanda Soden, Nikki Varney,
Helen Woods, Harriet Worthington
Thank you to those people who did an
inspection or two.

Marketing & PR
Emily Enright, Tessa Glover
+44 (0)117 204 7801
marketing@sawdays.co.uk

Production PagebyPage Co. Ltd.
Maps Maidenhead Cartographic Services
Printing Pureprint, Uckfield
Distribution Travel Alliance, Bath
dmcentee@morriscontentalliance.com

Cover: La Roche d'Esteil, page 300

France

Bed & Breakfast, Hotels, Châteaux

Hôtel Panache,
page 113

Contents

Manoir de la Malartrie, page 299

A word from Alastair Sawday

According to research 75% of French people holiday in – France! The question is not why they do so, but why wouldn't they? France is so big, so diverse, that you can wallow in mountains and lakes, cities rich in culture and beauty, miles of sandy beaches and sleepy shuttered towns amid lavender fields. You'll also find some of the best cycling routes in Europe and surprisingly clear roads for old-fashioned motoring. How lucky those French are, and how lucky we are to be so close.

Photo: Iris Thorsteinsdottir

This book is a first edition, bringing our special B&Bs and Hotels and Châteaux together in one glorious gathering. We sing the praises of the finest of mansions to the humblest of homes. We've visited every one of them and met the owners so we know you'll be looked after with huge generosity. You'll eat well too; table d'hôte is back so make sure you join in with this wonderful tradition. The markets in France are irresistible and almost every small town still has its own, mercifully intact. Each market day is a celebration of food from the region you are in – cheeses, meats, fresh vegetables – and more and more each year is organically produced.

'Wellbeing' is the buzz-word these days and we are urged to spend more time outdoors connecting with nature. From many of these special places you can wander through hushed forests, climb mountains and hills, swim in deep lakes, cycle along quiet poplar-lined roads and barely see another soul. But wellbeing comes from contact with other human beings too, and as technology takes over so the art of conversation will decline if we allow it. To sit with other guests in the owners' own beautiful surroundings, enjoying a happy, cultural exchange over a good meal with wine, is one of life's great riches. Whether you choose a grand château, a family-run hotel or a rural bed and breakfast we can almost guarantee your much-needed *bonnes vacances*. You will have learned, too, why the French holiday in their own beautiful country.

Alastair Sawday

How we choose our Special Places

It's simple. There are no rules, no boxes to tick. We choose places that we like and are fiercely subjective in our choices. We also recognise that one person's idea of special is not necessarily someone else's so there is a huge variety of places, and prices, in the book. Those who are familiar with our Special Places series know that we look for comfort, originality, authenticity, and reject the insincere, the anonymous and the banal. The way guests are treated comes as high on our list as the setting, the architecture, the atmosphere and the food.

INSPECTIONS
We visit every place in the guide to get a feel for how both house and owner tick. We don't take a clipboard and we don't have a list of what is acceptable and what is not. Instead, we chat for an hour or so with the owner and look round – closely (it involves bouncing on beds, looking at linen, testing taps). It's all very informal but it gives us an excellent idea of who would enjoy staying there and our aim is to match places and guests. If the visit happens to be the last of the day, we may stay the night. Once accepted, properties are re-inspected every three to four years so that we can keep things fresh and accurate.

FEEDBACK
In between inspections we rely on feedback from our army of readers, as well as from staff members who are encouraged to visit properties across the series. This feedback is invaluable to us and we always follow up on comments.

So do tell us whether your stay has been a joy or not, if the atmosphere was great or stuffy, the owners and staff cheery or bored. The accuracy of the book depends on what you, and our inspectors, tell us. A lot of the new entries in each edition are recommended by our readers, so keep

Château de Lerse, page 258

telling us about new places you've discovered too. Please email us on hello@sawdays.co.uk.

However, please do not tell us if the bedside light was broken, or the shower head was scummy. Tell the owner, immediately, and get them to do something about it. Most owners are more than happy to correct problems and will bend over backwards to help. Far better than bottling it up and then writing to us a week later!

SUBSCRIPTIONS

Owners pay to be part of Sawday's, but we only include places that we like and

DISCLAIMER

We make no claims to pure objectivity in choosing these places. They are here simply because we like them. Our opinions and tastes are ours alone and this book is a statement of them; we hope you will share them. We have done our utmost to get our facts right but apologise unreservedly for any mistakes that may have crept in.

You should know that we don't check such things as fire regulations, swimming pool security or any other laws with which owners of properties receiving paying guests should comply. This is the responsibility of the owners.

Talvern, page 177

find special for one reason or another, so it is never possible for anyone to buy their way onto these pages. Nor is it possible for an owner to write their own description. We will say if the bedrooms are small, or if a main road is near. We do our best to avoid misleading people and keep up our reputation for reliability.

Do remember that the information in this book is a snapshot in time and may have changed since we published it; do call ahead to avoid being disappointed. For many more photos, as well as special offers and our latest collections, visit www.sawdays.co.uk.

Using this book

FINDING THE RIGHT PLACE FOR YOU
All these places are special in one way or another. All have been visited and then written about honestly so that you can decide for yourselves which will suit you. Those of you who swear by Sawday's books trust our write-ups precisely because we don't have a blanket standard; we include places simply because we like them. But we all have different priorities, so do read the descriptions carefully and pick out the places where you will be comfortable. If something is particularly important to you then check when you book: a simple question or two can avoid misunderstandings.

MAPS
Each property is flagged with its entry number on the maps at the front. These maps are a great starting point for planning your trip, but please don't use them as anything other than a general guide – use a decent road map for real navigation. Most places will send you detailed instructions once you have booked your stay. If you are using a satnav make sure you have the right postcode.

SYMBOLS
Below each entry you will see some symbols; they are explained at the very back of the book. They are based on the information given to us by the owners. However, things do change: bikes may be under repair or a new pool may have been put in. Please use the symbols as a guide rather than an absolute statement of fact and double-check anything that is important to you – owners occasionally bend their own rules, so it's worth asking if you may take your child or dog even if they don't have the symbol.

Wheelchair access ☬ – Some of our owners are keen to accept wheelchair users and have made provision for them. However, this does not mean that

wheelchair users will always be met with a perfect landscape, nor does it indicate that they have been officially assessed

Manoir de la Fèvrerie, page 156

for such a status. You may encounter ramps, a shallow step, gravelled paths, alternative routes into some rooms, a bathroom (not a wet room), perhaps even a lift. In short, there may be the odd hindrance and we urge to call and make sure you will get what you need..

Limited mobility 🚶 – The limited mobility symbol shows those places where at least one bedroom and bathroom is accessible without using stairs. The symbol is designed to satisfy those who walk slowly, with difficulty, or with the aid of a stick. A wheelchair may be able to navigate some areas, but these places are not fully wheelchair friendly. If you use a chair for longer distances, but are not too bad over shorter distances, you'll probably be OK; again, please ring and ask. There may be a step or two, a bath or a shower with a tray in a cubicle, a good distance between the car park and your room, slippery flagstones or a tight turn.

Children 🧍 – The child symbol shows places which are happy to accept children of all ages. This does not mean that they will necessarily have cots, high chairs, etc. If an owner welcomes children but only those above a certain age, we have put in these details, too. These houses do not have the child symbol, but even these folk may accept your younger child if you are the only guests. Many who say no to children do so not because they don't like them but because they may have a steep stair, an unfenced pond or they find balancing the needs of mixed age groups too challenging.

Pets 🐕 – Our pet symbol shows places which are happy to accept pets. Do let the owners know that you'd like to bring your pet – particularly if it is not the usual dog! Be realistic about your pet – if it is nervous or excitable or doesn't like the company of other dogs, people, chickens, or children, then say so.

Owners' pets 🐈 – This symbol is given when the owners have their own pet on the premises. It may not be a cat! But it is there to warn you that you may be greeted by a dog, serenaded by a parrot, or indeed sat upon by a cat.

Château de la Ruche, page 218

Practical Matters

TYPES OF PLACES

Hotels can vary from huge, humming and slick to those with only a few rooms that are run by owners at their own pace. In some you may not get room service or have your bags carried in and out; in older buildings there may be no lifts. In smaller hotels there may be a fixed menu for dinner with very little choice, so if you have dishes that leave you cold, it's important to say so when you book your meal. If these things are important to you, then do check when you book. Some places have rooms in annexes or stables, barns or garden 'wings', some of which feel part of the house, some of which don't. If you have a strong preference for being in the throng or for being apart, check those details. Consider your surroundings, too: rambling châteaux may be cooler than you are used to; city places and working farms may be noisy at times; and that peacock or cockerel we mention may disturb you. Some owners give you a front door key so you may come and go as you please; others like to have the house empty between, say, 10am and 4pm. Remember that B&Bs are people's homes, not hotels.

Don't necessarily expect:
- a lock on your bedroom door
- gin and tonic at 2am
- your room cleaned, bed made and towels changed every day
- a private table at breakfast
- access to house and garden during the day
- an immediate response to your booking enquiry

ROOMS

Bedrooms – We tell you if a room is a single, double, twin/double (i.e. with zip and link beds), suite (a room with space for seating or two rooms sharing a bathroom), family room (a double bed + single beds), or triple (three single beds). If 'antique beds' sound seductively authentic, remember they are liable to be antique sizes too (190cm long, doubles 140cm wide); if in doubt, ask, or book a twin room (usually larger). Owners can often juggle beds or bedrooms, so talk to them about what you need before you book. It is rare to be given your own room key in a B&B and your room won't necessarily have a television.

Bathrooms – Most bedrooms in this book have an en suite bath or shower room; we only mention bathroom details when they do not. So, you may have a 'separate' bathroom (yours alone but not in your room) or a shared bathroom. Under certain entries we mention that two rooms share a bathroom and are 'let to same party only'. Please do not assume this means you must be a group of friends to apply; it simply means that if

La Maison d'Alice, page 298

you book one of these rooms you will not be sharing a bath with strangers. For simplicity we may refer to 'bath'. This doesn't necessarily mean it has no shower; it could mean a shower only. If these things are important, please check.

MEALS

Unless we say otherwise, breakfast is included. This will usually be a good continental breakfast – traditionally fresh baguette or pain de campagne with apricot jam and a bowl of coffee, but brioche, crêpes, croissants, and homemade cake may all be on offer too. Some owners are fairly unbending about breakfast times, others are happy just to wait until you want it, or even bring it to you in bed.

If you are staying in a B&B no meals should be expected apart from breakfast unless you have arranged them in advance. Many B&Bs offer their guests a table d'hôtes dinner – the same food for all and absolutely must be booked ahead. Some hotels serve lunch, most do Sunday lunch, the vast majority offer dinner. In some places you can content yourself with table d'hôte, in others you can feast on five courses. Some large hotels (and some posh private houses)

Auberge de Castel-Merle, page 301

will bring dinner to your room if you prefer, or let you eat in the garden by candlelight. Always ask for what you want and sometimes, magically, it happens.

PRICES AND MINIMUM STAYS
Most entries give a price PER ROOM with breakfast for two people. If this is not the case, we generally say so. The price range covers a one-night stay in the cheapest room in low season to the most expensive in high season. Some owners charge

more at certain times (during festivals, for example) and some charge less for stays of more than one or two nights. Some owners ask for a two-night minimum stay and we mention this where possible. Most small hotels do not accept one-night bookings at weekends and some owners ask for a two-night minimum stay always. Some places insist on three-night stays on bank holiday weekends.

The half-board price quoted is per person per night unless stated otherwise, and includes dinner, usually three courses. Mostly you're offered a table d'hôte menu.

Prices quoted are those given to us for 2019 onwards but are not guaranteed, so do double-check when booking.

Taxe de séjour is a small tax that local councils can levy on all paying visitors; it is rarely included in the quoted price and you may find your bill increased by €0.50–€2 per person per day to cover this.

PUBLIC HOLIDAYS
As well as the usual public holidays which we take in the UK, the French also celebrate on various other dates. It is likely that B&Bs and hotels will be booked up well in advance around these days, so do plan ahead if you are going to be travelling then.

1 May – Labour Day
8 May – Victory 1945 Day
Ascension Thursday and Whit Monday
14 July – Bastille Day
15 August – Assumption of the Blessed Virgin Mary
1 November – All Saints' Day
11 November – Armistice 1918 Day

BOOKING AND CANCELLATION
Do be clear about the room booked and the price for B&B, the stay and for meals. It is essential to book well ahead for July and August, and wise for other months. If you practise the last-minuting habit which seems to be spreading, you deprive

Chalet Colinn, page 379

yourself of choice and make life harder for your hosts. Owners may send you a booking form or contrat de location (tenancy contract) which must be filled in and returned, and commits both sides. Requests for deposits vary; some are non-refundable, some owners may charge you for the whole of the booked stay in advance.

Some cancellation policies are more stringent than others. It is also worth noting that some owners will take this deposit directly from your credit/debit card without contacting you to discuss it. So ask them to explain their cancellation policy clearly before booking so you understand exactly where you stand; it may well avoid a nasty surprise.

Remember that the UK is one hour behind France and people can be upset by telephone enquiries coming through late in their evening.

PAYMENT
Cash is usually the easiest way to pay. Virtually all ATMs in France take Visa and MasterCard. Some owners take credit cards but not all. If they do, we have given them the appropriate symbol. (Check that your particular card is

acceptable.) Euro travellers' cheques will usually be accepted; other currency cheques are unpopular because of commission charges.

TIPPING
B&B owners do not expect tips, but staff in a larger hotel might. If you've loved your stay at a particular place do leave a positive review on the website.

ARRIVALS AND DEPARTURES
If you're arriving at a B&B let the owners know roughly what time you will arrive (normally after 4pm), as most hosts like to welcome you personally. Be on time if you have booked dinner; if, despite best efforts, you are delayed, phone to give warning. In hotels housekeeping is usually done by 2pm, and your room will usually be available by mid-afternoon. Do try and agree an arrival time in advance or you may find nobody there.

CLOSED
When given in months this means the whole of the month(s). So, 'Closed: November–March' means from 1 November to 31 March.

Manoir de Kerledan,
page 180

General map

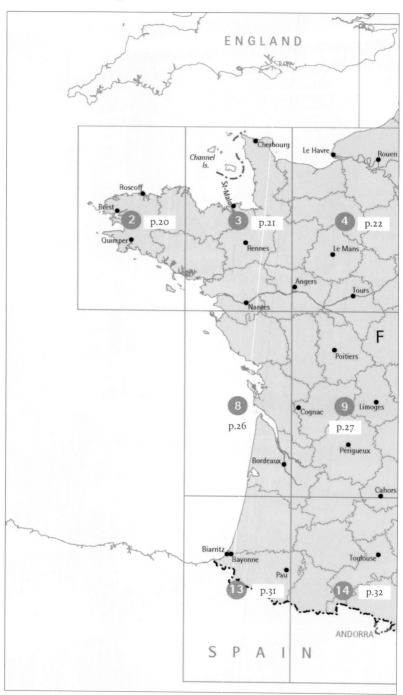

Toul Bleiz, page 181

Map 1

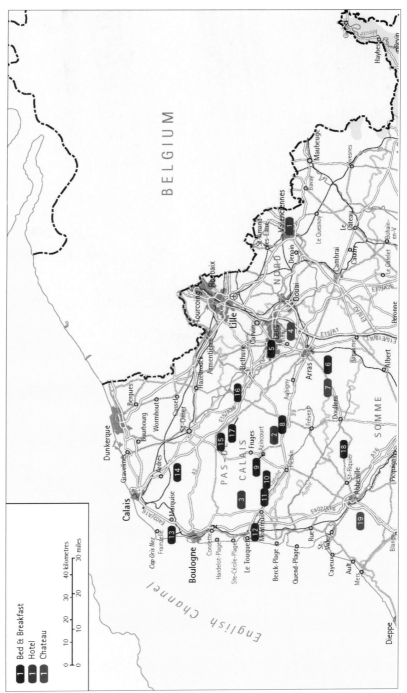

© Maidenhead Cartographic 2019

Map 2

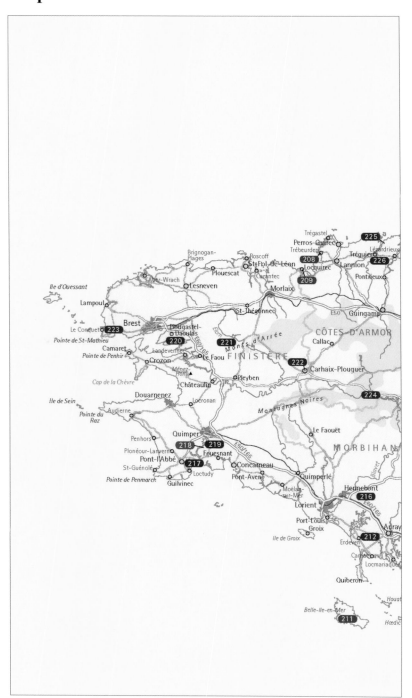

Map 3

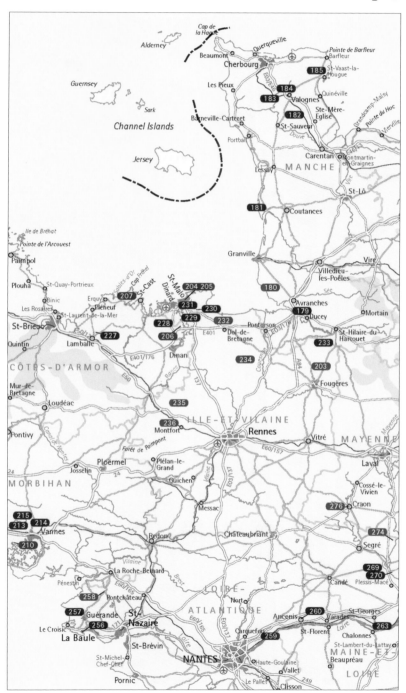

Map 4

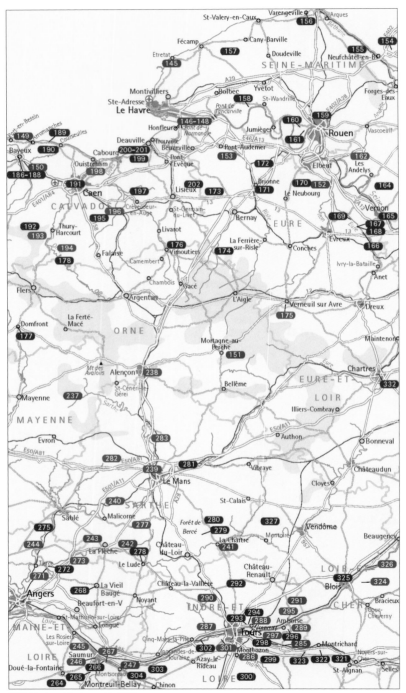

Map 5

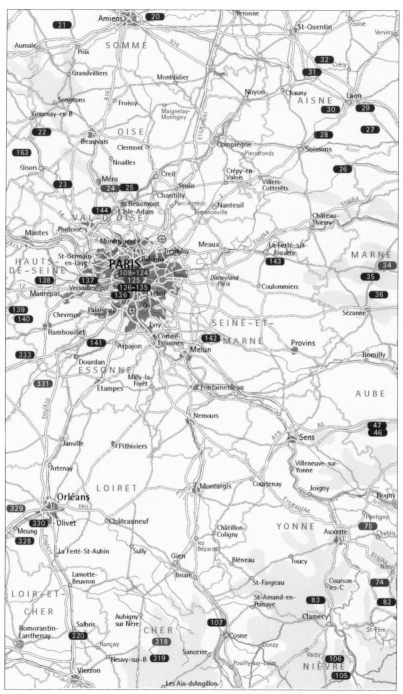

Map 6

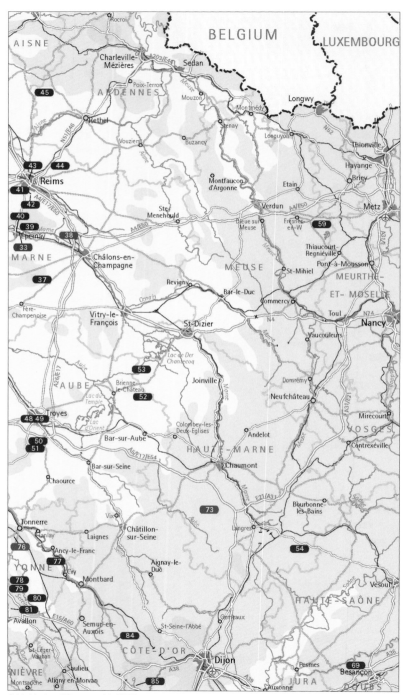

Map 7

© Maidenhead Cartographic 2019

Map 8

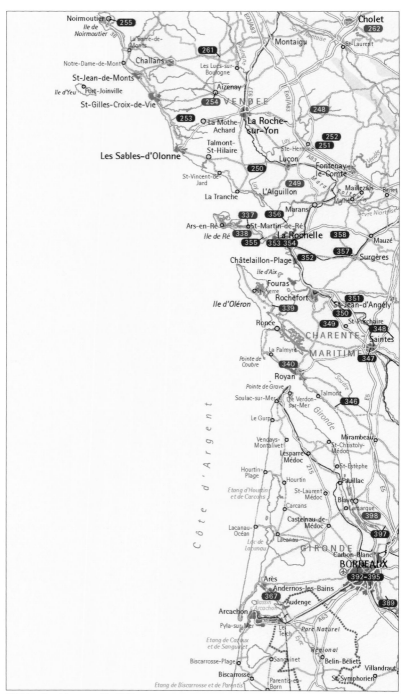

Map 9

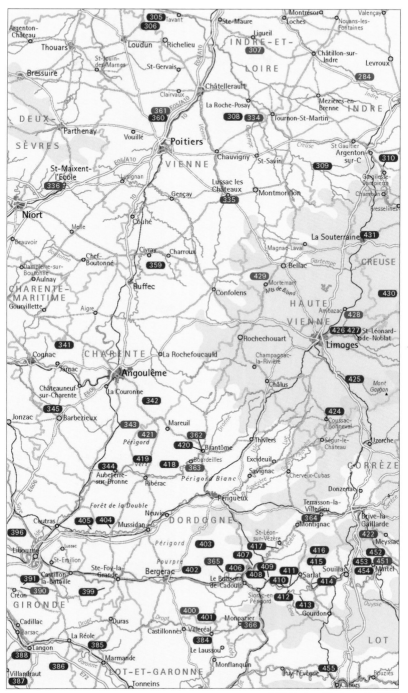

Map 10

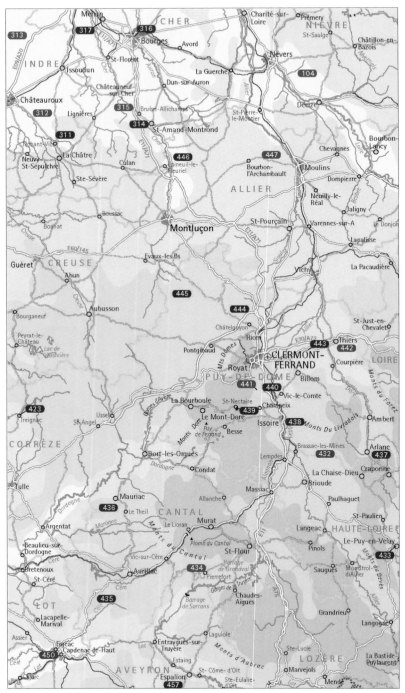

Map II

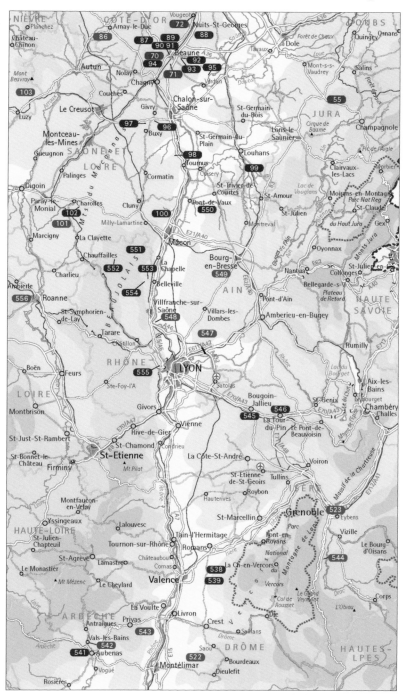

Map 12

Map 13

Map 14

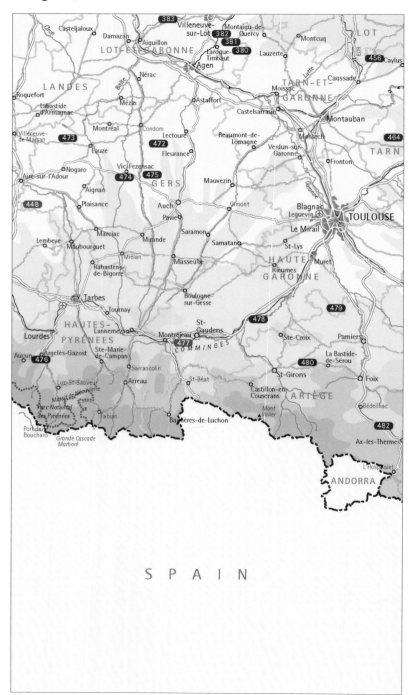

Map 15

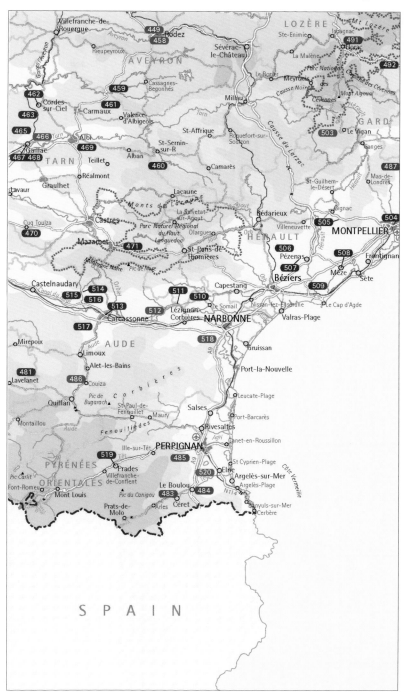

SPAIN

© Maidenhead Cartographic 2019

Map 16

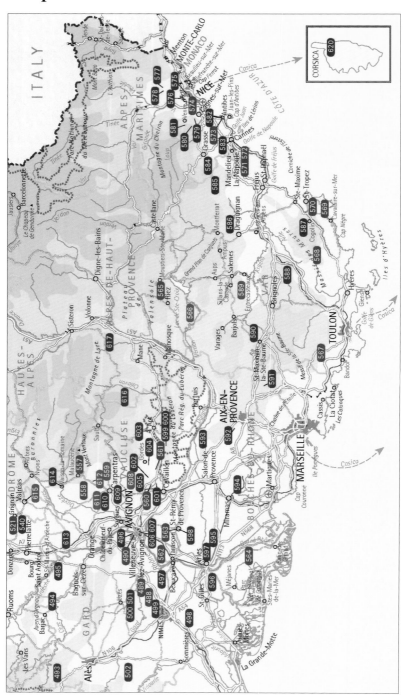

The North
Picardy

Auberge du Bon Fermier

Forget your stilettos, the cobbles in the flowered courtyard continue into the deeply attractive bar and restaurant of this 16th-century island in a rebuilt town. It is a maze of passageways, burnished beams and tiny staircases. A copper washbasin greets you at the top of the stairs leading to the rooms. Looking down from a glassed-in corridor, you can almost hear the clatter of hooves arriving in the courtyard, now a quiet terrace for afternoon tea and snacks; the passengers jostling between Paris and Brussels were probably delighted to be delayed at this bustling staging inn. Bedrooms are all differently quirky, one with tapestried curtains and walls, another with red bricks and wooden struts, some not too well lit, all with baths and bathrobes. There are two larger, lighter ground-floor rooms with post-modern lamps and tables. Downstairs, where a suit of armour guards a wooden reception dais, the evenings sparkle when the main restaurant is lit by candles. Monsieur Beine takes great trouble devising new menus with his chef and most diners would raise a glass in his direction.

Rooms	14 doubles: €98-€119.
	2 singles: €81-€99.
Meals	Breakfast €10.
	Lunch & dinner €26-€52.
Closed	Rarely.

Monsieur Beine	
Auberge du Bon Fermier,	
64 rue de Famars,	
59300 Valenciennes, Nord	

Tel	+33 (0)3 27 46 68 25
Email	beinethierry@hotmail.com
Web	www.bonfermier.com

La Cour de Rémi

Owner Sébastien cooks superb modern French dishes from scratch and the restaurant buzzes throughout the year – non-residents are welcome too. If you don't fancy getting out of bed in the morning, warm brioche and other good things can be delivered to your door. Walk or cycle (there are bikes to borrow) through 37 acres of green parkland, or get in the car for abbeys, châteaux, gardens, WWI sites. The coast is a 40-minute drive for blustery walks, wild swimming and seal spotting. Return to cool bedrooms and opulent bathrooms: one suite has a jacuzzi, another has two baths side by side. Aim to stay in the treehouse – wrapped round a sycamore, with a big decked balcony under the leaves – it's the business!

Rooms	6 doubles: €85-€100. 3 suites for 2: €140-€160. 1 treehouse for 2: €160.
Meals	Breakfast €12.50. Dinner €30. Wine €15-€100.
Closed	Christmas.

Tel	+33 (0)3 21 03 33 33
Email	sebastien@lacourderemi.com
Web	www.lacourderemi.com

Sébastien de la Borde
La Cour de Rémi,
1 rue Baillet,
62130 Bermicourt, Pas-de-Calais

ENTRY 2   MAP 1

Auberge d'Inxent

Sommelier in a restaurant in Lille, Jean-Marc won a Perrier contest on the luck of a draw. Off he tripped with his young wife and two children to a most emerald green valley and claimed a whitewashed, geranium-spilled, 18th-century country inn. Order a trout on the vine-covered terrace and back comes a live one in a bucket from their trout farm across the road by the river. Needless to say Jean-Marc's exceptional wine list and creative use of local produce should lead to a prolonged stay (the nearby ramparts of Montreuil sur Mer are well worth a visit). Inside: wonky beams and low ceilings, a battery of copper pans behind the old zinc counter, deep green walls in the smaller dining room (our favourite), and all the cosiness of a modest country kitchen with open fires on chilly days. Bedrooms are snug, smallish and beamy, furnished with repro cherrywood antiques and refreshed with modern leather and wicker; bathrooms are spacious and airy. This may not be grand-chic but it's an endearing address: an uncommon treat to find such good food combined with such perfect service.

Rooms	3 doubles, 2 twins: €79. Dinner, B&B €76-€114 p.p. Extra bed/sofabed €20 p.p. per night.
Meals	Breakfast €12. Lunch & dinner €25-€42.50. Restaurant closes same dates as auberge.
Closed	Christmas, New Year.

Laurence & Jean-Marc Six
Auberge d'Inxent,
318 rue de la Vallée de la Course,
62170 Inxent, Pas-de-Calais

Tel	+33 (0)3 21 90 71 19
Email	auberge.inxent@wanadoo.fr
Web	www.auberge-inxent.fr

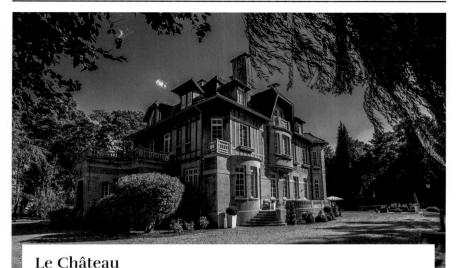

Le Château

This peaceful 'Manoir' is a harmonious home surrounded by parkland and field. Set in a small village, it was built in 1928 to replace a château destroyed in WWI; the Vimy War Memorial is close by. Light pours in through Art Deco windows and interiors have been enhanced by Madame's modern good taste. Sofas face a cosy log-burner in the monumental hall, bedrooms are immaculate (satin sheets, electric shutters, smart antiques). On the first floor you can step out onto a terrace and sit in the sun, enjoying the view over the park. Wake to wonderful breakfasts with plenty of choice at a table set with porcelain: charcuterie and cheese from local farms, yogurt, jam, homemade cake and juice, viennoiserie, freshly-baked bread, cereals and fruits. Light dinners are served on a tray in your bedroom or sometimes in the hall in front of the fire – or it's just a five-minute drive to a restaurant. Charming hosts offer bikes and umbrellas; Arras with its famous Grand Place is 15 minutes' drive; historic, lively Lille, with its clutch of botanical gardens to roam, is half an hour. It's a luxurious stopover en route to Calais too. *Parking on-site. Children over 10 welcome.*

Rooms	2 doubles: €125-€149. 1 suite for 2: €139-€159.
Meals	Dinner, 3 courses with apéritif, €28, by arrangement. Restaurants 10km.
Closed	15-28 August.

Mobile	+33 (0)6 22 19 87 25	**Jannick Blavier**
Email	lechateau62580@gmail.com	Le Château,
Web	www.lechateau-fresnoy-en-gohelle.com	9 rue du Puits,
		62580 Fresnoy en Gohelle, Pas-de-Calais

ENTRY 4 MAP 1

Ferme du Moulin

Terraced houses in front, a perfect little farmyard behind, the most welcoming of hosts within – sweet Agnès greets you with impeccable manners and old-fashioned hospitality – she's delighted to sit and chat in her homely kitchen. Your home town is marked with a pin on her map of Britain alongside her other treasured guests from across the Channel. The modest, authentically timeworn house is stuffed with much-loved collections and her genuine chambres d'hôtes – a threatened species – are family-furnished, floral-papered, draped with all sorts and conditions of crochet; the loo is across the landing. Breakfasts are good, too. Quiet, restful stays can be spent strolling into lovely, laid-back Liévin, close to the coast, war cemeteries and battlefields. Louvre-Lens Museum is a mere kilometre away, with art borrowed from the Paris collection.

Le Manoir de Bellacordelle

A grand arch leads to a traditional little manor house, so the salon and dining room are unexpected – a lively zebra painting, saffron yellow and black velvet seats, leopard print fabrics. It's vibrant but still hugely comfortable, with Dorothée your helpful host (husband Xavier, teenage son, two gentle dogs and a cat complete the family). Two serene rooms lie up a hidden staircase under the sloping roof, in soft greys and touches of pink. The suite in a separate wing is great for families. It's all perfectly placed for the Louvre-Lens or WWI sites on the Somme. Arras is even closer, 20 minutes away for meals out. *One hour exclusive spa time for every night booked. Parking on-site.*

Rooms	1 double, 1 triple both with separate bath or shower, sharing wc: €48-€58.		**Rooms**	2 doubles: €120. 1 suite for 4: €140. Extra bed €20 per night.
Meals	Restaurants 500m.		**Meals**	Restaurants 10km.
Closed	Rarely.		**Closed**	Rarely.

Tel	+33 (0)3 21 44 65 91		**Tel**	+33 (0)6 47 75 24 37
Mobile	+33 (0)6 81 04 46 96		**Email**	d.hego@orange.fr
			Web	www.bellacordelle.fr

Madame Agnès Dupont
Ferme du Moulin,
58 rue du Quatre Septembre, 62800 Liévin,
Pas-de-Calais

Dorothée Hego
Le Manoir de Bellacordelle,
19 rue de Bellacordelle, 62173 Rivière,
Pas-de-Calais

ENTRY 5   MAP 1

ENTRY 6   MAP 1

Château de Saulty

The re-lifted stately face looks finer than ever in its great park and apple orchards (15 varieties); it is a truly lovely setting. Inside, a warm, embracing country house with a panelled breakfast room, an amazing, museum-worthy, multi-tiled gents' cloakroom and, up the wide old stairs, quietly luxurious bedrooms, some huge, furnished with printed fabrics and period pieces. Be charmed by wooden floors and plain walls in sunny tones, perhaps an old fireplace or a mirrored armoire. Quiet and intelligent, Sylvie is a natural at making guests feel at home.

Le Loubarré

The period of each piece shows on its face, so you expect the elegantly coffered ceilings, the deeply carved woodwork, the vast Louis XIII dresser... but nothing prepares you for the neo-gothic stone fireplace! The rooms in the stables, some up, some down, are pretty and spotless, each with good fabrics, some antiques, a neat shower room, and you can use the comfortable family sitting room. Madame loves telling tales of the house and its contents, and has two dogs, a few goats and four donkeys; be aware there's a weekend car-racing track in the valley, though. Both your hosts work constantly on their beloved house.

Rooms	1 double: €75. 2 triples: €85. 1 family room for 4: €100. Singles €65.
Meals	Restaurants 16km.
Closed	January.

Rooms	1 double, 2 twins: €62.
Meals	Guest kitchen. Restaurants within walking distance.
Closed	Rarely.

Tel	+33 (0)3 21 48 24 76
Email	chateaudesaulty@nordnet.fr
Web	www.chateaudesaulty.com

Emmanuel & Sylvie Dalle
Château de Saulty,
82 rue de la Gare, 62158 Saulty,
Pas-de-Calais

Tel	+33 (0)3 21 03 05 05
Email	mcvion.loubarre@wanadoo.fr
Web	www.loubarre.com

Marie-Christine & Philippe Vion
Le Loubarré,
550 rue des Montifaux, 62130 Gauchin
Verloingt, Pas-de-Calais

La Gacogne

Enter a 1750 arched orangery (the tower) filled with a very long table, an open fire and 101 curiosities. Alongside teddies are chain-mail bodices, longbows, crossbows and similar armoured reminders of nearby Agincourt (Azincourt). It is a treat to be received in this most colourful and eccentric of parlours for hearty continental breakfasts (the seed cake is delicious!), hosted by motherly Marie-José and knightly Patrick who've lived here for years. Small bedrooms in the outbuilding are farmhouse simple with heavy-draped medieval touches, a lush garden melts into a conifer copse and your hosts are utterly charming.

Un Matin dans les Bois

He bakes delicious brioche, she adores birds and will take you to the marches, there are cats, dogs, ducks and plans for horses, and four-year-old Archie to make friends with. The house, concealed in woods with rolling hill views, dates from the 15th century. Bedrooms, scattered between barn, stables and pigeonnier, are inspired, one with a wall of glass, another with a bedhead of silver birch trunks; beds are big, deep, sumptuous. There's a restaurant to walk to and a guest kitchen in a rustic-chic extension. Swing in the tree chairs, swim a lap in the pool, wander the woods with a lantern from your room. Magical! *Minimum stay: 2 nights in high season.*

Rooms	2 doubles: €80.	**Rooms**	3 doubles: €148.
	1 family room for 3: €90.		1 suite for 4: €180-€230.
Meals	Restaurant 1km.		Singles €120.
Closed	1 November – 31 March.	**Meals**	Restaurants 3km. Guest kitchen.
		Closed	Rarely.

Tel	+33 (0)3 21 04 45 61	**Tel**	+33 (0)6 52 89 55 56
Email	fenetgeoffroy@aol.com	**Email**	info@unmatindanslesbois.com
Web	www.gacogne.com	**Web**	www.unmatindanslesbois.com

Patrick & Marie-José Fenet
La Gacogne,
62310 Azincourt, Pas-de-Calais

M & Madame Dubrulle
Un Matin dans les Bois,
100 Impasse le Fresnoy, 62990 Loison sur créquoise, Pas-de-Calais

ENTRY 9   MAP 1   ENTRY 10   MAP 1

Ferme du Saule

Guests have called Le Saule 'a little treasure'. And we know that the Trunnets' smiles are genuine, their converted outbuilding handsome and perfectly finished (down to mosquito nets on windows), the ground-floor rooms solidly traditional, the beds excellent, the dayroom proud of its beautiful armoire, and you get your own little table for breakfast. Monsieur and his son are only too happy to show you the flax production process (it's fascinating); young Madame looks after her three little ones and cares beautifully for guests. Proclaimed "the best cowshed I've ever stayed in" by one happy visitor.

Le Pré Rainette

Relax with beautiful colours around you – turquoise, striking purples, soft Egyptian reds – and admire the abundance of old wood found in brocantes and used throughout to soften the interiors. 'Violette' is a perfect family room or spacious for a couple; 'Hortense' and 'Lilas' share a super modern shower room; 'La Petite Maison' has huge windows overlooking a small lake. Anne-Marie and Christophe, intelligent, helpful hosts, built the long red-roofed house in 2003, and named it 'tree frog prairie' after the quietly croaking wildlife. Have a go at rowing, use the pool, borrow bikes, or use the beach hut at Le Touquet – bliss.

Rooms 2 doubles: €62. 1 suite for 4: €90-€105. 2 family rooms for 3: €75. Tourist tax €0.70 p.p. per night. Extra bed/sofabed €15 p.p. per night. Singles €50.	**Rooms** 1 suite for 2, 1 suite for 4: €120-€210. 1 apartment for 4: €150-€250.
Meals Restaurants 6km.	**Meals** Restaurants 3km.
Closed Rarely.	**Closed** 11 November – 15 March (open Christmas & New Year).

Tel +33 (0)3 21 06 01 28
Email atrunnet@gmail.com
Web www.ferme-du-saule.com

Trunnet Family
Ferme du Saule,
20 rue de l'Église, 62170 Brimeux,
Pas-de-Calais

Mobile +33 (0)6 48 18 90 83
Email prerainette@hotmail.fr
Web www.prerainette.com

Anne-Marie de Gastines
Le Pré Rainette,
1515 Grande Rue, 62170 Sorrus,
Pas-de-Calais

ENTRY 11 MAP 1

ENTRY 12 MAP 1

La Villa Sainte Claire

Friendly Catherine lends you bikes – so pedal off to Wimereux, a sweet seaside town a mile down the road. Then return to this 18th-century house in the lee of a village church, its long elegant façade distinguished by perfectly beshuttered tall white windows. The bedrooms are fresh, spacious and uncluttered, with views to the beautiful front garden; it's a treat to stroll the rambling grounds, dotted with statues, punctuated by topiary. Wake to fresh local croissants and homemade jams; set off for the markets and shops of Boulogne... and a lovely lunch in the historic old town. The coastline is wild and wonderful.

Le Manoir

The trompe l'œil and frescoed friezes are lavish, from the dining-room panelling to the staircase 'marble'. Although it's known in the village as "Le Château" it's not really big but, with the original details intact, it is a historian's delight. All four bedrooms (one a two-room family suite, another an elegant tribute to Africa) have been beautifully refurbished, combining fine antiques with modern fabrics. It has a soft, embracing atmosphere, excellent bathrooms and soothing garden views to box parterre and trees. Welcoming Sylvie and Pierre offer delicious table-d'hôtes dinner, and a living room just for guests.

Rooms	2 doubles: €98. Extra bed/sofabed €15-€25 p.p. per night. Additional room available for 2 children. Cot available.	**Rooms**	3 doubles: €80-€140. 1 suite for 4: €110.
Meals	Restaurant 50m.	**Meals**	Dinner with wine, €28-€40.
Closed	15 December – 31 January.	**Closed**	Rarely.

Tel	+33 (0)3 21 91 99 58	**Tel**	+33 (0)3 21 82 69 05
Email	contact@villa-sainte-claire.fr	**Email**	pierre.breemersch@wanadoo.fr
Web	www.villa-sainte-claire.fr	**Web**	www.lemanoirdebonningues.com

Catherine Debatte
La Villa Sainte Claire,
11 rue du Presbytère, 62126 Wimille,
Pas-de-Calais

Sylvie & Pierre Bréemersch
Le Manoir,
40 rue de Licques, 62890 Bonningues lès
Ardres, Pas-de-Calais

ENTRY 13 MAP 1

ENTRY 14 MAP 1

Les Dornes

Table d'hôtes round the convivial table is the
inspiration behind this B&B – which, this
couple do so well, being perfectionists.
Dinner, locally sourced, sounds delicious,
while vegetables come from an immaculate
potager. The interiors of their new but
traditional village house are equally
manicured: the L-shaped living room; the
bedrooms, colour-themed and French-cosy,
two on the ground floor, their tiles topped by
rugs, two under the eaves with honey-
coloured boards; all large and super-
comfortable. Historic St Omer is a must –
for music and markets, bric-a-brac and
breweries. Tremendous value.

Le Château de Philiomel

Unwind on a 15-acre estate – the owners
live next door – in immaculate solitude.
Overlooking parkland and lake, this
commanding Italianate mansion has the
right ingredients (pillars, portico, marble
fireplaces) to give you grand ideas, yet is run
with a light, friendly touch. Large lofty
bedrooms, uncarpeted, uncluttered, are
hotel-spotless in muted colours and the suite
has its own balcony. You wake to delicious
breakfasts at private tables in a light-flooded
dining room with white walls and polished
parquet, and you can stroll into town for
dinner. With the A26 close by, this is a really
nice stopover en route to Calais.

Rooms	3 doubles, 1 twin: €70.
Meals	Dinner with wine, €25; not Sundays.
Closed	Rarely.

Rooms	3 doubles: €90-€100. 1 suite for 2: €130. Singles €75-€95. Extra bed/sofabed €25 p.p. per night.
Meals	Restaurants 2km.
Closed	Rarely.

Tel	+33 (0)3 21 95 87 09
Email	lesdornes@lesdornes.com
Web	www.lesdornes.com

Jaqueline & Gilles Blondel
Les Dornes,
520 rue des Deux Upen, Upen d'Aval,
62129 Delettes, Pas-de-Calais

Tel	+33 (0)3 21 61 76 76
Email	contact@philiomel.com
Web	www.lechateaudephiliomel.com

Frédéric Devys
Le Château de Philiomel,
Rue Philiomel,
62190 Lillers, Pas-de-Calais

ENTRY 15   MAP 1

ENTRY 16   MAP 1

Les Cohettes

Fanny and her big dog Dune are welcoming and this old farmhouse very peaceful. It's a good stopover to or from Calais and just an hour from the Eurotunnel. If you stay longer there are WWI battlefields and plenty of museums to explore within an hour's drive. Wander the big garden with lawns and mature trees under which you can link up with others for summer pétanque or play billiards and table tennis inside. Unwind in two guest sitting rooms; bedrooms are in the long low attic or the snug suite with its own patio. If it's a full house there can easily be a dozen around the huge table for breakfast – croissants, yogurt, boiled eggs and home-made jams. It's worth staying in for Fanny's table d'hôtes or you can walk into the village for simple meals. Restaurants are a ten-minute drive.

Les Mazures

An architect-designed eco house, whose beauty lies in its simplicity. And the garden is glorious, a blaze of colour and form – rock, Japanese and wild flower, carefully gauged scent and colour combos to attract bees, butterflies and other such beasties. Bright white bedrooms have their own entrance and are immaculate, paired with sparkling bathrooms. At the heart, an airy open-plan living room that guests share with owners Peter and Vincent whose nationalities (English and French) are reflected in their cooking – tasty regional and British. Birdwatching, markets and WWI cemeteries are nearby. Fresh, peaceful, convivial.

Rooms	3 doubles, 1 twin: €60-€70. 1 family room for 4: €65-€119. 1 studio for 2: €65. Singles €55.		**Rooms**	2 doubles, 1 twin: €65.
Meals	Dinner with wine, €27. Guest kitchen.		**Meals**	Dinner with wine, €21. Restaurant 4km.
Closed	Rarely.		**Closed**	Rarely.

Tel	+33 (0)3 21 02 09 47		**Tel**	+33 (0)3 22 32 80 52
Email	ginabulot@gmail.com		**Email**	info@lesmazures.com
Web	www.lescohettes.fr/en/		**Web**	www.lesmazures.com

Fanny Bulot
Les Cohettes,
28 rue de Pernes,
62190 Auchy au Bois, Pas-de-Calais

Peter Clark & Vincent Caplier
Les Mazures,
2b rue de la Prairie,
80370 Beaumetz, Somme

Château de Béhen

Donkeys to stroke, bicycles to hire and ponies to ride: families will be in clover. It's authentic and unpretentious here; many guests stop on their way south – you're just a short hop from the motorway but the feel is very quiet and rural. Friendly Norbert-André is a good cook and you can all eat together or at single tables if you prefer; cheeses are local, vegetables are just-picked, banquets can be arranged. He also organises temporary exhibitions of local art in the salon and dining room. Stroll through the parkland surrounding the house; visit the swans in the pond or the farm animals. Saddle up one of the horses and enjoy a guided trek – for a day or even two – or you can hike or cycle. Historic Abbeville is a ten-minute drive and the coast with lovely Bay of the Somme nature reserve is half an hour.

Le Macassar

Le Macassar is named after the rare ebony used in the drawing room panelling. This gem of a house was restyled in the Twenties and Thirties to please a pretty young wife – but it's more 'femme fatale' than blushing belle. Suave bathrooms, bed linen, feather duvets – only the best. The master suite is the epitome of Art Deco glamour, the ash and bird's-eye maple furniture set off by turquoise velvet walls and contemporary art. Under sloping beams, one wonderfully intimate, sophisticated room is decked in taupe, cocoa and pale blue, its exotic bathroom through an ornate Moorish door. Downstairs, admire the gorgeously varied art, the books and glassware, the textures and the tones. Outside: a flowering Italianate courtyard, a fountain, a haze of lavender. Your hosts are truly charming and Amiens is close. *Over 12s welcome.*

Rooms	2 doubles, 1 twin: €129-€154. 1 suite for 2: €188-€210. 2 family rooms for 4: €190-€252.		**Rooms**	1 double: €200. 4 suites for 2: €220-€295.
Meals	Dinner with wine, from €43; book 2 days ahead.		**Meals**	Hosted dinner, 4 courses with champagne & wine, €55 (Sunday evenings only). Groups on request. Restaurants 5-minute walk.
Closed	Rarely.		**Closed**	Rarely.

Tel	+33 (0)3 22 31 58 30	**Tel**	+33 (0)3 22 48 40 04
Email	norbert-andre@cuvelier.com	**Email**	bookings@lemacassar.com
Web	www.chateau-de-behen.fr/en-GB/	**Web**	www.lemacassar.com

Cuvelier Family
Château de Béhen,
8 rue du Château,
80870 Béhen, Somme

Deborah Murphy
Le Macassar,
8 place de la Republique,
80800 Corbie, Somme

ENTRY 19   MAP 1

ENTRY 20   MAP 5

Les Chambres d'Aumont

Staying here, in the grounds of your kind host's stately 18th-century château is wonderfully relaxing. There's a serene, uncluttered feel to Stéphanie's interior design and you look out from light bedrooms on the estate stables and grounds; the wooded hills beyond entice you to lace up your walking boots. At breakfast there's a spread of homemade jams, cakes, cheeses and charcuterie... take some home from the Sunday market in nearby Poix de Picardie. Amiens, with its gothic Cathedral, is also a foodie city (macaroons a speciality) with excellent restaurants like Brasserie Jules and Chez Rosa. Go in December for the largest Christmas market in northern France. Follow the WWI Circuit of Remembrance and visit the wildlife reserve of the beautiful Somme Bay, complete with seal colony.

Rooms	3 doubles: €95. 1 family room for 4: €115-€135.
Meals	Restaurant 10km.
Closed	Christmas, New Year.

Tel	+33 (0)3 22 90 67 16
Email	stephanie@chambresdaumont.fr
Web	www.chambresdaumont.fr

Stéphanie Danzel d'Aumont
Les Chambres d'Aumont,
2 rue d'Hornoy,
80640 Aumont, Somme

ENTRY 21 MAP 5

Les Chambres de l'Abbaye

Chloé and her artist husband have the most unusual, delightful house in a village with a fine Cistercian abbey. You are free to roam a series of beautiful rooms downstairs, read a book in the pale blue formal salon, admire Jean-François' striking, exciting pictures (though sadly illness is making it harder for him). The family suite is on the first floor, the two doubles higher up; all are fresh, and immaculate. You should eat well: much is homemade, including walnut wine and liqueur from their own trees. Walk it off round the partly unmanicured garden with its summerhouse and pond. It's a fascinating house and a pleasure to stay here.

Rooms	2 doubles: €96-€105. 1 family room for 3: €105-€130. Singles €86-€96. Extra bed/sofabed €30 p.p. per night.
Meals	Dinner with wine & coffee, €25-€35; by arrangement.
Closed	23 December – 27 December.

Tel	+33 (0)3 44 81 98 38
Email	comte.resa@free.fr
Web	www.chambres-abbaye.com

Chloé Comte
Les Chambres de l'Abbaye,
2 rue Michel Greuet,
60850 St Germer de Fly, Oise

ENTRY 22 MAP 5

Le Clos

This lovely 18th-century farmhouse, whitewashed and Normandy-beamed, sits in a very pretty garden reached via a door in the wall. Indoors, you find a remarkably fresh, open-plan and modernised interior, with a comfortable sitting room to share. Garden lovers will enjoy visiting Monet's gardens at Giverny, about 45 minutes' drive away, or perhaps picturesque Gerberoy; you can walk or cycle around here too. Trains to Paris leave from a nearby station. Return for dinner with your hosts: three courses of classic French cuisine served beside the old farm fireplace. Philippe, the chef, receives much praise. Chantal, a retired teacher, keeps you company.

Château de Fosseuse

The de Montmorency family built this place in the 1560s; Françoise (nicknamed Fosseuse) was one of Henri IV's better-known mistresses. It is filled with lovely things: a momumental stone staircase ushers you past antique Turkish rugs and rich wall hangings, find a secret staircase behind panelling, sleep in canopied bedrooms with enormously high ceilings and glorious views. It's not strictly formal thanks to your warm, cultured hosts who genuinely enjoy sharing their home. There's a vast selection of historic reference books and plenty of advice on where to visit. Enjoy bountiful breakfasts and homemade preserves, gumboots for guests by the door and Michelin stars a short drive. Paris is 45 minutes – the train to the Gare du Nord is a hop away; medieval villages, Giverny and craft markets are near.

Rooms	3 family rooms for 3: €60-€72.	**Rooms**	1 double: €95-€100.	
Meals	Dinner with wine, €27; light dinner with cheese, dessert and wine, €20.		1 family room for 4: €120-€170. 1 triple: €95-€130. Singles €85.	
		Meals	Restaurant 5km.	
Closed	3 weeks in winter.	**Closed**	Rarely.	

Tel	+33 (0)3 44 49 92 38	**Tel**	+33 (0)3 44 08 47 66
Email	philippe.vermeire@wanadoo.fr	**Email**	chateau.fosseuse@orange.fr
Web	www.leclosdefay.com	**Web**	www.chateau-de-fosseuse.com

Philippe & Chantal Vermeire
Le Clos,
3 rue du Chêne Noir,
60240 Fay les Etangs, Oise

Shirley & Jean-Louis Marro
Château de Fosseuse,
60540 Fosseuse,
Oise

ENTRY 23   MAP 5

ENTRY 24   MAP 5

La Maison & L'Atelier

In the lush countryside outside of Chantilly – famed for its château, horse racing, lace and cream – lies a typical village house in unusual style. Clare's creative energy swirls around in the bold cubes and stripes, trompe l'oeil tiles, designer chairs and leafy plants. Carlos crafted the solid wood kitchen table at which you breakfast on home baked goodies, fresh fruits and juices from the village bakery or dine on a light charcuterie platter and a glass of good wine. Cats snooze by the fireplace in a light-filled sitting room bright with paintings by artist friends. And you will sleep well in one of two exquisite bedrooms overlooking a beautiful garden.

Ferme de Ressons

Ressons is home to a warm, dynamic, intelligent couple who, after a hard day's work running this big farm (Jean-Paul) or being an architect (Valérie) and tending three children, will ply you in apparently leisurely fashion with champagne, excellent dinner and conversation; they also hunt. The deeply carved Henri III furniture is an admirable family heirloom; bedrooms (two en suite) are colour-coordinated, views roll for miles and sharing facilities seems easy. A house of comfort and relaxed good manners (smoking is in the study only), whose decoration and accessories reflect the owners' travels.

Rooms	2 doubles: €120. Singles €100.
Meals	Dinner with wine, €25. Restaurants 15-minute drive.
Closed	Rarely.

Rooms	2 doubles, 1 twin, sharing bath & 2 wcs; 1 twin, with bath, sharing wc: €55-€80.
Meals	Dinner €19. Wine €14; champagne €18.
Closed	Rarely.

Mobile	+33 (0)6 80 04 38 04
Email	hello@lamaisonetlatelier.com
Web	www.lamaisonetlatelier.com/en/

Clare Howarth
La Maison & L'Atelier,
26 rue des Croix,
63530 Crouy-en-Thelle, Oise

Tel	+33 (0)3 23 74 71 00
Mobile	+33 (0)6 80 74 17 01
Email	ferryressons@orange.fr

Valérie & Jean-Paul Ferry
Ferme de Ressons,
02220 Mont St Martin,
Aisne

La Grange

Hidden down lanes, behind an undulating wall, glimpsed through wrought-iron gates, is this big converted barn; Tony and Thierry have been looking after guests, with great pleasure, for years. Rambling gardens and a bountiful vegetable plot run down to wide open pasture. Under the high glass atrium of the breakfast room lies the heart of the house with wood-burner, piano and windows opening to undulating views, while peaceful and immaculate bedrooms hop from fabric-swathed opulence to a more simple country elegance. Hosted dinners are convivial and delicious; Reims, rich in history and gastronomy, is under an hour.

La Quincy

An old family home, faded and weary yet timeless and romantic. All is peaceful, and Marie-Catherine is natural and quietly elegant. Find a mellow, laid back atmosphere; corridors cluttered with books, magazines and traces of family life lead to an octagonal tower, its great double room and child's room across the landing imaginatively set in the space. A handsome antique bed on a polished floor, charming chintz, erratic plumbing and two parkland views will enchant you. Shrubs hug the feet of the 'troubadour' château, the garden slips into meadow, and summer breakfast and dinner (good wine, book ahead) are in the lived-in orangery.

Rooms	2 doubles: €79. 1 apartment for 4: €149.		**Rooms**	1 family room for 3: €70-€110. Pets €8.
Meals	Dinner, 4 courses with wine, €29. Restaurant 10 km.		**Meals**	Occasional dinner with wine, €25.
Closed	Rarely.		**Closed**	Rarely.

Tel	+33 (0)3 23 25 82 42		**Tel**	+33 (0)3 23 54 67 76
Email	lagrangecuiry@orange.fr		**Email**	la.quincy@yahoo.fr
Web	www.lagrangecuiry.fr		**Web**	laquincy.free.fr

Tony Bridier & Thierry Charbit
La Grange,
6 impasse des Prés,
02160 Cuiry les Chaudardes, Aisne

Jacques & Marie-Catherine Cornu-Langy
La Quincy,
02880 Nanteuil la Fosse,
Aisne

ENTRY 27 MAP 5

ENTRY 28 MAP 5

Le Clos

Genuine country hospitality and warmth are yours in the big old house. Madame is kindly and direct; Monsieur is the communicator (mainly in French), knows his local history and loves the hunting horn. His 300-year-old family house is cosily unposh: floral curtains, French-papered walls, original wainscotting, funny old prints in bedrooms, comforting clutter in the vast living room, posters in the corridors. The master bedroom is superb, others are simple and fine; one has a ship's shower room, all look onto green pastures. And there's a pretty lake for picnics across the narrow road.

Domaine de l'Étang

The village on one side, the expansive estate on the other, the 18th-century wine-grower's house in between. There's a civilised mood: Monsieur so well-mannered and breakfast served with silver and fine china in the comfortably elegant guest dining room. Wake to church-spire and rooftop views in rooms with soft comfort where, under sloping ceilings, French toile de Jouy is as inviting as English chintz (your hosts spent two years in England). Bathrooms are frilled and pretty. Shrubs hug the hem of the house, a pool is sunk into the lawn behind and Laon trumpets one of France's first gothic cathedrals.

Rooms	2 doubles, 1 twin: €50-€60. 1 suite for 5: €70-€120. Extra bed €20. Pets, €5 per pet per night.
Meals	Occasional dinner with wine, €22.50 per person.
Closed	Mid-October to mid-March, except by arrangement.

Rooms	2 doubles, 1 twin: €60-€75.
Meals	Restaurant 50m (closed Mondays).
Closed	Rarely.

Tel   +33 (0)3 23 24 80 64
Email   leclos.cheret@club-internet.fr
Web   www.lecloscheret.com

Michel & Monique Simonnot
Le Clos,
02860 Chérêt,
Aisne

Tel   +33 (0)3 23 24 44 52
Email   gitemons@sfr.fr
Web   www.domainedeletang.fr

Patrick Woillez
Domaine de l'Étang,
2 rue St Martin,
02000 Mons en Laonnois, Aisne

Domaine Le Parc

This 18th-century mansion built on castle foundations is now a family-run guest château run in the spirit of a B&B. There are ten lawned, tree'd and statued acres here and a brick-walled belvedere terrace with soaring views. Inside, wander between a gracefully decorated dining room, breakfast room and library, and a sitting room. Up the spiral staircase are the classically decorated bedrooms. Strong colours with floral fabrics stand out against striped or patterned walls; smart bathrooms have jacuzzi baths; old bottles on the window ledges and an antique hobby horse add whimsical touches to the décor. New owners Jedy and Damien have backgrounds in hospitality so will look after you beautifully. Don't miss the fortified churches and great Gothic cathedrals. *Babes-in-arms and over 10s welcome.*

Rooms	3 doubles, 2 twins: €75-€95. Extra bed/sofabed €25 p.p. per night.
Meals	Dinner set menu with wine, €38; booking required for first night.
Closed	Rarely.

Tel   +33 (0)3 23 56 55 23
Email contact@domaineleparc.fr
Web   www.domaineleparc.com

Jedy Bergman & Damien Maillet
Domaine Le Parc,
Rue de Quesny,
02800 Danizy, Aisne

La Commanderie

Up here on the hill is a Templar hamlet and a millennium of history: an enclosed farmyard, a ruined medieval chapel, a tithe barn – and this modern house. José-Marie, an unharried grandmother of generous spirit, loves the history, harvests her orchards and vegetables, and welcomes genuinely. Bedrooms and bathrooms are in plain farm style but open the window and you fall into the view that soars away on all sides. Homely, authentic, simple and great value – but not for you if you need all mod cons and aren't keen on dogs. One guest said, "Like staying with a dear family member". Enjoy a breakfast of baguette, homemade jam, yogurts and muesli, then head off to explore. Saint-Quentin, a listed art and history town is a half-hour drive, Reims with its cathedral and champagne houses is about an hour.

Rooms	1 double: €55-€60. 2 family rooms for 4: €60-€70.
Meals	Restaurants 10km.
Closed	Last week October to February, except by arrangement.

Tel   +33 (0)3 23 56 51 28
Email carette.jm@wanadoo.fr
Web   www.gite-templier-laon.fr

José-Marie Carette
La Commanderie,
Catillon du Temple,
02270 Nouvion & Catillon, Aisne

Champagne
– Ardenne

La Villa Eugène

On the prestigious Avenue de Champagne, this 19th-century mansion was the home of champagne magnate Eugène Mercier; old family photos still line the staircase and the staff can tell you which room belonged to whom. Then there's the décor, an enticing balance of traditional French with contemporary touches: walls the colour of whipped cream, furniture Louis XVI or 'colonial' (dark wood, leather and wicker), soft yielding curtains, gracious parquet floors. There's modernity in flat-screens and WiFi, pampering in the bathrooms – all a good size – with fluffy towels and luxurious products by Keiji; it definitely earns the five stars of which the owner is so proud. The buffet breakfast is an array of homemade cakes, tarts, yogurts and breads, served in the light-filled conservatory – whose mosaic floor has been lovingly restored – or in the garden with its heated summer pool, colourful beds and young palm trees. Just 30 minutes from Reims and its mesmerising cathedral, a smart launch pad for the three major Routes de Champagne. After a day's exploring return to the luxurious cocoon that is the bar.

Rooms	15 twin/doubles: €160-€398.
	Extra bed/sofabed €36 p.p. per night.
Meals	Breakfast €21. Restaurants 2km.
Closed	Never.

Tel	+33 (0)3 26 32 44 76	**Agnès Rafik**
Email	info@villa-eugene.com	La Villa Eugène,
Web	www.villa-eugene.com	82-84 avenue de Champagne,
		51200 Épernay, Marne

Château d'Étoges

Étoges, used as a stopover by French kings on journeys east, is a moated 17th-century château: travel through the wrought-iron gates then over the footbridge to a little island fortress, transformed into a hotel by the family who have lived here for generations. The grounds are lovely, too, with their fountains, lawns and ponds. It is, indeed, fit for a king, from the fully French rooms with their delicious fabrics and linen to the elegant meals with home-grown veg. Opulent bedrooms glow with antiques and fresh flowers, some have four-posters and two have mezzanine beds over bathrooms; rooms in the orangery have less character. The handsome restaurant, also in the orangery, has a majestic fireplace and, fittingly, deep orange curtains. If you fancy breakfast in bed, smart staff will bring it to your lace-covered table: breads, croissants, jams, fruit. If you prefer to breakfast downstairs, take your pick from the buffet and drift onto the terrace. This intimate hotel is right in the middle of champagne-growing country; easy for cycling and fishing, too, with a well-stocked lake a ten-minute drive.

Rooms	26 twin/doubles: €139-€340.
	2 suites for 2: €300-€380.
Meals	Breakfast €20.
	Lunch & dinner €45-€89.
	Children's meals €20.
	Wine €20-€200.
Closed	Christmas, 22 January – 13 February.

Marie Champenois
Château d'Étoges,
4 rue Richebourg,
51270 Étoges, Marne

Tel   +33 (0)3 26 59 30 08
Email   contact@etoges.com
Web   www.etoges.com

Ferme de Bannay

Auprès de l'Église

The deep-country house in the pretty village brims with new chintz and old beams. Bedrooms dressed in ivory and white have quilted bedcovers and scatter cushions; sprays of artificial flowers brighten nooks and crannies; and there's a bathroom behind a curtain. Little English is spoken but the welcome is so endearing, the generosity so genuine, the food so delicious, that communication is easy. Just a few cows on the farm now, and the odd tractor passing, but the vegetable garden is handsome and much of the produce ends up on your (delightfully antique) plate. *Bikes available to rent – please book 2 days in advance.*

New Zealanders Michael and Glenis do excellent table d'hôtes and love sharing their restored 19th-century house full of surprises: some walls are unadorned but for the mason's scribbles. The upstairs suite is separated by a fabulous wall of bookcases and an attic stair, the ground floor has a French country feel. Another big, cleverly designed room leads off the courtyard where you sit in the shade of birch trees and dine (and enjoy a champagne aperitif). Oyes church has no chiming clocks: you'll sleep deeply here. Plenty of fun and funky brocante yet the comforts are modern. Charming Sézanne is a 20-minute drive.

Rooms	1 suite for 2 with kitchen: €98-€164.
	1 triple: €74-€94.
	1 quadruple: €74-€114.
	Extra bed/sofabed €20 p.p. per night; €18 for child.
Meals	Dinner with wine, €42; with champagne €61. Restaurant 3km (weekdays), 12km (weekends).
Closed	Rarely.

Rooms	2 suites for 2: €130-€170.
Meals	Dinner with wine, €40.
	Children's dinner, 2 courses, €10.
Closed	Rarely.

Tel	+33 (0)3 26 52 80 49
Email	leschambresdemuguette@orange.fr

Tel	+33 (0)3 26 80 62 39
Email	titusprod@me.com
Web	www.champagnevilla.com

Muguette & Jean-Pierre Curfs
Ferme de Bannay,
1 rue du Petit Moulin,
51270 Bannay, Marne

Glenis Foster
Auprès de l'Église,
2 rue de l'Église,
51120 Oyes, Marne

Au Pré du Moulin

The big 1789 farmhouse deep in the country has been in the Coulmier family for two generations. Luckily, one half of the main house has been given over to guests; an interconnecting suite (poppy-print wallpaper, wooden floors) provides family-sized space to match a child-friendly garden. Elsewhere, rooms are French 'rustic chic' to a tee: white lacquered bedsteads and cornflower-blue floral details in one; stylish dark wood and Burgundian limestone with tiny black cabochons in another. Valérie and Didier are lovely, friendly and knowledgeable hosts and will share delicious organic home-grown fare with you.

Château de Juvigny

Oozing old-world charm, this handsome 1705 château wraps you in its warmth. The family have occupied one wing for 200 years and, thanks to Brigitte, it has a wonderfully easy-going elegance. There are chandeliers, polished floorboards, wainscotting and antiques, old-fashioned bathrooms, cracked floor tiles, rustic outbuildings. Bedrooms, in the old servants' quarters, are informally stylish with marble fireplaces, pretty bedcovers and views over the park, the formal gardens and the lake. You breakfast, colourfully, beneath a vast (and deteriorated!) portrait of an ancestor. Charming, unfussy country comfort.

Rooms	1 double: €55-€70. 1 triple: €55-€85. 1 suite for 4: €90-€115. Extra bed/sofabed €20 per person per night.		**Rooms**	3 doubles, 1 twin: €110-€150. 1 suite for 4: €160-€220. Extra bed/sofabed €30 p.p. per night.
Meals	Dinner with wine, €30.		**Meals**	Restaurant 10km.
Closed	Christmas & New Year.		**Closed**	Mid-October to 1 April, except by arrangement.

Tel	+33 (0)3 26 64 50 16
Email	reservation@aupredumoulin.fr
Web	www.aupredumoulin.com

Valérie & Didier Coulmier
Au Pré du Moulin,
4 rue du Moulin,
51130 Clamanges, Marne

Mobile	+33 (0)6 78 99 69 40
Email	information@chateaudejuvigny.com
Web	www.chateaudejuvigny.com/en-GB/

Brigitte Caubère d'Alinval
Château de Juvigny,
8 av du Château,
51150 Juvigny, Marne

Domaine Sacret

Bubble 8

A dynamic, humorous and creative couple, these two. James was born into a small champagne dynasty and started the B&B as a natural extension of his wine-tasting sessions. Their large newly-done rooms go from coolly sober to dramatically red, all with character and great bathrooms. The bar-restaurant-salon is as big and welcoming as James himself. He runs champagne tastings every evening and serves delicious platters of local specialities at the long convivial table. Happy wine buffs relax in leather chesterfields or at the bright red pool table, and Mr Supercat lords it over all. A happy place to be.
Parking on-site.

These are classic apartments d'hôtes so choose between looking after yourself – there are good kitchens – or friendly owner Pascale can bring over whatever you ask for at breakfast time: fresh croissants from the bakery, charcuterie and cheese. Step into town for exploring, treat yourselves to a delicious meal or drive out into champagne country for a trail through all the houses and taste copious different cuvées. Culture seekers will head for Reims and the cathedral. As soon as you leave town you're among the vines and winding quiet roads perfect for cycling. It's peaceful for the middle of town and Pascale can organise a champagne tasting in the vaulted cellar for you. Those in the middle floor apartment can have a sundowner on the terrace and watch the town settle down for the night.

Rooms	3 doubles, 1 twin/double: €160-€190.
Meals	Dinner with champagne €80 for 2. Restaurants 5-minute walk.
Closed	23 December – 26 December, 30 December – 2 January.

Rooms	1 apartment for 2, 1 apartment for 4: €139-€259. 1 studio for 2: €109-€169. Extra sofabed available in attic apartment.
Meals	Breakfast €15. Restaurants 2-minute walk.
Closed	Never.

Tel   +33 (0)3 26 56 99 20
Email   james-chevillet@orange.fr
Web   www.champagne-sacret.com

James Chevillet
Domaine Sacret,
3 rue Billecart,
51160 Ay, Marne

Mobile   +33 (0)6 80 84 38 42
Email   pascale.lelong@live.fr
Web   www.bubble8.fr

Pascale Lelong-Macra
Bubble 8,
8 rue des Berceaux,
51200 Épernay, Marne

ENTRY 39   MAP 6

ENTRY 40   MAP 6

Les Bulles Dorées

The ethos may be that of a boutique hotel but the feel is cosy and the welcome homely all thanks to Heidi, who presses a flute of champagne upon you on arrival and offers you a whistle-stop tour... the warehouse is fascinating! Owner Didier takes over in the evenings. Upstairs, a vast sofa dominates the vaulted living room and the bedrooms are big, airy, contemporary and beautiful. Expect Italian wallpapers, retro coffee tables, wooden floors, modish colours, and the château next door peeping through the trees. As for breakfast, it awaits in a glass room overlooking the garden; don't miss the pâté en croûte Ardennais.

Domaine Ployez-Jacquemart

The grand old mansion sits in green, serene gardens near the outskirts of a small champagne village; Ployez-Jacquemart is an exceptional domain whose fizz ranges from buttery-rich to fruity-fresh. Courteous staff (who live off site) serve breakfast at one big table, and show you to bedrooms decorated in impeccable French style. Ask for one that faces the vineyards ('Nature', distinguished by its gentle colours and polished boards, is on the first floor, 'Savane' and 'Provence' are on the second). The communal spaces are chic, the gardens are elegant, the breakfasts are delicious and you can wander at will.

Rooms	2 doubles: €160-€170. 2 family rooms for 3, 1 family room for 4: €195-€260.		**Rooms**	3 doubles, 1 twin: €145-€160. 1 family room for 4: €220-€230.
Meals	Restaurant next door.		**Meals**	Gourmet dinner €135; minimum 6 guests. Restaurants 10km.
Closed	Never.		**Closed**	20 December – 19 January, 8 August – 21 August.

Tel	+33 (0)6 03 20 33 20		**Tel**	+33 (0)3 26 61 11 87
Email	contact@lesbullesdorees.com		**Email**	contact@ployez-jacquemart.fr
Web	www.lesbullesdorees.com/en/		**Web**	www.ployez-jacquemart.fr

Heidi Ramuz
Les Bulles Dorées,
32 Rue de Reims,
51500 Rilly-la-Montagne, Marne

Laurence Ployez
Domaine Ployez-Jacquemart,
8 rue Astoin,
51500 Ludes, Marne

ENTRY 41   MAP 6

ENTRY 42   MAP 6

La Demeure des Sacres

A privileged spot for a privileged mansion. Reims Cathedral is 150 yards away: you can see it from the balcony of the Suite Royale. All the rooms are 'royale' here: suave, spacious, voluptuous; the quietest facing the garden. Courteous Céline cares for house, family and guests and offers an elegant breakfast buffet of homemade cookies, crêpes and jams in the classical dining room (at one table, or several – you choose), or on the terrace on summer days, overlooking lawn, roses, shrubs and swings. You get minibars, safes, superb bathrooms, snow-white linen... and a sweeping Art Deco day room. *Parking 50m.*

La Closerie des Sacres

An easy drive from Reims, these former stables have changed radically. Large, cool, downstairs areas – the mangers and tethering rings remain – are pale-tiled with dark leather sofas, games and books, an open fire, a glass-topped dining table, wrought-iron chairs. And you can do your own cooking in the fully fitted kitchen. Bedrooms are solid oak-floored, draped and prettily coloured with well-dressed beds, cushions, teddy bears, electric blinds and jacuzzi baths. The Jactats have farmed here for generations and tell of the rebuilding of their village in 1925. Take time to talk, and play boules in the sheltered garden.

Rooms	2 twin/doubles with separate shower & wc: €175-€180. 2 suites for 2: €255-€275. Extra bed/sofabed €35 p.p. per night.
Meals	Restaurants within walking distance.
Closed	Rarely.

Rooms	1 double: €94. 1 suite for 5: €120-€180. 1 triple: €94-€115. Singles €78-€100.
Meals	Guest kitchen available. Restaurants 2km.
Closed	Rarely.

Mobile	+33 (0)6 79 06 80 68
Email	contact@la-demeure-des-sacres.com
Web	www.la-demeure-des-sacres.com

Céline Songy
La Demeure des Sacres,
29 rue Libergier,
51100 Reims, Marne

Tel	+33 (0)3 26 02 05 05
Email	contact@closerie-des-sacres.com
Web	www.closerie-des-sacres.com

Sandrine & Laurent Jactat
La Closerie des Sacres,
7 rue Chefossez,
51110 Lavannes, Marne

Le Presbytère de Sévigny

You'll love your hosts: Jatin, attentive and hands-on; Laurence, easy, serene and a good cook (try her nougat ice cream!). The wing of their 19th-century presbytery, once used for christenings and confirmations, has become a plush and pretty gîte, with bedrooms that can be rented individually. Extremely cosy and comfortable, they come in fashionable muted colours or in Asian style; mattresses are deep and firm, and garnished with square French pillows. Downstairs are the sitting and dining rooms, elegant and cool. The village is remote with a 13th-century church; beyond are the vineyards of Champagne.

Domaine du Moulin d'Eguebaude

A delightful mill – and trout farm. The secluded old buildings in the lush riverside setting are home to a fish restaurant, several guest rooms and 50 tons of live fish. Delicious breakfast and dinner are shared with your enthusiastic hosts, who started the business 40 years ago; groups come for speciality lunches, anglers come to fish. Bedrooms under the eaves are compact, small-windowed, simply furnished, decorated in rustic or granny style, the larger annexe rooms are more motel-ish. Lots of space for children, and good English spoken. More guest house than B&B.

Rooms	3 doubles: €85-€95. 1 triple: €95-€130. Children under 6 free. Cot available free. Reductions on stays over 3 nights.	
Meals	Dinner, 3 courses, €28. Restaurants 11km.	
Closed	Rarely.	

Rooms	2 doubles, 1 twin: €77-€82. 2 family rooms for 4: €112-€128. 1 triple: €87.	
Meals	Dinner with wine, €28. Guest kitchen.	
Closed	Rarely.	

Tel +33 (0)3 24 72 26 31
Email info@lepresbyteredesevigny.com
Web www.lepresbyteredesevigny.com

Laurence & Jatin Janray
Le Presbytère de Sévigny,
7 rue du Cabas,
08220 Sevigny-Waleppe, Ardennes

Tel +33 (0)3 25 40 42 18
Email moulineguebaude10@gmail.com
Web en.moulineguebaude.com

Alexandre & Sandrine Mesley
Domaine du Moulin d'Eguebaude,
36 rue Pierre Brossolette,
10190 Estissac, Aube

ENTRY 45 MAP 6

ENTRY 46 MAP 5

Villa d'Othe

Sink into a sofa in the airy sitting room with a glass of champagne from Laurence's bar. There's an excellent restaurant 9km away, and a pizza place in the village; but we suggest you dine in. This is a modest house that's been luxuriously revived; to enter is a wonderful surprise. All is immaculate and guaranteed to soothe, from the gliding glass doors to the art. Bedrooms – two downstairs, two under the eaves – exude a zen-like charm. You are in the undulating, forested Pays d'Othe, known for its cider trails and just eight minutes away from the Champagne route. Walk, cycle, ride (there's stables down the road) and revel in the apple blossom in spring. Soak up the history of 16th-century Troyes, treasured for its timbered houses and its cathedral. Return to the pretty garden and pool – good for families.

Rooms	3 twin/doubles: €90-€100. 1 suite for 2: €170. Extra bed/sofabed €30 p.p. per night.
Meals	Dinner by arrangement: contact Laurence to book and for prices.
Closed	Rarely.

Tel	+33 (0)6 24 42 37 87
Email	villadothe@gmail.com
Web	www.villa-d-othe.com

Laurence Houdre
Villa d'Othe,
8 rue Eugénie Geoffroy,
10190 Estissac, Aube

La Maison M

Handsome and traditional outside, smart and spacious inside. Add big-hearted hosts and views over the canal in charming old Troyes and you've quite a find. Ex-farmer Bruno did most of the renovation: immaculate bathrooms, clever storage and recovery of original parquet, wrought iron and marble. And with Michelle's design flair – hugely comfortable beds, modern pieces, bold papers and fabrics – rooms are attractive, fresh and comfortable. Revel in the grand, Belle Époque style of the three reception rooms; linger over breakfast, in the conservatory perhaps. There's a spa, sauna and sports room – and a swimming pool's planned. *Parking on-site.*

Rooms	5 doubles: €115-€160.
Meals	Restaurant 1-minute walk.
Closed	25 August – 4 September.

Tel	+33 (0)3 25 46 30 97
Email	contact@maisonmtroyes.com
Web	maisonmtroyes.com

Michelle Meunier
La Maison M,
3 quai la Fontaine,
10000 Troyes, Aube

Le Jardin de la Cathédrale

A gorgeous setting for this 18th-century house and courtyard garden in front of the medieval cathedral. Interiors are stunning and colourful; light floods in from large windows in the drawing and dining rooms. Wake up early (the bells!) in bedrooms which will delight and surprise: stained glass windows, incredible light hangings, vast beams, high ceilings and zingy wallpapers and fabrics. Oh, and a gigantic stuffed goose. At breakfast you feast on fresh pastries and bread with butter from Echiré and jams and honey from the Aube. Step outside for wonky half-timbered houses and the whole lovely town. Very special.

Domaine de la Creuse

You're well away from the main road but only a short walk from the village in this stone farmhouse dated 1742. B&B rooms are in various outbuildings set around a pretty courtyard with trees, shrubs and flowers: each is different but all have exposed oak beams, half-timbered walls, comfortable seats with views and fresh white embroidered cotton sheets on good thick mattresses. All have a seating area too. Breakfast is in the airy dining room, or the rambling garden – smiley Madame makes her own jams and yogurts and buys the best croissants and bread from the local artisan baker. Golf, walks, cycling and watery fun are all near.

Rooms	5 doubles: €180-€210.
Meals	Restaurants 2-minute walk. Afternoon tea available.
Closed	Never.

Rooms	2 doubles: €115-€135. 2 suites for 2: €130-€200. 1 family room for 4: €135-€205. Extra bed/sofabed €15-€30 p.p. per night.
Meals	Gluten-free breakfasts on request. Restaurants 15-minute drive.
Closed	Rarely.

Tel	+33 (0)6 11 12 26 76
Email	laetitia@jardindelacathedrale.com
Web	www.jardindelacathedrale.com

Laetitia Krumenacher
Le Jardin de la Cathédrale,
12 place Saint Pierre,
10000 Troyes, Aube

Mobile	+33 (0)6 07 89 99 49
Email	deroin.thevenin.ph@wanadoo.fr
Web	www.domainedelacreuse.fr

Marie-Christine Deroin-Thevenin
Domaine de la Creuse,
Ferme de la Creuse,
10800 Moussey, Aube

ENTRY 49   MAP 6

ENTRY 50   MAP 6

A L'Aube Bleue

Madame is a collector of intriguing finds (including the Peugeot 203). Her two family-friendly garden-facing bedrooms make good use of compact space: one has a double bed on the mezzanine floor and children sleep below; the other, pretty in pale colours, sleeps three. The disabled access room is larger, also simply furnished, with a baldequin bed. You breakfast at one big table next to the kitchen. Do arrange a meal in the sheltered outdoor dining area, too; it's fun and hung with agricultural bits and bobs, and the food will be good. All in a quiet village, in open country 18km south of medieval Troyes.

La Pierre Écrite

The Nachbroun, kindly people, simply love mills. This one began life in the 13th century – property then of the Earl of Champagne – and its history entwines with village folklore. Your upstairs room – modern retro style with painted panelling, brocante prints and a big monochrome shower room – overlooks the mill pond: a treat for all seasons whether dizzying with dragonflies or mist rising on a frosty morning. Breakfast is a grand spread of sweet and savoury; there's a corner kitchen downstairs, a garden barbecue, and a decent restaurant you can easily walk to in attractive, historic and watery Soulaine Dhuys.

Rooms	1 double: €69. 1 triple: €86. 1 family room for 4: €101. Singles €59. Dinner, B&B €25 extra p.p. Extra bed/sofabed €20 p.p. per night.
Meals	Dinner with wine & coffee, €29; children over 5, €9; under 5, €6.
Closed	Rarely.

Rooms	2 doubles: €85. Tourist tax €0.60 per adult/per night.
Meals	Restaurant within walking distance.
Closed	Rarely.

Tel   +33 (0)3 25 40 29 58
Email   contact@chambres-hotes-aube-bleue.fr
Web   www.chambres-hotes-aube-bleue.fr

Christine Degois
A L'Aube Bleue,
6 rue du Viard,
10320 Assenay, Aube

Mobile +33 (0)6 80 91 61 31
Email   lapierreecrite@orange.fr

Jean-Claude Nachbroun
La Pierre Écrite,
Le Moulin, 4 rue des Tanneries,
10200 Soulaine Dhuys, Aube

ENTRY 51   MAP 6

ENTRY 52   MAP 6

Domaine de Boulancourt

This large and splendid farmhouse is irresistible. For fishermen there's a river, for birdwatchers a fine park full of wildlife (come for the cranes in spring or autumn); for architecture buffs, the half-timbered churches are among the "100 most beautiful attractions in France". Bedrooms are comfortable and handsome; afternoon tea is served by the piano in the elegant panelled salon; and dinner, including fresh fruits and vegetables from the garden, local meats, cheeses and wine, is prepared by your delightful hosts. You will feel like a member of the family. *No card payments; please pay in cash or cheque on arrival.*

Le Relais du Puits

Regular guests of Michel and Évelyne in their tiny medieval village in Champagne will find this charming couple in a 'new' 200-year-old home. Just three rooms now, all reflecting Évelyne's quirky humour: snow-white 'Romantic', 'Belle-Époque', extravagant 'Medieval'; with a gothic, dark orange décor, daggers and tapestries. Bathrooms are gorgeous and the garden large. After 18 years your hosts know just what guests want, whether it's free internet, a roaring fire in the sitting room, or bicycles for the surrounding forests and country lanes.

Rooms	3 doubles: €85-€95.
	1 family room for 4: €125.
	1 single: €75. Extra bed/sofabed
	€20 p.p. per night. 10% discount
	for longer stays.
Meals	Restaurants nearby,
Closed	21 November – 2 May.

Rooms	1 double; 1 twin with separate
	bath: €76. 1 quadruple: €86-€129.
	Extra bed €20. Cot €12.
Meals	Restaurant 8km.
Closed	Rarely.

Tel	+33 (0)3 25 04 60 18
Email	dom.boulancourt@wanadoo.fr
Web	www.domaine-de-boulancourt.com

Philippe & Christine Viel-Cazal
Domaine de Boulancourt,
Le Désert,
52220 Longeville sur la Laines, Haute-Marne

Tel	+33 (0)3 25 88 80 50
Email	e.m.poope@orange.fr
Web	www.le-relais-du-puits.com

Évelyne & Michel Poope
Le Relais du Puits,
15 rue Augustin Massin,
52500 Pressigny, Haute-Marne

ENTRY 53 MAP 6

ENTRY 54 MAP 6

Lorraine
Alsace
Franche Comté

Maison Zugno, page 68

Maison Zugno

Look forward to a delicious dinner sourced from fine local ingredients. Each dish, cooked by Nicholas, served by Laurence, is beautifully presented – as is everything at this small intimate hotel. Take a glass of 'Jura blanc' to the great wood-burner downstairs; enjoy a continental breakfast on the terrace. Sunny bedrooms and suites, including one for families, lie peacefully at the back, each overlooking a meadow with trees. The old coaching inn on the route to Switzerland has been restored impeccably by its owners. The Jura is a very beautiful area, while Poligny (5km) is one of its most charming towns. Along with foodie capital Arbois (20km), the town is a gastronomic delight; a visit to 'les fruitières', the cheese and wine producing cooperatives, is a must. Follow with a hearty lunch in town, then lose the pounds being sporty: there are tennis courts right opposite the hotel.

Rooms	2 doubles, 2 twin/doubles: €120-€165. 2 suites for 2: €160-€180. 1 family room for 3: €165-€185. Dinner, B&B €106-€136 p.p. Extra bed/sofabed €15 p.p. per night.
Meals	Breakfast €10. Dinner €36.
Closed	Christmas, 1 January – 15 January, 31 March – 9 April, 1 September – 10 September.

Laurence Zugno
Maison Zugno,
Les Monts de Vaux,
39800 Barretaine, Jura

Tel   +33 (0)3 84 53 10 31
Email krieger.laurence@gmail.com
Web   www.maison-zugno.com/en/

ENTRY 55   MAP 11

Le Saint Barnabé – Hôtel & Spa

At the top of its peaceful valley, under the guidance of attentive and efficient owners, the whole hotel now has modern, clean lines: gone are the traditional Alsatian frills. Food is important here, and good. Éric is the chef. Trained with France's best and chef at Château d'Isenbourg for some years, he uses local, biodynamically-grown ingredients whenever he can. Clémence tends the colourful garden and can also advise on what to do between the Vosges hills and the Alsace plain: there are typical villages and wine-growers to visit, excellent hiking, bike rides and good fishing places (they also have mini-golf on the spot, and a spa with hammam). The ferny woods are full of paths and burbling brooks and there's skiing in season. Rooms, quietly elegant and comfortable, are of two kinds: in the main house they are big, sometimes in rich, dark colours, with smashing bathrooms and the odd balcony; in the separate building behind, they are smaller, with a shower each – and cheaper! A great place for nature lovers and gourmets, the Saint Barnabé is completely quiet – bar the birdsong – and carefully eco-friendly.

Rooms	26 twin/doubles: €86-€199. Extra bed/sofabed €25 p.p. per night.
Meals	Lunch €22.90, Mon-Sat. Picnic on request. Dinner €29-€78 plus à la carte. Restaurant closed 1 week in July, and 2 weeks in Jan/Feb.
Closed	24-25 December, part of January & part of March.

Tel	+33 (0)3 89 62 14 14
Email	hostellerie.st.barnabe@wanadoo.fr
Web	www.le-stbarnabe.com

Clémence & Éric Orban
Le Saint Barnabé – Hôtel & Spa,
53 rue de Murbach,
68530 Buhl, Haut-Rhin

ENTRY 56   MAP 7

Hôtel à la Ferme – L'Aigle d'Or

In a simple, colourful Alsatian village, this typical old farm is framed by shrubs, roses, manicured hedges and a pretty brick terrace. The welcome from the family, who have been here for generations, is as gracious as the setting. Bedrooms, in the main house or converted outbuilding, are splendid: a good size and comfortable, they have polished floorboards, oriental rugs and fine beds, one carved in Alsatian style. In the new, exquisitely decorated stable suites you'll find timber balconies, wonderful fabrics and an even greater sense of luxury. Here, too, are the spanking new Aigle d'Or restaurant and the breakfast room, where Jean-Philippe's delicious brioches and pastries are served. His father mans the bar, his mother and grandmother help in the kitchen, Brigitte meets and greets, Jean-Philippe is master chef and the food is outstanding. Chalked up on the board are escargots, foie gras, asparagus in season, choucroute, tarte flambée, apfelstrudel. Then retire to the wainscotted guest salon, warmed by a fine ceramic stove. A superb place run by a family that is professional, enthusiastic, endearing.

Rooms	12 doubles: €99-€156.
	3 suites for 2: €156-€210.
Meals	Breakfast €16.50.
	Lunch & dinner €33.50-€89.50 (except Monday eve & Tuesdays). Wine €25.
Closed	Rarely.

Jean-Philippe & Brigitte Hellmann
Hôtel à la Ferme – L'Aigle d'Or,
10 rue du Château,
67150 Osthouse, Bas-Rhin

Tel	+33 (0)3 90 29 92 50
Email	hotelalaferme@wanadoo.fr
Web	www.hotelalaferme.com

ENTRY 57   MAP 7

Auberge de la Cholotte

In a wooded valley filled with chattering birds, deer, foxes and wild boar sits a spacious pink sandstone farmhouse framed with bright blue shutters and rambling wisteria. A happy spot and spectacular in the autumn sunshine. Both the dining room with open-fire and the wood-panelled restaurant are open to the public and they host regular concerts here. Angelika serves up hearty local produce: ham baked in hay, local rabbit and trout, organic veg and German pastries; she'll even cook the mushrooms you forage from the forest. Stay for supper and some music or head to restaurants in Gerardmer or Saint Dié. Like the communal spaces, all five bedrooms have a rustic chic feel, artistic colour combinations and paintings on the walls; all are on the first floor with harmonious views of pond, garden or forest. There's much to do here: the Vosges mountains are nearby, the pilgrim's path – Saint Jean de Compostela – passes the house, there are heaps of gardens, good walking and fishing. Such peace and quiet and such a friendly couple running the show, no wonder guests return again and again.

Rooms	3 doubles, 1 twin, 1 family room for 3: €90-€100.
Meals	Dinner €25. Wine €18-€32.
Closed	Rarely.

Tel	+33 (0)3 29 50 56 93	**Angelika & Patrick Colin**
Email	auberge@lacholotte.com	Auberge de la Cholotte,
Web	www.lacholotte.com	44 La Cense de Saint Dié,
		88600 Les Rouges Eaux, Vosges

Les 3 Officiers

The prosperous looking manor by the church (once a modest farmhouse) has become a splendid B&B. Tea in the salon with Frederick – Anglophile furniture restorer with a great sense of humour – is civilised and fun, while dinner at the big table (homemade orange wine, local organic produce) with both hosts, and perhaps other guests, is a gorgeous feast. As for the bedrooms, they have been designed in the spirit of the house, one à la Napoleon III, the other Louis Philippe. Towels are snowy, bed linen crisp and all is generous and bright. Wake to fruit compotes served on antique china, head out to explore, then come home to a beautiful box-hedged garden. *Parking available.*

Château d'Alteville

This château was built in 1698 for one of Napoleon's generals and the two paintings that hang in the Louis XVI salon were gifts from the Emperor himself. The house has been in David's family for nearly a century and he's a genuinely charming and welcoming host. Enjoy the peace and quiet lazing on the terrace or in the library, or play a game of billiards perhaps – or pull on your hiking boots and follow your nose through the woods and round the ponds. Stay in for splendid candlelit dinners in the majestic dining room in the company of your host. Cycling and walking holidays can begin here, and David is happy to supply maps and suggestions. You can drive to Dieuze for shops and restaurants in ten minutes; Nancy, Strasbourg and Metz are within an hour.

Rooms	2 doubles: €90. Singles €80. Extra bed €30 per night.
Meals	Dinner, 3 courses with wine, €29; children under 7, €15. Restaurant 5km.
Closed	Rarely.

Rooms	4 doubles, 1 twin: €91.
Meals	Dinner €31-€38.50, by arrangement. Wine €5-€15.
Closed	Rarely.

Email	les3officiers.resa@orange.fr
Web	www.chambres-3officiers-lorraine.com

Frederick Metz
Les 3 Officiers,
Rue de Verdun,
55210 Woel, Meuse

Tel	+33 (0)3 87 05 46 63
Email	chateau.alteville@free.fr
Web	www.chateaudalteville.com

David Barthélémy
Château d'Alteville,
Tarquimpol,
57260 Dieuze, Moselle

La Noisetière

Sandra and Jean-François make you feel immediately at home in this peaceful, relaxing place. They live at one end of the barn (you're in the other) and will look after you at mealtimes when you'll all sit together to enjoy regional specialities and plates of typical Lorraine home cooking. Downstairs is one of the B&B bedrooms – sweet and charming, with a cosy sitting area and lots of books – while upstairs in the loft is the self-catering gîte with its whirlpool bath and sauna; it's a quirky layout, but it works. All share the lovely garden, with a pond and a terrace for relaxing. Days can be spent at the crystal museums at Baccarat and Meisenthal, exploring Strasbourg or Nancy (an hour by train) or the area's war history. Ask for details of cycle tracks – there are endless options. *Min. stay: 2 nights; 7 in high season.*

Maison d'hôtes La Vallée

Caroline and Patrick welcome you to their little corner of the German-French border with convivial breakfasts around the family table and evening meals at the weekends: local meat, veg and goat's cheese from a nearby farm. The surrounding villages and valleys are dotted with good Alsatian restaurants. Fabulously wild walks up and down the forested slopes of the Vosges Mountains are just a short drive away, as is charming Strasbourg. Borrow bikes and plan a circuitous route to finish at the goat's farm for Sunday lunch and a cheese tasting, or visit one of the village vineyards to sample aromatic Alsace wines. Winter visitors can drop in on the Christmas markets along the Route des Vins; in summer there are picnic spots in the lovely sloping gardens here. *Minimum stay: 2 nights in high season.*

Rooms	1 hayloft for 2, 1 cottage for 4: €71–€100. €50 cleaning fee. Breakfast hamper for 2 also available in the Hayloft.
Meals	Restaurants in the village, 1.5km.
Closed	Rarely.

Rooms	1 cottage for 2, 2 cottages for 4: €110–€150.
Meals	Dinner €30, Fri-Sun evenings. Restaurants 5-minute drive.
Closed	Rarely.

Tel	+33 (0)6 60 54 49 82
Email	sandra.noisetiere@orange.fr
Web	www.lanoisetiere.com/welcome.html

Sandra Colin
La Noisetière,
5 rue d'Arzviller,
57565 Niderviller, Moselle

Email	info@lavallee.com
Web	www.21-lavallee.com/?lang=en

Caroline & Patrick Hürlimann
Maison d'hôtes La Vallée,
21 rue de la Vallee,
67520 Kuttolsheim, Bas-Rhin

ENTRY 61   MAP 7

ENTRY 62   MAP 7

86 rue du Général de Gaulle

A real old Alsatian farmhouse in the wine-growing area where you can be in a beautiful, bustling village street one minute and your own peaceful little world the next. It is on a main road but the bedrooms are in the guest wing at the back, protected by the courtyard. Their simplicity is reflected in the price. Your friendly hosts retired from milk and wine production in order to have more time for guests; breakfast is served in the garden or in the dining room, and Paul makes a wicked eau de vie. A useful place to know at the start of the Route des Vins, and close to gorgeous, glamorous Strasbourg.

Bluets et Brimbelles

You feel welcome the moment you step into this renovated mountain house by the village church. Oak, spruce and larch abound, many features have been preserved and all is cosy. Catherine and Thierry love to speak English and do bountiful table d'hôtes at the long table, or on the terrace in summer (the gardens are delightful). She is a chef and pâtissier, produces for local shops and teaches courses in the large spotless kitchen. He is proud possessor of a fleet of 2CVs and a 1947 Traction Avant – book a private tour and set off to explore the mountains with the roof down... Return to log fires, delicious beds, drenching showers.

Rooms	3 doubles: €40-€44. Extra bed €8.
Meals	Restaurants within walking distance.
Closed	Rarely.

Rooms	2 doubles: €80-€90. 1 suite for 4: €90-€150. 1 family room for 5: €80-€120. Extra bed/sofabed €20 p.p. per night.
Meals	Dinner with wine, €25. Restaurants 2-minute walk.
Closed	Rarely.

Tel +33 (0)3 88 87 52 94
Email goetz.paul@wanadoo.fr

Paul & Marie-Claire Goetz
86 rue du Général de Gaulle,
67520 Marlenheim,
Bas-Rhin

Mobile +33 (0)6 32 09 99 78
Email bluetsetbrimbelles@orange.fr
Web www.bluetsetbrimbelles.com

Catherine Habersetzer
Bluets et Brimbelles,
4 rue de l'Eglise,
67420 Saulxures, Bas-Rhin

ENTRY 63 MAP 7

ENTRY 64 MAP 7

Ambiance Jardin

In a small Alsatian village is an 18th-century house surrounded by an exquisite garden. Gravel paths wander past bird-filled trees and charming benches, clipped shrubs and secret corners. Pierrette and Jean-Luc, warm, friendly and fluent in several languages, have set aside a barn with four first-floor bedrooms – immaculate, spacious and overlooking the garden. Wake to homemade pâtisseries and jams, served all morning at rustic tables. Cycle your way through Alsace's vineyards, hop on a ferry and cross the Rhine, or come as a group and take the barn over; there's a cosy sitting room and kitchen downstairs. *Parking on-site.*

La Haute Grange

On the side of a hill, looking down the valley, this 19th-century farmhouse is surrounded by forests and wildflower meadows. Rural and indulging all at once, it is a place for de-stressing, with deeply comforting bedrooms, subtle and spicy colours, and the whole house filled with the smell of baking in the morning. The large sitting room has an open fireplace, an honesty bar and hundreds of books; step onto the patio and enjoy the heart-lifting views. A warm, polyglot couple, Margaret and Philippe will help you plan days of discovery. There are a great selection of restaurants less than 15 minutes away by car. *Minimum stay: 2 nights at weekends & in high season.*

Rooms	4 doubles: €88-€98. Extra bed €20 p.p. per night. 10% discount for stays of 7 nights or more.
Meals	Restaurants 2-minute walk.
Closed	Rarely.

Rooms	3 doubles, 1 twin/double: €110-€150. Singles €95-€135.
Meals	Restaurants 6km.
Closed	4 January – 23 March.

Tel	+33 (0)3 88 74 84 85
Email	contact@ambiance-jardin.com
Web	www.ambiance-jardin.com

Pierrette Kieny
Ambiance Jardin,
12 rue de l'Abbé Wendling,
67230 Diebolsheim, Bas-Rhin

Tel	+33 (0)3 89 71 90 06
Email	lahautegrange@aol.com
Web	www.lahautegrange.fr

Margaret & Philippe Kalk
La Haute Grange,
La Chaude Côte,
68240 Fréland, Haut-Rhin

ENTRY 65   MAP 7

ENTRY 66   MAP 7

Maison d'Hôtes du Parc

Appreciate the finer things in life in Emmanuel and Mark's 1860s riverside home: gourmet cuisine, gorgeous gardens, inspired design. Polished, harmonious interiors waft with shades of mushroom, raspberry and moss, with period antiques, exquisite objets, a harp in the vast salon, a grand piano in the library. Fine china appears at four-course dinners as you chat over tender lamb cutlets with garden thyme. Rooms and suites are cosily sumptuous, views spilling over well-tended gardens of scampering roses, manicured hedges, a summer house and potager. Beyond centennial trees is a gem: Le Corbusier's sensually spiritual chapel.

La Maison de Juliette

There are bikes to borrow and the countryside is a mere 500m ride away. The moment you enter the gardens of this charming edge-of-town house, built for a wealthy family in 1904, all feels peaceful. Your hosts – she with perfect English – are among the warmest we know, their generosity extending from homemade brioche at breakfast to billowing whiter-than-white muslin and tip-top mattresses. Bathrooms are minimalist with an antique touch; the two double rooms have a shared kitchen and doors opening onto a terrace. Breakfast can be served outside or in the conservatory – gluten and dairy-free if preferred. Guests love it here.

Rooms	2 doubles, 1 twin: €110-€130. 1 suite for 2: €130. 1 single: €79.
Meals	Dinner, 4 courses, €25. Restaurants nearby.
Closed	Rarely.

Rooms	2 doubles: €80-€90. 1 family room for 4: €95-€155. Extra bed/sofabed €25 p.p. per night.
Meals	Restaurants 1km. Guest kitchen.
Closed	Rarely.

Tel	+33 (0)3 84 63 93 43
Email	leparc-egeorges@wanadoo.fr
Web	en.hotesduparc.com/

Emmanuel Georges
Maison d'Hôtes du Parc,
12-14 rue du Tram,
70250 Ronchamp, Haute-Saône

Tel	+33 (0)3 81 91 88 19
Email	maisondejuliette@orange.fr
Web	www.maisondejuliette.fr

Françoise Gauthé
La Maison de Juliette,
8 rue des Combes St Germain,
25700 Valentigney, Doubs

ENTRY 67 MAP 7

ENTRY 68 MAP 7

Les Egrignes

Refinement, loving care and high craftsmanship: you are welcomed to this exquisite home by Julien, a gentle soul now at the helm, whose parents breathed new life into this lovely old manor house. Myriad auctions were combed for fine rugs, antique mirrors, modern paintings, piano; you'll find thick curtains, pretty desks, carved armoires and soft sofas in vast pale-walled bedrooms and deluxe bathrooms. The garden is a marvel, the half-wheel potager is especially breathtaking. You'll eat well too – big breakfasts of baguette and granary bread, croissants, eggs, homemade jams, juice, different kinds of charcuterie from the Haut-Doubs area, a cheese platter with perhaps local Comté, Morbier and Roucoulons. Tasty table d'hôtes as well with herbs from the garden – all prepared by Julien, who has also opened a small bar in the sleepy village. Marnay is the nearest town (four kilometres), where you can buy local produce at a good épicerie – great for picnics. Besançon is a 30-minute drive – you can visit the cathedral with its unique 70-dial astronomical clock and there are heaps of fine restaurants. *Parking on-site.*

Rooms	1 suite for 2, 1 suite for 3, 1 suite for 5: €110-€135. Extra bed €45. Cots available €15.
Meals	Dinner, 3 courses, €32; by arrangement.
Closed	1 November – 28 February.

Tel	+33 (0)3 84 31 92 06
Email	info@les-egrignes.com
Web	les-egrignes.com

Julien Lego-Deiber
Les Egrignes,
2 route d'Hugier, 70150 Cult,
Haute-Saône

ENTRY 69   MAP 6

Burgundy

Château de Voudenay, page 90

Le Clos du Colombier

Reach out of your bedroom window and pluck the grapes. Well, almost. This handsome town house – all pale-pink plaster and sky-blue shutters – sits in a sea of vineyards in the heart of Burgundy, surrounded by legendary names: Beaune, Pommery, Meursault... You've come to the right place for wine-tasting or stocking up your cellar. Equally, you can check out a few châteaux, take a slow bike ride or just doze around the pretty pool. Although a hotel, the place has the feel of a relaxed, though rather smart, gîte. Bedrooms – some in a separate annexe – are airy and understated with tiled or polished-wood floors, cool whites and pale greys accented with, say, a splash of purple or charcoal. Sleek contemporary furnishings mix with vintage finds – perhaps a Baroque-style mirror or elegant writing desk – and all have garden or vineyard views. Some rooms have high ceilings and marble fireplaces. Stylish bathrooms have home-made organic soaps and soft bathrobes. Breakfast is continental and includes local honey, evening meals are available in the summer only. When the wine-tasting gets too much, chill out in the little spa overlooking the vines. *Parking on-site.*

Rooms	8 doubles: €150-€185.
	4 suites for 2: €210-€270. Extra
	bed/sofabed €30-€45 p.p. per night.
Meals	Breakfast €17.
	Dinner €32-€38; children €14.
	Restaurants 3-minute walk.
Closed	12 November – 28 February.

Tel	+33 (0)3 80 22 00 27	**Philippe & Véronique Barthelmebs**
Email	contact@closducolombier.com	Le Clos du Colombier,
Web	www.closducolombier.com	1 rue du Colombier,
		21630 Pommard, Côte-d'Or

ENTRY 70 MAP 11

Le Clos

A rustic-style hotel where you can have breakfast on the terrace overlooking the manicured *jardin de curé*. Then choose your suntrap in the garden – it's full of hidden corners; or wander, shaded by generous trees, among the quaint agricultural machinery that sculpturally dots the lawns. This white-shuttered farmhouse, in a peaceful semi-rural area, has been renovated to reveal exposed limestone walls and massive rafters; note the charming country breakfast room and the light and lofty sitting room whose ancient tiles have been garnished with oriental rugs and sofas. Big, neat, carpeted bedrooms have matching floral bed linen and curtains, some fine antique bedsteads and the odd exotic touch. Bathrooms are spotless and there are no half measures: big tubs, walk-in showers, an abundance of towels. There's no restaurant here, though there is a bar and a pretty village just down the road. Montagny lès Beaune is deep in wine country – and when you've had your fill of burgundies and beaunes, there are mustards to try in a nearby village. Beaune is conveniently close. *Charging ports for electric cars available.*

Rooms	20 twin/doubles: €110-€145.
	5 suites for 2: €165-€180.
	Singles €110-€180.
	Extra bed/sofabed €15 p.p. per night.
Meals	Breakfast €16.
	Restaurants 100m & 3km.
Closed	24 December – 1 January.

Monsieur & Madame Humbert
Le Clos,
22 rue Gravières,
21200 Montagny lès Beaune, Côte-d'Or

Tel	+33 (0)3 80 25 97 98
Email	hotelleclos@wanadoo.fr
Web	www.hotelleclos.com

Hôtel de Vougeot

Rows of vines sweep down an incline, surround the Château de Clos de Vougeot, and come to an abrupt halt at the back doorstep of this spotless place, whose 16 rooms inhabit three modest clusters of buildings; ask for a view of château and vines. For centuries, Clos de Vougeot was considered the finest of all burgundies; the Cistercian monks planted some of the vines in the 12th century and the cloister, cellar and vast presses are among the most interesting examples of architecture in Burgundy (it's fabulous at harvest time). Alain speaks excellent English and is a great host, but you are mostly on your own here with a key to come and go as you please. The staircase could be awkward for the very young or very old, and there's no sitting area; however, the terrace has marvellous views. Inside, everything has been kept simple and clean, the rough outlines of dark timbers contrasting with white walls, light coloured bedspreads, parquet floors and teak furniture. The buffet breakfasts and the cold supper platters are delicious – or splash out on a Michelin-starred table in the next village, the perfect end to a great day.

Rooms	12 doubles: €69-€133.
	1 family room for 5: €156-€167.
	1 triple: €88-€129.
	2 quadruples: €137-€148. Extra
	bed/sofabed €19 p.p. per night.
Meals	Buffet breakfast €12.
	Cold platter €22. Wine from €15.
Closed	Rarely.

Tel	+33 (0)3 80 62 01 15
Email	contact@hotel-vougeot.com
Web	www.hotel-vougeot.com

Alain Senterre
Hôtel de Vougeot,
18 rue du Vieux Château,
21640 Vougeot, Côte-d'Or

ENTRY 72   MAP 11

Château de Courban

This ambitiously renovated 19th-century mansion – with a 17th-century dovecote bearing witness to an even older heritage – was transformed into its present incarnation by Jérôme and Frédéric's father, perfectionist Pierre Vandendriessche. Most of the rooms are in the original mansion and flaunt a wide variety of styles, from the bold and bright to the floral and cosy, all tastefully harmonised and generously comfortable: recessed bedheads, draped four-posters, crisp colour schemes and carefully chosen prints. Newer buildings vaunt more contemporary design; rustic chic comfort and their own verandas. Bathrooms feature claw-foot tubs in some, walk-in showers with monsoon heads in others. Cuisine here is in the hands of award-winning chef Takashi Kinoshita. Try the great things he does with truffles and lobster, inter alia, in the expansive restaurant, the orangery or the veranda; breakfast should be enjoyed in bed with the shutters wide open. There are relaxed, formal gardens to one side, and an inviting infinity pool (and thoroughly kitted-out spa) to the other. Take all the time you can.

Rooms	14 twin/doubles: €99-€209.
	10 suites for 2: €149-€400.
	Dinner, B&B €60-€100 p.p.
	Extra bed/sofabed €30 p.p. per night.
Meals	Breakfast €19. Dinner €47-€95.
	Wine €40-€1250.
Closed	24 December – 26 December.

Famille Vandendriessche
Château de Courban,
7 rue du Lavoir Courban,
21520 Courban, Côte-d'Or

Tel	+33 (0)3 80 93 78 69
Email	contact@chateaudecourban.com
Web	www.chateaudecourban.com

Hôtel de la Beursaudière

Monsieur Lenoble's attention to detail is staggering. Not content with creating a buzzing, cheerful restaurant he has lovingly transformed a priory and farm buildings – stables, dovecotes, stone structures on varied levels, wooden verandas topped with red-patterned Burgundian roof tiles – into a very seductive hotel. Each bedroom has a trade for a theme: a typewriter and old books for the 'writer'; antique irons for the 'laundress'; horse and ox collars for the 'ploughman'; vine-decorated wooden panels for the 'wine-grower'. The walls have been lightly skimmed in plaster in natural shades of ochre, pigeon-egg grey or light yellow. Floors are terracotta or flagstone, stone walls are painted, rafters exposed and windows round or cottage square with curtains of vintage linens and lace. Beds are king-size, mattresses are excellent and TVs are hidden in antique cabinets. Most bathrooms are open plan so as not to detract from the beams and volumes. There is even a sheltered sun lounge on the terrace only overlooked by sparrows. A nice place to sit and sample your chilled choice picked up in Chablis.

Rooms	6 doubles, 5 twins: €85-€125.
Meals	Breakfast €10.
	Lunch & dinner €20.50-€43.50.
	Wine €15-€100.
Closed	Last 3 weeks January.

Tel	+33 (0)3 86 33 69 70
Email	message@beursaudiere.com
Web	www.beursaudiere.com

Monsieur & Madame Lenoble
Hôtel de la Beursaudière,
5-7 rue Hyacinthe Gautherin,
89310 Nitry, Yonne

Château de la Resle

Built for a dignitary who lost his head in the French Revolution, this handsome house sits on an impeccable estate of landscaped gardens, neat, gravelled, lavender-lined paths, plus *orangerie*, pond and hornbeam maze. Johan and Pieter, your smiley, engaging, humorous hosts, came from Holland several years ago and have made everything elegant, modern and stylish. A fine stone staircase with a wrought-iron banister leads to spacious, minimally furnished rooms painted in muted hues of moss and deep-blue; views ponder over the gardens to hilly horizons, and fabulous modern art hangs on the walls. A further huge suite with a fine dressing area lies under dramatic roof carpentry in a cottage outside. Bathrooms are spotless white with state-of-the-art showers, pale pebble floors, beautiful accessories and chunky towels. Tuck into breakfast in the vast dining room with its dark walls and limestone flags, then work it off in the first-floor fitness room. Or set off for the vineyards and the wine tastings, the pretty villages with their ancient half-timbered houses, the walks and the cycle rides. Fabulous in every way. *Over 16s welcome.*

Rooms	1 double, 1 twin/double: €195-€295. 3 suites for 2, 1 suite for 4: €250-€475. Extra bed/sofabed €50 p.p. per night.
Meals	Dinner available on request, depending on occupancy. Restaurant 2km.
Closed	1 November – 1 March.

Johan Bouman & Pieter Franssens	**Mobile**	+33 (0)6 86 11 29 22
Château de la Resle,	**Email**	info@chateaudelaresle.com
89230 Montigny la Resle,	**Web**	www.chateaudelaresle.com
Yonne		

ENTRY 75 MAP 5

Château de Béru

Château life as you'd dream it, and windows that survey vineyards for miles. Home to the Comtes de Béru since 1627, the estate includes a working vineyard. Harvested by hand, the grapes are grown naturally, mostly organically – a delectable extra as you tour the cellars. It's a place that transports you to another era, yet the choice antiques and tasselled tie-backs harmonise with contemporary backdrops: raw brickwork and pretty fabrics, fresh linens, chic bathrooms; we loved 'Havane'. Have breakfast in the sitting-dining room or in bed. Dinner is available in the wine bar at the 16th-century stables.

Le Petit Village

You are on the outskirts of a medieval village close to the Armançon river and this is perfect for families. Choose between Spring Cottage or Coach House – each has attractively decorated rooms with oak beams, flagstone floors, great mattresses and good fabrics. Bathrooms are clean and modern and there's a play barn full of toys. Breakfast is served at one convivial table – freshly baked bread and pastries or the Full Monty from Annabella's trusty Aga. She will cook you a delicious dinner too if you ask. Warm, friendly hosts, a heated shared pool and private gardens make this is a jewel. Enchanting.

Rooms	3 doubles: €150-€180. 1 suite for 5: €250-€270. Singles €150-€170. Extra bed €15-€25 p.p. per night.		**Rooms**	1 double; 1 double with separate bathroom: €70-€80. 1 cottage for 4, 1 cottage for 6: €125-€150.	
Meals	Dinner €40, by arrangement. Wine €20-€50. Restaurant 7km.		**Meals**	Breakfast €8-€10. Dinner, 4 courses, €25. Restaurant 3km.	
Closed	Rarely.		**Closed**	Rarely; self-catering only in August.	

Tel	+33 (0)3 86 75 90 43		**Tel**	+33 (0)3 86 75 19 08
Email	laurencedeberu@gmail.com		**Email**	le-petit-village@orange.fr
Web	www.chateaudeberu.com		**Web**	www.le-petit-village.com

Laurence & Athénaïs de Béru
Château de Béru,
32 Grande Rue,
89700 Béru, Yonne

Annabella Ware
Le Petit Village,
33 route de Genève,
89160 Fulvy, Yonne

Carpe Diem

Tranquil villages are close in this refreshingly unspoilt corner of Bourgogne: Vézelay and its abbey, quaint Noyers, and epicurean Dijon just a day trip away. Through the gate all is verdant with vines and the garden is perfect for evening strolls. You eat convivially on the pretty terrace or in the grand dining room with Patrick and Eric hosting you warmly. Vegetables are home grown, everything is cooked from scratch. Breakfast is as delicious – homemade yogurt, freshly-baked cakes, local meats and cheeses. You're in gorgeous countryside and the village perches on the river Serein so you can walk without coming across busy roads. Noyers is 9km away and one of the most beautiful villages in France. Return to romantic bedrooms with fine paintings and antiques, either in the house or the stables. *Over 12s welcome.*

Le Verger

You're in the middle of a proper Burgundian village by the church. Rooms are filled with character and beautiful things – a dining room with a wonderful beamed ceiling, a sitting room with Persian rugs, vast fireplace, pink tiled floor. Charming Alan and Rosemary give you breakfasts with homemade jams at one big table, outdoors in fine weather. Bedrooms – one in one house, two in the other – are fresh as a daisy and warm as toast with fine antiques and good art – one packed with books from floor to ceiling. Explore culture, taste wine, nip to Epoisses for some remarkably smelly cheese. A super place to stay.

Rooms	4 doubles, 1 twin/double: €75-€110. Singles €66-€90.
Meals	Dinner with wine, €38; not Thursdays. Restaurants 4km.
Closed	Rarely.

Rooms	1 double, 1 family room for 3 sharing bathroom: €80-€90. 1 family room for 3: €80-€90.
Meals	Restaurants 3km.
Closed	Rarely.

Tel	+33 (0)3 86 33 89 32
Email	carpediem.ser@gmail.com
Web	www.b-and-b-burgundy.com

Patrick Cabon
Carpe Diem,
53 Grande Rue,
89440 Massangis, Yonne

Mobile	+44 (0)77688 40313
Email	piazza@btinternet.com
Web	www.burgundyhols.com

Alan Ravenscroft & Rosemary Stones
Le Verger,
9-11 rue du Gravelain,
89440 Coutarnoux, Yonne

ENTRY 78   MAP 6

ENTRY 79   MAP 6

Maison Crème Anglaise

From a Tintin collection to the dogs, Custard and Crumble, this gracious old house is full of surprises. Swallows nest in a medieval archway, a staircase winds up a tower and the garden falls steeply away giving unforgettable views. Sumptuous rooms are bright with flowers, bedrooms are pretty, cosy, comfy, appealing and the charming bathroom is shared. Graham and Christine, open, enthusiastic, entertaining, hands-on, go the extra mile for their guests and hold evening recitals and exhibitions for local artists in the courtyard. The garden pool is delicious, the hilltop village is historic, the peace is a balm.

La Cimentelle

After an astoundingly beautiful drive you reach this handsome family house built by titans of the cement industry at the turn of the last century: now a pool sits on top of the old factory. Come for extraordinary food (both hosts are gourmet cooks), thoughtfulness, friendly chat and the loveliest rooms. Three are works of art and a touch of fun: a Murano mirror, an antique desk, pink faux-baroque wallpaper and stunning white linen curtains. Swish bathrooms shine with monogrammed towels and showers of Italian mosaic. Family suites at the top of the house are huge. Don't miss it, you'll need at least two nights. *Please see owner's website for online booking.*

Rooms	2 doubles, 1 twin sharing bathroom: €80-€90.
Meals	Buffet supper available on request. Special events catered for. Restaurants 6km.
Closed	Rarely.

Rooms	7 doubles: €95-€125. 2 family rooms for 6: €170-€370. Singles €80-€115. Extra bed/sofabed €35 p.p. per night.
Meals	Dinner with wine, €46. Guest kitchen and terrace also available.
Closed	Rarely.

Tel	+33 (0)3 86 32 07 73
Email	grahambattye@maisoncremeanglaise.com
Web	www.maisoncremeanglaise.com

Graham & Christine Battye
Maison Crème Anglaise,
22 Grande Rue,
89420 Montréal, Yonne

Tel	+33 (0)3 86 31 04 85
Email	lacimentelle@orange.fr
Web	www.lacimentelle.com

Nathalie & Stéphane Oudot
La Cimentelle,
4 rue de la Cimentelle,
89200 Vassy lès Avallon, Yonne

ENTRY 80   MAP 6

ENTRY 81   MAP 6

Girolles les Forges

Beyond the hamlet's church, in gardens where birds sing and hens roam, is a blue-shuttered 'maison de maître.' Corinne and Christian love nothing more than to share their life and their home, its regal sitting room, its elegant dining room, its long table laden with seasonal fruits, organic breads and homemade jams at breakfast. Discover historic Avallon and the fine wines of Chablis; return to polished boards, lush linen, a soothing massage. One bedroom is at the top of the steep dovecot stair, three are in the house, and the cellar suite, off the garden, is stunning. As for dinner, don't miss it: Christian is a fabulous chef.

Auberge de la Tuilerie

Surrounded by acres of woodland and pasture, a blissfully remote Burgundy farmhouse with charming rooms. Retired journalist Lee has transformed her historic home into a mellow countryside retreat. Parquet floors and oak beams endure in light, spacious bedrooms filled with antiques; each has a sparkling modern bathroom. Lee's bountiful vegetable garden provides much of the produce for superb regional meals eaten communally. Only birdsong disturbs the deep peace, so go slow and laze by the inviting pool, explore the wild gardens, take a siesta... or head out to Vézelay hilltop village or medieval Clamecy. Wonderful. *Minimum stay: 2 nights in high season. Pets by arrangement.*

Rooms	3 doubles: €83-€104. 2 suites for 4: €104-€156. Extra bed/sofabed €20 p.p. per night.	**Rooms**	3 doubles, 2 twin/doubles: €95. Singles €75-€95. Extra bed/sofabed €20 p.p. per night.
Meals	Dinner with wine, €45; children €12. Restaurants 7km.	**Meals**	Dinner €38. Restaurant 4km.
Closed	Rarely.	**Closed**	Rarely.

Tel   +33 (0)3 86 33 59 61
Email girolleslesforges@orange.fr
Web   www.girolleslesforges.com

Christian & Corinne Sauer
Girolles les Forges,
8 rue Bouchardat,
89200 Girolles, Yonne

Email auberge.tuilerie@gmail.com
Web   www.auberge-tuilerie.com

Lee Yanowitch
Auberge de la Tuilerie,
La Tuilerie,
89480 Andryes, Yonne

ENTRY 82 MAP 5

ENTRY 83 MAP 5

L'Étoile Argentée

In a courtyard where coaching horses once rested, now there are colourful gardens where children can play. Breakfast out here on croissants and homemade jams, or sit out with a glass of wine and a book from the library. In winter, cuddle up by the wood-burner amid Monsieur's choice of antiques and paintings. South-facing bedrooms, up wide oak stairs, are elegantly decorated by Madame, an interior designer. Two have modern en suite showers but loos are shared. Table d'hôte is popular – guests often ask for the recipes – and you can book cooking lessons. There's a pool and tennis and happy days can be spent fishing, golfing and walking in pristine countryside. *Male dogs welcome. Smoking permitted outside.*

Domaine de Serrigny

Just yards from a pretty stretch of the Burgundy Canal, a fine 18th-century house with high walls and magnificent views to perfect little Châteauneuf en Auxois. Charles and Marie-Pascale are stylish, informal and huge fun; so is their house. Fabulous antiques, interesting art and textiles, space outside for children to cavort. Bedrooms are a beautiful mix of styles with something for everyone, from grand salon to zen attic; all are delightful, bathrooms are bliss. Relax in the garden with its big lawn, colourful pots, decked pool and tennis court; have breakfast here or in the large open-plan sitting/dining room. Heaps of charm.

Rooms	1 twin/double, 1 twin, sharing wc; let to same party only: €65-€95. 1 twin/double with separate bathroom & wc: €65-€95. Dinner, B&B €95-€120 p.p.. Extra bed/sofabed €15 p.p. per night.	**Rooms**	1 double: €112-€117. 1 family room for 4: €132. Children under 8 free. Extra bed €18.
Meals	Dinner €25, by arrangement. Wine €12-€20.	**Meals**	Auberge opposite (closed Mondays).
Closed	Rarely.	**Closed**	Rarely.

Tel	+33 (0)3 80 30 70 52	**Tel**	+33 (0)3 80 49 28 13
Email	letoileargentee@gmail.com	**Email**	chaillot.mp@wanadoo.fr
Web	www.letoileargentee.com	**Web**	www.manoir-de-serrigny.com

Isabelle van Delft
L'Étoile Argentée,
2 av Carnot,
21350 Vitteaux, Côte-d'Or

Marie-Pascale Chaillot
Domaine de Serrigny,
Lieu dit le Village, Route Départementale,
21320 Vandenesse en Auxois, Côte-d'Or

ENTRY 84   MAP 6

ENTRY 85   MAP 6

Château de Voudenay

Cecile bought this 12th-century château as a shell, without ceilings or stairs, and over the years has created an open-plan interior combining exposed beams, elaborate chandeliers and mismatched furniture with modern artworks and sculptures. Discover a vast, theatrical space, with plenty of space to spread out – play billiards in the salon, read or play board games next to the huge fireplace in the corner, explore the rambling grounds and sit out on the shaded terrace. A welcome basket includes teas and coffees, and typical French breakfast with fruit from the orchard is served around the dining room table. You can arrange to have dinner from a private chef or drive to Arnay-le-Duc, ten minutes away, for restaurants – Chez Camille is good. *Minimum stay: 2 nights.*

La Saura

For those wishing to escape to a sweet Côte d'Or village near Beaune – and some of the world's greatest wines – come here. The house and stables are charming and peaceful, the renovation is recent, the décor is delicious, the pool is a boon. Irresistible Madame smiles easily and loves her guests, gives you generous breakfasts before the log fire and big airy bedrooms with classic colours and lavish touches – and views; there's also a conservatory for guests with books, magazines, games and TV. Bed linen is antique and embroidered, towels carry the La Saura logo, paths lead into the hills. Bliss. *Minimum stay: 2 nights June-Sept. Children over 10 welcome. Pets by arrangement.*

Rooms	6 doubles: €100-€130. Extra bed €25 p.p. per night. Cot available at no charge.	**Rooms**	1 double: €110-€125. 1 suite for 3: €130-€145. Extra bed/sofabed €35 p.p. per night.
Meals	Dinner, 3 courses with wine, €25-€30.	**Meals**	Dinner available by arrangement. Restaurant nearby, open Fri & Sat evenings.
Closed	5 January – 31 March.	**Closed**	30 November – 28 February.

Tel	+33 (0)6 03 74 53 86	**Tel**	+33 (0)3 80 20 17 46
Email	cecileperry123@gmail.com	**Email**	la-saura@wanadoo.fr
		Web	www.la-saura.com

Cécile Perry
Château de Voudenay,
9 rue de la Volaine,
21230 Voudenay le Château, Côte-d'Or

Jocelyne-Marie Lehallé
La Saura,
Route de Beaune,
21360 Lusigny sur Ouche, Côte-d'Or

Les Hêtres Rouges

A pretty old Burgundian hunting lodge, 'Copper Beeches' stands in a walled garden full of ancient trees; and its village setting is a delight. There's an unexpected air of Provence inside: beautifully judged colour schemes (Madame paints), fine furniture, numerous *objets*, a tomcat or two. Your hosts extend a warm, genuine yet ungushing welcome to the weary traveller, and can organise wine tours that are perfect for you. Up a steep stair are low-ceilinged rooms with dark character and fine linen. Breakfast has the savour of yesteryear: yogurt, fresh bread, homemade jam, delicious coffee.

Rooms	1 twin/double, 1 twin: €95-€105. Extra bed €32.
Meals	Restaurants 8km.
Closed	Rarely.

Le Clos des Roseaux

Bernard and Annick are so welcoming, inviting you to enjoy their home and gardens. The house, built for the master of the châteaux in 1860, has deep history which can be felt throughout; it's easy to imagine its heyday with vines planted up to the terrace. Burgundy's cellars are its main draw but its charms extend beyond wine. Gentle countryside for walking, cycling, photography and birdwatching surrounds you. Just a five-minute drive from the house is the Route des Grands Crus, stretching for 30km through ancient villages and vineyards. Closer is handsome, cobbled Beaune with its colourful tiled roofs. Breakfasts of homemade jam, cakes and fruit from the orchard will set you up for a day of sipping and swirling in the vineyards. Gather up a picnic and bring it back to enjoy in the extensive gardens.

Rooms	1 double: €100-€125. 1 family room for 4: €140-€170. Extra bed/sofabed €35 p.p. per night.
Meals	Restaurants 15-minute walk.
Closed	21 December – 6 January.

Tel	+33 (0)3 80 62 53 98
Email	leshetresrouges@free.fr
Web	www.leshetresrouges.com

Jean-François & Christiane Bugnet
Les Hêtres Rouges,
10 route de Nuits, Antilly,
21700 Argilly, Côte-d'Or

ENTRY 88   MAP 11

Tel	+33 (0)3 80 22 14 08
Email	annick.desroseaux@gmail.com
Web	www.leclos-desroseaux.com

Annick des Roseaux
Le Clos des Roseaux,
1 rue de l'eglise,
21200 Chorey les Beaune, Côte-d'Or

ENTRY 89   MAP 11

Sous le Baldaquin

Once Yves – the perfect host – swings open the huge doors of his townhouse in the heart of Beaune, the 21st-century disappears, the serene garden tugs at your soul and peace descends. Play the count, countess or courtesan as you mount the stone stair to your small perfect cocoon, past walls and ceiling painted in pale trompe-l'œil allegory. Gracious and elegant are the aubergine and willow-green taffeta drapes and beribboned baldaquin, charming the bathroom with its ancient double-basin, beautiful the view to the rambling roses. To call this romantic is an understatement – and Yves is the nicest host.

Les Jardins de Loïs

The owners are wine buffs and their pride and joy is their cellar. Inside this 200-year-old house every detail delights, while bedrooms, reached by a splendid exterior stair, are lavish and beautiful. Antique armoires flatter oriental rugs, Italian bathrooms are immaculate with monsoon showers, and the garden suite is housed in a private outbuilding with its own sitting room and huge bath. Breakfast and homemade jams are enjoyed in the elegant, airy dining room. Stroll Beaune's ancient cobbles, sample the fruits of the region's wine capital. Then retire with a bottle of their own fine burgundy to a gem of a half-hectare garden.

Rooms	1 double: €100-€110. Extra bed €25.
Meals	Restaurants 5-minute walk.
Closed	Rarely.

Rooms	3 doubles: €165. 2 suites for 2: €185-€195.
Meals	Restaurant 150m.
Closed	25 December – 20 January.

Tel	+33 (0)3 80 24 79 30
Email	yves.cantenot@laposte.net
Web	www.souslebaldaquin.fr

Yves Cantenot
Sous le Baldaquin,
39 rue Maufoux,
21200 Beaune, Côte-d'Or

ENTRY 90   MAP 11

Tel	+33 (0)3 80 22 41 97
Email	contact@jardinsdelois.com
Web	www.jardinsdelois.com

Anne-Marie & Philippe Dufouleur
Les Jardins de Loïs,
21200 Beaune,
Côte-d'Or

ENTRY 91   MAP 11

La Terre d'Or

The night view of twinkling Beaune, five minutes down the hill, is glorious. The Martin family – Jean-Louis and Christine now joined by son Vincent – run three wonderful houses, each surrounded by mature trees and a terraced garden. The modern, multi-levelled main house has five large and lovely bedrooms while the stone cottage, for B&B or self-catering, is traditional, the third house being more independent. The noble old beams and rosy tommette floors frame a fine contemporary look warmed with stylish lighting, crisp linen and polished country pieces. The honeymoon suite has a private piece of garden. It's bliss to relax on the main terrace and gaze across vineyards to the ramparts of old Beaune. Down a wildflower path is a family-run restaurant.

Le Clos Champagne Saint Nicolas

Le Clos is nicely set back from the main road and Beaune is a ten-minute stroll. Built to take guests, the new wing has spanking new bedrooms, modern bits in the bathrooms and a salon overlooking the garden. Fabrics, bedding and antiques reveal Anne as a woman of taste who thinks of everything, even a guest kitchen for your morning spread of homemade jams, cake, croissants, bread, yogurt and fresh fruit. Bruno has a passion for vintage cars, especially if they're English. Knowledgeable natives and hospitable hosts, they fill you in on the sights, restaurants and vineyards over a welcoming cup of tea or some fresh juice.

Rooms	1 twin: €200-€230. 4 suites for 2: €165-€280. 1 cottage for 4, 1 cottage for 6: €360-€480.
Meals	Breakfast €13. Picnic available. Restaurant 400m.
Closed	Rarely.

Rooms	1 double, 2 twin/doubles: €110-€130. Extra bed/sofabed €10 p.p. per night.
Meals	Guest kitchen. Restaurants within walking distance.
Closed	Rarely.

Tel	+33 (0)3 80 25 90 90
Email	jlmartin@laterredor.com
Web	www.laterredor.com

Vincent, Christine & Jean-Louis Martin
La Terre d'Or,
Rue Izembart La Montagne,
21200 Beaune, Côte-d'Or

Tel	+33 (0)3 80 61 24 92
Email	closchamp.stnicolas@free.fr
Web	closchamp.stnicolas.free.fr

Bruno & Anne Durand de Gevigney
Le Clos Champagne Saint Nicolas,
114 ter route de Dijon,
21200 Beaune, Côte-d'Or

ENTRY 92   MAP 11   **ENTRY 93   MAP 11**

Clos Saint Jacques

Wine-lovers' heaven! In a magnificent, ancient village this 18th-century winery looks its handsome 300-year-old self, but has all the right mod cons. Your engaging, enthusiastic and knowledgeable hosts are keen to share their local contacts; Monsieur is in the wine trade, Madame takes huge care of guests with memorable breakfasts and big, deeply comfortable beds. Lovely rooms, in the old worker's house and *cuverie*, are either rustic and beamed or more brightly modern; everyone's welcome to relax in sofas by the fire. Pilgrims bound for Santiago gathered in Meursault and the tradition of hospitality continues.

Jan's Place

Sitting pretty, opposite the ancient church and right on the river – with its own jetty – Jan's home is comfortably quirky, and spotless. In what was once the village inn you've a little warren of downstairs rooms with a huge collection of vinyl, loads of books, French, Dutch, Danish and English antiques; country breakfasts and dinners, served beautifully, in the kitchen or on one of the terraces. Peaceful bedrooms, up winding stairs, with gentle views; two cosy under the eaves – and bathrooms both properly modern and pleasingly retro. Take to the river, go cycling, explore Besançon and the vineyards of the Côte d'Or. *Pets by arrangement.*

Rooms	3 apartments for 2, 1 apartment for 4: €98-€198. Extra bed €20 only for Sous les Etoiles.
Meals	Restaurants 3-minute walk.
Closed	Rarely.

Rooms	3 doubles: €105-€125. 1 family room for 4 with separate shower room: €150. Extra bed/sofabed €18 p.p. per night.
Meals	Dinner, 3 courses, €25; by arrangement. Restaurants 6km.
Closed	31 October – 31 January.

Mobile +33 (0)6 08 93 25 82/(0)6 80 99 10 91
Email contact@clossaintjacques.fr
Web www.clossaintjacques.fr

Anne & Denis Duveau
Clos Saint Jacques,
1 rue Pierre Mouchoux,
21190 Meursault, Côte-d'Or

Tel +33 (0)9 63 60 14 46
Email jcreuvers@gmail.com
Web www.jansplaceinburgundy.jimdo.com

Jan Reuvers
Jan's Place,
Quartier de l'Eglise 8/10,
71350 Ecuelles, Saône-et-Loire

ENTRY 94   MAP 11

ENTRY 95   MAP 11

Domaine de Nesvres

There are Michelin stars in Chagny, châteaux all around and the Route des Vins beyond the door; this is a great spot for a civilised holiday. In the small village of St Désert, at the end of the private driveway, you stay on a fortified farm steeped in history and owned by a lovely French couple. Outside is vast and full of rustic charm; inside is cosy and comfy. Find billiards, books, beams, a sitting room for guests (games, music, WiFi, TV), five airy bedrooms (the family room with good antiques) and Adeline's delicious food, perhaps homemade 'pain d'épices' at breakfast, and poulet de Bresse at dinner.

L'Orangerie

Enter gardens that are secluded, charming, full of colour. Light spills into the sitting room through arched vine-clad windows while cream walls and Indian rugs add to the simple elegance of this *maison de maître*. Antiques and travel are the owners' passion: a grand staircase, interesting paintings and oriental fabrics add up to a mix of styles that work beautifully. Bedrooms vary in size and have lovely seersucker linen and antique prints; bathrooms are classically tasteful. Terraced lawns lead down to the heated pool, lavish breakfasts include unusual homemade jams, and the wonderful Voie Verte cycle route runs nearby. *Minimum stay: 2 nights. Children over 12 welcome.*

Rooms	1 double, 1 twin: €75-€85. 1 family room for 3, 1 family room for 4: €85-€140. 1 triple: €85-€115. Pets €5 p.n.
Meals	Dinner with apéritif & wine, €35. Restaurants 5km.
Closed	Rarely.

Rooms	3 twin/doubles: €80-€110.
Meals	Hosted dinner with wine, €25-€40. Restaurants 4km.
Closed	3 November – 17 March.

Tel	+33 (0)3 85 47 98 93
Email	micourcenet@aol.com
Web	domainedenesvres.jimdo.com

Adeline & Michel Courcenet
Domaine de Nesvres,
Route de Buxy,
71390 Saint-Désert, Saône-et-Loire

Tel	+33 (0)3 85 47 91 94
Email	info@orangerie-moroges.com
Web	www.orangerie-moroges.com

David Eades & Niels Lierow
L'Orangerie,
20 rue des Lavoirs Vingelles,
71390 Moroges, Saône-et-Loire

ENTRY 96   MAP 11

ENTRY 97   MAP 11

Le Crot Foulot

Gutsy Jan and Annie sold their prize-winning restaurant in Brussels and filled their cellar while putting the finishing touches to this handsome wine-grower's house. Golden stones outside, a clean minimalism inside: Belgians always seem to pull this off with flair. An elegant glass and wood staircase leads to muted bedrooms with delicate pale timbers revealed and glorified. In the open kitchen you can watch Jan whip up his mussel mousse while a farmyard chicken sizzles with citrus fruits in the oven. Annie will have brought up the perfect nectar for the menu. All is well in Burgundy tonight!

La Ferme de Marie-Eugénie

Marie-Eugénie and Dominique give you light-flooded rooms in their pretty half-timbered barn which looks out over a big lawned garden. Bedrooms are comfortable with much family art; there's an inviting, books-and-magazines salon and a slick dining-kitchen where you eat. The cooking is legendary, changing with the seasons but always with the freshest local ingredients: roasted Bresse chicken, cheese from the rugged Jura mountains, wines from Beaune, all served around a big shared table. Potter around Louhans' market and count the 157 arches of the arcaded street – the longest in France – or make day trips to Brancion's hilltop chapel, the tiny wine producing villages around Chardonnay, Tournus' famous abbey or Beaune's colourful Hospice.

Rooms	3 twin/doubles, 1 twin: €110-€140. 1 family room for 3: €168-€198.
Meals	Dinner €39. Wine from €15.
Closed	November – February.

Rooms	3 doubles, 1 twin: €135. Extra bed/sofabed €30 p.p. per night.
Meals	Dinner €35. Wine €25-€70. Restaurants in Louhans, 9km.
Closed	Christmas.

Tel	+33 (0)3 85 94 81 07
Email	info@crotfoulot.com
Web	www.crotfoulot.com

Annie Coeckelberghs & Jan Hostens
Le Crot Foulot,
71240 Jugy,
Saône-et-Loire

Tel	+33 (0)3 85 74 81 84
Email	info@lafermedemarieeugenie.fr
Web	www.lafermedemarieeugenie.fr

Marie-Eugénie Dupuy
La Ferme de Marie-Eugénie,
225 allée de Chardenoux,
71500 Bruailles, Saône-et-Loire

Le Clos de Clessé

Set in superb gardens (mature olive trees, clipped box hedges, gravel paths, stone-edged beds, delicious roses) the old manor by the church is the life's dream of delightful Tessy and André, Cordon Bleu cooks both – don't miss dinner! Two gorgeous cottages with split-level bedrooms overlook the garden and there's a pretty, bare-beamed guest room in the main house. Natural stone, old fireplaces, terracotta tiles and flagstones worn satin-smooth offset modern fittings and antique pieces perfectly. Vineyards and châteaux galore... though the tempting and secluded pool may be as far as you'll get. *Minimum stay: 2 nights in high season. Pets by arrangement.*

Château de Vaulx

Vaulx was described in 1886 as "well-proportioned and elegant in its simplicity". It is as lovely now and in the most beautiful position, high on a hill with views that stretch to distant mountains. Delightful Marty will escort you to the west wing then create a delicious dinner. Expect big bedrooms full of character, a panelled drawing room with chandeliers, a huge dining room with fresh flowers, and manicured lawns and box balls tightly topiaried – stroll down the romantic avenues in dappled sunlight. In the village, a 13th-century bell tower; nearby, one of the best chocolate makers in France (monthly tastings and lessons).

	Le Clos de Clessé	Château de Vaulx
Rooms	1 double: from €110. 2 cottages for 4: €190-€215. Singles €105-€125. Extra bed/sofabed €30 p.p. per night.	2 doubles: €110-€130. 2 family rooms for 4: €149. 1 apartment for 5: €195. Extra bed €36-€100 p.p.
Meals	Dinner, 4 courses with wine, €50; available twice a week. Children under 12, €20. Restaurant 3km.	Dinner €33. Wine €20. Restaurant 3km.
Closed	Rarely.	Rarely.

Tel	+33 (0)3 85 23 03 56	+33 (0)3 85 70 64 03
Email	info@closdeclesse.com	marty@chateaudevaulx.com
Web	www.closdeclesse.com	www.chateaudevaulx.com

Tessy & André Gladinez
Le Clos de Clessé,
11 place de l'église,
71260 Clessé, Saône-et-Loire

Marty Freriksen
Château de Vaulx,
71800 St Julien de Civry,
Saône-et-Loire

La Tour

The terraced garden is brimful of stepping
stones and flowers, ginger tabbies wend
through the irises, bucolic views stretch
across undulating pastures: this is a deeply
rural ensemble. June, widely travelled, kind,
attentive, a great reader and lover of art in all
its forms, lives in a long stone farmhouse in
a cluster of outbuildings that go back to
1740. The airy two-bedroom suite in its own
wing has a fine stone fireplace on its ground
floor; floorboards are honey-coloured, the
bathroom is a treat, and scrumptious
breakfasts are served on charming country
china. Lovely.

Château de Villette

Coen and Catherine – he Dutch, she
Belgian – fell in love with this little château,
then had their wedding here: they love their
adopted country. They've opened just five
rooms to guests (the suites are twin-
roomed) so they can spoil you properly.
And get to know you over dinner. (Though,
should you prefer a romantic dinner for
two, they'll understand.) Bedrooms, large,
light and airy, with warm colours and
polished floors, are dressed in château-
style finery. Views sail out of great
windows to meadows and woodland and
families will love it. Beaune and the
vineyards lie temptingly close.

Rooms	1 family suite for 3: €85-€95. Extra bed €15.
Meals	Dinner with wine, €24. Vegetarian meals available. Restaurants 7km.
Closed	Rarely.

Rooms	3 doubles: €195-€265. 2 suites for 5: €340-€410.
Meals	Dinner €55, book ahead. Wine €18-€100.
Closed	15 September – 31 March.

Tel	+33 (0)3 85 25 11 67
Email	bibbyjune@gmail.com
Web	www.latourbandb.com

June Bibby
La Tour,
71120 Marcilly La Guerce,
Saône-et-Loire

ENTRY 102   MAP 11

Tel	+33 (0)3 86 30 09 13
Email	catherinestork@chateaudevillette.eu
Web	www.chateaudevillette.eu

Catherine & Coen Stork
Château de Villette,
58170 Poil,
Nièvre

ENTRY 103   MAP 11

Château de Prye

The rooms are vast, the marble stables are palatial and the corridors heave with antlers and stag heads from previous ancestors; the history is intriguing. The young Marquis and Marquise have joyfully taken up the challenge of running both château and estate (they breed Charolais cattle) and host their guests with grace. Each cavernous bedroom is furnished with splendid antiques; bathrooms are en suite. Take a peek at the château kitchen... from here breakfast is dispatched to an oak-panelled dining room with sumptuous views. This rambling château with its woodlands, gentle river and trees is dreamy... relish the fairy tale.

La Villa des Prés

Deep in real peace-wrapped country, this place of secluded old-style comfort and breathtaking views of the Morvan has new and rightly enthusiastic Dutch owners: it's gorgeous. Inside are open fires, antique beds, sympathetic period decorations, antique linen and super modern showers. Rooms are vast and there are two salons, one gloriously golden green, for lazing about. A baronial double stair leads down to the fine garden and the ha-ha where, rather endearingly, chickens may be roaming. A base for church, château and vineyard visits – a peaceful paradise.
Minimum stay: 2 nights.

Rooms	3 doubles, 2 suites for 4: €115-€190.
Meals	Dinner €35. Wine €8-€105.
Closed	Mid-October to mid-April.

Rooms	5 twin/doubles: €80-€105.
Meals	Complimentary dinner with wine for 7-night stays (Sun only). Guest kitchen. Restaurant 3km.
Closed	Rarely.

Tel	+33 (0)3 86 58 42 64
Email	info@chateaudeprye.com
Web	www.chateaudeprye.com

**Magdalena & Antoine-Emmanuel
du Bourg de Bozas**
Château de Prye,
58160 La Fermeté, Nièvre

Tel	+33 (0)3 86 29 03 81
Email	villa-des-pres@orange.fr
Web	www.villa-des-pres.com

Kees & Inge Stapel
La Villa des Prés,
Route de Corbigny,
58420 St Révérien, Nièvre

ENTRY 104   MAP 10

ENTRY 105   MAP 5

Jardin d'Amis

From this peaceful spot, meander through gentle countryside to reach wine tastings, visit the hill town of Vézelay with its Benedictine abbey or to canoe from Saint-Père. Return to a homely place, where guests have a separate entrance and a living room, as well as access to a handy fridge and microwave. 'Gamay' on the ground floor has its own little courtyard terrace for quiet relaxation, and there's a big garden with fruit and vegetable patches and spaces for outdoor dining. Lovely Irish hosts Anne and Stuart offer boulangerie goodies, homemade jam, eggs and yogurts from the nearby farm for breakfast, and serve up good value dinners too. *Pets by arrangement.*

Le Prieuré Saint Agnan

Beneath the bell tower of Cosne sur Loire's historic church, five characterful B&B rooms in an old Benedictine priory. Surrounded by tranquil gardens, the handsome stone building stands on the banks of the Loire, within walking distance of the town's restaurants, and a cycle ride from Sancerre and Pouilly Fumé vineyards. Bedrooms are spacious and colourful, with river or courtyard views, and immaculate en-suite shower rooms. A continental breakfast, including local goat's cheese and ham, is served at a large wooden table in the light-filled dining room or in the garden. Take a dip in the heated pool or explore local châteaux. *Parking on-site.*

Rooms	2 doubles, 1 twin/double: €76. Singles €66. Extra bed/sofabed €26 p.p. per night.	**Rooms**	5 doubles: €120-€150. Extra bed/sofabed €30 p.p. per night.
Meals	Dinner, 4 courses with apéritif & wine, €30.	**Meals**	Restaurants within walking distance.
Closed	1 November – 31 March.	**Closed**	Rarely.

Tel +33 (0)3 86 26 88 02
Email anne.irwin@orange.fr
Web www.jardindamis.com

Anne Irwin
Jardin d'Amis,
2 bis rue de Grenois,
58420 Asnan, Nièvre

Email leprieuresaintagnan@gmail.com
Web www.prieuresaintagnan.com

Gilles Cégretin
Le Prieuré Saint Agnan,
1 rue des Forges, Impasse du Prieuré, Place St Agnan, 58200 Cosne sur Loire, Nièvre

ENTRY 106   MAP 5

ENTRY 107   MAP 5

Hôtel Panache, page 113

Le Relais du Louvre

Look down the throats of gargoyles, soak up the history. The Revolutionaries printed their newsletter in the cellar; the place inspired Puccini's Café Momus in *Bohême*. It is utterly delightful and so are the charming young managers who greet you from the antique desk. Everywhere, antiques and oriental rugs complement the modernity of firm beds and perfect bathrooms. Front rooms look onto the church's Gothic flights of fancy and along to the austerely neo-classical Louvre; others give onto a light-filled patio. Top-floor junior suites have space for a sofabed, pastel walls, exuberant upholstery and heaps of light from mansard windows. Smaller rooms are luminous, fresh and restful – yellow, a favourite colour, brings sunny moods into small spaces. Various rooms connect to make family suites. You feel softly secluded and coddled everywhere. The sense of service is highly developed and, as there is no dining room, breakfast comes to you.

Rooms	14 twin/doubles: €165-€389. 1 suite for 2, 1 suite for 3, 1 suite for 4: €235-€540. 4 singles: €135-€225. On each floor 2 rooms interconnect to make a family suite.
Meals	Breakfast €15 (until 2pm). Dinner €10-€30 (6pm-3am). Wine €8. All room service only.
Closed	Never.

Sophie Aulnette
Le Relais du Louvre,
19 rue des Prêtres St Germain l'Auxerrois,
75001 Paris

Tel   +33 (0)1 40 41 96 42
Email contact@relaisdulouvre.com
Web   www.relaisdulouvre.com

Hôtel Molière

This is an enchantingly French hotel. The big lobby/salon is smart and rather grand with its *faux-marbre* columns, potted palms and bucket chairs, and the staff at reception are hugely competent and friendly; the young owners infuse the place with their intelligent enthusiasm. The breakfast room is a delight, and deep red curtains frame the leafy, cobbled courtyard. There's also a small, deep-chaired salon round the corner for your quiet moments, perhaps with an old book. Brand new bedrooms are super modern and grand with plush, bold carpets, velvet sofas and bucket chairs, white linen, white walls, antique-look portraits and chandeliers. Bathrooms (some separated from the bedroom by a glass wall) vary in size but all are modern; those in the suites dazzle with rectangular double sinks, huge tubs and swish Italian showers. Interesting paintings, books and ornaments give the hotel a well-cared-for feel. You're in the heart of Paris and can walk to everything – soak your aching limbs in the spa when you return. Everyone loves the Molière.

Rooms	14 doubles, 10 twin/doubles: €215-€410. 3 suites for 4: €500-€610. 2 triples: €345-€410.
Meals	Breakfast €14. Restaurants nearby.
Closed	Never.

Tel	+33 (0)1 42 96 22 01
Email	info@hotel-moliere.fr
Web	www.hotel-moliere.fr

Patricia & Rémy Perraud
Hôtel Molière,
21 rue Molière,
75001 Paris

ENTRY 109 MAP 5

Hôtel Jeanne d'Arc Le Marais

Make haste if you want to experience the last breath of that dying species, the two-star Parisian hotel. The Jeanne d'Arc, always one of the friendliest and best-placed of the bunch, has a talented new owner who will soon be wielding her design flair and filing for an upgrade. She has already lifted the façade with glorious torrents of geraniums – the neighbours love them too. Hurry if you want to enjoy fresh croissants beneath the extravagantly kitsch bling-before-bling mirror in the airy breakfast room, a landmark for generations of Paris-loving guests. The hallway has already been beautified with soft pinky-mushroom paint over a gleaming white dado, some shower rooms have been done up with smart white tiles and trendy strips of brown wafer slices while others await their turn in their spotless but fuddy-duddy dated garb of bubbly tiles and reedy pictures. The staircase will soon match the hallway, all bedding is to be renewed and the brocante-style furniture mix brought up to date, but not at the price of the essence of the place, its cosy friendliness and superb value for the lively, trend-conscious Marais quarter.

Rooms	17 doubles, 10 twin/doubles: €150-€250. 2 family rooms for 4: €220-€420. 5 singles: €90-€120. Extra bed €40.
Meals	Breakfast €8. Restaurants next door.
Closed	Never.

La Réception
Hôtel Jeanne d'Arc Le Marais,
3 rue de Jarente,
75004 Paris

Tel	+33 (0)1 48 87 62 11
Email	information@hoteljeannedarc.com
Web	www.hoteljeannedarc.com

Hôtel du Jeu de Paume

The Île Saint Louis is the most exclusive 17th-century village in Paris and this renovated 'tennis court' – three storeys soar to the roof timbers – is one of its most exceptional sights. Add genuine care from family owners, fresh flowers, time for everyone and super staff. Regulars will be stunned – and delighted – by the recent revamp, which sees sleek designer furniture set under ancient beams, bright colours flung across stone walls, new large built-in cupboards and funky lighting to show off contemporary art. Some rooms feature beautiful beams, one gives onto a little garden; number 109's bed perches on a high platform. We love it – for its sense of history, eccentricities, aesthetic ironies, peaceful humour and feel of home; and for its unconventional attitudes and relaxed yet thoroughly efficient staff. The serene, spacious lounge has low armchairs in chocolate and red, modern art and Lemon Blues the black retriever; breakfast is beneath magnificent timbers by faux Greek columns; work out or take a sauna in a new spa in the vaulted cellars. *Let Madame Heckel know if your stay spans a birthday or anniversary.*

Rooms	20 twin/doubles: €295-€360.
	7 singles: €195-€255.
	3 suites for 2: €560.
	2 apartments for 6: €620-€900.
Meals	Breakfast €20. Restaurants nearby.
Closed	Never.

Tel	+33 (0)1 43 26 14 18
Email	info@jeudepaumehotel.com
Web	www.jeudepaumehotel.com

Nathalie Heckel
Hôtel du Jeu de Paume,
54 rue St Louis en l'Ile,
75004 Paris

ENTRY 111   MAP 5

Hôtel Saint Paul Rive Gauche

A welcoming place with a flickering fire in the sitting room and a day-lit interior patio. With the Luxembourg Gardens a stroll away, bustling Saint Germain at the end of the street, and exceptional service and attention to detail (such as little cakes and organic croissants at breakfast), it's the favourite of many guests. Bedrooms come in different sizes – and that includes small, as with most Paris hotels. Those at the back have handsome views onto the classical façade of the famous Lycée St Louis, those in front look onto the ever-fascinating Rue Monsieur le Prince. Expect crisp white duvets and spotless bathrooms with real shower heads, L'Occitane en Provence soaps and towel heaters. There are stunning fabric wall coverings in each room; colours from these are picked out in the reupholstered period chairs; glass tables add a modern twist and some rooms have mobiles with free Europe use too. The little ground floor salon has quirky portraits with animal heads; the colourful breakfast cellar room can be used for meetings. The fourth generation of a Franco-British family has made the Saint Paul Rive Gauche a warm marriage of French elegance and English comfort.

Rooms	21 doubles, 7 twin/doubles; 2 rooms can interconnect: €178-€408. 2 family rooms for 3, 1 family room for 4: €328-€486. Singles €158-€258. Child bed available in 2 family rooms.
Meals	Buffet breakfast €10-€16. Restaurants nearby.
Closed	Never.

Valérie Benigno
Hôtel Saint Paul Rive Gauche,
43 rue Monsieur le Prince,
75006 Paris

Tel	+33 (0)1 43 26 98 64
Email	contact@hotelsaintpaulparis.com
Web	www.hotelsaintpaulparis.com

ENTRY 112 MAP 5

Grand Hôtel des Balcons

Les Balcons has the lot: an idea of service that produces tea on winter afternoons and a daily feast of a breakfast (cooked specials, organic yogurt, fruit salad, espresso), that's free on your birthday. Owners and staff appear to work with lightness and pleasure. Having decorated their Art Nouveau hotel by taking inspiration from the floral 1890s staircase windows, Jean-François and directrice Marie run the place with great charm. Rooms are simple yet pleasing and those that have already been updated are lovely. The five big family rooms have smart décor and modern lamps, parquet floors and two windows, decent bathrooms (slowly but surely being updated); singles have new walk-in showers. Some rooms are tiny but purpose-made table units use the space judiciously, amusing prints decorate the walls and front rooms have balconies with planted window boxes. At the back, you may be woken by the birds. An eagle eye is kept on maintenance, beds are firm, colours and fabrics simple and bright. Remarkable value, super people, and bang in the heart of the Latin Quarter. *Minimum stay: 2 nights at weekends & in high season.*

Rooms	16 doubles inc. 1 ground floor room with wheelchair access, 13 twins: €155-€220. 5 family rooms for 4: €275. 15 singles: €105-€200.
Meals	Breakfast €12. Restaurants nearby.
Closed	Never.

Tel	+33 (0)1 46 34 78 50
Email	grandhoteldesbalcons@orange.fr
Web	www.balcons.com

Jean-François André
Grand Hôtel des Balcons,
3 rue Casimir Delavigne,
75006 Paris

ENTRY 113   MAP 5

Hôtel Le Clément

This cute little hotel has been in the same family for 100 years and Madame Charrade, should you be lucky enough to meet her, is the gentlest hotelier you could hope to meet (her staff are less personal). More living room than lobby is the inviting sitting area off the new breakfast room, with fireplace, gleaming wood panelling and bookshelves. From the higher floors, the view across the St Germain marketplace to the towers of St Sulpice church is super. These rooms at the top have loads of character with their sloping ceilings, though little space and thin walls, and access is by narrow stairwell or even narrower lift! Back rooms have no view, of course, except over the pretty planting at the bottom of one of the lightwells (the hotel occupies two connecting buildings), but peace is guaranteed. Madame's decorative style is southern cottage: small spriggy or floral prints, harmonious fabrics, good colour combinations – midnight-blue and ivory, Provençal red and orange – and crisp, white piqué bedcovers; bathrooms are often tiled in colourful mosaic. A hotel of good value – from which reaching all the sights is a breeze.

Rooms	12 doubles, 6 twins: €136-€175. 5 triples: €193.
Meals	Buffet breakfast €13. Restaurants nearby.
Closed	Never.

Patricia & Rémy Perraud
Hôtel Le Clément,
6 rue Clément,
75006 Paris

Tel	+33 (0)1 43 26 53 60
Email	info@hotel-clement.fr
Web	www.hotel-clement.fr

Hôtel Dauphine Saint Germain

You will find food for mind and body here, a superb breakfast buffet included in the price, a thoughtful academic atmosphere in the bar later in the day, a youthful joie-de-vivre at all times; the new owner's family photographs help create this vibe. There are some interesting contemporary drawings, prints and photographs as well as traditional baroque-style lamps and furnishings. Under the guidance of the delightful and efficient manager, Inga, the staff are young, dynamic and welcoming. With their 17th-century beams and many-splendoured fabrics, the bedrooms, all different, feel both elegant and personal. Snuggle into the softness of timeless Jouy-cloth walls and moulded mahogany alcoves, admire the harmony of grey and pink with swags and tassels to match, rejoice in your luxurious marble-topped bathroom. The top-floor junior suite has, of course, the best view over Paris' renowned rooftops to Notre Dame cathedral on one side and St Germain des Prés on the other. You will be happy to return after a day's work or museum-tramping to this utterly Parisian hotel in the heart of the fashion and café-life district.

Rooms	29 twin/doubles: €100-€350.
	1 suite for 2: €250-€450.
	Extra bed €25.
Meals	Breakfast €12; children under 12, €6.
	Restaurants next door.
Closed	Never.

Tel	+33 (0)1 48 87 62 11
Email	hotel@dauphine-st-germain.com
Web	www.dauphine-st-germain.com

La Réception
Hôtel Dauphine Saint Germain,
36 rue Dauphine,
75006 Paris

ENTRY 115   MAP 5

La Villa Saint Germain

A showcase of contemporary French design that screams trendy Saint Germain. Step in to soberly studied forms and colours: a blocky black desk, soft silky chestnut curtains, a curvy steel stair rail, ochre-flecked stone floor slabs; gentle music too, and grey and café latte chairs on a teak floor by the bar. Staff are appropriately young, bright, attentive. Bedrooms reflect Saint Germain's split personality: the drama of wine red, brown, white; the gentleness of ivory, beige. Materials are rich and yielding – thick burgundy curtains folded back on silk linings, 'crocodile'-skin bedheads, fluffy white duvets against scarlet walls. (If you like your room with extra personality, ask for a newly redesigned one on the fourth floor, where shelves groan with modern white objets and funky lighting gleams on half-moon tables.) And the details: room numbers light-projected by the door, monogrammed linen, superb designer bathrooms in chrome and ground glass. The bar is peaceful, the lift speedy, and breakfast is down the 1930s-look stairs in a stylish rich red space. It all feels so good and the cool Left Bank laps at your feet.

Rooms	17 doubles, 10 twins: €180-€390. 4 suites for 2: €390-€560.
Meals	Buffet breakfast €16-€22. Restaurants nearby.
Closed	Never.

Christine Horbette
La Villa Saint Germain,
29 rue Jacob,
75006 Paris

Tel   +33 (0)1 43 26 60 00
Email hotel@villa-saintgermain.com
Web   www.villa-saintgermain.com

Le Petit Chomel

Owners Georges and Charlotte Ferrero cleverly create a private house vibe in their boutique hotels – Le Petit Chomel is a delight, and manager Mathieu Renaudin and team are warmly helpful. Style and elegance are their trademarks, and contemporary touches mix with lovely old things in an effortless way. Mme Ferrero hunts out flea market pieces and has a great eye for colour and comfort. Sink into a big sofa or bright orange chair in reception, relax by glowing lamps and vases of flowers; coffee tables invite lingering. The breakfast lounge is a wonderful space to sit in too – shelves of books and sculptures, china and vibrant art. There's something beautiful in every corner. Bedrooms vary in size, but all have beds with bright throws and more eclectic fun; find bathrobes in bigger rooms. Suites, on the sixth floor, have sitting rooms with paintings, a purple, cushion-strewn sofa perhaps, a dumpy china bird here and there; some have balconies with rooftop views. You're in the heart of Montparnasse, next door to Les Botanistes, named best bistro in 2014, and steps from luxurious department store Bon Marché.

Rooms	11 doubles, 10 twin/doubles: €175-€350. 2 suites for 2: €270-€390. Extra bed €40.
Meals	Breakfast €14. Restaurants 1-minute walk.
Closed	Never.

Tel	+33 (0)1 45 48 55 52
Email	chambre414@hotmail.com
Web	www.lepetitchomel.com/en

Mathieu Renaudin
Le Petit Chomel,
15 rue Chomel,
75007 Paris

ENTRY 117   MAP 5

Hôtel de Varenne

Step into the little green cul-de-sac with its ivy covered walls, hidden fountain and exquisite canopy over the entrance door and you will feel like Alice in Wonderland; you have tumbled into an oasis of peace and calm, far from the hustle bustle of the city streets. The front doors slide open, the reception desk is a friendly antique writing table, two bronze statues grace antique chests of drawers and a handsome gilt-studded balustrade leads you upstairs. There's a traditional hotel feel to the bedrooms and most of them (the quietest) look onto the courtyard where breakfast or an evening drink is a delight. Most are a reasonable size for Paris and all have a desk and a chair. Monsieur Pommier is a man of detail and classic taste: green, gold, blue or wine red are the classic figured bedspreads while curtains repeat the colour schemes – certainly no design surprises. There are framed prints of Parisian monuments and well-kept bathrooms with plenty of shelf space. Four bigger rooms give onto the street; slightly less quiet than the rest. The charming staff will always go out of their way to make your stay special.

Rooms	16 doubles, 10 twins: €154-€380. Extra bed/sofabed €40 p.p. per night. Private car park €30 per day.
Meals	Breakfast €12. Restaurants nearby.
Closed	Never.

Jean-Marc Pommier		**Tel**	+33 (0)1 45 51 45 55
Hôtel de Varenne,		**Email**	varennehotel@gmail.com
44 rue de Bourgogne,		**Web**	www.hoteldevarenne.com
75007 Paris			

ENTRY 118   MAP 5

Hôtel Panache

Young, fun Paris meets 30s New York with Belle Époque touches, and more... in this handsome 18th-century building. It's in a residential, not-so-touristy area with boutique shops, bars and eateries of many nationalities so you can happily stay close or be by down by the Seine in no time (Metro line 1, the Folies Bergère and Musée Grévin are all nearby). Sassy interior design: bold geometric patterns in wallpaper and rugs, retro-style furniture, lighting and dark paint works well, sometimes quirkily, around the internal architecture, like its wooden beams and iron girders. So, bedrooms come in all shapes and sizes, and with triple-glazed windows; some have balconies for two to sit out on and ponder the day. Good, solid bathrooms have tiny mosaic to subway-style tiling. The ground floor has a quiet drawing room and a corner bar and restaurant: huge windows, dark floorboards, dark velvets, colour pop armchairs, that serves breakfast, brunch, and dinners of imaginative modern, seasonal dishes, and the best of the quartier's pastries, breads, cheeses, coffees. And staff are super-friendly. Exciting.

Rooms	8 doubles, 14 twin/doubles: €150-€280. 6 suites for 2: €280-€450. 2 family rooms for 4: €280-€400. 6 singles: €95-€190. 4 triples: €170-€300.
Meals	Breakfast: €18. Lunch €24-€29. Dinner: €50.
Closed	Never.

Tel	+33 (0)1 47 70 85 87
Email	hotel@hotelpanache.com
Web	www.hotelpanache.com

Sofia Benarous
Hôtel Panache,
1 rue Geoffroy-Marie,
75009 Paris

ENTRY 119   MAP 5

Hôtel Paradis

A ten-minute walk from Eurostar's Gard du Nord – south towards the Marais – is a youthful hotel in a quirky 'quartier' where everything is on the up. Behind the handsome façade and the eye-catching awning is a hotel of friendliness and French-designer charm. Enter the lobby that divides the breakfast room in two to find clean-limbed sofas, minimalist chairs and striking modern wallpapers. Here, continental buffet breakfast is served – coffee, baguettes, and just-baked croissants. Bedrooms make it all the way to the top and are reached by many stairs, or a lift that squeezes in two. (Note, the lift stops at the sixth floor, so if your room's under the roof on the seventh, you hike the final stair.) Bedrooms overlook the central courtyard or the street – less quiet but more fun; however, windows are double-glazed, and the street is no main thoroughfare. Bedheads are boudoir-biscuit shaped, carpets are modish, colours are moody blue or scarlet and white. Most rooms are small (this is Paris!) so splash out on a suite if you can. And if you fancy a sweet view of the Sacré Coeur, ask for the suite on the sixth floor.

Rooms	23 doubles: €100-€220.
	7 singles: €90-€180.
	6 triples: €120-€250.
Meals	Breakfast €12.
	Restaurants 2-minute walk.
Closed	Never.

Amel Dunker	**Tel**	+33 (0)1 45 23 08 22
Hôtel Paradis,	**Email**	hotel@hotelparadisparis.com
41 rue des Petites-Écuries,	**Web**	www.hotelparadisparis.com
75010 Paris		

ENTRY 120   MAP 5

Hôtel le Relais Montmartre

There are good reasons why artists still live in this village, tucked in behind the Sacré Coeur, that giant marshmallow of a church. It could be the views over the rooftops of Paris, or the meandering little streets, or Montmartre's transformation at dusk as bistros, bars and clubs come into their own. It deserves much more than an afternoon visit so book into this little jewel and the secrets of this rediscovered neighbourhood will be revealed. Just up from Amélie's celebrated café, tucked into a sweet side street, the entrance is discreet. Elegance and intimacy blend in the lobby with fireplace and antique desk; the sofa, the period chairs and the curtains are an extraordinary mix of rich fabrics; the small trellised patio set with sunny yellow garden furniture is the cherry on the cake. It feels like someone's home and anglophone Vincent knows every café and gallery by heart. In the rooms, find deep armchairs, quilted headboards and curtains in quiet pastels or reds, pinks and greens, mixed and matched with care. The mattresses are dreamy, the staff are delightful; this is simple luxury at its best.

Rooms	26 doubles: €119-€249. Extra bed/sofabed €25 p.p. per night.
Meals	Breakfast €15. Restaurants nearby.
Closed	Never.

Tel	+33 (0)1 70 64 25 25
Email	contact@relaismontmartre.fr
Web	www.relaismontmartre.fr

Samia Mobarek
Hôtel le Relais Montmartre,
6 rue Constance,
75018 Paris

ENTRY 121   MAP 5

Hôtel Eiffel Trocadéro

Paris's latest eco hotel, sister to the Gavarni, is a gem with Eiffel Tower views, beautiful new rooms and impressive water, energy and materials-saving credentials. Under Xavier Moraga's committed baton, there is inventive use of led lighting, intelligent fittings in small spaces and a fun choice of décor – he's even bought an electric van so guests can take a green tour of the city. Landing walls, done in metallised limewash, glow softly under hand and eye. Choose a soberly chic modern-classic room in quiet grey, brown or caramel stripes with a sensuously padded wall behind the bed, or a joyous, hand-painted backdrop of giant flowers – turquoise, fuchsia, mimosa – matching velvet curtains and floor-level lighting; take the Eiffel suite and you'll feel you are sitting on top of the tower. Many are connected to the latest in eco-friendly air treatment and have recycling showers or jacuzzi baths in their excellent (unchanged) marble bathrooms. Organic breakfast is in the jaunty black and white basement, fine French food with oriental tinges is in the stunning ground-floor restaurant with its variegated seating and living walls. A delight.

Rooms	11 doubles, 5 twin/doubles: €220-€350. 1 suite for 4: €500-€650. Family apartment €400-€520.
Meals	Breakfast, 3 types, €8-€18 (free for Sawday's guests!). Child's breakfast €9-€12. Lunch from €23; dinner à la carte. Wines €20-€200.
Closed	Never.

Xavier Moraga
Hôtel Eiffel Trocadéro,
35 rue Benjamin Franklin,
75116 Paris

Tel   +33 (0)1 53 70 17 70
Email reservation@hoteleiffeltrocadero.com
Web   www.hoteleiffeltrocadero.com

Hôtel Gavarni

The neat little Gavarni has heaved itself up the hotel ladder on ropes of rich draperies, smart bathrooms and (mostly) refurbished bedrooms. It's also growing more eco-friendly by the year. Bedrooms are slowly being done up – so ask for one that's had a makeover – they are light and airy, painted in pastel colours, have original artwork on the walls and look very modern. Suites are big and traditional with jacuzzis and massage shower panels, fine canopies and beautiful furniture – supremely French with Eiffel Tower views – yet never overdone. The first-floor rooms are less luxurious but the quality is the same: thick lovely carpets, finely stitched quilts, heavy curtains and good little pieces of furniture. The triumph is those little bathrooms which have gained so much space with their utterly ingenious made-to-measure red 'granite' basin, shower and loo. Xavier, the dynamic young manager, is dedicated to making the Gavarni as 'green' as possible and a terrific organic, fairtrade breakfast is served in the conservatory; energy is renewable and all cleaning is done with eco-friendly ingredients.

Rooms	10 doubles, 6 twins: €160-€190. 3 suites for 2, 1 suite for 4: €220-€450. 4 family rooms for 4: €400-€520. Singles €110-€160.
Meals	Breakfast €15. Restaurants nearby.
Closed	Never.

Tel	+33 (0)1 53 70 17 70	**Xavier Moraga**
Email	reservation@gavarni.com	Hôtel Gavarni,
Web	www.gavarni.com	5 rue Gavarni,
		75116 Paris

`ENTRY 123   MAP 5`

Hôtel Passy Eiffel

The first owner was a passionate bee-keeper so he perhaps picked a place with a bit of nature as a centrepiece. When you step off the smart shopping street you can certainly believe that Passy was just a little country village a hundred years ago. Breathe deeply in this calm atmosphere, a restful mix of old-fashioned and contemporary styles where nothing is overdone. Lounge in the glassed-in veranda where you can see a darling gardener's cottage across the tiny cobbled yard. There is a comfortable salon and an inviting breakfast room off the panelled hall which give onto the street through arching windows. Rooms are decorated in firm but unaggressive colours with floral quilts and curtains. The family rooms have large windows, some of which provide an excellent view of the Eiffel Tower. Beams and timbers frame the upper floors; furniture is cane and wood; storage space behind mirrored folding doors is good. On the courtyard side, you look down onto the hotel's green patio and the next-door neighbour's very well-kept garden. Lovely staff, too.

Rooms	46 twin/doubles: €99-€285. 3 family rooms for 3: €209-€340.
Meals	Breakfast €14. Restaurants nearby.
Closed	Never.

Christine Horbette
Hôtel Passy Eiffel,
10 rue de Passy,
75016 Paris

Tel	+33 (0)1 45 25 55 66
Email	contact@passyeiffel.com
Web	www.passyeiffel.com

Château de Bourron

Surrounded by perfectly clipped yew and box topiary, the early 17th-century château built on fortress foundations is hugely warm and inviting. Louis XV and his regal in-laws once met here; now it is owned by a charming young family. Inside is a feast of original Versailles parquet, oriental rugs and period pieces, exquisite fabrics and elegant tapestries. Breakfast tables are laid in a fine big ground-floor room that leads to the cosy guest sitting room. Upstairs, bedrooms in perfectly chosen bold colours display pale marble bathrooms – some with draped free-standing tubs – handsome fabrics and fitting period-style furniture: five-star stylishness in a château setting. On the first floor is the library, with panelled walls and shelves laden with leather-bound tomes. Outside, there are more treasures to uncover. The 80 acres of walled gardens and woodland are extraordinary... statues of Ceres and St Joseph, a chapel in one of two small pavilions, and the St Sévère spring supplying moat, canal and village wash-house. Your friendly hosts will tell the stories. Beyond lie the pretty village and the great forest. *Free shuttle service between Bourron train station and Château. .*

Rooms	8 twin/doubles: €180-€520. Extra bed/sofabed €25 p.p. per night.
Meals	Breakfast €16. Dinner €33.
Closed	Rarely.

Tel	+33 (0)1 64 78 39 39	Comte & Comtesse Guy de Cordon
Email	bourron@bourron.fr	Château de Bourron,
Web	www.castle-paris.com	16 av Blaise de Montesquiou,
		77780 Bourron Marlotte, Seine-et-Marne

ENTRY 125   MAP 5

Martinn – Key2Paris

A gem of a pied-à-terre for two, right in
the middle of old Paris. Step through the
secluded cobbled courtyard to this ground-
floor flat; the door opens into the small,
uncluttered bedroom with a book-filled
living room beyond. Find a joyful yellow
bedcover matching a copy of Monet's 'La rue
Montorgueil', a snazzy bathroom and a
corner kitchen for preparing your own meals
after Martinn's welcoming breakfast; all is
beautifully decorated. The neighbourhood
teems with busy brasseries, pavement cafés,
fashionable shops; easy stroll to Pompidou
centre, Louvre, the Marais. Martinn is
charming, and eager to share Paris with
you. *Minimum stay: 3 nights. Over 23s only.
No parties.*

Bonne Nuit Paris

Absolute Paris, 300-year-old timbers, crazy
wonky stairs and modern comforts,
independent rooms and a warm welcome,
little streets, friendly markets: it's real
privilege. Charming, intelligent Jean-Luc
serves his honey, Denise's jams and fresh
bread in their generous, rambling living
room upstairs. To each room, be it ground
or first floor, a colourful shower, a lot of
quirk (the last word in creative basins), an
appealing mix of antique woodwork and
modern prints, and a sense of seclusion.
Simplicity, panache and personality,
attention and service: these are the
hallmarks. No communal space, but a
lovely peaceful courtyard.

Rooms	1 apartment for 2-3: €95-€167. Extra bed/sofabed available €40 for 3-7 nights. Reduction in nightly price for longer stays.	**Rooms**	2 doubles: €175-€225. 2 triples: €275-€300. Extra bed €75.
Meals	Dinner, €45 per person (with wine), by arrangement. Restaurants within walking distance.	**Meals**	Restaurants within walking distance.
Closed	Never.	**Closed**	Rarely.

Mobile	+33 (0)6 03 48 29 29	**Tel**	+33 (0)1 42 71 83 56
Email	info@key2paris.com	**Email**	jean.luc@bonne-nuit-paris.com
Web	www.key2paris.com	**Web**	www.bonne-nuit-paris.com

Martinn Jablonski-Cahours
Martinn – Key2Paris,
Rue d'Argout,
75002 Paris

Denise & Jean-Luc Marchand
Bonne Nuit Paris,
63 rue Charlot, Le Marais,
75003 Paris

Notre Dame district

At the end of the street are the Seine and the glory of Notre Dame. In a grand old building (with a new lift by the 17th-century stairs), the two unaffected rooms, one above the other, look down to a little garden. The mezzanined family room has its bathroom off the landing; a simple breakfast of shop-packed items is laid here. Upstairs is the smaller room: bed in the corner, timeworn shower room and your own entrance. Madame is polyglot, active and eager to help when she is available; she leaves breakfast ready if she has to go out. She appreciates the variety of contact guests bring. A gem in the heart of Paris. *Minimum stay: 2 nights.*

Les3chambres

Vibrant colour, family antiques and atmosphere are here thanks to Laurent's flair for interiors (he's a lighting designer) and his love of meeting people. He's also a walking encyclopaedia on Paris. After pâtisserie, homemade jam and excellent coffee, explore Paris using Laurent's specially-designed map: the main sights, places to eat, museums and markets on one side; three neighbourhood walks on the other. Return to discuss your day over a glass of wine and canapés in the library/living room. You'll feel like a local staying in this residential neighbourhood but it's very central: Gare du Nord is only a ten-minute walk away; the department stores on Boulevard Haussmann are 15 minutes and the Louvre is 30 minutes.

Rooms	1 double: €95. 1 family room for 4 with separate bathroom & breakfast area: €130 for 4; €120 for 2.
Meals	Restaurants nearby. Continental breakfast left if owner has to go out (for family room). No breakfast for double but tea and coffee facilities provided.
Closed	Rarely.

Rooms	3 doubles: €169-€209.
Meals	Restaurants within walking distance.
Closed	August.

Tel	+33 (0)1 43 25 27 20
Email	brichati@hotmail.com

Brigitte Chatignoux
Notre Dame district,
75005 Paris

Tel	+33 (0)1 42 47 07 42
Email	contact@les3chambres-paris.com
Web	les3chambres-paris.com/en/

Laurent Rougier
Les3chambres,
14 rue Bleue,
75009 Paris

Côté Montmartre

There's a gift of a view here: old Paris crookedly climbing to the Sacré Cœur. Your interesting, cultured, hosts, Isabelle and photographer Jacques, are well-travelled. Beautiful great tomes of Jacques' images of Paris, Morocco and various exotic destinations fill an entire shelf and his framed photos mingle with good eclectic art in their drawing/dining room. Breakfast may be in here, or out on the flowery, suntrap balcony. Your big white bedroom off the landing has an independent entrance; find a modern, airy space filled with more photos and books, lamps and colourful rugs – all peaceful in its rooftop seclusion.

52 Clichy

If you want conviviality for two, choose to share your host's stylish and peaceful top-floor flat, its immaculate blue bedroom and en suite bathroom with a private loo just over the passage. Rosemary will chat about her many-facetted traveller's life, serve breakfast on the pretty balcony or at the walnut table in her relaxing chiaroscuro living room. If you prefer privacy for two to four, choose the modern third-floor apartment in chocolate and fire-red and breakfast at your own table. Rosemary knows a million Parisian things and will point you to the Paris that suits you. You will be well cared for. *Please check owner's website for availability – owner's website is always up to date. Bags can be left with the owner all day at no extra charge.*

Rooms	1 double: €135-€150. Extra bed/sofabed €15 per night. Child's bed available, €15.	
Meals	Restaurants nearby.	
Closed	Rarely.	

Rooms	1 twin/double with separate wc: €125-€135. 1 apartment for 4: €160-€200.
Meals	Restaurants 100m.
Closed	Rarely.

Tel	+33 (0)1 43 54 33 09
Email	bravoisabelle@gmail.com
Web	www.cotemontmartre.com

Isabelle & Jacques Bravo
Côté Montmartre,
11 bis rue Jean Baptiste Pigalle,
75009 Paris

Tel	+33 (0)1 44 53 93 65
Email	rosemarylouise@52clichy.com
Web	www.52Clichy.com

Rosemary Allan
52 Clichy,
52 rue de Clichy,
75009 Paris

ENTRY 130 MAP 5

ENTRY 131 MAP 5

Studio Amélie

Villa Montabord

In Montmartre village, in a quiet street between bustling boulevard and pure-white Sacré Cœur, Valérie and her architect husband offer a super-chic and ideally autonomous studio off their charming, pot-planted and cobbled courtyard with your bistro table and chairs. A bed dressed in delicate red against white walls, an antique oval dining table, a pine-and-steel gem of a corner kitchen, a generous shower, a mirror framed in red. Valérie's discreet decorative flourishes speak for her calm, positive personality and her interest in other lands. A delicious Paris hideaway you can call your own. *Minimum stay: 3 nights.*

If ever there was a hidden treasure in Paris, La Cité des Fleurs is it! Imagine opening a gate onto a peaceful, private lane of grand houses and sumptuous gardens – the busy city melts away. All that's missing from this utterly untouched view of La Belle Epoque is a penny-farthing and children playing marbles... The Sciards are kind hosts with an eye for elegant detail. Red doors open to a hall of chequered tiles and stained glass; airy bedrooms have marble fireplaces and white linen. Breakfasts of homemade cakes, gourmet teas and viennoiserie are taken en famille in the dining room or internal courtyard. Visit nearby museums, wander Montmartre. *Underground parking 3-minute walk, €30 per day.*

Rooms	1 twin/double, with kitchenette: €98; €680 per week. Extra bed available.
Meals	Breakfast at the boulangerie next door. Guest kitchen. Restaurants 2-minute walk.
Closed	Rarely.

Rooms	4 doubles: €219-€239.
Meals	Restaurants 5-minute walk.
Closed	Rarely.

Email	studiodamelie@wanadoo.fr

Email	villamontabordparis@gmail.com
Web	www.villamontabordparis.com

Valérie Zuber
Studio Amélie,
Montmartre,
75018 Paris

Isabelle Sciard
Villa Montabord,
3 Cité des Fleurs,
75017 Paris

ENTRY 132   MAP 5

ENTRY 133   MAP 5

Copernic

Feel Parisian here with Sylvie and her husband. Enter the large limestone building and up the spiral staircase (or the tiny lift) to the third floor. Relax and chat in the modern-feeling large kitchen/living area, eat breakfast at a time to suit you, order dinner too – Sylvie is a grand cook. Bedrooms are all off the guest corridor: expect marble fireplaces, shelves filled with books, large mirrors, new mattresses and floor to ceiling windows with views to the quiet street. You're within walking distance of the tourist traps, super restaurants and shops, museums, galleries and the wide open spaces of the Bois de Boulogne.

Les Toits de Paris

The light-filled rooms, generous breakfasts and a most courteous owner are all of a lovely piece: quiet, clothed in gentle earthy colours, natural materials and discreet manners. You will feel instantly at ease in this cultured atmosphere. The attic room has a super-comfy bed, beautiful terracotta tiles and a darling little writing desk beneath the sloping beams; the beautiful bathroom has everything. Two family rooms for four and the studio (for three) have kitchenettes and sparkling shower rooms. Walk round 'the village', discover its quirky shops, its restaurants for all tastes and budgets – then head for the riches of central Paris.

Rooms	1 double, 1 twin: €200-€250. Singles €150-€180.
Meals	Dinner available. Restaurants 2-minute walk.
Closed	Rarely.

Rooms	1 double with single sofabed: €130. 2 family rooms for 4: €150-€180. 1 studio for 3: €130-€150. Extra bed €20.
Meals	Restaurants nearby.
Closed	Rarely.

Mobile +33 (0)6 95 09 14 27
Email sylvie.petitnivard@gmail.com

Sylvie Petit
Copernic,
39 rue Copernic,
75116 Paris

Mobile +33 (0)6 60 57 92 05
Email resa@chambrehotesparis.fr
Web www.chambrehotesparis.fr

Matthieu de Montenay
Les Toits de Paris,
25 rue de l'Abbé Groult,
75015 Paris

ENTRY 134 MAP 5

ENTRY 135 MAP 5

Le Clos des Princes

Paris is 20 minutes by train, Versailles 15 by motorway. Here, behind wrought-iron gates in an elegant suburb, the French mansion sits in an exuberant town garden of pergolas, box bushes and mature trees. Your kind, attentive hosts – she an ex-English teacher, he with a passion for Sully-Prudhomme – may give you the poet/philosopher's two-room first-floor suite; he lived here in 1902. Polished floorboards, pretty prints, choice antiques, all dance to the 19th-century theme. Breakfast unveils gorgeous porcelain. Outstanding. *Private parking on premises for guests staying in Sully Prudhomme and Poésie rooms. Guests staying in Céleste room will need to park in the street (free parking).*

Bed in Versailles

Versailles the one and only. The gilded palace grandeur, the tiny old-town backstreets, the great lake of the Swiss Guards and, in between, a discreet door opening to a big rambling house warmed by cultured parents, well-mannered student offspring, friendly pets and the smell of beeswax. Bathe in books, blasts of colour and art (Laure is an accomplished artist and dress designer); a garden too. Climb two gentle floors (pictures to absorb at every step) to large light rooms with views over the Royal Gardens. Add unusual family furniture and a superb new biscuity shower room: this genuine family B&B is a rare privilege.

Rooms 1 double: €110. 1 family room for 4: €120. 1 suite for 2: €130. Sofabed available for children.	**Rooms** 1 double, 1 twin/double, sharing bathroom; let to same party only: €140-€160. Cot €40 per night. Child's bed €60 per night
Meals Restaurant 400m.	**Meals** Restaurants within walking distance.
Closed Rarely.	**Closed** Rarely.

Tel +33 (0)1 46 61 94 49 **Email** ce.duprez@yahoo.com **Web** www.leclosdesprinces.com	**Tel** +33 (0)1 39 53 65 40 **Email** bedinversailles@gmail.com **Web** www.bedinversailles.com
Christine & Éric Duprez Le Clos des Princes, 60 av Jean Jaurès, 92290 Châtenay Malabry, Hauts-de-Seine	**Laure de St Chaffray** Bed in Versailles, 6 rue de la Quintinie, 78000 Versailles, Yvelines

ENTRY 136   MAP 5   **ENTRY 137   MAP 5**

Les Chambres de Beynes

À l'Ombre Bleue

With Paris and Versailles a short hop away, these charming, modern rooms suit explorers and business types. Owner Alexandra is kind and thoughtful and cooks for you by arrangement. There's a bedroom (up a spiral staircase) in the large 18th-century house and two more in the cottage across the pretty garden, one designed for wheelchair users. All are spotless and comfortable, with their own bathrooms and terraces. Choose a continental breakfast of delicious breads and pastries or a full English, either outside or in the dining room. You're a short stroll from shops and restaurants, and a twice-weekly table d'hôte showcases Alexandra's splendid cooking. *Parking on-site.*

Let the willows weep over the village pond; you go through the high gate into a sheltered paradise. The prettiest rooms have masses of old pieces, dolls, books, pictures to intrigue you, a chirruping garden with two rescue dogs to play with and the most caring hostess to provide an exceptional brunch. Have dinner too if you can (Catherine teaches cookery and sources locally: it's delicious). The miniature garden house is a lovers' dream: tiny salon downstairs, bedroom sporting superb bath up. Fulsome towels, extras of all sorts: charming, chatty Catherine thinks of everything.

Rooms	3 doubles: €95-€105. Singles €85-€95. Cot available.	
Meals	Dinner, 3 courses with wine, €25; Monday & Thurs only. Restaurants 5-minute walk.	
Closed	1 week in July.	

Rooms	1 double: €80-€100. 2 family rooms for 4: €80-€160. Singles €80-€90.
Meals	Dinner with wine, €30. Light supper €18.
Closed	Rarely.

Mobile	+33 (0)6 66 30 42 24
Email	alexandra@leschambresdebeynes.com
Web	www.leschambresdebeynes.com

Alexandra Joseph
Les Chambres de Beynes,
1 place de l'Estandart,
78650 Beynes, Yvelines

Tel	+33 (0)1 34 85 04 73
Email	catherine@alombrebleue.fr
Web	www.alombrebleue.fr

Catherine Forget-Pépin
À l'Ombre Bleue,
22 rue de la MareLes Pâtis,
78125 Mittainville, Yvelines

ENTRY 138   MAP 5

ENTRY 139   MAP 5

La Grange de la Guesle

In a hamlet of stone houses, electronic gates glide open to an immaculate farmhouse owned by Catherine and Michel. In the barn are four bedrooms with forest views, two up and two down (with private terraces), all linked by a steep spiral stair. They're big and stylish, with monsoon showers tucked behind half-height walls. Breakfast tables are laid with homemade breads and artisan jams, supper is good too, and the decked terrace is for all to share – you'll even find an infrared Japanese sauna. In this deeply rural setting you have bikes to borrow (mountain or electric) and a station 4km away – set off for Paris and Versailles! *Parking available on-site. Owner will collect guests from the station. Cot available.*

Nid de Rochefort

Wander among fruit trees in Stephane's tranquil walled garden; hard to believe that Paris is just 30 minutes by train. Wake to birdsong, and fabulous views of ancient Rochefort and the forest beyond. Breakfast is a convivial delight – feast on pancakes, pastries and honey (fresh from their own hives) in the elegant sitting room. Stylish, brightly painted doubles and a spacious family suite are split between the 18th-century house and a blue-shuttered cottage, or seek privacy in an extra room in the garden with its own kitchen: DIY breakfast, or sneak some from the house. Stroll to the unspoilt village for divine pastries.

Rooms	2 doubles: €125. 1 family room for 4: €105-€185. 1 triple: €105-€145. Extra bed/sofabed €40 p.p. per night. Sauna included for doubles; €15 for 2, in other rooms.
Meals	Dinner weekdays €27; Saturdays €47; by arrangement;. Kitchenette in barn. Restaurants 5km.
Closed	Rarely.

Rooms	3 doubles: €82-€90. 1 suite for 5: €115-€195. 1 studio for 2 with kitchenette: €120-€150. Singles €78-€105. Extra bed/sofabed €15 p.p. per night.
Meals	Restaurants in village
Closed	Rarely.

Mobile   +33 (0)6 15 02 83 21
Email   reservation@lagrangedelaguesle.fr
Web   www.lagrangedelaguesle.fr

Catherine Sergent
La Grange de la Guesle,
33 bis rue de la Forêt,
78125 Hermeray, Yvelines

Tel   +33 (0)1 78 97 02 82
Email   stephane.jacquerez@gmail.com
Web   www.lenidderochefort.fr

Stephane Jacquerez
Nid de Rochefort,
34 rue Guy le Rouge,
78730 Rochefort-en-Yvelines, Yvelines

ENTRY 140   MAP 5

ENTRY 141   MAP 5

Ferme de Vert Saint Père

Cereals and beets grow in wide fields and show-jumpers add elegance to the fine landscape. A generous farm courtyard surrounded by very lovely warm stone buildings encloses peace and a genuine welcome from hosts and labradors alike, here where Monsieur's family has come hunting for 200 years. Find family furniture (the 1900s ensemble is most intriguing) and planked floors in beautiful bedrooms, immaculate mod cons and a handsome guest living room where breakfast is served at a convivial table surrounded by honey, polished floors and oriental-style rugs. Utter peace, a remote setting, and a Michelin-rated auberge in the village.

Rooms	1 family room for 3: €78-€88. 2 apartments for 4: €122-€132.
Meals	Restaurant in village, 1.5km.
Closed	Christmas.

Tel +33 (0)1 64 38 83 51
Email mauban.vert@wanadoo.fr
Web vertsaintpere.com

Philippe & Jeanne Mauban
Ferme de Vert Saint Père,
77390 Crisenoy,
Seine-et-Marne

ENTRY 142   MAP 5

Le Clos de la Rose

For seekers of garden peace, for champagne and architecture buffs... A leafy retreat from crazed Paris, this gorgeous home is cool, quiet and stylishly homely. Its 200-year-old origins are celebrated: limewash, timbers, country antiques, a gathering of books. Bedrooms have pretty colours, vintage linen and patchwork charm, the adorable cottage (with kitchen) is ideal for a longer stay. Véronique makes jams and offers pâtisserie courses; she's happy to spend time chatting over apéritifs and dinner is a choice of three menus, finishing with local cheeses and homemade desserts. Champagne vineyards and historic Provins are nearby.
Pets by arrangement.

Rooms	2 doubles: €94-€146. 1 cottage for 3: €99-€181; B&B & self-catering available. Extra bed/sofabed €25 p.p. per night.
Meals	Breakfast €11. Dinner €29. Wine €20-€34. Champagne €32. Restaurant 10-minute drive.
Closed	Never.

Tel +33 (0)1 60 44 81 04
Email resa@clos-de-la-rose.com
Web www.clos-de-la-rose.com

Véronique & Brendan Culligan
Le Clos de la Rose,
11 rue de la Source, L'Hermitière,
77750 St Cyr sur Morin, Seine-et-Marne

ENTRY 143   MAP 5

Chez Jules & Léonie

All the bedrooms are named after artists with close links not just to the village of Valmondois but to Laurent's fascinating, cultured family. Three overlook a peaceful terraced garden and one the village square. The upstairs drawing room is pleasingly book-lined, breakfast includes Valmondois honey and is served in the big dining room at one sociable table. Laurent speaks excellent English and can give you plenty of tips about the village he loves so much. Wander to the village square for a spot of people-watching or a visit to the bakery and a café which does lunch. Beyond is beautiful countryside for walking and cycling, a riverside beach for swimming and hikes in the Park.

Rooms	2 doubles, 1 twin/double: €88-€105. 1 suite for 4: €105. Singles €68.
Meals	Dinner with wine, €28. Restaurants 10-minute drive.
Closed	Rarely.

Tel	+33 (0)1 34 69 51 60
Email	contact@chezjulesetleonie.fr
Web	www.chezjulesetleonie.fr/en

Laurent de Gaulle
Chez Jules & Léonie,
Place Honoré Daumier,
95760 Valmondois, Val-d'Oise

ENTRY 144 MAP 5

Normandy

Domaine Saint Clair, page 131

Domaine Saint Clair

For a romantic, lavish stay, this hotel has it all covered – lush rooms with a fairytale feel, sunny terrace with good views and a restaurant with ambitions for a Michelin star. Owner Mr Abodib is dynamic and friendly – his parents set up the hotel in the 1970s. Guests stay in the original turreted 'donjon', built in 1873, or next door in a red brick villa with pretty shuttered windows. Rooms and suites are eclectic, from quietly serene 'Paul' to vibrant red 'Marcel Proust' or military-themed 'Major'. There's a beautiful pool – bag a comfy recliner or dreamy daybed with floaty white curtains. If the weather is cooler, mellow with piped jazz in the calm of the conservatory, or pick a book from wall to ceiling shelves in the library. Outside, look out for the hotel cat as you explore the garden, steep and terraced with rose arches. There are eateries in the bustling, touristy town below, but treat yourself and dine in the restaurant here, where deep blue walls and a Persian rug bring the classic red velvets and white linens to life. You'll find elegant presentation, delicious local produce and an extensive wine list.

Rooms	15 twin/doubles: €120-€500.
	6 suites for 2: €120-€500.
Meals	Breakfast €15. Dinner €29-€75.
	Child €15-€25.
	Restaurants 10-minute walk.
Closed	Never.

Tel	+33 (0)2 35 27 08 23
Email	info@hoteletretat.com
Web	www.hoteletretat.com

La Réception
Domaine Saint Clair,
Chemin Saint Clair,
76790 Etretat, Seine-Maritime

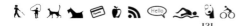

ENTRY 145   MAP 4

Les Maisons de Léa

You could almost do with a guide to steer you round the passageways, narrow stairs and twists and turns of this intriguing 16th-century building – once three fishermen's houses and a salt warehouse. Each of the bedrooms has its own decorative style – romantic, nautical, Baltimore, country; the attention to detail is exquisite. Imagine dreamy fabrics, limewashed walls, cushions on painted wicker, toys and chairs for children and a booklet for each guest on the treasures of Honfleur. Sample gourmet food in the hotel's new restaurant with blazing log fire in winter, or delicious home-made scones for afternoon tea. Breakfast is laid out in a red-walled room with views to the big square and the church of Sainte Catherine; on Saturdays, the food market leaps into action. Relax in the salon, spoil yourself in the spa or the (free) hammam, self-cater in the delicious Petite Maison. No lift – that would spoil the charm – and the car park is a few minutes' walk away, but staff will happily ferry bags to the upper floors. A total gem.

Rooms	43 twin/doubles: €155-€420. Extra bed/sofabed €20 p.p. per night.
Meals	Buffet breakfast €18. Lunch €24. Dinner €30-58. Restaurant closed Mon all day, Tues & Weds lunchtime.
Closed	Rarely.

La Réception		
Les Maisons de Léa,	**Tel**	+33 (0)2 31 14 49 49
Place Sainte Catherine,	**Email**	contact@lesmaisonsdelea.com
14600 Honfleur, Calvados	**Web**	www.lesmaisonsdelea.com

ENTRY 146   MAP 4

Hôtel Maison de Lucie

Named after the poet Lucie Delarue-Mardrus, who was born here, the 1850 house in the heart of Honfleur is shielded by a high wall. Sunshine illuminates panelled walls and leather sofas, the parquet'd salon has an Edwardian air and bedrooms, elegantly colour-themed, now expand into an adjoining house; those on the second floor overlook the estuary. Furnishings are immaculate – plum taffeta, burgundy velvet – beds are big and reading lamps won't spoil your eyes. Bathrooms are awash with potions and lotions, there are fresh orchids and vivid rugs, roll top baths and antique chests of drawers, and wide views over rooftops to the sea. Our favourite room is under the eaves, but they're all lovely. In the courtyard, the old caretaker's house is now a suite, its ground-floor sitting area furnished in a deliciously decadent 1930s manner; another room has a small new terraced courtyard area. Soak away your cares in the brick-walled jacuzzi spa; take your time over a great homemade breakfast of bacon, eggs, fruits, cheese, in bed or in the sun. Muriel's welcome is the cherry on the cake. *Parking €15 per night; 4 spaces.*

Rooms	9 doubles: €180-€220.
	3 suites for 2: €270-€360.
Meals	Breakfast €12-€18.
	Restaurants 300m.
Closed	Early to mid-December.

Tel	+33 (0)2 31 14 40 40
Email	info@lamaisondelucie.com
Web	www.lamaisondelucie.com

Muriel Daridon
Hôtel Maison de Lucie,
44 rue Capucins,
14600 Honfleur, Calvados

ENTRY 147   MAP 4

Le Manoir des Impressionnistes

As you watch the sun set over the Seine estuary, revel in the comfort and serenity of this charming 18th-century manor house, in the green embrace of a wooded hillside. There are bedrooms on all three floors; some peep from beneath the gables of the stone-tiled roof, others gaze boldly from the half-timbered façade and you can choose between sea and garden views. Each room is individually decorated with simplicity and taste, unmistakably French, with snowy bed linen and oriental rugs on warm-hued floors; bathrooms are a riot of thoroughly modern marble. In the terracotta-tiled breakfast room, a buffet table loaded with organic local produce is a welcome start to the day, but your evenings belong to the spectacular dining room. Beneath ancient wooden beams, in the flickering light of the gothic limestone fireplace, crisp linen and white china frame gourmet meals of Gallic splendour. English owner Bridget is thoughtful, warm and friendly, and leaves a welcome note and fresh fruit and flowers in your room. The name? You're a mile from the picturesque port of Honfleur, cradle of Impressionism.

Rooms	2 doubles, 8 twin/doubles: €125-€395. 1 family room for 3: €485. Extra bed/sofabed €20 p.p. per night.
Meals	Breakfast: €21 in restaurant; €15-€24 room service. Lunch €32-€79. Dinner €49-€79. Wine from €32. Restaurants 1.5km.
Closed	Never.

Bridget Boelen	**Tel**	+33 (0)2 31 81 63 00
Le Manoir des Impressionnistes,	**Email**	contact@le-manoir.com
Phare du Butin, Route Adolphe Marais,	**Web**	www.manoirdesimpressionnistes.eu
14600 Honfleur, Calvados		

Ferme de la Rançonnière

Drive through the narrow arch into the vast courtyard and history leaps out to grab you. This was originally a fortified stronghold – the tower is 13th-century – to protect against English reprisals after Duke William of Normandy conquered England... exposed timbers and limestone floors announce the Norman heritage. Each courtyard building houses eight to ten rooms. The amazing suite has stone steps down to a double bedroom then up a spiral stair to a children's room in the tower with tiny windows. Handsome, solid furniture combines with pieces that are plainer, and rustic-medieval is the look: a butter churn in the corridor, an awe-inspiring armoire, a well-worn kneading trough: reminders that this was a working farm. Off the huge breakfast room and restaurant is a vaulted, stone-flagged sitting area with a log fire at one end: great spot for after-dinner coffee. The bright breakfast room and terrace face south to catch the morning sun. Young, friendly, professional Isabelle Sileghem and her husband keep this place humming, with help from a devoted staff. It's big and rooms vary: book ahead for the best.

Rooms	21 twin/doubles: €60-€200. 1 suite for 2: €140-€270. 13 triples: €128-€228. Extra bed/sofabed €28 p.p. per night.
Meals	Breakfast €12. Lunch €24. Dinner €30.80-€42.80. Wine €15-€40. Restaurant closed 3-25 January.
Closed	Rarely.

Tel	+33 (0)2 31 22 21 73
Email	ranconniere@wanadoo.fr
Web	www.ranconniere.fr

Isabelle & Koen Sileghem
Ferme de la Rançonnière,
Route de Creully, Arromanches,
14480 Crépon, Calvados

ENTRY 149 MAP 4

Hôtel Tardif

A mid 18th-century house in the centre of Bayeux, this is an architectural jewel. It was built for a botanist who worked at Versailles and specimen trees still stand in the grounds. In those days, carriages would rumble through the archway and enter the central 'cour d'honneur'; still cobbled, the yard is an exquisite spot from which to glimpse a fascinating range of building styles. Delighted to share all he knows about this house and its history, Anthony, with impeccable English, is an exceptionally generous young host. Inside are white walls, parquet étoile floors and a curved and suspended staircase, one of only two in France. And such beautiful things: antiques and tapestries, brocade chairs and gilt-framed mirrors, a grand piano and a chandelier from Compiègne where the Empress Josephine lived. Bedrooms are elegant, spacious and sober, in keeping with the history. One bedroom, on the first floor, is a listed 'monument historique', its panelling immaculately revived in regulation browns and golds. Other rooms have pale stone walls; all are uncluttered and serene. What value!

Rooms	6 doubles: €125-€280.
	1 suite for 4: €250-€390.
	Extra bed €20.
Meals	Breakfast €10.
	Restaurants walking distance.
Closed	Christmas.

Anthony Voidie
Hôtel Tardif,
16 rue de Nesmond,
14400 Bayeux, Calvados

Tel	+33 (0)2 31 92 67 72
Email	hoteltardif@orange.fr
Web	www.hoteltardif.com

ENTRY 150   MAP 4

Villa Fol Avril

Once a stopover for travellers passing on this peaceful road, the 19th-century staging post became a petrol station some years ago; now it's been rescued by the Sicres. Since leaving Paris, this energetic couple have added modern touches to authentic features and created a beautiful, bright hotel. Sunshine pours in through windows overlooking the pretty village's rosy-coloured roofs, and handcrafted furnishings pop up everywhere. Bedrooms are bold and individual, all with elaborately carved key fobs and something to make you go "ooh". In one, an oak ladder leads to a high mezzanine – great fun for kids. The exposed timbers upstairs are magnificent and some remnants from the coach house's old life have been given a new lease of life: an ancient hayrack and shutters have become quirky headboards. Bathrooms are equally distinctive, with yellow tiles. Fresh local produce is served in the restaurant or on the garden terrace; look out for snails from the local 'escargotière'. Venture into the Perche for plenty of surprises: forested walking tracks, fairy-tale manoirs and the famous Percheron horses.

Rooms	4 doubles, 2 twins: €90-€130. 6 suites for 2: €120-€180. 1 triple: €125-€170.
Meals	Breakfast €13. Dinner €25-€45. Wine €20-€60. Restaurants 8km.
Closed	Never.

Tel	+33 (0)2 33 83 22 67
Email	contact@villafolavril.fr
Web	www.villafolavril.fr

Monsieur & Madame Sicre
Villa Fol Avril,
2 rue des Fers Chauds,
61110 Moutiers au Perche, Orne

ENTRY 151   MAP 4

Manoir de Surville

The estate's handsome buildings span the 16th to the 19th centuries, and sit amid lush lawns and trees in bucolic Normandy countryside. The old stones and wood beams breathe elegance and a light-filled reception room, with its fireplace, books and chessboard, sets the welcoming tone. You'll be well looked after by gentle, multilingual hosts Hugues and Camille – and by talented chef Magalie, who serves creative four-course menus on advance reservation. The French concept of 'cocooning' floats through eleven fresh rooms and suites spread over two buildings and themed in imaginative colours like rose pink, honey orange and mimosa yellow. Accessible 'lime green' room has a suntrap terrace, while others are upstairs, with two cute 'cocoon' rooms with open baths under steeply sloping eaves. You can pamper yourself in modern granite bathrooms, and make full use of the basement wellness area with its steam and sauna cabins, and showers enhanced by light and music. The surrounding forested countryside offers walking, cycling and horse-riding, golf in 18-hole courses and an aquatic complex in Louviers. *Pets by arrangement.*

Rooms	9 doubles: €180-€275.
	2 suites for 3: €260-€365.
Meals	Breakfast included. Dinner €49-€55;
	Thurs, Fri & Sat eve only.
Closed	15 October – 31 October.

Camille & Hugues Oeyen
Manoir de Surville,
82 rue Bernard Petel,
27400 Surville, Eure

Tel	+33 (0)2 32 50 99 89
Email	contact@manoirdesurville.com
Web	www.manoirdesurville.com

ENTRY 152 MAP 4

Le Petit Coq aux Champs

The thick thatch roof of this Norman-style farmhouse is a fitting end to your journey into the countryside to find it. Only after a trek down a long village lane and parking among the azaleas and rhododendrons do you really catch sight of the elusive hotel itself. Extensions to the original timbered building give it an eclectic air despite the ubiquity of the thatch and in contrast with the motif of the eponymous cockerel, represented in every form from sculpture to tapestry. The bedrooms are simpler, with understated comfort and modern bathrooms lit up by the occasional antique and most rooms sporting balconies where the lush vegetation gives shade and privacy. The garden however, as with most of the hotel, is centred around providing for the restaurant. Here you find a menu as diverse as the décor is constant. The rustic, cosy dining room serves up not just fowl but foie gras, lobster, veal sweetbreads and beef fillet throne among others. If the occasionally hefty prices make you head for town, then historic Rouen and coastal Deauville, both around 40 minutes away, will sate all your senses on any budget.

Rooms	10 doubles, 5 twin/doubles: €119-€192. Dinner, B&B €45 extra p.p. Extra bed/sofabed €27 p.p. per night.
Meals	Restaurant on-site. Dinner €32-€70. Restaurants 7km.
Closed	16 December – 31 January.

Tel	+33 (0)2 32 41 0419
Email	info@lepetitcoqauxchamps.fr
Web	www.lepetitcoqauxchamps.fr

Fabienne Huard
Le Petit Coq aux Champs,
400 chemin du Petit Coq,
La Pommeraie Sud, 27500 Campigny, Eure

ENTRY 153 MAP 4

Le Moulin de l'Epinay

Lynn and Duncan's three-storey mill house is surrounded by farmland and apple orchards, and although you're near the A28 and A29 there's no hint of traffic noise. Visit in autumn and join in with the cider harvest, when all the neighbours come together to help. Guests gather together for breakfast around a long table in the relaxed living room or in the conservatory next door. Don't miss Lynn's four-course dinners, served in the lovely outdoor dining barn in summer – veg from the garden, Neufchâtel cheese, puddings with fruit from the garden and perhaps some of Duncan's home-distilled Calvados to finish. The pretty garden has three bridges crossing a stream and a little waterfall, and the indoor pool is great for a swim year-round. The nearest village is a couple of fields away, there are lovely châteaux to visit, and the Normandy coast is less than an hour's drive away. *Children over 3 welcome*

Rooms	1 double; 1 twin with separate bathroom: €75. 1 suite for 2: €90. 1 family room for 3: €85-€105. Singles €70. Extra bed available €25 p.p. per night. Tourist tax €0.40 p.p. per night (above 13 y/o).
Meals	Dinner €30.
Closed	Sundays, Mondays, 1 October, 17 December – 31 January, 12 – 14 June.

Lynn Birtles
Le Moulin de l'Epinay,
16 chemin du Moulin,
76270 Ste Beuve-en-riviere, Seine-Maritime

Tel	+33 (0)2 32 97 13 01
Email	ilbaumoulin@hotmail.com
Web	www.moulin-epinay.com/en/home.html

ENTRY 154 MAP 4

23 Grand Rue

Madeleine – energetic, vivacious – welcomes you with interesting conversation and a fine dinner table dressed in silver. Set back from the road behind fence and clipped hedge are three immaculate, classically furnished bedrooms: books and fresh flowers, a calvados nightcap on the landing. There's a conservatory for breakfast with long, lovely views, a cosy front room for relaxing, drinks in the garden and French suppers in the dining room. You can walk from the door to the fairy-tale château of Mesnières-en-Bray, pedal along the Avenue Verte through rich farmland, visit local gardens or take bracing clifftop walks along the Normandy coast. Monet's dreamy landscapes, Dieppe, Rouen, Somme, Honfleur: all are wonderfully close.

Rooms	2 doubles, 1 twin: €75. Singles €65.
Meals	Dinner with wine, €30.
Closed	Rarely.

Tel	+33 (0)2 32 97 06 31
Email	info@23grandrue.com
Web	www.23grandrue.com

Madeleine Mitchell
23 Grand Rue,
76270 Mesnières en Bray,
Seine-Maritime

ENTRY 155   MAP 4

St Mare

A fresh modern house under a steep slate roof in a lush green sanctuary; it could not be more tranquil. The garden really is lovely and worth a wander – a tailored lawn, a mass of colour, huge banks of rhododendrons for which the village is renowned (three of its gardens are open to the public). Claudine runs home and B&B with effortless efficiency and gives you homemade brioches for breakfast; smiling Remi leads you to guest quarters in a freshly wood-clad house reached via stepping stones through the laurels. Bedrooms are comfortable, sunny, spotless, shining and utterly peaceful – two are big enough to lounge in.

Rooms	2 suites for 4, 1 suite for 5: €90-€150. Extra bed €20 p.p. per night.
Meals	Restaurants 20-minute walk.
Closed	Rarely.

Tel	+33 (0)2 35 85 99 28
Email	claudine.goubet@chsaintmare.com
Web	www.chsaintmare.com

Claudine Goubet
St Mare, Route de Petites Bruyères, 1 chemin des Sablonnières, 76119 Varengeville sur Mer, Seine-Maritime

ENTRY 156   MAP 4

Le Clos du Vivier

The lush garden shelters bees, bantams, sleek cats and a phenomenal variety of shrubs and flowering plants. Madame tends to her guests, with respect for everyone's privacy and offers guidance on hiking; there's also tennis and fishing nearby. She is an intelligent, active and graceful person, her bedrooms, some under sloping ceilings, are cosily colourful, her bathrooms big and luxurious, her breakfast richly varied. After a jaunt, you can read their books, relax among the lovely antiques or make tea in the breakfast room. The cliffs at Étretat are 20 minutes away. *Minimum stay: 2 nights. Pets by arrangement.*

Mille Roses

Poised on a hillside gazing south over the Seine, this proud red-brick mansion was once home to opera tenor Placide Poultier. Now Patsy will welcome you in; a teacher and guide, she is well versed in local history and happy to share the local secrets over a light breakfast. At the top of the house are two modern, simple twin bedrooms and a sitting room where you can browse a guide book over a cup of tea; bathrooms are separate but private and everything is spotless. Outside, a huge copper beech and blue cedar sprinkle shade into a lush, sloping garden where a barbecue and hammock promise lazy summer afternoons. *Pets by arrangement.*

Rooms	1 twin/double: €130.
	1 triple: €130. Singles €30.
Meals	Restaurants in Valmont, 1km.
Closed	Rarely.

Rooms	2 twins both with separate bathrooms, sharing living area: €85-€95.
Meals	Restaurant nearby.
Closed	March – May & October/November.

Tel	+33 (0)2 35 29 90 95
Email	le.clos.du.vivier@wanadoo.fr
Web	www.le-clos-du-vivier.com

Dominique Cachera-Gréverie
Le Clos du Vivier,
4 chemin du Vivier,
76540 Valmont, Seine-Maritime

Tel	+33 (0)2 32 70 44 32
Email	patsy.musto8@orange.fr
Web	www.frenchencounters.com

Patsy Musto
Mille Roses,
9 rue Jean Le Gaffric,
76490 Villequier, Seine-Maritime

ENTRY 157   MAP 4

ENTRY 158   MAP 4

Chambres avec Vue

The elegant black door hides a little house of treasures, curios, art and character, an easy walk (25 minutes) from the centre of Rouen. Dominique, full of energy and enthusiasm, has a flair for decoration – as her paintings, coverings and light, bright furniture declares. Oriental rugs on parquet floors, French windows to balcony and garden, bedrooms brimful of interest. Nothing standard, nothing too studied, a very personal home and leisurely breakfasts promising heavenly surprises. The house's hillside position in this residential area is equally special. Great value, great views.

Le Brécy

Jérôme has happy childhood holiday memories of this elegant 17th-century manor house; he and delightful Patricia moved to join grand-mère who had been living here alone for years. A long path flanked by willows leads down to the Seine: perfect for an evening stroll. One suite is on the ground floor, in classically French coral and cream, its windows opening to a walled garden; the second, equally refined, is in the attic. Breakfast is when you fancy: brioches, walnuts, fresh fruit in a pretty green-panelled room. Ask about the Abbey and walks to its gardens. A charming rural paradise just 15 minutes from Rouen Cathedral.

Rooms	3 doubles: €65. Singles €50.		**Rooms**	1 suite for 2, 1 suite for 3: €99-€127.
Meals	Restaurant 1km.		**Meals**	Restaurant in village.
Closed	Rarely.		**Closed**	Rarely.

Tel	+33 (0)2 35 70 26 95		**Tel**	+33 (0)2 35 32 00 30
Email	chambreavecvue@free.fr		**Email**	lebrecy@gmail.com
Web	chambreavecvue.online.fr		**Web**	www.lebrecy.com

Dominique Gogny
Chambres avec Vue,
22 rue Hénault,
76130 Mont St Aignan, Seine-Maritime

Jérôme & Patricia Lanquest
Le Brécy,
72 route du Brécy, 76840 St Martin de
Boscherville, Seine-Maritime

Manoir de Captot

The drive curves through paddocks and pillared gates to this serene 18th-century mansion. The forest behind may ring with the stag's call, the heads and hooves of his kin line the grand staircase. The fine classic French interior is peacefully formal: a gorgeous primrose-yellow dining room with an oval mahogany table for breakfast feasts, a collection-filled drawing room, a beautiful first-floor bedroom with the right curly antiques and pink Jouy draperies. Michelle cherishes her mansion and resembles it: gentle, attentive, courteous. Giverny is near, Rouen and its heaps of lovely restaurants are ten minutes away. *Children over 10 welcome.*

Château de Bonnemare

A Renaissance gatehouse leads to a remarkable 16th-century brique de St Jean façade as you enter the grounds of this enticing 'monument historique'. Alain and Sylvie, generous and charming, have restored two elegant ground-floor rooms in the north wing, and two with listed decoration on the first floor. Find French classical elegance, chandeliers, mouldings, deep mattresses and pleasing modern bathrooms. Breakfast in the vaulted Great Kitchen with embroidered napkins, fresh fruits and flowers, pâtisserie and homemade jams. The estate walls enclose chapel, farm, cider press, bakery, barns and 44 acres of park and woodland. Grand.

Rooms	1 double, 1 suite for 2: €95-€115. Extra bed/sofabed €30 p.p. per night.		**Rooms**	1 double: €130-€155. 3 suites for 3: €190-€245. Extra bed/sofabed €25 p.p. per night.
Meals	Restaurant 900m walk in Rouen, 10-minute drive.		**Meals**	Shared guest kitchen. Restaurant 6km.
Closed	Rarely.		**Closed**	1 December – 15 February.

Tel	+33 (0)2 35 36 00 04	**Tel**	+33 (0)2 32 49 03 73
Email	captot76@yahoo.fr	**Email**	sarlbonnemare@nordnet.fr
Web	www.captot.com	**Web**	www.bonnemare.com

Michelle Desrez
Manoir de Captot,
42 route de Sahurs,
76380 Canteleu, Seine-Maritime

Sylvie Vandecandelaere
Château de Bonnemare,
990 route de Bacqueville,
27380 Radepont, Eure

ENTRY 161 MAP 4

ENTRY 162 MAP 4

La Lévrière

This farmhouse, in a quaint corner of Haute-Normandie, is surrounded by a green paradise of orchards and summer and winter vegetable patches. Organic produce and simple living are the buzzwords in the Languignons' bolthole, and you breakfast on wholemeal bread and crusty baguette, jams and fruit – all homemade or grown, and accompanied by local honey, farm yogurt and heart-shaped Neufchâtel cheese. Relax in the grassy gardens, cross over the stream and duck under the long tendrils of the white willow and hazel to explore the footpaths at the end of the garden. Three airy bedrooms overlook a central courtyard - larger families can take over the whole place, but it's private enough for a romantic long weekend of gentle pedalling through the villages of the thickly forested valley.

Chambres d'hôtes de la Bucaille

In a small hamlet surrounded by 600 acres of land is a farmhouse where Sophie and her children live, and a four-square brick mansion for the guests. You'll find a breakfast room, sitting room and TV room downstairs, and five bedrooms up, with choice fabrics, period furniture and fine new bathrooms. Breakfast is served on antique tablecloths and white china, and elegant wallpapers and north African rugs are scattered throughout. All feels polished, pleasing, and hospitable. Say hello to the horses, borrow the bikes, visit Richard the Lionheart's Château Gaillard; it's one of many historic sites.

Rooms	3 suites for 2: €95-€105. Extra bed €30 p.p. per night
Meals	Restaurant 5km.
Closed	Rarely.

Rooms	1 double, 3 twin/doubles: €80-€110. 1 apartment for 5: €90-€150.
Meals	Restaurant 8km.
Closed	Rarely.

Tel	+33 (0)2 32 27 04 78
Email	hello@normandyrooms.com
Web	www.normandyrooms.com

Monsieur & Madame Languignon
La Lévrière,
24 rue Guérard,
27140 Saint Denis Le Ferment, Eure

Tel	+33 (0)2 32 54 58 45
Email	hamot.jerome@orange.fr
Web	www.chambres-hotes-labucaille.com

Sophie Hamot
Chambres d'hôtes de la Bucaille,
2 rue Jean Lucas,
27700 Guiseniers, Eure

La Réserve

You will like Valérie, lively mother of four, and her quietly refined house. And after breakfast at the big guest table you will want to stay forever. Over home-grown eggs and homemade jams, cake of the day, cheeses, charcuterie and fruit kebabs, conversations flourish, friendships bud. Outside, limewash walls stand among lavender-edged lawns and orchards, kindly Flaubert the Leonberger ambles, cows graze; inside are grey woodwork and gorgeous rooms, superb beds, handsome rugs on parquet floors, fine antiques and touches of brocante. Monet's ineffable gardens are just down the hill.

Les Hautes Sources

Three golden farmhouses around a central lawned terrace, with views that sail over the valley to a distant church spire: an incomparable setting. Enthusiastic Amaury and Audrey arrived with their family in 2012 and give you three bedrooms in the second house and a family cottage in the third: uncluttered, gorgeous, luxurious. Imagine decorative floors, white-painted beams, muted colours and snowy linen. Wake to five homemade jams that include apple caramel, set off for Monet's beautiful Giverny, wander the lovely gardens, splash in the pool, sink into sofas by the great stone fire. You will unwind here.

Rooms	1 double, 4 twin/doubles: €110-€170. Extra bed, under 11s €25; over 11s, €45. Whole property can be rented for groups and events.	
Meals	Restaurants 1km. Meals for groups available, on request.	
Closed	End of October to end of March, except by arrangement.	

Rooms	1 twin/double, 1 twin: €130-€150. 1 suite for 2: €170-€180. 1 cottage for 5: €200-€210.
Meals	Restaurants 3km.
Closed	Rarely.

Tel	+33 (0)2 32 21 99 09
Email	mlreserve@gmail.com
Web	www.giverny-lareserve.com

Valérie & François Jouyet
La Réserve,
27620 Giverny,
Eure

Tel	+33 (0)6 72 84 91 89
Email	amaury.detilly@hotmail.fr
Web	www.les-hautes-sources.fr

Amaury de Tilly
Les Hautes Sources,
32 rue Roederer,
27120 Ménilles, Eure

Clos de Mondétour

Les Logis du Moulin

Tiny church to one side, lazy river behind, views to weeping willows and majestic limes – the house oozes grace and tranquillity. Grégoire and Aude have created a calm, charming atmosphere inside: this is a family home. Lofty, light-drenched bedrooms with polished floorboards, antiques and monogrammed bed linen are beautifully refined; bathrooms are light and luxurious. The living area, with a striking tiled floor and bold colours, is a restful space in which to settle in front of a log fire – or enjoy a special breakfast among fresh flowers and family silver. Aude's horses graze in the meadow behind.

Welcome to a serene green paradise – a converted water mill and burgeoning B&B. Across deckchair'd lawns linked by meandering paths (clogs and umbrellas provided!) are two separate cottages, sober, simple, fresh and warm; total tranquillity. In the first, the main bedroom is downstairs and the single is up, leading through to a rustic-stylish shower. In the converted bread oven, bucolically on the river bank, is a double with an extra bed for child. Find floors of rosy terracotta, arched windows hung with muslin, pretty beds topped with quilts. In the handsome dining room, gentle Elisabeth serves a breakfast worth lingering over; and you can, until 11am. *Pets by arrangement.*

Rooms	1 double, 1 twin/double: €130. 1 family room for 4: €100-€150. 1 triple: €140.
Meals	Restaurants 2km.
Closed	Rarely.

Rooms	1 double: €85.1 suite for 3: €105. Singles €65-€70. Extra bed/sofabed €15 p.p. per night.
Meals	Assiette gourmande with cider, €16. Restaurant 3km.
Closed	Rarely.

Tel   +33 (0)2 32 36 68 79
Email   aude.jeanson@closdemondetour.com
Web   www.closdemondetour.com

Aude Jeanson
Clos de Mondétour,
17 rue de la Poste,
27120 Fontaine sous Jouy, Eure

Tel   +33 (0)2 32 26 06 07
Email   elisabeth.lamblardy@orange.fr
Web   www.leslogisdumoulin.fr

Elisabeth Lamblardy
Les Logis du Moulin,
4 rue du Moulin,
27120 Fontaine sous Jouy, Eure

ENTRY 167   MAP 4

ENTRY 168   MAP 4

La Ferme des Isles

Approach this sprawling 19th-century farm through a watercolour of mills, meadows and bridges... friendly French hosts await with a menagerie of four-legged friends. With vintage chairs, suspended lamps, billiards and book-filled mangers, it's perfect for fun social soirées and François's four-star dinners. Beams break up modern bedrooms – a triangular bath and a sunburst bed will astound you. Breakfast in the cavernous barn (on goat's cheese, grainy breads, garden fruits); end the day amongst fireplaces, convivial tables and chesterfields in stone-walled sitting and dining rooms. For nature lovers, couples and families – huge fun. *Minimum stay: 2 nights at weekends.*

Au Vieux Logis

They are full of character and terribly French, this artist owner and her crooked house marked by the slings and arrows of 500 years: wonky floorboards, bathrooms among the beams, old-fashioned floral bedrooms and a sensuous garden full of old favourites: lilac and honeysuckle, luscious shrubs and fruit trees. Set in the middle of the village, the quiet old house has an atmosphere that inspires ease and rest. (Saint-Exupéry, author of the *Le Petit Prince* and a friend of Madame's father, stayed here.) Madame, a good, generous soul, was once an antique dealer so breakfast is served on old silver.

Rooms	5 doubles: €110-€170. Singles €105-€165. Extra bed/sofabed €20-€30 p.p. per night.
Meals	Dinner, 4 courses with wine, €47.50. Restaurants 300m.
Closed	Rarely.

Rooms	2 doubles: €55. 1 triple: €80. 1 quadruple: €100.
Meals	Dinner €17. Wine €15.
Closed	Rarely.

Tel	+33 (0)2 32 36 66 14
Email	lafermedesisles@gmail.com
Web	www.lafermedesisles.com

François & Sophie Breban
La Ferme des Isles,
7 chemin des Isles,
27490 Autheuil Authouillet, Eure

Tel	+33 (0)2 32 50 60 93
Email	levieuxlogis5@orange.fr
Web	www.levieuxlogis.fr

Annick Auzoux
Au Vieux Logis,
27370 St Didier des Bois,
Eure

ENTRY 169   MAP 4

ENTRY 170   MAP 4

Manoir d'Hermos

The sedately old-French bedrooms with
good antiques and satin touches in the
16th-century house (in Madame's family for
100 years) are large, light and lovely.
All sit in peace by pastoral meadows, a
birdy orchard and spreading lake. Béatrice
is full of spontaneous smiles, puts flowers
everywhere, organises big parties on a
theme (not when B&B guests are here),
serves good breakfasts and brunches at
one table and keeps four gentle donkeys.
The orchards produce cider and trees are
being carefully and meticulously planted to
Napoleonic plans discovered in the
archives. A super place to stay, filled with
interesting history.

Le Logis des Monts

The house, picturesquely timbered and
behind wrought-iron gates, lies on the edge
of a hamlet. The setting is rural; the large
garden is delightful. Françoise and her
Spanish greyhound are the friendliest hosts.
The sitting room has overhead beams and
the colourful, immaculate bedrooms are in
the guest wing, the cosiest under the eaves.
After a fine continental breakfast – brioche,
homemade jams, fruit salad – served in the
conservatory at flexible times, set off for
Rouen, Honfleur and glamorous Deauville.
Table d'hôtes is offered Monday to Friday on
request – don't miss it: Françoise is an
excellent cook.

Rooms	1 suite for 3 with kitchen: €108.
	1 quadruple: €94-€138.
Meals	Restaurants 2km.
Closed	Rarely.

Rooms	2 doubles: €68.
Meals	Dinner with drinks, coffee &
	apéritif, €25 (Monday-Friday).
	Restaurants 7km.
Closed	Rarely.

Tel	+33 (0)2 32 35 51 32
Email	contact@hermos.fr
Web	www.hermos.fr

Béatrice & Patrice Noël-Windsor
Manoir d'Hermos,
27800 St Éloi de Fourques,
Eure

Tel	+33 (0)2 32 57 25 88
Email	lelogisdesmonts@orange.fr
Web	www.lelogisdesmonts.fr

Françoise Hannedouche
Le Logis des Monts,
26 impasse des Monts Nord,
27520 Theillement, Eure

Les Clématites

It's impossible not to feel happy in this maison de maître (one of several that housed Norman ribbon weavers), set in the fields of the Normandy plains, with a dreamy garden and a cider producer next door. Breakfast is at a long table and includes freshly-squeezed orange juice, good coffee and delicious pastries. Your hosts, courteous and charming, will happily tell you about the region, starting with Bernay, 20 minutes away: it has a medieval abbey and the oldest church in Normandy. Cormeilles too is close, a pretty place with a calvados distillery to visit. This is great walking and cycling territory and criss-crossed with quiet roads, so pack up a picnic and discover sleepy villages. Return to a panelled drawing room and lofty bedrooms with views of the garden and the fields beyond. Peacefulness reigns.

Rooms	1 double, 1 twin: €74. Singles €70.
Meals	Restaurants nearby.
Closed	Rarely.

Tel	+33 (0)2 32 45 46 52
Email	la.charterie@orange.fr
Web	monsite.orange.fr/la.charterie

Marie-Hélène François & Hughes de Morchoven
Les Clématites,
11 route de Duranville, Hameau de la Charterie,
27230 St Aubin de Scellon, Eure

ENTRY 173   MAP 4

Le Clos du Guiel

Marika and Pierre live in a 19th-century mansion on the edge of a country town and have converted two outbuildings in the garden into B&B spaces. All have separate entrances, some have balconies or terraces, and the pretty garden has a river running through it. Stroll to the house for charcuterie, cheeses, cold meats, pastries and homemade jams, surrounded by antiques and bric-a-brac – Marika and Pierre are passionate collectors. Walk to restaurants for lunch and dinner or rustle up something simple in your kitchenette. Ask your hosts about hikes, horse riding and fishing nearby. The town centre has a deli, grocery and bakery, or you can drive to Bernay in 20 minutes for supermarkets, antique shops and trains into Paris (1hr 20 mins). For the ferry, Caen is an hour and a half away.

Rooms	1 twin: €90. 2 suites for 2: €120; suites can also be self-catering, €95 per night. Professional cosmetic treatments and massages available.
Meals	Restaurant 3-minute walk (closed Wednesday evening).
Closed	4 September – 30 September, 29 November – 9 December.

Tel	+33 (0)6 86 53 96 59
Email	marika@leclosduguiel.fr
Web	leclosduguiel.fr

Marika Koch
Le Clos du Guiel,
2 rue de l'Eglise,
27390 Montreuil l'Argillé, Eure

ENTRY 174   MAP 4

Château de la Puisaye

A fine château which oozes 18th-century elegance (pale façade, shuttered windows) in 27 acres of rural bliss. Find large airy bedrooms with antiques, huge mantelpiece mirrors, glass-panelled doors that flood spaces with light; ivory paintwork and snowy linen create an ordered calm. The salon and library have elaborate woodwork and the dining room, with its gleaming table and silver candlesticks, invites you to linger over breakfast, a feast of homemade pastries, jams and cooked dishes. Lounge in the book-filled library, borrow a bike and pedal the grounds; swim in the heated pool or relax in the infra-red sauna among delicious aromatherapy oils. *Pool open May-September.*

Rooms	3 doubles, 1 twin: €98-€128. 1 suite for 4: €185.
Meals	Restaurants 4km.
Closed	Rarely.

Tel +33 (0)2 32 58 65 35
Email info@chateaudelapuisaye.com
Web www.chateaudelapuisaye.com

Bruno & Diana Costes
Château de la Puisaye,
Lieu-dit La Puisaye,
27130 Verneuil sur Avre, Eure

ENTRY 175 MAP 4

Domaine de Pasiphae

This traditional farmhouse from the 1860s is set back from the road and surrounded by rambling gardens, so you'll feel like you're in the countryside even though you can stroll to good restaurants. Cecile and Frederic's home is stylish without feeling too formal. Breakfast is on the terrace or in the garden – bread, brioche and croissants from the local bakery, homemade jams, yogurt, compotes and cakes. While there are two sitting rooms with fireplaces and plenty of books, the garden is the main draw: more wild jungle than a formal garden, with a kids' play area, veg patch and two resident sheep. There are shops and two good restaurants in the nearby village, and you're perfectly located for the Normandy cheese trail. Cycle or walk the surrounding countryside, explore sweet towns, return to relaxed hospitality.

Rooms	3 suites for 2: €82-€102. Singles €75-€95.
Meals	Restaurants 5-minute walk.
Closed	Rarely.

Tel +33 (0)6 07 91 77 03
Email ledomainedepasiphae@gmail.com
Web domainedepasiphae.fr

Cecile Bussiere
Domaine de Pasiphae,
13 avenue Foch,
61120 Vimoutiers, Orne

ENTRY 176 MAP 4

Belle Vallée

Built in 1800, this very pretty house stands in acres of woods, pastures and landscaped gardens, with outbuildings (the owners' quarters) and cottage. Footpaths meander to a lovely walled orchard and a pristine kitchen garden complete with hens. Inside are corridors alive with books, five delightful bedrooms, spick and span bathrooms and a sitting room with a log fire – guests are comfortable here. In the panelled dining room, kind Richard and Victoria, both from the catering industry, serve French breakfasts at crisp tables. Domfront on its hill is wonderfully close, very French. *Children over 12 welcome.*

Manoir de Bénédicte

A really wonderful house, bursting with history and beautiful architecture. Bénédicte is warm, engaging and a delight to stay with, opening her home and also the impressive grounds in an informal, relaxed way. Light floods in to a rich red dining room with oak parquet floor and picture windows overlooking lawns and river; the salon is calming and has equally fine views; upstairs are lofty-ceilinged bedrooms with Persian rugs and family antiques. Breakfast is round the large table: freshly-squeezed orange juice, local cheeses, bread from the local bakery, homemade cakes and jams. Energetic walks abound – or just stroll the parkland. *Parking on-site.*

Rooms	5 doubles: €70-€90. Singles €65-€85.	**Rooms**	3 doubles: €125-€155. Extra bed €25.
Meals	Dinner available. Restaurants 5-minute drive.	**Meals**	Restaurants 3km.
Closed	Rarely.	**Closed**	5 November – 1 April.

Tel	+33 (0)2 33 37 05 71	**Mobile**	+33 (0)6 74 13 17 49
Email	belle.vallee@wanadoo.fr	**Email**	benedicte@lemanoirdebenedicte.fr
Web	www.belle-vallee.net	**Web**	www.lemanoirdebenedicte.fr/en/

Victoria & Richard Hobson-Cossey
Belle Vallée,
61700 Domfront,
Orne

Bénédicte de Saint Pol
Manoir de Bénédicte,
Les Planches,
61430 Cahan, Orne

2 Le Bois de Crépi

Madame's welcome is as cheerful and bright as her bedrooms – and she loves to cook. The Gavards' immaculate 1980s house, resting in one pretty acre (lawns, roses, little footbridge over the pond) is the perfect stopover: near the autoroute yet truly tranquil. Borrow bikes and cycle the 'voie verte' to Mont St Michel or spend the day in St Malo. Then come home to friendly table d'hôtes and a great-value menu that reflects the seasons. There's a guest sitting room to retire to, with guide books, games, TV; and bedrooms are under the eaves, warm, simple, characterful, with brand new beds and flowers. Bathrooms gleam.

Château de Chantore

Set in peaceful countryside and just 5km from the sea, this striking 18th-century château has been restored with great care by Bernard and Inaki. It is filled with startlingly bold colours, striking fabrics, fine paintings and antique pieces. Bedrooms have big canopied beds, marble fireplaces and spotless bathrooms with individual flourishes. You breakfast on fresh bread and apple cake from the local baker, honey from the estate hives and eggs from the chickens. Take the bikes for a spin, visit nearby seaside towns and discover bracing coastline before returning to supper on the terrace and a stroll through the grounds. *Parking on-site.*

Rooms	2 family rooms for 4: €57-€81. Singles €50. Extra bed/sofabed €12 p.p. per night. Under 3s free.	**Rooms**	2 doubles, 1 twin: €180-€220. 2 suites for 4: €260-€350. Extra bed/sofabed €50 p.p. per night.
Meals	Dinner, 3 courses with wine, €20. Children €10. Restaurants 1 km.	**Meals**	Restaurants 5km.
Closed	Rarely.	**Closed**	Rarely.

Tel	+33 (0)2 33 48 34 68	**Tel**	+33 (0)9 60 52 82 73
Mobile	+33 (0)6 65 31 99 99	**Email**	contact@chateaudechantore.com
Email	jpgavard@club-internet.fr	**Web**	www.chateaudechantore.com

Jean-Paul & Brigitte Gavard
2 Le Bois de Crépi,
Poilley,
50220 Près de Ducey, Manche

Bernard Legal
Château de Chantore,
50530 Bacilly,
Manche

Manoir de Coutainville

Le Petit Ruisseau

Secluded rooms with views over rooftops and sparkling seas are a traveller's joy. Add a cultured hostess, delectable dining and a 15th-century manoir and you have a dash of French magic. Through pale stone arches serenity awaits, genteel apéritifs ushering in five-course dinners that showcase fish and seafood. Sophie Véron provides spare wellies and captivating conversation, her fashion career informs her calm interiors – a rare mix of charm and luxury – and history resonates through every sea-view room. Downstairs in the annexe find library armchairs and a scullery kitchen. Stroll to Coutainville, watch the sailing boats.

In the hamlet of Le Douit is a 350-year-old house, rather grand with its own little turret, a delicious piece of Norman history. Linda's welcome is generous and warm, and her knowledge of World War II second to none; her father-in-law was a renowned photojournalist and his black and white photos are captivating. There are books, antiques, squishy sofas too, and a kitchen with a big old Aga. Linda loves real food so her suppers and dinners reflect the seasons and you can eat under the old walnut tree in summer. All this, feather quilts, fresh flowers and deep mattresses, and a young garden backed by pastures – enchanting!

Rooms	2 doubles; 1 twin with separate shower: €200-€280. 1 suite for 4, 1 suite for 5: €250-€410. Dinner, B&B €259-€339 p.p. Extra bed/sofabed €50-€100 p.p. per night.
Meals	Dinner with wine, €59.
Closed	Rarely.

Rooms	1 twin/double: €75-€80. Singles €50.
Meals	Dinner with wine & coffee, €35. Light supper €17.50. Restaurants 4km.
Closed	Rarely.

Tel	+33 (0)2 33 47 05 90
Email	sophie-veron@manoir-de-coutainville.com
Web	www.manoir-de-coutainville.com

Sophie Véron
Manoir de Coutainville,
2 rue de la Maugerie,
50230 Agon Coutainville, Manche

Tel	+33 (0)2 33 41 47 05
Email	lande.la@orange.fr
Web	www.normandybandb.co.uk

Linda Malindine
Le Petit Ruisseau,
9 chemin de L'Église,
50390 Biniville, Manche

ENTRY 181   MAP 3

ENTRY 182   MAP 3

Ferme de Banoville

Sarah, Andy, and their two young children
moved here four years ago. The aim is to
be self-sufficient so they've planted a
willow coppice and fitted solar panels.
Down a bumpy track from the village,
ringed by countryside, the rustic farmhouse
and outbuildings huddle round an ancient
oak and duck pond. At one end of the
family home find three simple bedrooms
(one en suite) and a guest salon/dining
room where you breakfast: eggs from the
hens, home-pressed apple juice, the usual
pastries. Part of the fun of staying is joining
your hosts for supper; perhaps lamb or
duck raised on the farm. You can explore
both coasts from here.

Manoir de Bellauney

Even the smallest bathroom oozes
atmosphere through its *œil de bœuf*.
The youngest piece of this fascinating
and venerably ancient house is over
400 years old; its predecessor stood on the
site of a monastery, the fireplace in the
lovely Medieval bedroom carries the coat
of arms of the original owners. To furnish
the rooms, your ex-farmer hosts hunted out
carved *armoires de mariage*, lace canopies,
footstools – and hung tapestry curtains at
the windows. They share their energy
enthusiastically between this wonderful
house, its small dense garden, and their
guests. Sheer comfort among warm old
stones.

Rooms	1 double; 2 doubles both with separate bathroom: €59-€60.
Meals	Dinner with wine & coffee, €19. Restaurants 5km.
Closed	Never.

Rooms	1 double: €70. 3 suites for 3: €90-€120.
Meals	Restaurants 4km.
Closed	November-April.

Tel	+33 (0)2 33 08 05 36
Email	banoville@gmail.com
Web	www.banoville.com

Sarah Beale
Ferme de Banoville,
50260 Négreville,
Manche

Tel	+33 (0)2 33 40 10 62
Email	manoirdebellauney@gmail.com
Web	www.bellauney.com

Christiane & Jacques Allix-Desfauteaux
Manoir de Bellauney,
50700 Tamerville,
Manche

ENTRY 183   MAP 3

ENTRY 184   MAP 3

Manoir de la Fèvrerie

Your blithe, beautiful, energetic hostess is a delight, forever indulging her passion for interior decoration. Her exquisite rooms are a festival of colours, textures, antiques and embroidered linen. It's a heart-warming experience to stay in this wonderful old Normandy farmhouse where the great granite hearth is always lit and a breakfast of superb local specialities is served on elegant china; there is a richly carved 'throne' at the head of the long table. Find a deep courtyard at the entrance, a pretty garden behind; soft countryside surrounds you and Barfleur and the coast is a short drive.

Le Petit Matin

You're on a residential street overlooking the Place Charles de Gaulle, a short walk from the astonishing 11th-century cathedral at the heart of this ancient town. Helpful Pascal has transformed his antique-filled handsome town house into a lovely place to stay with beautiful lawned gardens (for lazing in the shade or playing boules). Bedrooms are comfortable and elegant, full of space and light, each with their own smart modern bathroom – one on the ground floor has its own entrance and terrace. Breakfasts are a paean to the baker's art, with fruit, yoghurt, homemade jam and much more. Explore historic Bayeux.

Rooms	3 twin/doubles; extra children's room available: €75-€85. Extra bed/sofabed €25 p.p. per night. Fifth night offered free (not July/August).	
Meals	Restaurants 3km.	
Closed	Rarely.	

Rooms	4 doubles, 1 twin/double: €75-€140. Extra bed €50. Cot available.
Meals	Picnics available. Restaurants 5-minute walk.
Closed	Rarely.

Tel	+33 (0)2 33 54 33 53
Email	lafevrerie@orange.fr
Web	www.lafevrerie.fr

Marie-France Caillet
Manoir de la Fèvrerie,
4 route d'Arville,
50760 Ste Geneviève, Manche

Tel	+33 (0)2 31 10 09 27
Email	lepetitmatin@hotmail.fr
Web	www.lepetitmatin.fr/en/

Pascal Lebret
Le Petit Matin,
9 rue des Terres, Place Charles de Gaulle,
14400 Bayeux, Calvados

Clos de Bellefontaine

Come to be pampered and effortlessly spoiled at this elegant townhouse, a ten-minute stroll from the famous Tapestry. Bedrooms are chic and gracious with choice antiques, colours are mocha and white, floors polished parquet or seagrass. Choose the top floor for snugness and charm, the first floor for grandeur and space. With a walled garden and two handsome ground-floor salons – antiques, family photographs, help-yourself refreshments – to lounge around in, you'll not miss home. Carole's breakfasts, with homemade tarts, fruit compotes and cheeses, are the highlight of the stay.

Les Glycines

This lovely couple are kindness itself, she softly spoken and twinkling, he jovial, talkative, utterly French. Having retired from farming, they moved into the heart of Bayeux. You can glimpse the cathedral spires from their house, once part of the old bishop's palace. Beyond the gates and the wisteria, the door opens to a lofty beamed living room rejoicing in good antiques and a monumental fireplace; through another is the kitchen. Up the ancient stone stairs are pretty bedrooms – immaculate bedding, pastel-tiled showers – that look quietly over a pocket-handkerchief garden. Delicious breakfasts, history all around, and no need for a car.

Rooms	2 doubles, 1 twin: €135-€175. Extra bed/sofabed €20 p.p. per night.	**Rooms**	2 doubles: €71. 1 family room for 3: €98. Singles €61.
Meals	Restaurants nearby.	**Meals**	Restaurant 50m.
Closed	Rarely.	**Closed**	Rarely.

Mobile	+33 (0)6 81 42 24 81	**Tel**	+33 (0)2 31 22 52 32
Email	clos.bellefontaine@wanadoo.fr	**Mobile**	+33 (0)6 89 39 84 79
Web	www.clos-bellefontaine.fr	**Email**	louisfauvel@orange.fr

Carole & Jérôme Mallet
Clos de Bellefontaine,
6 rue de Bellefontaine,
14400 Bayeux, Calvados

Louis & Annick Fauvel
Les Glycines,
13 rue aux Coqs,
14400 Bayeux, Calvados

Le Mas Normand

A fun place to stay run with great warmth
by Sandrine. You're a stone's throw from
long sandy beaches and wild dunes. Return
to relax in a light modern conservatory with
books and games which leans against the
old stone garden wall, very comfortable
bedrooms accessed from the courtyard
and a pretty south-facing garden. Breakfast
is served at a large modern table and
includes breads and pastries from the local
boulangerie, cheeses, yogurt and
homemade cake. Hire bikes, explore with a
picnic (Sandrine can give you tableware),
visit the Memorial de Caen or the Bayeux
Tapestry. Mont St Michel is near enough
for a day trip.

La Malposte

Walk through the gates to this group of old
stone buildings in a garden of moss, trees,
hens, flowers, and little bridges over the
rushing stream. Patricia and Jean-Michel
live in the mill and you stay across the
water, in an elegantly rustic stable with
your own kitchen. Hire a boat at
Courseulles-sur-Mer (5km), swim in the
pool down the road, or explore interesting
Bayeux (22km). Its tapestry, commissioned
for the inauguration of the cathedral in
1077, is the jewel in its crown. Bed is at the
top of the spiral stair; let the mill stream lull
you to sleep. In the morning, wake to a
beautiful breakfast of croissants, fruits,
cheeses and Patricia's homemade jams.
The entire place is a work of art, and the
gardens are Jean-Michel's pride and joy.
Two nights may not be enough.

Rooms	1 double: €65-€90.
	2 cabins for 4: €65-€120.
	Extra charge for pets.
Meals	Restaurants 5km.
Closed	Rarely.

Rooms	1 double: €92. Singles €72.
	1 family room: €112 for 3;
	€148 for 4.
Meals	Guest kitchen. Restaurants 2km.
Closed	Rarely.

Tel	+33 (0)2 31 21 97 75
Email	lemasnormand@wanadoo.fr
Web	www.lemasnormand.com

Sandrine Thierry
Le Mas Normand,
8 impasse de la Rivière,
14114 Ver sur Mer, Calvados

Tel	+33 (0)2 31 37 51 29
Email	jean-michel.blanlot@wanadoo.fr
Web	www.lamalposte.com

Patricia & Jean-Michel Blanlot
La Malposte,
15 rue des Moulins,
14470 Reviers, Calvados

Chez Laurence du Tilly

Laurence has a passion for cool, contemporary style – and good food. Her central 18th-century townhouse has an elegantly hip salon – honesty bar, open fire, Danish chairs, music – then, up ancient spiral stairs to a choice of three apartments. The first floor is classic in white offset by modern pieces; the second has stripped boards and funky designer pieces; the cosy under the eaves one has animal skin rugs, black parquet and a roof top terrace. Beds are well dressed, bathrooms snazzy, kitchens state-of-the-art. Fab food can be delivered to your table. Ferry port is close, and Caen is a great little city to explore on foot. *Parking on-site.*

Le Gaudin

People return because it's fun to stay here with friendly Clive and Denise at the helm – and a long sociable table for superb dinners. Shooting through the centre of this 18th-century farmhouse is a chimney of 4,500 bricks. Clive knows: he built it! Every feature conveys the creativity of your British hosts. Exposed stone walls; an old manger, now a wine rack; Denise's upholstered coffee table; a doll's house in the sunny breakfast room. Deeply comfortable bedrooms have hand-sewn fabrics and fine French antiques. Fish in the wooded grounds; join the ancient pilgrims' walk to Mont St Michel; go canoeing in nearby Thury-Harcourt.

Rooms	1 apartment for 2, 2 apartments for 4: €150-€200. Extra bed/sofabed €25 p.p. per night.
Meals	Full breakfast extra €15. Dinner €25-€30. Restaurants 1-minute walk.
Closed	Never.

Rooms	3 doubles, 1 twin: €70-€90.
Meals	Dinner with wine, €38.
Closed	January-March.

Mobile	+33 (0)7 86 23 28 28
Email	chez-laurence@dutilly.fr
Web	www.chez-laurence.dutilly.fr

Laurence du Tilly
Chez Laurence du Tilly,
9b rue Pémagnie,
14000 Caen, Calvados

Tel	+33 (0)2 31 73 88 70
Email	bookings@legaudin.co.uk
Web	www.legaudin.co.uk

Clive & Denise Canvin
Le Gaudin,
Route d'Aunay,
14260 Campandré Valcongrain, Calvados

ENTRY 191   MAP 4

ENTRY 192   MAP 4

Château La Cour

Welcome to a 13th-century castle, once owned by the Ducs d'Harcourt, full of comfort and joy. There are Lloyd Loom chairs and marble fireplaces. Every room is stunning and faces the garden, one has a curved stair to a lavish bathroom. Breakfast includes home-grown fruits, homemade yogurt and eggs from the château's hens, while English china, damask and candelabra grace the dinner table. David's potager is a wonder; Lesley's cooking is delicious. The Cravens are conservationists, too; barn owls nest in the end wall and the birdwatching is fabulous. Don't miss the Normandy beaches, or Bayeux. *Children over 12 welcome.*

Château de la Pommeraye

A big shuttered mansion (1646 with later additions) surrounded by meadows and woodland, this part-moated house is flanked by 12th-century towers and outbuildings. Your ex-Parisian hosts, a young family, give you perfect bedrooms – find handsome carpets on polished boards, vast beds heaped with pillows, a selection of pictures (oils, icons, engravings) and classic porcelain hand basins. Downstairs: pale painted wainscoting and moss-green velvet chairs, log fires and stone flooring. Spa, golf and riding breaks can be arranged, there's 'Suisse Normande' for rock climbing and canoeing, Caen for culture and shopping.

Rooms	3 doubles, 1 twin: €160.
Meals	Hosted dinner with wine, €35-€50.
Closed	November – February.

Rooms	4 twin/doubles: €175-€225. 2 suites for 4: €245-€295. Extra bed €40.
Meals	Breakfast €19. Dinner by arrangement, 4 courses, €49. Restaurant 2-minute walk.
Closed	Rarely.

Tel	+33 (0)2 31 79 19 37
Email	info@chateaulacour.com
Web	www.chateaulacour.com

David & Lesley Craven
Château La Cour,
14220 Culey le Patry,
Calvados

Tel	+33 (0)2 31 69 87 86
Email	alexandre.boudnikoff@orange.fr
Web	www.chateaudelapommeraye.com

Alexandre Boudnikoff
Château de la Pommeraye,
14690 La Pommeraye,
Calvados

ENTRY 193 MAP 4

ENTRY 194 MAP 4

Ferme de la Ruette

The gates glide open to a gravelled sweep and a tree'd lawn, with an old stone cider press to the side. Elegant, compassionate Isabelle looks after house, garden, guests – and rescue cats and horses – with warmth and charm; Philippe, a friendly GP, fills the game larder. The barn houses two bedrooms plus a delightful family room under the rafters (up a steep private stair) and a cosy guest sitting room with a bar. Bedrooms have pretty striped wallpapers, seagrass floors and elegant Louis XV-style chairs, quirky objets on shelves and in crannies, beds dressed with white heirloom spreads. Vivacious, bustling Caen is an easy drive.

Ô Saisons, Ô Châteaux (Château de Cesny)

An elegant Pierre de Caen stone château surrounded by 11 acres of grounds. Guests stay in their own wing and your host lives in the opposite one. A long staircase leads to two double bedrooms and a suite for four. You will love the room with the cavernous en suite and the claw-footed tub and fresco. Assemble in the salon for breakfasts of fresh pastries, just-squeezed orange juice and cakes with apples from the garden, or in the snug for quiet evenings in front of the television. Ramble outside – there's lots of grass for boisterous offspring, a little stream, a walled orchard with roaming hens and a fenced-off lake with a boat. Explore the villages, head to the coast to stroll along the landing beaches or the streets of ritzy Deauville and Trouville-sur-Mer. Caen is a short drive – great for Channel crossings.

Rooms	2 doubles: €70-€80. 1 family room for 4 with kitchenette: €80-€90. Singles €60-€80. Extra bed/sofabed €10 p.p. per night.	**Rooms**	2 doubles: €130-€150. 1 suite for 4: €160. The suite's twin room can also be booked separately: €90.
Meals	Restaurant 5km.	**Meals**	Restaurants 3.5km.
Closed	Rarely.	**Closed**	1 January – 31 March.

Tel	+33 (0)2 31 78 11 82	**Tel**	+33 (0)6 64 84 33 23
Email	laruette@gmail.com	**Email**	chateau.normandie@orange.fr
Web	www.fermedelaruette.fr		

Isabelle & Philippe Cayé
Ferme de la Ruette,
5 chemin Haussé,
14190 Cauvicourt, Calvados

Marie-Laure Heuzey
Ô Saisons, Ô Châteaux (Château de Cesny),
33 rue Andre Lemaitre,
14270 Cesny-aux-Vignes, Calvados

ENTRY 195 MAP 4   ENTRY 196 MAP 4

Le Fresnay

Friendly owner Matteo Fabra has created a peaceful, stylish sanctuary surrounded by 18 acres of pasture, orchards, woodland and garden. Breakfast on fresh bread and pastries with homemade marmalade and organic estate honey on the terrace. You're deep in unspoilt French countryside – perfect for long walks through fields and woods. But you can explore the manor grounds first – there's a croquet lawn and a boating pond. Pack up a picnic and head to the coast for a day out, taste cider and calvados, return to an open fire and a comfy sitting room. Head to the nearby village (just a mile) for dinner. *Please note that we do not accept credit cards, only cash or transfers.*

Château de Bénéauville

Down the plane-flanked drive to an immaculate Renaissance château in harmonious grounds. Find painted 17th-century beams in perfect condition, heads of antelope and oryx surprising the walls, a panelled library, a powder-blue dining room, and fireplaces imposing and theatrical. Here live the Augais family, with horse, hens and handsome gundogs. In big peaceful bedrooms with tall windows are chestnut floors and grey-washed beams, oriental carpets, quilted bedspreads, boudoir armchairs, deep baths (with shower attachments) and exquisite curtain tassels. Take a dip in the discreet pool; set off for culture in Caen. Marvellous.

Rooms	2 doubles, 1 twin/double: €90-€110. Use of the kitchen for stays of 2+ nights.
Meals	Restaurants 2.5km.
Closed	Rarely.

Rooms	3 doubles: €210-€290. 1 suite for 5: €290-€440.
Meals	Restaurants 5km.
Closed	Rarely.

Mobile	+33 (0)6 89 82 95 40
Email	lefresnay@gmail.com

Matteo Fabra
Le Fresnay,
2630 chemin d'Englesqueville,
14340 Cambremer, Calvados

Tel	+33 (0)2 31 72 56 49
Email	reservation@chateaudebeneauville.fr
Web	www.chateaudebeneauville.fr

Philippe Augais
Château de Bénéauville,
Bénéauville,
14860 Bavent, Calvados

Le Clos aux Masques

Ceramic masks on the façade of this charming Norman B&B greet you with a smile. Delightful Anne and convivial Andrea have transformed this half-timbered longère into a peaceful rural retreat. Ancient beams remain in some cosy bedrooms, offset by white walls and colourful bed linen, but creatively tiled en suites are supremely modern and views soar over the big, lawned, garden. Huddle around the open fire in a sitting room furnished with antiques and comfy sofas. Feast on hearty breakfasts of fresh bread, local cheese and Sicilian pastries. Sandy beaches are close and you can borrow the family's beach hut at Blonville! *Minimum stay: 2 nights.*

Villa d'Eaux

You're right in town in a row of arty terraced houses hidden from the brisk breeze. Affable Valérie gives you hotel-inspired extras like piles of pillows and robes that envelop you – plans are afoot for a wine bar for tastings, plus yoga and cookery classes. Escape to a secluded spot on the terrace or join new friends around the communal table indoors for a continental breakfast of pastries, jam and honey and Normandy cheese and yogurt. Wander the market, amble to the sandy beach, hire bikes, visit the paleo museum. Small groups could take over the whole property – six bedrooms and seven sitting rooms, plus a rooftop glass atrium facing west for sunsets – though it's romantic enough for couples' escapes to enjoy the beaches at Deauville, charming Honfleur and peaceful coastal pedalling. *Min. stay: 2 nights.*

Rooms	2 doubles: €85-€115. 2 family rooms for 3, 1 family room for 4: €95-€169.
Meals	Restaurants 4km.
Closed	Rarely.

Rooms	5 doubles: €230-€320. 1 single: €200.
Meals	Restaurants 15-minute walk.
Closed	Rarely.

Tel +33 (0)9 72 44 02 06
Email contact@clos-aux-masques.com
Web www.clos-aux-masques.com

Anne & Andrea Acquanegra
Le Clos aux Masques,
Le Bourg,
14950 Saint Pierre Azif, Calvados

Tel +33 (0)6 40 93 63 21
Email valerie@villadeaux.com
Web villadeaux.com/en/home/

Valérie Carrat
Villa d'Eaux,
12 rue Michel d'Ornano,
14640 Villers-sur-Mer, Calvados

ENTRY 199 MAP 4

ENTRY 200 MAP 4

La Mascotte

In the animated seaside town of Villers sur Mer – next to legendary Trouville – is a 19th-century villa built by a librettist. An airy hall leads to a stylish sitting room with French windows to a terrace, and a table at which stupendous breakfasts are served: breads, pastries, fruits, yogurts, homemade waffles and jams. Your gentle, discreet hostess, a passionate golfer, can direct you to one of numerous courses. Then it's back to boudoir armchairs, comfy beds and polished parquet: the bedrooms (one with a balcony, one a roof terrace) are a joy – all overlook the garden and rooftops, all have distant views of the sea. *Parking on-site.*

Bergerie de la Moutonnière

Sheep graze behind this old bergerie in the grounds of your hosts' manor house. Cook al fresco in a rustic, open kitchen on the covered terrace; breakfast (you can order a hamper to be delivered) or dine here overlooking the beautiful garden with its huge linden trees is a very special treat. The suite is light, lofty and beamed; the little Bergère will bring you close to nature – leave the top part of the stable door open and watch the stars come out one by one. On chilly days light the wood-burning stove and plan your next adventures. Stroll through the garden and orchard to find bee hives, chicken and sheep. Hike through gentle, rolling countryside with munching cows and donkeys. Hop in the car for farmers' markets, superb old churches and the magnificent beach at Trouville.

Rooms	1 double, 1 twin/double: €100-€150. 1 family room for 4: €130-€190.
Meals	Restaurants 3-minute walk.
Closed	January or February.

Rooms	1 suite for 2, 1 double, let with suite to same party only: €95-€120.
Meals	Breakfast €10. Evening meals on request. Restaurants 4km.
Closed	Rarely.

Mobile	+33 (0)6 76 98 20 34
Email	contact@guesthouse-lamascotte.com
Web	www.guesthouse-lamascotte.com

Ségolène de la Serre
La Mascotte,
11 rue de la Comtesse de Béarn,
14640 Villers-sur-Mer, Calvados

Tel	+33 (0)2 31 62 56 86
Email	walthaus@mac.com
Web	www.bergerienormandy.com

Rudolf Walthaus
Bergerie de la Moutonnière,
295 chemin du Mesnil,
14590 Le Pin, Calvados

ENTRY 201   MAP 4

ENTRY 202   MAP 4

Brittany

Château de la Ballue, page 186

Château du Bois-Guy

Stay in the main house itself or pick one of five eco-lodges around the lake with its ducks and geese. Animals rule the roost here; you may happen upon a pot-bellied pig in the car park, or find a door opened for you by a wily chocolate Lab. It's just how owners Michael and Mathias envisaged; they've put the finishing touches on their vision with a nine-hole eco golf course and a swimming pool. They're unfailingly generous: borrow golf clubs, bikes, umbrellas. Generosity extends to breakfast, a cornucopia of local produce (jam, eggs, cheese, pâtisserie), served in the dining room with lakeside views. Dinner, local and seasonal, also takes place here. Interiors are hip rather than historic, though big beams and yawning stone fireplaces hint at 15th-century roots. The grounds are perfect for a walk and there's a great gym, a driving range and yoga twice weekly; book a massage if you've had a long drive. You need your car for the coast but there's plenty on the doorstep; cycle for miles along the very peaceful Voie Verte or visit the American Cemetery.

Rooms	17 twin/doubles: €90-€179.
	2 family rooms for 4: €150-€180.
	5 cabins for 2: €160-€180. Extra
	bed/sofabed €10 p.p. per night.
Meals	Breakfast €14.
	Dinner, 3-courses, €45-€55.
Closed	Never.

Michael Linhoff & Mathias Haefeli
Château du Bois-Guy,
Lieu dit Bois-Guy,
35133 Parigné, Ille-et-Vilaine

Tel	+33 (0)2 99 97 34 60
Email	info@bois-guy.fr
Web	www.bois-guy.fr

Hotel les Charmettes

Two charming Belle Époque villas make up this lively, laid-back hotel. Each villa has eight rooms so some overlook St Malo's promenade and long sandy beach while others look onto a fairly quiet residential street. The area is well-heeled and, inside, owner Fabrice has been working hard to bring the place up-to-date. You'll find local art to buy on the walls, live music nights, bistro-style dishes flying out of the kitchen and small, individual, nautically themed bedrooms. The dining room is enticing with panoramic views out to sea; you eat here or on the terrace when the weather's fine. Breakfast is a generous continental spread of pastries, crepes, fruit, ham and cheese while dinner is mainly fresh-as-can-be seafood (it's open to the public too). Hire bikes to explore St Malo, hit the waves, get the ferry (or walk – it takes about four hours) to refined Dinard for lunch and a mooch around. This ticks all the boxes for a fantastic, affordable base with heaps to do nearby, and it's easy peasy for the Portsmouth ferry.

Rooms	10 doubles: €69-€130.
	5 triples: €89-€140.
	1 quadruple: €89-€130. Extra bed €10;
	cots available at no extra charge.
	Parking €7 per day.
Meals	Dinner €10-€25.
	Restaurants 5-minute walk.
Closed	November – February, except
	Christmas & New Year.

Tel	+33 (0)2 99 56 07 31	**Fabrice Chauvel**
Email	info@hotel-les-charmettes.com	Hotel les Charmettes,
Web	www.hotel-les-charmettes.com	64 bd Hebert,
		35400 Saint-Malo, Ille-et-Vilaine

ENTRY 204   MAP 3

Malouinière le Valmarin

The graceful *malouinière* was built in the early 18th century by a wealthy shipowner. Very near the ferry terminal, and in the centre of town, whence the urban buzz, this hotel has an unexpectedly large rose-filled garden with loungers and tables beneath mature cedars and the copper beech. Most bedrooms – light-filled with high ceilings, tall windows carefully draped to match the bedcovers – overlook the garden. Second-floor rooms have sloping ceilings and a cosier feel, with exposed beams, white walls and pale blue carpets. The indefatigable and cheerful Françoise and Bertrand refurbish a couple of rooms each winter. There are lavender bags in the wardrobes and plenty of books in French and English. Breakfast at the small yellow and blue dining tables or have your café-au-lait in bed and laze a bit before exploring the fabulous ramparts of the city or sunning on the nearby beaches. There's riding nearby and excellent thalassotherapy spas, or take an ocean ride to one of the Channel Islands – Sark is fascinating. Dinard, the 'Nice of the North', is a very short drive. Great value. *Secure parking available.*

Rooms	8 twin/doubles: €95-€165.
	4 family rooms for 5: €139-€215.
Meals	Breakfast €12. Restaurants nearby.
Closed	Never.

Françoise Nicolas-Quéric
Malouinière le Valmarin,
7 rue Jean XXIII, Saint Servan,
35400 Saint Malo, Ille-et-Vilaine

Tel   +33 (0)2 99 81 94 76
Email   levalmarin@wanadoo.fr
Web   www.levalmarin.com

Hôtel Manoir de Rigourdaine

At the end of the lane, firm on its hillside, Rigourdaine breathes space, sky, permanence. The square-yarded manor farm, originally a stronghold with moat and all requisite towers, now looks serenely out over estuary and rolling pastures, and offers a sheltering embrace. The reception/bar in the converted barn is a good place to meet the friendly, attentive master of the manor, properly pleased with his excellent conversion. A high open fireplace warms a sunken sitting well; the courtyard, a gravelled enclosure overlooking the estuary, is made for lounging in the sun; breakfast is at long tables laid with bright mats. Refurbished (or in the process) rooms are attractive and comfortable: Iranian rugs on plain carpets, coordinated contemporary-chic fabrics in pleasing colours, some fine old furniture, pale bathrooms with all essentials. Six ground-floor rooms have private terraces onto the garden – ideal for sundowners. Everywhere, atmosphere is lent by old timbers and antiques, and always the long limpid view. Great for families, cyclists, sailors, walkers. *Minimum stay: 2 nights at weekends & in high season. Children over 2 welcome.*

Rooms	10 doubles, 4 twins: €97-€105.
	3 triples: €117-€125.
	2 quadruples: €137-€145.
	Singles €89-€97.
Meals	Breakfast €9.50. Restaurants 4km.
Closed	4 November – 4 April.

Tel	+33 (0)2 96 86 89 96
Email	hotel.rigourdaine@wanadoo.fr
Web	www.hotel-rigourdaine.fr

Patrick Van Valenberg
Hôtel Manoir de Rigourdaine,
Rigourdaine, 22490 Plouër sur Rance,
Côtes-d'Armor

ENTRY 206   MAP 3

Hotel le Manoir Saint Michel

On a hillside overlooking wide white sands and wild coves is a 400-year-old sturdy stone 'manoir' with a long and varied history. Ducks wander the peaceful gardens, there's a small lake stocked with fish, wooden loungers dot the lawns and there are fine sea views from every angle. Inside, fresh flowers pretty up the reception and Monsieur and Madame greet you warmly: your hosts could not be nicer. Bedrooms vary in size and shape, not luxurious but comfortable and cosy, some traditional with floral fabrics and patterned carpets, others more contemporary. Bathrooms are spotless and small. Exposed stone walls add rusticity, antique armoires add character and there are 20 rooms to choose from so let the website guide you. Some are in the converted stables, some have sea views, some are on the ground floor. Take a ferry between St Malo and Dinard, visit the ancient, unspoilt Château de la Hunaudaye, come home to cakes and tea by the great log fire, and walk to dinner (take a torch!). Breakfasts are to die for: homemade croissants, yogurts and jams: Monsieur was once a pâtissier.

Minimum stay: 4 nights in high season.

Rooms	9 doubles, 2 twins: €85-€110. 3 triples: €90-€150. 1 quadruple: €108-€178. 2 cottages for 2, 1 cottage for 3, 1 cottage for 5, 1 cottage for 6: €90-€203.
Meals	Breakfast €11.50, children €5. Restaurant 800m.
Closed	November to March.

Jérôme Fournel
Hotel le Manoir Saint Michel,
38 rue de la Carquois, 22240 Fréhel,
Côtes-d'Armor

Tel	+33 (0)2 96 41 48 87
Mobile	+33 (0)6 26 87 54 05
Email	contact@manoirstmichel.com
Web	www.manoirstmichel.com

Ti al Lannec

Heaps of English antiques yet it is superbly French and fulsome: an Edwardian seaside residence perched on the cliff, its gardens ambling down to rocky coves and sandy beaches; fall asleep to waves and wind in the pines. (The beach club closes at midnight.) Inside, a mellow warmth envelops you in armfuls of drapes, swags and sprigs. Each room is a different shape and size, individually decorated as if in a private country mansion, with a sitting space, a writing table, a pretty bathroom and a view to the cypresses or, most wonderful, the sea. Expect florals, stripes, oriental rugs, white linen. Some bedrooms are big, with well-furnished white loggias, some are made for families with convertible bunk-bed sofas. Salons are cosily arranged with little lamps, mirrors, ornaments, old prints; the restaurant faces the sea and serves some pretty fancy and decorative food. The genuinely charming Jouanny family, immersed in the community and very mindful of their guests' welfare, have created a smart but human hotel with a lovely intimate spa by the indoor pool. Walk, swim, or just relax in this stunning setting.

Rooms	24 twin/doubles: €215-€400. 7 family rooms for 5: €308-€663. 2 singles: €156-€182. Extra bed/sofabed €49-€66 p.p. per night. Pets €13.50. Cot €16.50.
Meals	Breakfast €19. Children under 8 €11. Lunch, set menu, €28. Dinner, set menu, €48-€81; à la carte also available. Children's meals €18-€26.
Closed	Mid-November to March.

Tel	+33 (0)2 96 15 01 01
Email	contact@tiallannec.com
Web	www.tiallannec.com

Jouanny Family
Ti al Lannec,
14 allée de Mezo Guen,
22560 Trébeurden, Côtes-d'Armor

ENTRY 208   MAP 2

Grand Hôtel des Bains

Marine purity on the north Brittany coast: it's like a slightly snobby yacht club where you are an old member. The minimalist magician has cast natural spells of cotton, cane, wood, wool, seagrass: nothing synthetic or pompous. Sober lines, little ornamentation and restful colours leave space for the scenery, the sky pours in through walls of glass, the peaceful garden flows into rocks, beach and sea. Moss-green panelling lines the deep-chaired bar where a fire leaps in winter. Smallish, pale grey-panelled bedrooms have dark mushroom carpets and thick cotton stripes and checks, a four-poster here, a balcony there, nearly all have the ever-changing sea view. Bathrooms are due for refurbishment but bathrobes give you that four-star look on your way to the indoor seawater pool and treatment spa. Staff are smiling and easy, the ivory-panelled dining room with its sand-coloured tablecloths is deeply tempting. Spectacular coastal paths, a choice of beaches, yoga and spa retreats, even a writer's workshop – the luxury of space, pure elegant simplicity and personal attention are yours.

Rooms	36 twin/doubles: €201-€337. Singles €107-€277. Dinner, B&B €110-€332 p.p.
Meals	Dinner €37-€50.
Closed	Rarely.

Madame Nicol
Grand Hôtel des Bains,
15 bis rue de l'Église,
29241 Locquirec, Finistère

Tel	+33 (0)2 98 67 41 02
Email	reception@grand-hotel-des-bains.com
Web	www.grand-hotel-des-bains.com

Le Parc er Gréo

Fields, woods, sea and the coastal path are just yards away – all feels lovely and rural yet Vannes is a short drive. Owners Éric and Sophie built the neat modern building in the 1990s, but it's so well designed and decorated it feels like it's been in the family for ages. Warm colours, oriental rugs and fine family pieces sit easily in the smallish salon and dining room; these open onto terrace, garden and pool (heated and open all year round and sheltered by a high wall) – great places to relax or play with the children on the big lawn. Éric (who speaks excellent English) attentively prepares itineraries for guests: boating, swimming in the sea or inland exploration. His father's watercolours lend personality to all the rooms and the unusual candlesticks in the hall and ancestral portraits, including a large Velazquez–style child in a great gilt frame, are most appealing. Snug bedrooms, with a good mix of old and modern, are attractive in shades of red, green and salmon; nearly all have brand new bathrooms with spacious showers. Come by electric car and charge up at this easy, friendly place to stay. *Minimum stay: 2 nights in high season.*

Rooms	11 doubles: €79-€174. 1 suite for 4: €198-€278. 1 triple: €169-€209. Extra bed/sofabed €25 p.p. per night.
Meals	Breakfast €15. Restaurants 3km.
Closed	1 January – 15 February, 1 – 8 December.

Tel	+33 (0)2 97 44 73 03
Email	contact@parcergreo.com
Web	www.parcergreo.com

Éric & Sophie Bermond
Le Parc er Gréo,
9 rue Mané Guen, Le Gréo,
56610 Arradon, Morbihan

ENTRY 210   MAP 3

Hôtel La Désirade

Everyone loves an island and this one, with its wild windswept coast, is especially enticing. Battered by storms in winter, it is hot and gorse-scented in summer and the roads are silent. La Désirade, sheltered in its parkland, is made up of a new village of colourwashed houses round a pool. If leafy gardens, comfortable hotelly bedrooms and super bathrooms (white bathrobes, lashings of hot water) don't bring instant relaxation, the spa and massages surely will. Breakfast is served buffet-style in the breakfast room or by the pool; dinner, formal but excellent, is in the hotel restaurant across the lane. The young chef specialises in local dishes and the presentation is impeccable; wines are first-class too. Research the island's possibilities curled up in a wicker chair in the reception salon with its unexpectedly blue fireplace: there are lots of illustrated books. Ask your hosts about the 104 kilometres of coastal paths and cycle routes to choose from, while the beaches are a 20-minute walk away. Take your paintbox and you'll be in good company: Monet and Matisse both came to the island to paint.

Minimum stay: 2 nights in high season.

Rooms	14 doubles, 14 twins: €99-€285. 4 family rooms for 4: €190-€370. Extra bed/sofabed €30 p.p. per night.
Meals	Breakfast €18. Picnic lunch available. Dinner, 3 courses, from €34. Wine €24-€99.
Closed	Early November to early April.

Pierre & Bénédicte Rebour
Hôtel La Désirade,
Le Petit Cosquet, Bangor,
56360 Belle-Ile-en-Mer, Morbihan

Tel   +33 (0)2 97 31 70 70
Email   hotel-la-desirade@wanadoo.fr
Web   www.hotel-la-desirade.com

Les Chaumières de Kerimel

Kerimel is a handsome group of granite farm buildings in a perfect setting among the fields. Bedrooms are simple with patchwork bedcovers and pale curtains, beams, stone and some fine old furniture. The dining room is cottagey with dried flowers hanging from beams over a wooden table, a fire in the vast stone fireplace, breakfasts from grand-mère that promise an organic treat each day. Nicolas and family are gentle, generous and passionately eco-minded. He presses apple juice and brews beer with homegrown organic oats and hops, spring water from the land and a dash of spice; he's a dab hand at making crepes too. The standing stones of Carnac are minutes away, beaches, coastal pathways and golf course too. There are five bikes you can rent – join one of the many cycle routes nearby. *Minimum stay: 2 nights in high season. Pets by arrangement.*

Rooms	2 twin/doubles: €90-€100. 3 triples: €105-€115.
Meals	Crêpes supper with cider, €20. Restaurants 3km.
Closed	December to February.

Mobile	+33 (0)6 83 40 68 56
Email	chaumieres.kerimel@wanadoo.fr
Web	www.chambres-kerimel.com

Nicolas Malherbe
Les Chaumières de Kerimel,
9 Kerimel, 56400 Ploemel,
Morbihan

ENTRY 212　MAP 2

Le Clos du Gusquel

Bask by the pool watching the grazing sheep, stroll down to settle under the trees. Not far from the motorway, through fields on either side, you pass a little chapel and there is the house, architect designed and full of light. Find an open-plan living/dining area with a wood-burner for winter and a wall of glass for the view. And upstairs, in an independent part of the house: contemporary, luxurious guest rooms with views and plenty of space, a sauna on the landing, a mini cinema below. Christelle's breakfast, served on the decking in summer, is worth getting up for – croissants, crepes, eggs from the hens, homemade jams. It's a short drive to bars, boutiques and markets of beautiful old Vannes and Brittany's (almost) land-locked 'little sea', the Gulf of Morbihan. Catch a boat to the islands.

Rooms	2 doubles, 1 twin/double: €98-€129. Singles €89-€120. Self catering option for 6 in the guest wing, €945-€1680; minimum stay 7 nights.
Meals	Restaurants 3km.
Closed	Never.

Domaine de Coët Bihan

Close to beautiful, medieval Vannes and the Gulf of Morbihan, Jantine and Jacques' house lies in undulating country where horses, goats and Highland cattle graze and clematis clambers. Light-filled bedrooms, the most luxurious on the first floor, are crisp and comfy with pukka linen and top-class showers. Start the day with an organic à la carte breakfast of homemade jams, yogurts, eggs from the chickens and croissants, with cakes on Sunday. Have a nap in the enclosed gardens, sip an espresso in the tiny salon, enjoy the indoor pool. For dinner, there are many restaurants nearby and your hosts are happy to recommend some great-value ones serving local produce. *Minimum stay: 2 nights at weekends & in high season. Pets by arrangement.*

Rooms	4 doubles: €90-€105. Extra bed €15.
Meals	Cold platter €12-€20. Restaurants 4km. Kitchen & BBQ available.
Closed	Rarely.

Email	christelle@leclosdugusquel.com
Web	www.leclosdugusquel.com

Christelle Guérin
Le Clos du Gusquel,
Lieu-dit Le Gusquel,
56890 Plescop, Morbihan

Tel	+33 (0)2 97 44 97 22
Email	domainedecoetbihan@gmail.com
Web	www.chambredhotes-vannes.fr

Jantine Guégan-Helder
Domaine de Coët Bihan,
Lieu-dit Coët Bihan, Monterblanc,
56250 Vannes, Morbihan

Les Dames de Nage

Philippe has transformed this Breton farmhouse into an indulgent retreat; perfectly positioned between medieval Vannes, the Gulf of Morbihan and the wild Quiberon coast. A born host, you'll find him cultured and discreet. La Victoria and La Vasa (with a private terrace) are on a separate wing, each has a big window, sparkling bathroom and seriously comfortable bed. A delicious, local breakfast is served in the glass atrium overlooking the vibrant flower gardens. There's a gym, indoor pool, and spacious guest lounge with games and TV. While away hot days lazing on the wooden deck with cooling dips in the hot tub.

Talvern

Sit back on the terrace, lap up the peace, and savour a glass of Patrick's walnut wine. Strolling distance from the Château de Lannouan, whose farmhouse this once was, all you hear are birds, and all you see are trees and fields. The house is a solid stone longere, separated from the road by a grassy courtyard, with a lawn at the back where children can play, and a much-loved potager. Patrick, ex-Parisien chef, creates wonderful dinners held in house-party style. Christine, the talent behind the décor, is also the creator of breakfast's jams, which include an exotic spiced plum. There are walks in the woods, easy cycling for families, and white sand beaches to head for, on the 42 isles of the Gulf of Morbihan. You're also close to the hiking route which runs along the Ria d'Etel.

Rooms	4 doubles: €119-€178. Extra bed/sofabed at no charge.
Meals	Restaurants 3km.
Closed	Rarely.

Rooms	2 doubles, 1 twin/double: €72-€86. 2 suites for 4: €125-€130. Singles €72-€76. Extra bed/sofabed €25 p.p. per night.
Meals	Dinner with wine, €27.
Closed	Rarely.

Mobile	+33 (0)6 40 88 23 60
Email	prabet@orange.fr
Web	www.lesdamesdenage.com

Philippe Rabet
Les Dames de Nage,
Rescorles,
56390 Grand-Champ, Morbihan

Tel	+33 (0)2 97 56 99 80
Email	talvern@chambre-morbihan.com
Web	www.chambre-morbihan.com

Patrick Gillot
Talvern,
56690 Landévant,
Morbihan

ENTRY 215   MAP 3

ENTRY 216   MAP 2

La Ferme de Kerscuntec

You arrive, through wooded countryside, to an easy welcome and a feeling of tranquillity – hens strut the cottagey garden; the farm's 17th-century frame is full of charms. Take a room with a terrace for even more space, and sit out to ponder the day – with a glass of Anne's apple juice. She'll happily help you plan your time... be as sporty as you like; pretty much everything from golfing to angling is on hand. Without the car: there are cross-country paths and you're a stroll from the nearest sandy beach. It's a short drive to attractive fishing ports, villages and towns – see the catch landed at Le Guilvinec, take a boat from Bénodet to the Iles Glénan. Quimper and Concarneau are known for fine food and Sainte Marine's harbour-side eateries are nearby – fish, and crêpes, are specialities, of course. *Min. stay: 2 nights.*

Rooms	5 doubles: €90-€150.
Meals	Restaurant 2km.
Closed	Rarely.

Tel	+33 (0)2 98 51 90 90
Email	contact@lafermedekerscuntec.fr
Web	www.lafermedekerscuntec.fr/en/

Anne & Bruno Porhiel
La Ferme de Kerscuntec,
Kerscuntec,
29120 Combrit, Finistère

Château de Penfrat

You can hike freely around 100 hectares of forested parkland, and watch birds on the banks of the Odet. It's relaxing and peaceful, as is the château – a tall, handsome hunting lodge built by eccentric nobles, now owned by easy-going Patrick and Barbora. Here you can appreciate the simple pleasures of a good book, an easy chair and light jazz, and an apéro with your hosts and other guests. There's a retro feel to the dining room, with black and white photos and 50s brocante, and breakfast is typically French: bread, croissants, jams, fruit, local organic yoghurt, but also cheese and eggs. The estate is a lovely bubble – but burst out and explore: the nearby coast, the winding lanes and fish markets of Quimper, the architectural gems of Locronan, the artists' village of Pont-Aven. Massages are available too.

Rooms	1 double: €100-€120. 1 suite for 3, 1 suite for 4: €130-€180.
Meals	Restaurant 5km.
Closed	1 December – 3 January.

Email	info@penfrat.fr
Web	www.penfrat.fr

Barbora Kairyte & Patrick Viossat
Château de Penfrat,
25 chemin de Penfrat,
29950 Gouesnach, Finistère

ENTRY 217   MAP 2

ENTRY 218   MAP 2

Tregont Mab

There's a faded elegance about this 16th-century stone manor with its lingering smell of woodsmoke and grand features that whisper its fine heritage. Up a spiral staircase are three bedrooms – Anne de Bretagne, a suite for three with separate bathroom, Les Cordeliers for two, and Retour de Voyage for up to four. All are unfussy yet inviting. Breakfast is a treat in front of a crackling fire: fresh breads, pastries, local honey. Mme Voisard will gladly give you the grand tour, or you can wander free-range: find the little chapel in the grounds, cosy-up in the guest salon, explore the forest. Bustling Quimper and the coast are close. *Minimum stay: 2 nights in high season.*

Domaine de Moulin Mer

Joaquin has done wonders with Domaine de Moulin Mer, taking one of Brittany's elegant mansions and giving it a facelift worthy of its grandeur. City souls will revel in the sea air coming off the Atlantic and there's a wellness centre with hammam, jacuzzi et al, so you'll sleep soundly in your Louis XVI bed. You arrive through a gated entrance sheltered by palm trees and with graceful steps up to the front door. The gardens are yours to wander, abundant with olives and eucalyptus trees. Joaquin can provide (according to availability and his whim) inventive dinners using only the best local produce, just the thing for warming up after bracing coastal walks through the snoozy villages of this pin-drop quiet peninsula. *Minimum stay: 3 nights in high season.*

Rooms	1 double: €100-€120. 1 family room for 3, 1 family room for 4: €100-€160.
Meals	Restaurants 1km.
Closed	Rarely.

Rooms	2 doubles: €105-€145. 2 suites for 2: €145-€180. Singles €95-€170. Extra bed/sofabed €35-€45 p.p. per night. Tourist tax: €0.44 p.p. per night.
Meals	Dinner €33. Wine from €8.
Closed	Rarely.

Mobile	+33 (0)6 87 35 19 85
Email	contact@tregontmab.fr
Web	www.tregontmab.fr

Mai Voisard
Tregont Mab,
Chemin de Tregont Mab,
29000 Quimper, Finistère

Tel	+33 (0)2 98 07 24 45
Email	info@domaine-moulin-mer.com
Web	www.domaine-moulin-mer.com

Joaquin Lopez
Domaine de Moulin Mer,
34 route de Moulin Mer,
29460 Logonna Daoulas, Finistère

Kergudon Chambres d'Hôtes

On the outskirts of tiny Saint Cadou is a 17th-century presbytery flanked by two houses, a place of serenity and charm. Ben and David, generous to a fault, have created four immaculate gîtes at the end of the lane... and if you're a couple, you can do B&B. Choose between 'Hayloft' (kitchen, log-burner, sweet sunny garden) and 'Stable', an adorable studio with sliding doors to its own patio. Eggs Breton, porridge, fresh continental, full English – whichever breakfast you go for it'll be delicious, and delivered to your door. Fly-fish at lovely Lake Drennec (a 10-minute stroll) or hop on the bikes and cycle the Vélo Vert.
Minimum stay: 7 nights in high season.

Manoir de Kerledan

Everyone loves Kerledan, its gargoyles, its sophisticated theatrical décor, its owners' enthusiasm. Peter and Penny have made it stunningly original. Sisal and unstained oak, limed walls, the odd splash of antique mirror or gilded bergère with fake leopard skin create a mood of luxury and calm; stone-floored bathrooms are delicious, candlelit, cut-glass dinners are legendary. Sit by the great dining room fire, stroll in the lovely gardens (baroque courtyard, palisade hornbeam allée, potager), lounge in antique linen in a perfect bedroom and let yourself be pampered by your hosts: arrive as strangers, leave as friends.
Minimum stay: 2 nights in high season.

Rooms	2 doubles: €80-€100.
Meals	Dinner, 3 courses, €75. Restaurants 3km.
Closed	Rarely.

Rooms	2 doubles, 1 twin/double: €95-€115. 1 suite for 4: €120-€160.
Meals	Dinner, 2 courses, coffee & apéritif, €25. Wine from €10.
Closed	Mid-November to March.

Tel	+33 (0)2 98 24 16 98
Email	contact@kergudon.com
Web	www.kergudon.com

Ben Dickins
Kergudon Chambres d'Hôtes,
Hent Gorreker,
29450 Saint Cadou, Finistère

Tel	+33 (0)2 98 99 44 63
Email	kerledan@gmail.com
Web	www.kerledan.com

Peter & Penny Dinwiddie
Manoir de Kerledan,
Route de Kerledan,
29270 Carhaix Plouguer, Finistère

ENTRY 221 MAP 2

ENTRY 222 MAP 2

La Vinotière

Mature elegance meets modern chic at the 'end of the earth' in this 16th-century merchant's house teetering on the Finistère coast. Around it, Le Conquet bustles with fishermen and ferries, boutiques and the weekly Tuesday market. Inside, bathrooms have been cleverly squeezed into all bedrooms (some are sectioned from the room by half-glazed walls or low panels). Find exposed stone, customised furniture and oak shutters; bright oil paintings (for sale) add a splash. Children will love the jaunty boat theme of the bunk-bedded 'Petite Vinotière'. Walk the Kermorvan Peninsula, paddle on the local beach, have fishy fun at Brest's Océanopolis, a shortish drive. No outdoor space but adults can retire to the hotel's Salon de Thé for cakes and organic teas – the perfect pick-me-up before more exploring..

Toul Bleiz

A Breton 'longere' where light pours in through French windows and there are sweeping views from the outdoor deck of the summerhouse – a great place for a sundowner. You're surrounded by the Liscuis moorland and wildlife lovers will spot deer and rare birds like hen harriers in the summer. You breakfast in the stone built summerhouse which is all yours; on chilly mornings Julie lights the wood-burner to keep you cosy while you enjoy the lovely views, and candlelit evening meals are prepared by Jez. If you prefer to look after yourselves there's a barbecue and good local markets for stocking up. The village is near for exploring, Lake Guerlédan is wonderful to walk around and the Abbaye de Bon Repos is nearby. This is a tranquil place to unwind.

Rooms	5 doubles: €60-€135.
Meals	Breakfast €10. Light lunch available. Restaurants within walking distance.
Closed	Rarely.

Rooms	1 double: €75.
Meals	Vegetarian dinner with wine, 2 courses, €22. Picnic available. Summerhouse with kitchenette & BBQ.
Closed	Rarely.

Tel   +33 (0)2 98 89 17 79
Email info@lavinotiere.fr
Web   www.lavinotiere.fr

Joëlle Tromeur
La Vinotière,
1 rue Lieutenant Jourden,
29217 Le Conquet, Finistère

Tel   +33 (0)2 96 36 98 34
Email jezrooke@hotmail.com

Julie & Jez Rooke
Toul Bleiz,
22570 Laniscat,
Côtes-d'Armor

ENTRY 223   MAP 2

ENTRY 224   MAP 2

Manoir d'Hôtes de Troëzel Bian

A finely restored, peaceful old farmhouse, the manor is warm and comfortable. Your hosts, a chatty Franco-British couple who previously worked in science are loving their new life as B&B owners; founts of local knowledge they will advise you expertly to what to do and see – even starting you off on the coastal path or giving you a guided tour of Tréguier cathedral. Their gourmet dinners feature organic and home-grown produce with some novel twists on traditional French cuisine. With its suite-like bedrooms upstairs, two sitting rooms, original stone fireplace, a wood stove and lots of garden, this is a place to relax after your days exploring a beautiful part of the Breton coast. *Minimum stay: 2 nights in high season.*

Manoir de Coat Gueno

The 15th-century, country-cocooned manor house, close to fishing ports, headlands and long sandy beaches, is a treasure. Beautifully restored over decades, every detail has been considered yet Christian is not so precious that he stops the blue tits nesting in a nook in the stone work! The salon's 'lit clos' is a treat, as is the vast stone fireplace, crackling with logs in winter. Gaze from a florally furnished suite onto the lawns below, enjoy the splashing of the pool or the crack of the billiards. The games room and the charming cottage suite (with its own fire) are in the grounds, and your host is the perfect French gentleman. *Children over 7, who know how to swim, welcome.*

Rooms	4 twin/doubles: €85-€95. Singles €75-€85. Extra bed/sofabed €20-€30 p.p. per night.	
Meals	Dinner, 3 courses €25. Restaurants 10-minute walk.	
Closed	Rarely.	

Rooms	2 suites for 2: €110-€170. 1 cottage for 2: €100-€170. 10% discount on stays of 6 nights or more. 20% discount on stays in May/June.
Meals	Restaurants 4km.
Closed	September – April.

Tel	+33 (0)9 52 61 47 36
Email	ctrobian@gmail.com
Web	www.troezelbian.com

Armelle & Tony Sébilleau
Manoir d'Hôtes de Troëzel Bian,
Lieu dit de Troëzel Bian,
22610 Kerbors, Côtes-d'Armor

Tel	+33 (0)2 96 20 10 98
Email	coatguen@aol.com
Web	mapage.noos.fr/coatgueno

Christian de Rouffignac
Manoir de Coat Gueno,
Coat Gueno,
22740 Pleudaniel, Côtes-d'Armor

Le Manoir de la Villeneuve

Embraced by rolling lawns, wooded parkland and sweeping drive, this manor house seems untouched by the 21st century. Light airy pools of calm – high ceilings, tall windows, polished boards – are furnished with a contemporary elegance while plain walls, beams and tomette floors have been allowed to glow. Beautiful bedrooms have soothing colours, pretty antiques, delicious soaps, beams in some and sloping ceilings; the suite has a vast bathroom and its own salon. Breakfast handsomely at the convivial table, then explore Dinan, St Brieuc, the coast. Return for a dip in the new summer pool. Charming Nathalie oversees all. *Minimum stay: 2 nights; 3 in high season.*

Manoir du Clos Clin

Monsieur found this ancient, grand farmhouse derelict and has lavished huge attention on it. He's done it immaculately, from re-roofing and installing geothermal underfloor heating, to creating smart, comfortable and historically themed bedrooms and bathrooms; the Louis XIII-style four-poster is exemplary. Formal family portraits hang in the huge living room where you can gen up on things local and play the piano. Fresh breakfasts come from the open-plan kitchen. Pedal the cycle path to Dinan; you're on the outskirts of Pleurtuit, a couple of miles from Dinard. Return to lounge peacefully in the lawned garden, or immerse yourself in the hedge maze.

Rooms	3 doubles, 1 twin/double: €80-€150. 1 suite for 3: €130-€150.		**Rooms**	4 doubles: €72-€160. Singles €72-€160.	
Meals	Restaurant 2km.		**Meals**	Restaurants 500m.	
Closed	Rarely.		**Closed**	Rarely.	

Tel	+33 (0)2 96 50 86 32	**Mobile**	+33 (0)6 88 17 93 91
Email	manoirdelavilleneuve@wanadoo.fr	**Email**	gmacquart@orange.fr
Web	www.chambresaumanoir.com	**Web**	www.manoirclosclin.fr

Nathalie Peres
Le Manoir de la Villeneuve,
22400 Lamballe,
Côtes-d'Armor

Guy Macquart de Terline
Manoir du Clos Clin,
Le Clos Clin,
35730 Pleurtuit, Ille-et-Vilaine

ENTRY 227   MAP 3

ENTRY 228   MAP 3

Les Mouettes

House and owner are imbued with the calm of a balmy summer's morning, whatever the weather. Isabelle's talent seems to touch the very air that fills her old family house (and smokers are not spurned!). Timeless simplicity reigns; there is nothing superfluous: simple carved pine furniture, an antique wrought-iron cot, dhurries on scrubbed plank floors, palest grey walls to reflect the ocean-borne light, harmonious gingham curtains. Starfish and pebbles keep house and little garden sea-connected, whimsical mobiles add a creative touch. The unspoilt seaside village, popular in season, is worth the trip alone.

Malouinière des Trauchandières

This handsome manoir in big peaceful gardens has been lovingly restored by Claude, who speaks six languages, and equally well-travelled Agnès; both are charming and friendly – to you and your dog. Theirs is a fascinating house dating from 1510, with French windows opening to a south-facing terrace and a salon lined with oak panelling; relax by the blazing fire. Bedrooms, comfortable, traditional and upstairs, are dominated by dark ships' timbers; the port of St Malo is close, so are golden sand beaches – perfect for woofy walks. Breakfast is served beneath the chandelier and there's an annual garden party in the grounds. Marvellous. *Dogs welcome free of charge.*

Rooms	4 doubles, 1 twin: €58-€68.
Meals	Restaurants in village.
Closed	Rarely.

Rooms	4 twin/doubles: €80-€100. 1 suite for 4: €120-€130.
Meals	Hosted dinner with wine, €35. Restaurants in St Méloir, 5-minute drive.
Closed	Rarely.

Tel +33 (0)2 99 58 30 41
Email contact@les-mouettes-saint-suliac.com
Web www.les-mouettes-saint-suliac.com

Isabelle Rouvrais
Les Mouettes,
17 Grande Rue,
35430 St Suliac, Ille-et-Vilaine

Tel +33 (0)2 99 81 38 30
Email agnesfrancois@hotmail.com
Web www.les-trauchandieres.com

Agnès François
Malouinière des Trauchandières,
Albiville, St Jouan des Guérets,
35430 St Malo, Ille-et-Vilaine

ENTRY 229 MAP 3

ENTRY 230 MAP 3

Villa Saint Raphael

Emmanuelle and Antoine turned a ruin into a chic home with a handsome classical façade that belies modern interiors. The elegant, contemporary dining/sitting room is a lovely spot; breakfast here or in the walled garden on pâtisserie and lashings of coffee. A wide staircase sweeps you up to smart bedrooms all individually styled with accent wallpaper, cool art and objet; gleaming bathrooms are piled high with towels. You're in a leafy neighbourhood but you can stroll to restaurants and beach. Delightful Dinard, coastal walks and boat trips are all possible and it's easy peasy for the Portsmouth ferry.

Château de Mont Dol

An elegant, quietly sophisticated destination which will suit those who adore good food. The overall feel is one of unassuming good taste: find a large salon with chalky or exposed stone walls, an open fire, ecru and grey soft furniture and vases of hydrangeas – some gorgeous antiques too. Bedrooms are exquisite in a country style and with spick and span bathrooms. But you're here for the food – breakfasts of homemade yogurt, jams from the garden, croissants from the local bakery, and through the beautiful garden (low clipped box hedges, a fountain, gravel paths) you'll find the restaurant: a fixed menu, three courses, delicious. *Minimum stay: 2 nights at weekends & in high season.*

Rooms	3 doubles: €85-€150.
	2 suites for 2: €85-€175.
Meals	Restaurants 5-minute walk.
Closed	11 November – 11 December,
	13 January – 1 February,
	9 February – 24 February.

Rooms	4 doubles: €95-€125.
	1 family room for 4: €139-€165.
	Singles €95-€115.
	Extra bed €25 p.p. per night.
Meals	Dinner with wine, coffee & apéritif,
	€44. Restaurants 5-minute walk.
Closed	15 November – 2 February.

Mobile	+33 (0)6 20 52 83 19/ (0)9 53 03 45 09
Email	emmanuelle.delanoe@gmail.com
Web	www.villa-st-raphael-saint-malo.com

Emmanuelle Delanoë
Villa Saint Raphael,
19 rue des Fours à Chaux,
35400 St Malo, Ille-et-Vilaine

Mobile	+33 (0)6 24 31 87 49
Email	yannick.goulvestre@wanadoo.fr
Web	www.chateaumontdol.com

Yannick Goulvestre
Château de Mont Dol,
1 rue de la Mairie,
35120 Mont Dol, Ille-et-Vilaine

ENTRY 231   MAP 3

ENTRY 232   MAP 3

Les Touches

Elizabeth and Matthew's 18th-century cottage sits in three acres of garden on the edge of a small river valley and is surrounded by rolling countryside – a lack of light pollution makes for terrific star gazing. Breakfast around the large table in the kitchen includes bread, croissants, homemade jams, eggs from the hens, cheeses and charcuterie; the nearest restaurant is a 15-minute drive or you can stay in for delicious four-course dinners – aperitif, wine and digestif included. Read or play games by the wood-burner in the cosy guest sitting room; there's a kettle if you fancy a cup of tea. You can sit out in the garden, and children will love the swimming pool, swings and trampoline. You're perfectly near to sights in both Brittany and Normandy and it's a 45-minute drive to the coast.

Rooms	1 double: €80. 1 triple: €85-€103. 1 quadruple: €85-€121.
Meals	Dinner, 4 courses, €35; children €10.
Closed	1 December – 11 February

Tel +33 (0)9 62 66 94 16
Email enquiries@lestouches.info
Web www.lestouches.info/

Elizabeth François & Matthew Sebesteny-King
Les Touches,
35420 St Georges de Reintembault,
Ille-et-Vilaine

Château de la Ballue

Artists say this 1620s château inspires creativity – you may fall under its spell too. The formal gardens are listed and open to the public – a French reverie of bosquets and paths sprinkled with sculptures, gazing over Mont St Michel. Find a hidden spa, zen garden and pool. Baroque recitals may ring in the courtyard; inside, Purcell odes may float through elegant panelled rooms, over marble fireplaces, antique paintings, gilded mirrors and orchids. This is no museum, however, but a family home with spirited hosts who are passionate about the place. Drift off on dreamy canopied beds in fabulous bedrooms: perhaps bold red 'Victor Hugo' or blue-ferned 'Florence'; three have tented cabinets de toilette rather than separate bathrooms. Wake to a fine continental spread in the candle-lit breakfast room.

Rooms	3 doubles: €230-€250. 1 suite for 4: €305-€385. 1 triple: €290. Extra bed €40.
Meals	Breakfast €20. Restaurants 15km.
Closed	Rarely.

Tel +33 (0)2 99 97 47 86
Email chateau@la-ballue.com
Web www.la-ballue.com

Marie-Françoise Mathiot-Mathon
Château de la Ballue,
35560 Bazouges la Pérouse,
Ille-et-Vilaine

Château du Quengo

Anne, descendant of an ancient Breton family, and Alfred, who is Swiss, are passionate about animals, gardens, music, life! They welcome you open-armed to their inimitable house: a private chapel, a bio garden, rare trees, 1800s wallpapers, a carved staircase, a mosaic'd floor. She runs willow-weaving classes and plies you with homemade delights; he builds organs; both love the slow life. Bedrooms have antique radiators and are properly old-fashioned, our favourite being the suite. No plastic anything, few mod cons, just intelligent, humorous hosts and a house steeped in atmosphere, beauty and peace.

Château du Pin

The small château with its pretty faded shutters is now inhabited by the Josses. Modern furniture rubs shoulders with brocante finds, shelves burst with books and art, bold red walls brighten up the salon where breakfast is served. Up to soft-hued bedrooms, their swathes of ruched silk clasped by tassels, their beds delicious with hand-painted headboards and luxurious covers. Outside: masses of park and woodland for children to roam. A light supper is available at separate tables: a platter of smoked salmon, a hot gratin – ideal for the first night. You're within easy reach of the Emerald coast, the gulf of Morbihan, Dinard and St Malo. *Helipad available!*

Rooms	1 double: €82-€89. 1 suite for 5: €82-€165.	**Rooms**	1 double, 2 twin/doubles, 2 family rooms for 4: €88-€163. 1 cottage for 4: €140. Extra person €29.
Meals	Guest kitchen. Restaurants 1.5km.	**Meals**	Breakfast €14. Dinner €29, on request. Wine €10-€30. Restaurant 5km.
Closed	Rarely.	**Closed**	Rarely.

Tel	+33 (0)2 99 39 81 47	**Tel**	+33 (0)2 99 09 34 05
Email	lequengo@laposte.net	**Email**	contact@chateau-pin.fr
Web	chateauduquengo.free.fr	**Web**	en.chateau-pin.fr

Anne & Alfred du Crest de Lorgerie
Château du Quengo,
35850 Irodouër,
Ille-et-Vilaine

Marie-France & Jean-Luc Josse
Château du Pin,
Route départementale 125, La Veronnière,
35750 Iffendic, Ille-et-Vilaine

Château de Chambiers, page 213

Hôtel Oasis

Efficient anglophile Steve and his young wife Émilie run a happy ship. You couldn't fail to feel well cared for: spotless and well-equipped bedrooms, leather sofas in the bar and a personal trainer in the gym. The cosy, woody reception sets the tone, flaunting all the beams, joists, exposed stones and wafer-brick walls you'd expect from a restored farmhouse with outbuildings. Bedrooms are in the stable wing, some off a raftered corridor upstairs, others at ground level. All have old timbers, attractive repro country furniture, comfy armchairs, writing desks and immaculate bathrooms. The bar, which has an English pubby feel, serves very decent food and there's also a super pizzeria/grill in the courtyard. The lounge is snug with plants, piano and pool table and the breakfast room is a treat: red-clothed tables on a stone floor and a big stone fireplace crackling with logs. A shame to stay just a night, there's so much to see in the area, from the 24-hour race at Le Mans to the 14th-century château at Carrouges. And you could squeeze in a round of mini-golf before breakfast.
Friendly people, excellent value.

Rooms	8 doubles, 3 twins: €65-€140. 2 family rooms for 4, 1 family room for 6: €85-€140. Singles €50-€80. Extra bed/sofabed at no charge.
Meals	Breakfast €7.80. Light meals available.
Closed	Rarely.

Tel	+33 (0)2 43 03 28 67	**Steve & Émilie Chedor**
Email	oasis@oasis.fr	Hôtel Oasis,
Web	www.oasis.fr	La Sourderie,
		53700 Villaines la Juhel, Mayenne

ENTRY 237   MAP 4

Château de Saint Paterne

A marvellous mix of the Renaissance and the 18th century, a château abandoned for 30 years then rediscovered by an heir who gave up Provence for lovely Perche pastures. He and his wife, a charming couple, have redecorated with spirit, respecting the style and history of the building, adding a zest of southern colour to panelled, antique-filled rooms, pretty country furniture before ancient fireplaces and rough, hand-rendered finishes. Sitting, dining and first-floor bedrooms are in château-style, the Henri IV room (he had a mistress here, of course) has thrillingly painted beams; ancestors and *objets* adorn but don't clutter. The theatrical new tower room is worth every one of the 52 steps up and the attic floor is a fantasy among the rafters. Now there's a spectacular new room on the ground floor awash with Indian silks, and a dreamy dacha in the forest, heaven for two. Your host creates classic cuisine nuanced with contemporary flavours and exotic vegetables from his potager and calls his cookery courses *Liaisons Délicieuses*. A fine mixture of past and present values and superb high-energy hosts.

Rooms	5 doubles: €145-€175.
	5 suites for 2: €220-€260.
	Dinner, B&B €208-€386 p.p.
	Extra bed/sofabed €20 p.p. per night.
Meals	Breakfast €14. Dinner with apéritif & coffee, €49; book ahead.
	Wine €15-€49.
Closed	January to March; Christmas week.

Charles-Henry & Ségolène de Valbray	**Tel**	+33 (0)2 33 27 54 71
Château de Saint Paterne,	**Email**	chateaudesaintpaterne@wanadoo.fr
72610 Saint Paterne,	**Web**	www.chateau-saintpaterne.com
Sarthe		

Château de la Groirie

Turn down the elegant avenue, drive past the fishing lake and park up in front of a rather imposing 18th-century château, your home for the night – but not quite, as the bedrooms are in an ochre-washed stable block just to the side. The views are lovely from here, with rooms accessed off a little courtyard or up a flight of outdoor staircases; the upstairs rooms are the homeliest with nooks and beds under the eaves. Head across to the château for a thoroughly French breakfast of hams and cheeses served under a fresco of pastoral scenes, a reflection of the parkland outside the large windows. Explore the eclectic mix of formal gardens and established woods on foot and spy deer. If you don't want to go out you can ask for a supper tray and eat in your cosy bedroom, or picnic in the garden on warm evenings. Le Mans is just five minutes' drive away – with flying buttresses, stained glass windows and pointy Gothic houses.
Electric car charge points available.

Rooms	13 twin/doubles: €159-€500.
Meals	Supper available by arrangement. Restaurants 5-minute drive.
Closed	Rarely.

Mobile	+33 (0)6 75 08 97 08
Email	contact@chateaudelagroirie.com
Web	www.chateaudelagroirie.com/

Isabelle Come
Château de la Groirie,
72650 Trangé,
Sarthe

ENTRY 239   MAP 4

Château de Vaulogé

A fairy-tale place! The Radinis, from Milan, wanted their children to have an international education, eventually finding Vaulogé. Marisa and her delightful, amusing daughter Micol now run the place, Marisa devoting herself to the garden, her latest project being the horseshoe-shaped potager for fresh dinner produce. The original part of the château, where the family lives, was built in the 15th century. Vaulogé was later remodelled in troubadour style, giving it two circular pepperpot towers; when the shock waves of the Revolution had faded, the aristocracy reclaimed their houses. If it's space you're after, stay in 'Casanova': a huge round tower room, with terracotta floor and amazing, near-vertical beams – excellent for propping books on. (There are plenty of books: Marisa feels a house is not properly furnished without them.) There are other round rooms – 'La Grande Tour' is smaller, and ravishingly pretty. The whole place is enticing with flowers and little nooks and crannies, often put to good use as wardrobes or cupboards. The grounds are lovely, with lilies on the moat and a delicate stone chapel. *Pets by arrangement.*

Rooms	1 double: €230-€280. 4 suites for 2: €260-€320. Extra bed/sofabed €40-€70 p.p. per night.
Meals	Dinner with wine, €70; book ahead.
Closed	2 January – 31 March.

Micol Tassan Din
Château de Vaulogé,
72430 Fercé sur Sarthe,
Sarthe

Tel +33 (0)2 43 77 32 81
Email vauloge@mail.com
Web www.vauloge.com

Hotel de France

Beloved of car racing buffs, this charming hotel has been part of the Le Mans 24-hours story for ever. The nostalgia is spread by a history of champion drivers, film stars and world leaders, as well as some glorious old cars that have roared up to the front door. Its creeper-clothed face looks over the lovely town square, its bar clients spill onto the convivial pavement. An English classic-car enthusiast fell in love with the hotel years ago and... finally it was his. He renovated the Art Deco dining room, built a pretty pool beside the river and kept the head chef and barman whom everyone loved. Bedrooms have been beautifully refurbished: some have famous racing names, four-posters and damask wall fabric, all have brand-new bathrooms and fine attention to detail, all are excellent value. But motor racing isn't all: the châteaux of the Loire are an hour away; the bucolic valley has some fine historic buildings of its own, including Le Lude with its glorious furniture and gardens. Vineyard tours in an eccentric pre-war bus can be arranged; or bicycle trips, or hot-air ballooning...
Then back for a high-class dinner.
Pets by arrangement.

Rooms	22 doubles: €91-€139. 3 suites for 4: €140-€170.
Meals	Lunch menu découverte €35. Dinner, 4 courses, €39-42. Restaurants 1-minute walk.
Closed	Never.

Tel	+33 (0)2 43 44 40 16
Email	bienvenue@lhoteldefrance.fr
Web	www.lhoteldefrance.fr

La Réception
Hotel de France,
72340 La Chartre sur le Loir,
Sarthe

ENTRY 241   MAP 4

Auberge du Port des Roches

If you like the idea of idling with an evening drink by the slow green water, watching out for the odd fish, looking forward to an exceptionally good dinner, this is the place for you. Not grand, not the Loire – the Loir is a sweet, lovely and unsung river – but we can hear you saying: "Oh, what a pretty spot". Valérie and Thierry, who have been here for almost two decades, are young, very friendly, though a touch shy, and full of enthusiasm for their auberge. The lively little restaurant, which seats about 50 people in two rooms, and the riverside terrace heavy with roses and sweet-smelling climbers, are the star turns here, though Valérie is also justly proud of the effort she has put into the bedrooms and the way everything sparkles. Rooms are not large but done up in fresh colours with white bedcovers. Those at the back overlook the courtyard, those at the front face the Loir, double glazing separates you from the small road that runs past and peace reigns at night. This is a quiet, very French place to stay, within easy reach of the châteaux. All round superb value – and plenty of choice for vegetarians.

Rooms	9 doubles, 2 twins: €76-€130. 1 family room for 3: €106-€135.
Meals	Breakfast €8. Picnic available. Lunch & dinner €34-€50. Wine €15-€128. Restaurant closed Sun eve, Mon, & Tues lunchtimes.
Closed	Rarely.

Valérie & Thierry Lesiourd
Auberge du Port des Roches,
Le Port des Roches,
72800 Luché Pringé, Sarthe

Tel   +33 (0)2 43 45 44 48
Email   leportdesroches@orange.fr

Hôtel Haras de la Potardière

François, an architect specialising in restoring old buildings, Marie-Yvonne, relaxed and efficient, and their children live in a creeper-covered wing of this grand château. The entertaining brochure tells the family's story: François' grandfather built up a successful centre for training show jumpers alongside an established thoroughbred stud; then, in the nineties, after ten years of empty stables, La Potardière began taking in stallions for the summer. Now, horse-loving guests ride up on their own mounts from all over France... the fine approach includes mares and foals grazing beneath the oaks. Château bedrooms are a graceful mix of prettiness and elegance, polished parquet and fresh flowers; rooms in the stables are less formal, cosier and have their own wicker-furnished terrace. A glorious place for a horse-mad child – though all children love it here: fields, a safe and secluded pool, billiards, table football, a Wendy house full of toys. There's an honesty bar and relaxed seating, a piano you may play and sociable apéritifs on Saturdays.
The welcome is superb.

Rooms	3 twin/doubles: €100-€120.
	2 suites for 5: €180.
Meals	Breakfast €12. Cold platter €25; book ahead. Wine €28. Group dinners by arrangement.
Closed	Rarely.

Tel	+33 (0)2 43 45 83 47
Email	haras-de-la-potardiere@wanadoo.fr
Web	www.potardiere.com

François & Marie-Yvonne Benoist
Hôtel Haras de la Potardière,
Route de Bazouges,
72200 Crosmières, Sarthe

ENTRY 243 MAP 4

Château des Briottières

Deep in the Loire valley countryside, this 18th-century château, in the family for six generations, is an experience of opulence and splendour. It is now occupied by your host, the relaxed and endearing Monsieur de Valbray, his wife and children (most of them grown and flown), rightfully proud of their extraordinary home. A charming and laid-back place to stay, in spite of the grandiose surroundings, it has handsome interiors decorated in fine traditional French style. The grand drawing room is a symphony of rich red velvet with swathes of fine silk floating elegantly to the ground; sweep up the marble staircase to bedrooms beautifully adorned; many beds are canopied. many windows have sweeping estate views; there are candles everywhere. A local Crémant de Loire, served by Monsieur, is the perfect apéritif before a three-course meal, prepared by Madame (an exquisite cook) and served in the dining room by candlelight. A digestif can, on cool nights, be sipped in the drawing room where the log fire roars delightfully. In the grounds is a country-style Orangery with extra rooms in a more rustic style.

Rooms	7 doubles: €145-€250. 3 suites for 2, 1 suite for 4: €299-€400. 1 triple: €210-€270. 1 apartment for 6; no WiFi: €440-€470. 1 chalet for 2: €299-€389. Singles €129-€249. Dinner, B&B €224-€312 p.p. Extra bed/sofabed €20-€40 p.p. per night.
Meals	Breakfast €18. Dinner €50, book ahead. Wine from €18. Restaurants 10km.
Closed	15 November – 15 March.

François de Valbray
Château des Briottières,
49330 Champigné,
Maine-et-Loire

Tel	+33 (0)2 41 42 00 02
Email	briottieres@gmail.com
Web	www.briottieres.com

Château Le Prieuré

Relax on the restaurant terrace and raise a glass to the view: the languid Loire meanders below and the valley reaches into the distance. As for dinner, it is the creation of gourmet chef Richard Prouteau, served quite rightly in a dining room fit for kings. Guarded by stone lions, the 10th-century exterior of the priory has not changed. In contrast, the annexe next door is brand new. Bedrooms are divided between the annexe and the main house, 50m apart, but those in the house are unquestionably the finest: luxurious, flamboyant and huge fun. Enjoy tennis and mini-golf in the grounds, stroll down to the little village, borrow bikes and follow the river. Be sure to pop into Saumur for its Saturday market, discover the restaurants and galleries of Angers, and go home laden with the local Crémant.

Rooms	21 doubles: €109-€450. Sofa bed €35-€51 per night.
Meals	Breakfast €23. Lunch €25. Dinner €40-€80, children €19. Restaurant closed Monday-Tuesday (Oct-Mar).
Closed	Never.

Mobile	+33 (0)2 41 67 90 14
Email	prieure@younancollection.com
Web	www.younancollection.com/en/ chateau-le-prieure/hotel-loire.html

La Réception
Château Le Prieuré,
Rue du Comte de Castellane,
49350 Chênehutte-Trèves-Cunault,
Maine-et-Loire

ENTRY 245 MAP 4

Château de Verrières

Guests are full of praise for this elegant château, built in 1890 to host balls and grand soirées. In recent years it has been passionately, authentically, lavishly restored. The house stands in huge grounds – unusually so since it is right in the heart of old Saumur – and the charming new owners, Pascale and François, could not be more welcoming or more helpful. Bedrooms are lofty, lovely and filled with light. Every trace of modern updating – central heating, rewiring – has been artfully concealed, and generous curtains hang at huge windows overlooking the private park. Other rooms overlook the Cavalry School, where aristocratic officers used to hone their equestrian skills. The décor is classic French at its finest, apart from the contemporary and zen-like top-floor suite. Bathrooms are as luxurious, each one unique. There's a heated pool, and the garden is rather (wonderfully) wild – Pascale has plans to tame it; step into town – don't miss the Saturday market! Breakfasts include pastries, omelettes, ham, delicious pain perdu; good restaurants are on the doorstep. Worth every penny.

Rooms	8 doubles, 1 twin: €195-€415. 1 suite for 2: €343-€415. Singles €198-€390. Extra bed/sofabed €40 p.p. per night.
Meals	Breakfast €24. Restaurant 400m.
Closed	1 December – 31 January.

Pascale & François Hamelin
Château de Verrières,
53 rue d'Alsace,
49400 Saumur, Maine-et-Loire

Tel	+33 (0)2 41 38 05 15
Email	contact@chateau-verrieres.com
Web	www.chateau-verrieres.com

Hôtel & Spa La Marine de Loire

In a pretty little town on the banks of the Loire, this lovely hotel is casual, stylish and run with superb efficiency. Friendly, elegant Caroline bought the building five years ago and gave it a fabulous new look. With her flair for interior decoration she's clearly had fun: 'Sous la Lune' has glittering stars, 'Reflet' has a floaty airy feel, while driftwood and pebbles adorn others, decorated in chalky colours. There are super bathrooms and many have views over the river or the handsome courtyard. Suites are big and mostly come with mezzanine sleeping areas, although access to one is up some tricky stairs – check before you go. The large salon has a a relaxed homey feel with comfy sofas, fresh flowers and lots of plants. On the second Sunday of the month, in a long sunny room that gazes over the garden, enjoy brunch with heavenly terrine and sweet French treats from the local market. Later, explore narrow winding streets that take you up to the cliff face for stunning views. You're well placed for cycling, gardens and châteaux, but the cocktails at the bar will tempt you back.

Rooms	7 doubles: €150-€190.
	4 suites for 2: €250.
Meals	Breakfast €13-€16. Dinner €35.
	Restaurant 1km.
Closed	Rarely.

Tel	+33 (0)2 41 50 18 21	**Caroline Chagnaud**
Email	resa@hotel-lamarinedeloire.com	Hôtel & Spa La Marine de Loire,
Web	www.hotel-lamarinedeloire.com	9 avenue de la Loire, 49730 Montsoreau,
		Maine-et-Loire

`ENTRY 247   MAP 4`

Manoir de Ponsay

The family manor, a listed building, dates back to 1492: note the coat of arms over the door. Now both castle and hotel are run generously, and singlehandedly, by charming young Laurent, who was born here, and his Romanian wife Orelia. Outside is one of the oldest dovecotes in France, a peaceful pool and a hot tub, a tiny sauna, table tennis and bikes; the grounds are open and safe, the meadows stretch to the horizon. Inside, find an elegant room for candlelit feasts, a sitting room with billiards and a tapestry or two, a priest's hole for hiding revolutionaries, should any lurk, and a massive stone stair. This sweeps you up to five characterful suites, historic, traditional, their long windows overlooking the park, their armoires polished to perfection, their chintz bright, their fireplaces lit (when required); the 'Chambre à Baldequin' has an exquisite four-poster and there's fine new Italian-style shower in the largest room. Dinner is prepared, served and hosted by Laurent and Orelia; special wines can be ordered from the cellar. Beyond, the summer extravaganzas at Puy du Fou draw a million spectators every year.

Rooms	3 suites for 2, 1 suite for 3, 1 suite for 4: €68-€180.
Meals	Breakfast €9.50. Dinner €34.
Closed	November to April (open only by arrangement).

Laurent de Ponsay
Manoir de Ponsay,
85110 Chantonnay,
Vendée

Tel	+33 (0)2 51 46 96 71
Email	manoirdeponsay@gmail.com
Web	www.manoirdeponsay.com

Le Château de l'Abbaye

In the Marais Poitevin Regional Park, this *castel romantique* had been graciously managed by Danielle Renard for 32 years; now she, her son Renaud-Pierre and daughter-in-law Korakot make a delightful, welcoming trio. Discover bibelots and boxes, photographs and fresh flowers, Korakot's embroideries, furniture antique and new. Roosters can be found in every medium, shape and size; don't miss the bulging scrapbooks of drawings by guests and their children. Continental breakfast is on the veranda in summer; dinner at candlelit tables reflects the best seasonal produce (French menus by Danielle, Thai by Korakot). In the château, air-conditioned bedrooms are decorated to create cocoon-like spaces; extras include children's books and embroidered needlework, typical touches from these thoughtful hosts. Two big rooms in an outbuilding are more modern-oriental; one even has a waterbed. All have electronic extras, suites have their own garden and jacuzzi bath, there's a pool to laze in and a wellness space, too. You're just a 30 minute drive from La Rochelle and grand beaches of South Vendée.

Rooms	1 double, 5 twin/doubles: €99-€219. 1 family room for 4: €179-€359. 3 suites for 2 with jacuzzi and terrace: €189-€359. Singles €89-€189. Extra bed/sofabed €30 p.p. per night.
Meals	Breakfast €15. Dinner, 3 courses, €38-€42. Wine from €8/glass, €65/bottle, champagne €189.
Closed	Never.

Tel	+33 (0)2 51 56 17 56
Email	chateau-moreilles@orange.fr
Web	www.chateau-moreilles.com

Family Renard
Le Château de l'Abbaye,
85450 Moreilles, Vendée

ENTRY 249   MAP 8

Le Clos du Marais

Spot egrets, herons and storks as you gaze across to the marshes beyond Jacqueline and Gil's whitewashed home. At the edge of a historic village close to the Vendée coastline, this beautifully renovated 1700s longère has two elegant rooms for guests. Cheery blue 'Hortensia' has an en suite with a roll top bath and scented stuff for pampering; romantic 'Les Dimes' has a walk-in shower and its own sitting room with a pair of stylish leather armchairs. Breakfast on pastries, homemade jam and local honey in the dining room or by the heated pool; book ahead for Gil's superb three-course dinners. A delightful stopover when travelling south. *Minimum stay: 2 nights; 3 in high season. Over 17s welcome.*

La Maison de Landerie

Annie used to have her own restaurant in Devon so whether you are outside on her little stone terrace overlooking open fields and forest or inside at her long antique table, it will be a Cordon Bleu breakfast. Multi-talented Annie could open an antique shop: her lovingly collected artefacts decorate this sweet little farmhouse like a dream from the past. The paint work is gorgeous, the vintage linens are sumptuous, the towels are soft, the mattresses are from heaven. You can walk to town, pick a trail in the forest or rent a canoe and follow the lazy river Lay. Annie's dinners are renowned, even the Mayor comes to dine. *Children over 10 welcome.*

Rooms	2 doubles: €60-€105.
Meals	Dinner €30.
Closed	Rarely.

Rooms	2 doubles: €80.
Meals	Dinner with wine, €30.
Closed	Christmas.

Tel	+33 (0)2 28 14 01 12
Email	leclosdumarais@gmail.com
Web	www.leclosdumarais.com

Jacqueline & Gil Darlavoix
Le Clos du Marais,
10 rue du Communal,
85540 Curzon, Vendée

Tel	+33 (0)2 51 27 80 70
Email	richard.jory@wanadoo.fr
Web	www.lalanderie.com

Annie Jory
La Maison de Landerie,
La Réorthe,
85210 Sainte Hermine, Vendée

La Frelonnière

An elegant country house in a peaceful,
pastoral setting – who would not love it?
The 18th-century farmhouse, complete
with musket holes and open rafters, is
informal and delightful. Your English/Scottish
hosts are fun, friendly and intimately
acquainted with France – they brought
their children up here. Now they generously
open their living space to guests, their
serene pool and their exquisite Monet-style
garden. Quietly stylish bedrooms (coir
carpets, white walls, fresh flowers, silk
flourishes) are divided by a sofa'd library
on the landing. A gem.

Manoir de l'Eolière

The owners live in the handsome 18th-
century manoir, and the guests in the grey-
shuttered stables. But the setting is the
thing: three hectares of parkland where
birds trill, hares leap, and wild boar come
snuffling at night. Enjoy it all from the
comfort of your own spacious terrace.
Etienne is your host, highly professional,
easy to talk to, full of enthusiasm for his
family's new venture (his ancestors once
worked on the estate). The three ground-
floor bedrooms are airy and light, with
white walls, elegant colours, high rafters,
immaculate beds. They're spacious too –
Monarque's terrace alone is 50 sq metres!
Parking on-site.

Rooms	4 doubles: €80.
Meals	Dinner with wine, €25.
	Restaurants 11km.
Closed	Rarely.

Rooms	1 double: €95-€115.
	1 family room for 4: €125-€145.
	1 triple: €115-€135.
	Cot €15; extra bed €30, only in
	triple & family room.
Meals	Restaurants 1km.
Closed	1 November – 31 March.

Tel	+33 (0)2 51 51 56 49
Email	julie@lafrelonniere.fr
Web	www.bandbvendee.com

Julie & Richard Deslandes
La Frelonnière,
85410 La Caillère-Hilaire du Bois,
Vendée

Tel	+33 (0)2 51 33 69 83
Email	contact@manoir-eoliere.fr
Web	www.manoir-eoliere.com

Etienne Chaillot
Manoir de l'Eolière,
L'Eolière,
85220 Landevieille, Vendée

Château de la Maronnière

Friendly Marie and François have excelled in restoring their luxurious, 18th-century château. Oak parquet is warm underfoot, copper leaf chandeliers light the circular hall and a stuffed fox surprises on the spiral staircase. Many rambling acres of green-fingered Eden await; take a wildlife walk or pluck cherries by the pool. Stylish shared spaces are immaculate with a baby grand in residence; Le Petit Bois has carved antique furniture; La Rotonde is marble grey with unusual panelling. Textiles and trimmings are sumptuous, bath robes fluffy; throw open the shutters and the views pour in. Stroll into Aizenay – or dine here. *Minimum stay: 2 nights.*

Blanc Marine

A dreamy coastal light shimmers over the whole flat island, then comes the Atlantic breeze to blow happy birds, boaters and cyclists in all directions. Even in thronging summer, peace reigns inside the scented garden of this smart, comfortable modern house where each originally-furnished B&B room has its own entrance and wee hedged terrace. Delightful and enthusiastic, Jane makes guests feel very welcome; you will get to know her and the others over breakfast at one big table in the family living room. Binge on seafood and rare local potatoes, swim off wide sandy beaches, explore rock pools in this ideal holiday place.

Rooms	1 double, 2 twin/doubles: €125-€140. 1 suite for 4: €220. Extra child bed €25.
Meals	Dinner with wine, €35. Restaurants 500m.
Closed	Rarely.

Rooms	5 doubles; 2 can interconnect: €85-€155. Extra bed available in 1 room, €25. Bikes available, €10 p.p. per day.
Meals	Brunch €10. Restaurants 10 min walk.
Closed	Rarely.

Mobile	+33 (0)6 25 02 00 55
Email	dhalluinmh@gmail.com
Web	www.chateauvendee.com

François-Xavier & Marie-Hélène d'Halluin
Château de la Maronnière,
Route des Sables,
85190 Aizenay, Vendée

Tel	+33 (0)2 51 39 99 11
Email	contact@blanc-marine.net
Web	www.blanc-marine.net

Jean & Jane Dalric
Blanc Marine,
1 bis rue de l'Acquenette,
85330 Noirmoutier, Vendée

Villa La Ruche

Benoit's carefully restored 1903 villa is three minutes' walk from the famous beach of La Baule, at the peaceful end of the bay. Its swimming pool takes up most of the palm-fringed courtyard and its rooms – ground floor Les Pins, the biggest – are classy in an old-meets-new way: bold modern wallpaper, polished, original floorboards, local art. Bathrooms are generous, and striking – one's very New York 20s, another is lined with huge marble tiles. Breakfast jams and cakes are a homemade treat in the conservatory; the salon has an open fire, books, games, hot drinks. Your charming host, passionate about La Baule, will guide you. *Parking available on very quiet street.*

Le Manoir des Quatre Saisons

Welcome to a manoir with a fascinating history, and a delightful and attentive host. Jean-Philippe offers swimming robes and drinks by the pool on summer days, and leisurely breakfasts at the big table with eggs and cereals as well as local choices. Recently refreshed rooms (some in two-storey cottages in the grounds, some with kitchens, some with sea views) are colourfully co-ordinated with a traditional feel – stripes, patterns, French flourishes; little dishes of local fudge are a lovely extra. Beach, river and town are walkable but children (and dogs) will love romping in the garden with its many secret corners. *Minimum stay: 2 nights July/Aug & bank holiday weekends.*

Rooms	3 doubles: €95-€149.	
Meals	Restaurants 3-minute walk.	
Closed	Rarely.	

Rooms	3 doubles, 1 twin: €75-€95.	
	1 quadruple: €95-€105.	
	Extra bed €20.	
Meals	Restaurants 1.5km.	
Closed	Rarely.	

Mobile	+33 (0)6 18 65 18 24
Email	contact@villa-laruche.com
Web	www.villa-laruche.com

Benoit Colin
Villa La Ruche,
6 bis avenue du Général Berthelot,
44500 La-Baule-Escoublac, Loire-Atlantique

Mobile	+33 (0)6 87 33 43 86
Email	manoirdes4saisons@gmail.com
Web	www.le-manoir-des-quatre-saisons.com

Jean-Philippe Meyran
Le Manoir des Quatre Saisons,
744 bd de Lauvergnac,
44420 La Turballe, Loire-Atlantique

Château de Coët Caret

Come for a taste of life with the French country aristocracy – it's getting hard to find; the family have lived here for 13 generations. Gwénaël greets you on arrival and is on hand when needed. The château is tucked into the woods and 100 hectares of parkland with plenty of paths for wandering: serenity is guaranteed. Bedrooms are lived-in but comfortable; 'Saumon', under the eaves, comes with binoculars for the birds. Start the day with excellent bread, jams and coffee in the wonderful breakfast room. Gwénaël is full of tips and you are in the Brière Regional Park where water and land are inextricably mingled and wildlife abounds.

Belle Couronne

A short walk from a small wine town, and tucked away from the neighbours, is an elevated, turretted Belle Époque villa where, thanks to kind hosts Gerdie and Jan, all is calm and serene. A suit of shining armour guards the front door, two elegant tables await for breakfast, and a curved stair leads to tip-top bedrooms in traditional French style, mirror images of each other. Large windows open to sweeping Loire views, beds are pristine, towels snowy white, and bathrooms stunningly contemporary. Explore the vineyards, spin off on the bikes, return to stylish seating beneath the trees and lazy laps in the tranquil pool.

Rooms	3 doubles, 1 twin: €85-€120.
Meals	Restaurants 2-10km.
Closed	Rarely.

Rooms	2 doubles: €120.
Meals	Dinner available.
	Restaurants 2-minutes walk.
Closed	Christmas.

Tel	+33 (0)2 40 91 41 20
Email	coetcaret@gmail.com
Web	www.chateaudecoetcaret.com/en/

Gwénaël de La Monneraye
Château de Coët Caret,
44410 Herbignac,
Loire-Atlantique

Tel	+33 (0)2 28 16 13 12
Email	contact@bellecouronne.fr
Web	www.bellecouronne.fr

Jan & Gerdie Liebreks
Belle Couronne,
4 rue des Grands Coteaux,
44850 Le Cellier, Loire-Atlantique

Loire-Séjours

An 18th-century townhouse run with love and pride by Breton Aline and London-Scot Andrew. Their home has a friendly feel; the sitting room has grand piano, parquet and books, elegant bedrooms have good beds. They know western Loire well – it's part of the old kingdom of Brittany and steeped in Celtic history. Continental breakfast is delicious: organic coffee, homemade jams and cakes, artisan bread and viennoiseries. The Loire à Vélo route is on the doorstep, Nantes is nearby; discover the vineyards of Muscadet and Coteaux d'Ancenis, and relax with a glass of wine in the pretty tiered garden on your return – Andrew might entertain you with his bagpipes!
On street parking.

Logis de Richebonne

Monsieur's parents bought this old *logis Vendéen* when he was six. Years later, researching the history of the house, he found his family had owned it in 1670! In the hall, Madame's family tree goes back to the 14th century. Both are warm, welcoming and not at all grand and the old house is full of personal touches: Madame painted the breakfast china and embroidered the beautiful tablecloths. Vast bedrooms have peaceful views and quantities of fresh and dried flowers. The suite is ideal for a family, the huge grounds hold two pretty ponds (unfenced) and a barbecue: you may picnic here. Wonderful all round.

Rooms	2 doubles, 1 twin: €75. Singles €65.
Meals	Restaurants within walking distance.
Closed	Christmas, New Year, Easter, Bank Holidays.

Rooms	2 doubles: €75. 1 suite for 5: €75-€147. Extra bed €20.
Meals	Picnic possible. Restaurant in village, 1.5km.
Closed	Rarely.

Tel	+33 (0)9 64 40 47 46
Email	info@loire-sejours.fr
Web	www.loire-sejours.com

Andrew Treppass
Loire-Séjours,
196 rue du Général Leclerc,
44150 Ancenis, Loire-Atlantique

Tel	+33 (0)2 40 04 90 41
Email	adeternay@wanadoo.fr
Web	www.logisderichebonne.com

Alain & Françoise de Ternay
Logis de Richebonne,
7 impasse Richebonne,
44650 Legé, Loire-Atlantique

ENTRY 260   MAP 3

ENTRY 261   MAP 8

Château de la Frogerie

It's not often you can pretend to be medieval royalty but ascending the fabulous spiral staircase to your turret bedroom presents the ideal opportunity! Overlooking glorious Loire countryside, this petite château dates back to the fifteenth-century. Panelled-walls, a moat and parquet floors create historical atmosphere but charming owners, Jean-Christophe and Raymond-Pierre, have ensured that modern comfort co-exists. Antique beds are dressed in fine linen; cosy leather armchairs surround the fireplace and there's a pool shaded by ancient walls. Breakfast like a king on pastries, milk from the local Jersey herd and honey from the château's hives. *Parking on-site.*

La Rousselière

A hymn to peace, permanence and gentle living. The superb garden is Monsieur's pride and joy; château-like reception rooms open one into another – glass doors to glass doors, billiards to dining to sitting – like an indoor arcade; family portraits follow you everywhere; Mass is still said once a year in the chapel. But it's never over-grand. Bedrooms are highly individual with their antiques and hand-painted armoires (courtesy of an artistic sister), many bathrooms are new and Madame is the most delightful smiling hostess and a fine cook (veg, meat and eggs all home-grown). Your lovely hosts join you for an aperitif before dinner.

Rooms 3 doubles: €89-€159.	**Rooms** 2 doubles, 2 twins: €100.
1 family room for 4: €221-€284.	1 family room for 4: €150.
Singles €78-€146.	**Meals** Dinner with wine, €30.
Meals Restaurant 6km.	**Closed** Rarely.
Closed Rarely.	

Tel +33 (0)2 41 30 60 67
Email contact@chateau-frogerie.fr
Web www.chateau-frogerie.fr

Jean-Christophe Robert
Château de la Frogerie,
49360 Maulévrier,
Maine-et-Loire

Tel +33 (0)2 41 39 13 21
Email larousseliere@unimedia.fr
Web www.anjou-et-loire.com/rousseliere

François & Jacqueline de Béru
La Rousselière,
49170 La Possonnière,
Maine-et-Loire

La Grande Maison d'Arthenay

Micaela was in the hotel trade, Sue worked at a Sussex winery, now they run an idyllic B&B on a former Saumur wine estate. The tours of their cellars and of the region are unmissable. The house dates from 1706, the potager is organic, and the outbuildings create a delicious hollyhock'd garden off which two rustic-chic bedrooms lie. The two in the house are equally lovely, one with an extra bed on the mezzanine: tuffeau walls, deep mattresses, soft beautiful colours. Start the day with a convivial breakfast (fresh figs, eggs from their hens), end it with a twice-weekly wine-tasting dinner at the big table.

Manoir de Boisairault

Our inspector had an *Alice Through The Looking Glass* moment as she stepped off the street, through the unremarkable gate and into the wonderful gardens – a series of secret 'rooms' – that surround this elegant, 18th-century, cloistered manor. A labyrinth of caves, typical of the region, lies below and guests sometimes dine there with Jean-Pierre and Béatrice – your cultured, interesting hosts. Pray for the camembert sprinkled with pastis, cooked in the fire's embers – it's divine. Inside are an attractive dining room and three pretty bedrooms; the ground-floor one – all Louis XV – is particularly enchanting.

Rooms	3 twin/doubles: €110-€120. 1 suite for 4: €125-€140. Singles €95-€97.	**Rooms**	2 doubles: €125. 1 family room for 4: €200-€230.
Meals	Dinner with wine, coffee, tea & liqueur, €57 (Sunday & Monday only).	**Meals**	Hosted dinner with wine €35; children under 10, €15. Restaurants 10 km.
Closed	November – March.	**Closed**	1 November – 29 March.

Tel	+33 (0)2 41 40 35 06	**Mobile**	+33 (0)6 08 93 85 61
Email	resv@lagrandemaison.net	**Email**	contact@manoir-de-boisairault.com
Web	www.lagrandemaison.net	**Web**	www.manoir-de-boisairault.com

Micaela Frow & Sue Hunt
La Grande Maison d'Arthenay,
Rue de la Cerisaie, Arthenay,
49700 Saumur, Maine-et-Loire

Jean-Pierre Delmas
Manoir de Boisairault,
8 rue de Pas d'Aubigné,
49260 Le Coudray Macouard, Maine-et-Loire

ENTRY 264 MAP 4

ENTRY 265 MAP 4

La Sterne de Loire

Véronique, who paints, is loving settling into the medieval village, gleaning crockery and furniture from brocantes and her own grandparents to bring a new life and soul to this delightfully eclectic 15th-century house. On a road beside the Loire, it has direct sightings of swooping "sternes" (terns), an authentically ancient atmosphere, small bedrooms with huge personality and pretty showers, a splendid fireplace with its original bread oven in the dark beamed dining room – and masses of steps. Your cosmopolitan, polyglot hostess knows all the fascinating things to do and see here.

Château de Beaulieu

Set back from the banks of the river Loire lies a château of character and charm, a perfect reflection of its delightful owners. The house was built in 1727 and the décor, traditional and authentic, captures the romance of that earlier age. Five bedrooms lead off an oak-beamed corridor and range from the dramatic to the cosy and intimate. Find antique armoires, ornate fireplaces, bold colours and dreamy views of the large, tree-brimmed garden – with a lovely pool and a small prospering vineyard. Snuggle down with a book from the library, try your hand at billiards, visit historic Saumur and the treasures of the Loire valley are legendary – you can visit the châteaux on horseback! We'd stay for the atmosphere and company alone.

Rooms	4 doubles: €95-€105. 1 triple: €130-€140.		**Rooms**	4 doubles: €120. 1 suite for 4: €160-€190.
Meals	Restaurants 5-minute walk.		**Meals**	Restaurants 1km.
Closed	5 November – 6 April.		**Closed**	November to Easter.

Tel	+33 (0)6 63 11 28 12		**Tel**	+33 (0)2 41 50 83 52
Email	lasternedeloire@gmail.com		**Email**	info@chateaudebeaulieu.fr
Web	www.lasternedeloire.com		**Web**	www.chateaudebeaulieu.fr

Véronique van Eetvelde
La Sterne de Loire,
26 rue des Ducs d'Anjou,
49400 Souzay-Champigny, Maine-et-Loire

Conor & Mary Coady-Maguire
Château de Beaulieu,
98 route de Montsoreau,
49400 Saumur, Maine-et-Loire

ENTRY 266 MAP 4

ENTRY 267 MAP 4

Les Bouchets

It's spotless now, with all mod cons, gleaming antiques, open fires and vases of fresh flowers. The house was a ruin when the Bignons found it but they managed to save all the old timbers and stones. The result is a seductively warm cheerful house with bedrooms cosy and soft, two upstairs, one with an entrance off a garden where swings invite children to play. Passionate about food, they used to run a restaurant where Michel was chef; note the coppers in the kitchen/entrance hall, and memorabilia in the family sitting room. Géraldine, bright, friendly and organised... and serving beautiful homegrown or local food and the wines of Anjou.

La Croix d'Étain

Frisky red squirrels decorate the stone balustrade, the wisteria is a glory in spring, and the wide swooshing river cascades over the weir. It feels like deep country yet this handsome manor has urban elegance in its very stones. Panelling, mouldings, subtly muted floor tiles bring grace; traditional French florals add softness. It looks fairly formal but sprightly Madame loves having guests and pampers them, in their own quarters, with luxury. Expect plush, lacy, flowery, carpeted bedrooms, three with river views, all with sunny bathrooms. The yacht-side setting is stunning – it could be the Riviera.

Rooms	1 double, 1 twin/double: €72-€88. 1 family room for 4: €130.
Meals	Dinner with wine, €29.
Closed	Rarely.

Rooms	1 double, 3 twin/doubles: €85-€110. Singles €75. Extra bed/sofabed €25 p.p. per night.
Meals	Dinner with wine €30, except on Sundays; by arrangement. Crêperie 50m.
Closed	Rarely.

Tel	+33 (0)2 41 82 34 48
Email	geraldinebignon@gmail.com
Web	www.lesbouchets.com

Michel & Géraldine Bignon
Les Bouchets,
49150 Le Vieil Baugé,
Maine-et-Loire

Tel	+33 (0)2 41 95 68 49
Email	croix.etain@loire-anjou-accommodation.com
Web	www.loire-anjou-accommodation.com

Jacqueline & Auguste Bahuaud
La Croix d'Étain,
2 rue de l'Écluse,
49220 Grez Neuville, Maine-et-Loire

ENTRY 268 MAP 4   ENTRY 269 MAP 3

Manoir du Bois de Grez

An ancient peace lingers over the fan-shaped cobbled courtyard, the old well, the little chapel: the Manoir oozes history. Your doctor host, a talented gardener, and his charming wife, much-travelled antique-hunters with imagination and flair, offer guests warm generous bedrooms (including a superb family room) hung with well-chosen oriental pieces and paintings in good strong colours that reflect the garden light. Most wonderful of all are the specimen tree'd gardens, their great grassy carpets embracing a small lake. You share a big sitting room with your lovely hosts, lots of plants and a suit of armour.

Château de Montreuil sur Loir

An 1840s neo-gothic delight, now a listed historical monument, in a 16-hectare, deer-roamed park, a river for swimming and rowing, and a film set of an interior. The sitting room is splendidly 'medieval', the panelled drawing room pure 18th century, taken whole from a château, with superb hangings and immensely high doors. This was once a self-sufficient country estate with chapel, dovecote and mill (remains still visible). Large, lofty bedrooms have authentic wooden floors and carpets, antique cupboards, bucolic river views. Your hosts speak good English, are gracious, refined and humorous, and always there to receive guests.

Rooms	2 doubles, 1 twin: €90-€110. 1 family room for 4: €110-€150.	**Rooms**	3 family rooms for 3: €100-€145. Singles €90-€100. Cot €20.
Meals	Picnic on request. Guest kitchen. Restaurant 1.5km.	**Meals**	Dinner with wine, €40.
Closed	Rarely.	**Closed**	15 October – 15 April.

Tel	+33 (0)2 41 18 00 09
Email	cesbron.boisgrez@wanadoo.fr
Web	www.boisdegrez.com

Marie Laure & Jean Gaël Cesbron
Manoir du Bois de Grez,
Route de Sceaux d'Anjou,
49220 Grez Neuville, Maine-et-Loire

Tel	+33 (0)2 41 76 21 03
Email	renardalice@hotmail.fr
Web	www.anjou-loir.com/en/

Marc & Alice Renard
Château de Montreuil sur Loir,
49140 Montreuil sur Loir,
Maine-et-Loire

ENTRY 270 MAP 3

ENTRY 271 MAP 4

Domaine de Bré

A classically French family home in a hamlet surrounded by gentle countryside. Handsome, shuttered, with a rose-filled garden, the 18th-century house is filled with beautiful objects collected by the owners on their travels. You sleep in a cottage next door – which has seating if you prefer to be private – and is distinctly oriental in design. It's a sociable sort of place. Meals are shared with other guests and you may use the reception rooms in the house – pick a book from the shelves and find a spot inside or out to sit. Breakfasts are homemade and home-laid, packed lunches can be rustled up and dinners are locally-sourced and delicious. Gentle walks through the garden extend to strolls through meadows and quiet lanes. Historic Angers with its pretty medieval streets is a half hour drive; châteaux and vineyards are all near.

Château de Chambiers

Another marvellous family château, this one surrounded by a deep forest. Smiling Madame (a good cook, and wonderful with children) speaks perfect English, is proud of her gardens and her big, beautiful rooms; she is a talented designer. Bedrooms have delicious antiques, one a French-Caribbean mahogany bed, floors are 18th-century oak with *terre cuit* borders – exquisite; some of the baths, washstands and fittings are period originals, so it's a huge treat to stay here if you appreciate history. There's a panelled *salon de thé*, a billiards room and books, and a playhouse and organic potager in the garden. Un coin de paradis! *Well-behaved pets welcome, €12.50 per night.*

Rooms	1 double: €130.
Meals	Dinner €30. Child €15. Packed lunch available. Restaurants 20-minute drive.
Closed	Rarely.

Rooms	1 double: €128-€206.4 family rooms for 3: €120-€206. Extra bed/sofabed €28 p.p. per night.
Meals	Dinner, 3-4 courses, €36.50-€49.50; children under 9, €14.50.
Closed	Rarely.

Email	lise.donon@gmail.com
Web	www.domainedebre.com

Tel	+33 (0)2 41 76 07 31
Email	info@chateauchambiers.com
Web	www.chateauchambiers.com

Lise Donon
Domaine de Bré,
49140 Seiches sur le Loir,
Maine-et-Loire

Anne & Élie Crouan
Château de Chambiers,
49430 Durtal,
Maine-et-Loire

Château du Plessis Anjou

You can lift off from the grounds in a balloon; some of the finest châteaux and wineries of the Loire are within easy reach. Sixteenth-century Le Plessis has been welcoming guests for years. Dinner, brought to a long table in a dining room grandly furnished with Roman Empire frescoes, might include duck with apricots, cheese, a crisp fruit tart. One bedroom is striking with oriental rugs and the bed in a deep alcove; others have lofty beamed ceilings. Children are welcome and the Renouls have two of their own, hence the playground and the trampoline, the rabbits and the goat. Madame invites children to gather breakfast's eggs, and the pool hides in the grounds; the trees are sublime. Terra Botanica is a 15-minute drive.

La Maison du Roi René

The famous old auberge has become a charming B&B. Scrunch up the drive serenaded by soft roses to a lovely welcome from Madame. Part medieval, part 18th century, like the village around it, it has corners, crannies and a stunning central stone fireplace. The Valicourts – they speak four languages!- are the happy new owners of these magnificent oak doors and rosy tomette floors; bedrooms are beamed and very pleasing – one opens to the garden, three to the tower. There's a pretty paved terrace for breakfast with viennoiseries and a room of auberge proportions for a light supper of cold meats and local specialities.

Rooms	3 doubles: €105-€180. 2 suites for 2: €220-€250. Extra bed/sofabed €25-€35 p.p. per night.
Meals	Hosted dinner €48. Wine €20-€240.
Closed	Rarely.

Rooms	2 doubles, 1 twin: €70-€85. 1 suite for 2: €80. Extra sofabed available in twin.
Meals	Supper tray available, €15. Restaurant 100m.
Closed	Rarely.

Tel	+33 (0)2 41 95 12 75
Email	plessis.anjou@wanadoo.fr
Web	www.chateau-du-plessis.com

Valérie & Laurent Renoul
Château du Plessis Anjou,
49220 La Jaille Yvon,
Maine-et-Loire

Tel	+33 (0)2 43 70 52 30
Email	roi-rene@orange.fr
Web	www.chambrehote-roi-rene.fr

Dominique de Valicourt
La Maison du Roi René,
4 Grande Rue,
53290 Saint Denis d'Anjou, Mayenne

Château de Craon

Such a close and welcoming family, whose kindness extends to include you. It's a magnificent place, with innumerable expressions of history, taste and personality, and gracious Séverine and Bertrand, young parents, treat you like friends. A sitting room with sofas and a view of the park, an Italianate hall with sweeping stone stair, classic French bedrooms in lavender, blue, cream... an original washstand, a canopied bed, a velvet armchair. Everywhere a feast for the eyes; paintings, watercolours, antiques. Outside, 40 acres of river, meadows, lake, ice house, tennis court, pool, and a potager worth leaving home for.

Château de Montaupin

Outside, a virginia creeper has the façade in its clutches – to pretty effect! Inside, wine and conversation flow. Mme David is friendly and welcoming and adores her house, family and guests. There's a laid-back feel, a cluttered elegance, a faded decor; the atmosphere is that of a happy household. A suspended spiral staircase leads to the upper floors and the best suite is right at the top, its roof timbers exposed. Families will feel at home. Breakfasts are robust and table d'hôtes is classic French, with much produce from the garden. Be sure you try the family wines!

Rooms	3 doubles, 1 twin: €120-€160. 1 suite for 4: €180-€260. 1 single: €80. Extra bed/sofabed €35 p.p. per night.
Meals	Restaurants within walking distance.
Closed	November – March.

Rooms	2 doubles: €75-€80. 2 suites for 4: €80-€155. 1 triple: €75-€105. Extra bed/sofabed €25 p.p. per night.
Meals	Dinner with wine, €22.50.
Closed	Occasionally.

Tel	+33 (0)2 43 06 11 02
Email	chateaudecraon@wanadoo.fr
Web	www.craoncastle.com

Séverine & Bertrand de Guébriant
Château de Craon,
53400 Craon,
Mayenne

Tel	+33 (0)2 43 87 81 70
Email	chateaudemontaupin@wanadoo.fr
Web	chateau-de-montaupin.e-monsite.com

Marie David
Château de Montaupin,
72330 Oizé,
Sarthe

ENTRY 276   MAP 3

ENTRY 277   MAP 4

5 Grande Rue

On Le Lude's Grande Rue is a nobleman's house built around 1650, in its own walled garden, sunny and peaceful; from many of the windows you can glimpse the Château. Simon and Susan pay huge attention to detail, love having guests, offer tea, cakes or wine on arrival, and give you one of five big comfortable bedrooms upstairs. All have immaculate linen, sparkling bathrooms and original button cushions made by Susan. There's an illuminated dining terrace and a wonderful salon to come home to, and long, leisurely breakfasts to wake to. Wine caves and châteaux abound, including Bauge's with its 17th-century apothecary.

Le Moulin de St Blaise

A house of surprises: mill machinery in the dining room; vast bread oven in the kitchen; fruit and vegetable plot like a Garden of Eden. Come here for fantastic fresh food (dinners, too), the sounds of water, and freedom. Huge beamed dining and sitting rooms have books, games, billiards – and space for children to play. More space on the terrace and in the meadow and garden; keep an eye on children by the river. Airy, white bedrooms have garden and vineyard views; most have smart shower rooms. Friendly owners will point you to Le Mans, lakeside beach, châteaux. Catch fish for supper, or relax with a book and the rushing water.

Rooms	4 doubles, 1 twin: €75-€99.
Meals	Dinner, 3 courses with wine, €27. Restaurants 50m.
Closed	Rarely.

Rooms	1 double, 2 twins: €79-€149. 1 family room for 3: €89-€149. Extra bed/sofabed €25-€35 p.p. per night.
Meals	Dinner with wine, €25. Restaurant 1km.
Closed	1 November – 28 February.

Tel	+33 (0)2 43 94 92 77
Email	info@5granderue.com
Web	www.5granderue.com

Simon & Susan Wachter
5 Grande Rue,
72800 Le Lude,
Sarthe

Tel	+33 (0)2 43 46 78 05
Email	philelaine2007@yahoo.co.uk
Web	www.moulinstblaise.com

Elaine Love Miles
Le Moulin de St Blaise,
72340 Chahaignes,
Sarthe

ENTRY 278   MAP 4

ENTRY 279   MAP 4

Le Chaton Rouge

The Le Mans race track is less than ten miles away; in St Pierre du Lorouer life is lived at a slower pace. Opposite the church is a house that combines château grandeur with a cottagey feel – thanks to cheerful, generous, imaginative Sarah. Relax in the courtyard, climb the steps to the walled garden. Sarah is a fabulous cook and uses vegetables from her garden and organic and seasonal local produce whenever possible – make sure you book dinner. There's a real fire for winter, an outdoor dining room for summer, and, up a sweeping stair, the bedrooms – fresh, white and uncluttered. There's a studio on the top floor too – ideal for longer stays. *Children over 5 welcome. Breakfast normally 8am-10am.*

La Maison du Pont Romain

Cross Montfort's exquisite stone bridge to this pretty house on the banks of the river. Enter the grounds and forget the world in heavenly peace among very old trees. Gentle Madame saved it all from ruin and gives you two comfortable rooms upstairs, privately off the courtyard, both with fine armoires. The suite in the old stables (salon below, bedrooms above) has a charming late 18th-century feel. There are delicious jams at the big table for breakfast and a family salon for guests. You can visit the lovely, unsung villages and vineyards of the Sarthe. For children? Forest animals at Pescheray and an aquapark in the village.

Rooms	2 doubles; 1 double with separate shower: €90-€150. 1 family room for 4: €160-€200. Singles €70.
Meals	Lunch €10. Dinner €25, by reservation only. Restaurant 20m.
Closed	Rarely.

Rooms	2 doubles: €70-€82. 1 suite for 3: €132. Extra bed/sofabed €20 p.p. per night.
Meals	Dinner with wine & coffee, €25.
Closed	Rarely.

Tel	+33 (0)2 43 46 21 37
Email	sarah@lechatonrouge.com
Web	www.lechatonrouge.com

Sarah Carlisle
Le Chaton Rouge,
4 rue du Calvaire,
72150 Saint Pierre du Lorouer, Sarthe

Tel	+33 (0)2 43 76 13 46
Email	chantal-paris@wanadoo.fr
Web	www.le-pont-romain.fr

Chantal Paris
La Maison du Pont Romain,
26 rue de l'Église,
72450 Montfort le Gesnois, Sarthe

ENTRY 280   MAP 4

ENTRY 281   MAP 4

Château d'Eporcé

Grand and pure 17th century with a moat and magnificent avenue of trees leading to the door. Yet you discover a laid-back, lived-in atmosphere with three salons for guests and little change for 50 years. Find lofty ceilings, antiques, books, engravings and butterfly collections galore. Meals are easy-going, with drinks before and tea in the lounge afterwards. Bedrooms are charmingly faded; all face the sun and have lovely park views and rather eccentric, ancient bathrooms. First-floor rooms are the ones to go for – proper château stuff. Anglophile Rémy is a charming host; his gardens handsome, formal, wonderful. Pack a woolly jumper in the winter...

Château de la Ruche

Turning into the long drive your first glimpse of La Ruche, in the peaceful isolation of its pretty park will gladden weary travellers. You're treated to restored 18th-century elegance along with luxurious beds and bathrooms, quirky vintage finds (Tim's a keen 'up-cycler'....) and drawing rooms to repair to. Rebecca loves to cook so do dine in – on the best local and seasonal food; French-inspired with English twists; preceded by a friendly cocktail. Breakfasts are generous too with great pastries and preserves. Arrange a special celebration here, or a Le Mans group visit and every detail will be seen to. Take the path to the Sarthe river or hop in the car to visit local villages and châteaux. Swim in the lake at Sille-le-Guillaume; head for the Alpes Mancelles for kayaking, hiking, biking.

Rooms	2 doubles, 1 twin/double: €90-€150.
Meals	Dinner with wine, €40.
Closed	Rarely.

Rooms	1 double: €175. 1 suite for 2: €200-€250.
Meals	Dinner, 4 courses, €30.
Closed	Rarely.

Tel	+33 (0)2 43 27 70 22
Email	eporce@wanadoo.fr
Web	www.chateau-eporce.com

Rémy de Scitivaux
Château d'Eporcé,
Éporcé,
72550 La Quinte, Sarthe

Tel	+33 (0)6 35 55 10 50
Email	rebecca@chateaudelaruche.com
Web	www.chateaudelaruche.com

Rebecca Jones
Château de la Ruche,
72290 Teille,
Sarthe

Loire
Valley

Château de Beauvois, page 223

Château du Boisrenault

Built by a 19th-century aristocrat as a wedding present for his daughter – well overdue, she'd had two sons by the time it was finished – Boisrenault may be turreted, noble and imposing on the outside but it's a family home within. Furniture, objects, pictures, all have a story to tell – and there's no shortage of hunting trophies and stags' heads on the wall. Reception rooms are lofty, with huge fireplaces. One sitting room has a baby grand; another, smaller and cosier, is lined with books. As for the bedrooms, each is an adventure in itself. Named after the family's children and grandchildren, they feature a hotchpotch of pieces from different periods, including some excellent antiques; two apartments upstairs have their own fitted kitchens. A delicious pool is discreetly tucked away behind trees in the lovely grounds; table tennis and table football are a godsend on rainy days. Meals, cooked by Elfie, are served at a vast table in the dining room; be sure to book if you'd like dinner.

Rooms	2 doubles, 1 twin: €90-€116. 3 family rooms for 3, 1 family room for 4: €116-€150. 2 apartments for 5: €528-€556. Extra bed available €15 p.p. per night.
Meals	Dinner €25, by arrangement. Wine from €20.
Closed	Rarely.

Elfie Massé & Colas de Decker
Château du Boisrenault,
36500 Buzançais,
Indre

Tel	+33 (0)2 54 84 03 01
Mobile	+33 (0)6 89 30 44 16
Email	boisrenault@wanadoo.fr
Web	www.boisrenault.fr

Le Cheval Blanc

Bang in the middle of Loire châteaux country, the famous 19th-century staging inn has always been an hotel – but much has changed in the last few years. The main square is now mostly pedestrianised, so the place is brilliantly quiet, and the rooms, all on the first floor, have been beautifully revamped by the new owners. Decorated and furnished with imagination, flair and lots of original timbers, the rooms are all different: from a cleancut 21st-century palette to a more traditional draped look. This is contemporary chic in a highly sophisticated yet unfussy manner. Bathrooms are state-of-the-art stylish, one room has its bathtub and shower proudly centre-stage in the room. Your charming and dynamic hosts are breathing new life into these old bones – fast. The restaurant, long known as one of the best in the region, is furnished and decorated with elegant simplicity so that you can concentrate on the gastronomic delights on your plate. In fine weather, the pretty inner courtyard has peace and shade for breakfast and dinner – and the sheltered pool is a great bonus.

Rooms	7 doubles: €87-€145. 2 suites for 2: €185-€205. Singles €78-€98.
Meals	Breakfast €12. Dinner €32-€58. Wine list €26.50-€47. Restaurant closed Monday & Tuesday. Restaurants within walking distance.
Closed	January.

Tel	+33 (0)2 47 30 30 14
Email	aguinoiseau@lechevalblancblere.fr
Web	www.lechevalblancblere.fr

Claire & Alain Guinoiseau
Le Cheval Blanc,
5 place Charles Bidault,
37150 Bléré, Indre-et-Loire

ENTRY 285 MAP 4

Domaine de la Tortinière

It seems unreal, this pepperpot-towered château on a hill above the Indre, the bird-filled woods where wild cyclamen lay a carpet in autumn and daffodils radiate their light in spring. Then there's the view across to the stony keep of Montbazon; this is an exceptional spot with tennis, a heated pool, fishing or rowing on the river, too. Bedrooms are decorated with flair and imagination, be they in the château or in one of the several outbuildings. The smallest is enchanting in its elegant simplicity and fine fabrics; the pavilions, for playing shepherdesses, are charming and beautifully furnished. Bathrooms are luxurious, some smaller than others. For wet nights there's an underground passage to the orangery where you dine – with a dining terrace for summer. Soft lighting, panelled reception rooms, deep comfort and discreet friendliness here in this real family-run hotel: the warm, humorous owners are genuinely attentive, their sole aim to make your stay peaceful and harmonious. Discover the unsung mills and villages of the Indre.

Rooms	25 doubles: €125-€340. 7 suites for 2: €250-€460.
Meals	Breakfast €20. Dinner €36-€82. Restaurant closed Sunday evenings November-March.
Closed	19 December – 13 February.

Xavier & Anne Olivereau
Domaine de la Tortinière,
Les Gués de Veigné, 37250 Montbazon,
Indre-et-Loire

Tel	+33 (0)2 47 34 35 00
Email	contact@tortiniere.com
Web	www.tortiniere.com

Château de Beauvois

The Younan family bought this impressive 17th-century chateau in 2016 – their third in and around the Loire valley – and have spent every moment since gently updating it. Now all the large bedrooms are deliciously comfortable with reproduction antique furniture, pretty printed wall fabrics, charming nooks and crannies and long views of the grounds. One room is in the original mediaeval tower. Breakfast is a hot and cold buffet affair served in the elegant dining room (which doubles as a ballroom) or out on the terrace if the weather is fine. It's worth booking dinner too; the chef has been here for 20 years and turns out beautifully presented traditional French fare. And there's a glorious beamed and chandeliered sitting room for *apéritifs* or post supper brandies. The approach is gorgeous: from the picturesque town of St Etienne you drive through a woodland valley to arrive at this stately château ringed by verdant countryside with a formal knot garden and fountains. A friendly, laid back feel pervades and the best of the Loire is on your doorstep.

Rooms	2 doubles, 12 twin/doubles: €145-€309. 2 suites for 2: €195-€389. 8 family rooms for 3: €259-€345. Extra single bed available in some rooms €40 p.p. per night; free for children.
Meals	Breakfast €23.
Closed	Never.

Tel	+33 (0)2 47 55 38 71
Mobile	+33 (0)2 47 55 50 11
Email	beauvois@younancollection.com
Web	www.younancollection.com

Le Réception
Château de Beauvois,
Route de Beauvois,
37230 Saint Etienne de Chigny,
Indre-et-Loire

ENTRY 287 MAP 4

Domaine des Bidaudières

Sylvie and Pascal have made their mark on this classic, pale-stone former winegrower's property. Now helped by their son, they produce a small quantity of wine from their vineyard on the terraced land above the house while cypress trees standing on the hillside behind give it an Italian feel. Sylvie, casually elegant and outgoing, lends sophistication to the whole place not least the bedrooms – fresh, carpeted and contemporary, each decorated in Designers Guild fabric. Some are light, south-facing and have valley views, while the very private suite, once a cave dwelling, is delightfully rustic in character – and has a private terrace for the views. The den-like sitting room, cosy with a wood-burner in the old fireplace (and a billiard table) is also hewn out of the rock. Enjoy breakfast in the stone-flagged conservatory, then while away the afternoon by the splendid south-facing swimming pool on the lower terrace next to the orangerie (you can reach the pool by the lift in the main house). Sun beds are separated by small bushes for privacy and every detail is given attention.

Rooms	4 doubles, 1 twin: €130-€150.
	1 suite for 3: €150.
	1 apartment for 4: €170.
	1 cottage for 4: €180.
	1 bothy for 4: €150.
Meals	Restaurants 2km-15km.
Closed	Rarely.

Pascal & Sylvie Suzanne
Domaine des Bidaudières,
Rue du Peu Morier, 37210 Vouvray,
Indre-et-Loire

Tel	+33 (0)2 47 52 66 85
Mobile	+33 (0)6 07 79 25 31
Email	contact@bidaudieres.com
Web	www.bidaudieres.com

Château des Arpentis

This superb neo-Gothic château (with 14th-century origins) lies just outside Amboise, yet you are immersed in countryside: the grounds are vast and secluded. Behind, a cliff face is hewn with caves, one of which has become a family suite: sensational, like something out of a fairy tale. To the front: the view! From a sward of lawn and an elegant pool (accessed by a tunnel) the eye is drawn to a lake shrouded by woodland and explored via a riddle of trails. A sense of the regal pervades the interiors; and, as befitting an old hunting lodge, there are hunting trophies in some of the corridors. A cosy guest sitting room feeds into a billiard room (each with a magnificent painted fireplace); the sunny dining room, opening to the terrace, exudes an elegant simplicity and is a beautiful backdrop for breakfast. Each bedroom is marvellous, including a huge raftered suite with its tower annexe and in-room tub. All have gorgeous furnishings, gleaming bathrooms, views over the grounds. Sylvie Suzanne (the owner, and great fun) spends a lot of time here; unsurprisingly, she can't keep away.

Rooms	9 doubles: €140-€210.
	2 suites for 4: €230-€395.
	2 family rooms for 2: €160-€205.
	1 apartment for 5: €355.
Meals	Restaurants 3km.
Closed	Rarely.

Tel	+33 (0)2 47 23 00 00	
Mobile	+33 (0)6 07 79 25 31	
Email	contact@chateaudesarpentis.com	
Web	www.chateaudesarpentis.com	

Pascal & Sylvie Suzanne
Château des Arpentis,
37530 Saint Règle,
Indre-et-Loire

ENTRY 289 MAP 4

La Mère Hamard

Watch the world from your window, the locals clutching their baguettes on their way home. Two pretty townhouses in the centre of a quiet little village, this has been a restaurant-hotel since it was bought in 1903 by a remarkable widow, Madame Hamard, who built up an excellent reputation – Parisian actors loved it and the Duke of Windsor passed by. New owners Alice and Olivier have a gastronomic background and are full of energy and enthusiasm. They've already redecorated the restaurant in restful, contemporary tones – bedrooms are next but all are spotless, comfortable and attractive. The two big ground-floor rooms are tasteful; upstairs there are pale walls and light, bright fabrics; the two smallest rooms under the roof are charming in simple country style; the 'chalet' room over the restaurant is completely different with its wood-slatted walls, and cheerful checked fabrics. Another reason to stay is the seriously good food, traditional with original touches. It's popular with the locals so book your table at weekends. An excellent place to start a family holiday or spend a few days exploring the area. *Parking on-site. Storage available for guests' bikes and golf bags.*

Rooms	7 twin/doubles: €93-€99. 4 family rooms for 4: €128-€158. Dinner, B&B €206-€232 p.p. Extra bed/sofabed €20 p.p. per night.
Meals	Breakfast €14; children €9. Lunch €24. Dinner €35-€69. Restaurant closed Sunday evenings 15 October-15 April. Restaurants 5km.
Closed	Never.

Alice & Olivier Loize
La Mère Hamard,
37360 Semblançay,
Indre-et-Loire

Tel	+33 (0)2 47 56 62 04
Email	reservation@lamerehamard.com
Web	www.lamerehamard.com

Le Fleuray Hôtel & Restaurant

The Newington family hotel is a haven of peace surrounded by fields and grazing cows. The basics at Le Fleuray are ideal: a solid, handsome old manor house with duck pond and barns, mature trees and bushes, swimming pool, hot tub, tennis, kid's park and bikes – all that's needed. Then there's the country-house mood: lightly floral sofas into which you can sink, bookcases, prints and flowers. The rooms in the converted barns are just right for families; slightly cut off from the rest, they have French windows opening onto the garden so each has an individual patio. Those in the main building are a bit smaller but cosy and spotless, with queen-size beds. In summer, you can dine on the terrace. In winter, apéritifs are served in front of a log fire. A young French chef, who comes with quite a pedigree, produces a delicately inventive and well-presented cuisine; the restaurant is one of the most popular in the area. Expect a genuine welcome from family and staff – they know the best châteaux to visit and some lovely walks. Amboise is a short hop away.

Rooms	9 twin/doubles: €78-€168. 2 suites for 6: €188-€260. 12 family rooms for 5: €128-€218.
Meals	Breakfast €15; children €9. Dinner €29-€39; children from €16. Wine €18-€24.
Closed	4 November – 20 November, 23 December – 26 December.

Tel	+33 (0)2 47 56 09 25
Email	contact@lefleurayhotel.com
Web	www.lefleurayhotel.com

Newington Family
Le Fleuray Hôtel & Restaurant,
Fleuray, 37530 Cangey-Amboise,
Indre-et-Loire

ENTRY 291 MAP 4

La Louisière

Simplicity, character and a genuine welcome make La Louisière special. Madame, natural and unpretentious, is a great hostess and knows lots about the local area. The traditional bedrooms have well-chosen colour schemes and neat-as-a-pin bathrooms; touches of fun, too. Surrounded by chestnut trees, the farmhouse backs onto the gardens of the château and is wonderfully quiet; beautiful Ronsard roses climb up the walls of the cart shed and there are eggs to collect from Madame's hens. Tennis nearby, bikes, tractors, horses and an old-fashioned playground – it's bliss for children and a fuss free atmosphere for parents.

La Falotière

A cave suite! Hewn long ago into the rock beside a bell-topped presbytery, deliciously cool and light, it's a spacious retreat. Step from private courtyard to sitting room with big fireplace and old bread oven, smart wicker chairs, red lamps, tiled floors. Burrow through to a cushioned, red-carpeted bedroom sculpted into whitewashed rock; soak in a theatrical free-standing bath. Locals and walkers, your delightful hosts serve home-laid eggs at breakfast, enjoy sharing their lovely shady garden and this intriguing town, wedged in a gully ten minutes from Tours amid the Loire's vineyards and châteaux. Private, unique, fantastic. *Minimum stay: 2 nights in high season.*

Rooms	1 double: €65. 1 triple: €83. 1 suite for 5: €119. Singles €55-€65. Extra bed/sofabed €18 p.p. per night.
Meals	Auberge 800m (Tuesday/Thursday only & Friday lunch). Restaurants 10km.
Closed	Rarely.

Rooms	1 suite for 2: €130.
Meals	Restaurant 150m.
Closed	Rarely.

Tel	+33 (0)2 47 24 42 24
Email	andree.campion@orange.fr
Web	www.louisiere.racan.org

Andrée Campion
La Louisière,
37360 Beaumont la Ronce,
Indre-et-Loire

Mobile	+33 (0)6 50 65 41 49
Email	jpdanderieux@gmail.com
Web	www.falotiere.com

Dominique & Jean-Pierre Danderieux
La Falotière,
51 rue du Docteur Lebled,
37210 Rochecorbon, Indre-et-Loire

Bagatelle

A graceful 18th-century house in a charming setting close to the famous white wine vineyards of Vouvray. Lena and her young family moved from Paris and love their new home. Choose between rooms in the house or memorable ones carved into the stone cliff outside. All have painted furniture and art; the main suite has wonderful views over the garden. Wake to breakfast in the elegant dining room or outside in the sunshine: fresh juice, pastries, local yogurt, perhaps ham, cheese and eggs. Roam the garden, enjoy the large pool, and head out for Tour market, Loire canoeing, Beauval zoo and Lulu Parc.

Château de Nazelles

A charming 16th-century manor house in the centre of the village with a shady courtyard and a winding track leading to woodlands and vineyards. House and garden are an exuberant mix of formal and informal, contemporary and traditional. Steps and pathways entice you through a series of 'secret' gardens, doorways cut in high hedges offer intriguing glimpses of the Loire valley. Rooms are a delight, furnished with simple understated elegance to fully show off the character of the house and the breakfast room is serene with a low, beamed ceiling. Great breakfasts, delightful hosts; even the pool is special. *Access to the drive is quite narrow.*

Rooms	1 double: €95. 4 suites for 2: €130-€150. Extra bed/sofabed €20 p.p. per night. 20% off your room rate from the 3rd night.
Meals	Restaurants 15-minute walk.
Closed	Christmas, New Year.

Rooms	4 doubles: €115-€160. 2 suites for 4: €240-€320. Extra bed/sofabed €30 p.p. per night.
Meals	Summer kitchen. Restaurants 3km.
Closed	Rarely.

Mobile	+33 (0)6 62 45 46 16
Email	lena.lebras@gmail.com
Web	www.bagatelle-vouvray.com/en/

Léna Le Bras
Bagatelle,
77 rue du Petit Coteau,
37210 Vouvray, Indre-et-Loire

Tel	+33 (0)2 47 30 53 79
Email	info@chateau-nazelles.com
Web	www.chateau-nazelles.com

Véronique & Olivier Fructus
Château de Nazelles,
16 rue Tue-La-Soif,
37530 Nazelles, Indre-et-Loire

Manoir de la Maison Blanche

Woods, fields and giant sequoias surround this historic property on the edge of town. Stroll up to the paddock to find friendly ponies and llamas to pat – Lulu the big house dog is very gentle too. B&B rooms are divided between two long low houses separated by a furnished courtyard: a family suite on one side, two doubles on the other. (One is on the ground-floor, the other under the roof.) Breakfast, served in a pleasant communal room with five tables, includes two kinds of brioche and bread and homemade jams. Walk into pretty Amboise – it takes about 20 minutes. People travel far for its Sunday market, and its château, commanding a spur above the Loire. Leonardo da Vinci visited in 1515 and stayed until his death in 1519; from here, Francois I launched the French Renaissance.

Château de Pintray

Instant charm at the end of the long leafy avenue. This intimate château glows with personality and peculiarity yet this is no museum-piece: delightful Anne looks after the B&B while Jean Christophe produces some of the region's best sweet and dry white wines; enjoy the tastings. Stuffed full of character, bedrooms have super comfy beds on carpeted floors and bathrooms big old roll top tubs and walk-in showers. Tuck in to a splendid breakfast at the convivial table – alongside the Guignol puppet theatre! – before setting off for the great châteaux: Chenonceau, Amboise, Villandry and Azay le Rideau, all within an hour's drive.

Rooms	2 doubles: €102.		**Rooms**	2 doubles: €115.
	1 suite for 4: €128. Singles €91.			1 family room for 4: €115-€165.
	Extra bed/sofabed €26 p.p. per		**Meals**	Restaurant 2km.
	night.		**Closed**	Rarely.
Meals	Guest kitchenette.			
Closed	Rarely.			

Tel	+33 (0)6 88 89 33 66		**Tel**	+33 (0)2 47 23 22 84
Email	annick.delecheneau@wanadoo.fr		**Email**	marius.rault@wanadoo.fr
Web	www.lamaisonblanche-fr.com		**Web**	www.chateau-de-pintray.com

Annick Delécheneau
Manoir de la Maison Blanche,
18 rue de l'Epinetterie,
37400 Amboise, Indre-et-Loire

Anne Ricou & Jean Christophe Rault
Château de Pintray,
RD 283, Lussault sur Loire,
37400 Amboise, Indre-et-Loire

Le Clos de Fontenay

Sweep up the wooded drive to the formal garden to be greeted by Madame, or one of her grown-up children brushing up their English... and know you have entered an enchanting place. The graceful château sits in wooded splendour on the banks of the Cher – and you can see it the river from the suitably châteauesque bedrooms. Breakfast well on a wisteria-shaded terrace by the pool, or in the elegant dining room where you can tuck into a rather fine dinner too. Borrow bikes (masses to see within pedalling distance), play billiards in the fab games room or just have a wander: it's the most relaxed of places.

Manoir de Chaix

Up a quiet lane, embraced by woodland and fields, an exceedingly fine manor house with dovecot, orchard, barn, pool and flourishing potager. Friendly Dominique welcomes you in, and treats you to a wonderful table d'hôtes. Spacious beamed bedrooms – four reached via a stone turret stair – are full of traditional comfort, and the dining room is inviting, with blazing logs, light-flooded windows and a great big convivial table. This is the Loire and there are châteaux by the hatful: Chenonceau, Loches, Amboise, Azay le Rideau, Villandry. A great find, and good value. *Pets by arrangement.*

Rooms	2 twin/doubles; 2 doubles with separate bathroom: €99-€179. Extra bed €30. Cot and highchair free of charge.		**Rooms**	2 doubles, 1 twin: €80-€85. 1 family room for 4: €85-€130. 1 triple: €100-€120.	
Meals	Restaurants 5km.		**Meals**	Dinner with wine, €27. Restaurants 5km.	
Closed	Rarely.		**Closed**	Rarely.	

Tel	+33 (0)2 47 57 12 74		**Tel**	+33 (0)2 47 43 42 73
Email	contact@lechateaudefontenay.fr		**Email**	manoirdechaix@sfr.fr
Web	www.lechateaudefontenay.fr		**Web**	www.manoir-de-chaix.com

Nathalie Carli
Le Clos de Fontenay,
5 Fontenay,
37150 Bléré, Indre-et-Loire

Dominique Casaromani-Fillon
Manoir de Chaix,
Lieu dit Chaix,
37320 Truyes, Indre-et-Loire

ENTRY 298   MAP 4

ENTRY 299   MAP 4

Cèdre et Charme

Château du Vau

A treat! Lively, intelligent conversation, good food and music in elegant surroundings. The du Garreaus love sharing their fine 19th-century townhouse with its big bosky garden, and helping guests discover the riches of Touraine and the Loire Valley. Bright, serenely stylish bedrooms, with excellent bedding and bathrooms, are a seamless blend of period and modern (two inter-connect). The table – outdoors or in – is beautifully dressed for friendly meals focused on regional and homemade food. Children can eat separately and romp safely; there's an enticing, enclosed pool to look forward to – after a châteaux-cycling day?

At the end of a long bumpy drive is a house of great character run with good humour: delightful philosopher Bruno has turned his family château into a stylish refuge for travellers. Two large, light bedrooms have been redecorated with seagrass and family memorabilia round splendid brass bedsteads; others remain, very comfortably, in their traditional, distinguished garb. And then there are the beautifully crafted treehouses: oriental in the oak tree, African in the cedar, breakfast hampers delivered at the end of a rope... Dinners showcase estate produce. There's a fine pool, and a golf course opposite. With 118 hectares of grounds it is very hard to imagine that you're only 15 minutes from Tours. On fine summer evenings take a supper tray à la Glyndebourne to a favourite corner of the vast grounds.

Rooms	2 doubles, 3 twin/doubles: €125. Singles €115. Extra bed/sofabed €20-€30 p.p. per night. Cot €10 per night. Interlinking rooms can be booked together for families.
Meals	Dinner with wine, €20-€30.
Closed	Never.

Rooms	3 doubles: €130-€140. 1 family room for 4: €175-€190. 2 treehouses for 2: €100-€140. 1 triple: €175. Extra bed/sofabed €30 p.p. per night.
Meals	Restaurants nearby.
Closed	Rarely.

Mobile	+33 (0)6 32 15 19 31
Email	contact@cedre-et-charme.fr
Web	www.cedre-et-charme.fr

Anne du Garreau
Cèdre et Charme,
17 Grand Rue, 37320 Saint Branchs,
Indre-et-Loire

Tel	+33 (0)2 47 67 84 04
Email	info@chateau-du-vau.com
Web	www.chateau-du-vau.com

Bruno Clément
Château du Vau,
37510 Ballan Miré,
Indre-et-Loire

ENTRY 300 MAP 4

ENTRY 301 MAP 4

Le Chat Courant

A handsome 18th-century family house on the river Cher just opposite Villandry and with its own lovely garden (whose birdsong drowns out occasional train noise). Bedrooms are pretty and stylish: the double in the converted cottage opens to the swimming pool, the suite in the main house has fine antique furniture. Éric – who is also a keen photographer – has created garden enchantment here with old species of apple trees, a walled vegetable garden, a wisteria-clad pergola, a formal boxed flower garden, and a semi-wild garden beyond, all surrounded by woodland and pasture where the families' horses peacefully graze.

La Chancellerie

Bernard and Claire have a real sense of hospitality and love their charming old manor house, backed by trees and lawns, fronted by pretty parterres. Talented musicians, they host concerts and masterclasses too (note the five pianos!). Bedrooms lie in the more humble wing but the family suite is in the house – large and lofty with a splendid stone fireplace. All is immaculate, the food is delicious, there are wine tastings in the cellars (the best local bottles) and beautiful Chinon is a 15-minute drive. Swim in the nearby river or in your friendly hosts' heated pool; hire canoes and float down the Vienne. *Parking on-site.*

Rooms	1 double: €85-€90.
	1 family room for 5: €120-€195.
Meals	Restaurant 5-minute drive.
Closed	Rarely.

Rooms	3 doubles: €100-€120.
	1 suite for 2, 1 suite for 5: €135-€220.
Meals	Dinner, 2-4 courses with wine, €23-€37. Restaurants 1km.
Closed	Rarely.

Tel	+33 (0)2 47 50 06 94
Email	infos@le-chat-courant.com
Web	www.le-chat-courant.com

Éric Gaudouin
Le Chat Courant,
37510 Villandry,
Indre-et-Loire

Tel	+33 (0)2 47 95 46 76
Email	info@lachancellerie.com
Web	www.lachancellerie.com

Claire & Bertrand Pelourdeau
La Chancellerie,
37420 Huismes,
Indre-et-Loire

ENTRY 302   MAP 4

ENTRY 303   MAP 4

La Pénesais

Michèle and Jean-Jacques are the best kind of urban refugees. They retired early from high-stress jobs in Paris after falling in love with this elegant house in a wonderful, less-beaten part of the Loire Valley. Warm and fascinating, they will communicate their love of this new life over delicious breakfast of fruit salad, homemade cakes and jams, or homely French dinner. There's a comfortable grey and red salon, most attractive with its throws and cushions and fine stone fireplace. Then, up a colourful staircase are excellent bedrooms. The airy first-floor rooms give onto the pretty courtyard, the quirky rooms under the eaves have great tree-trunk rafters and share a stylish bathroom. Visit châteaux, vineyards and wonderful Fontevraud Abbey, go kayaking or cycling from Chinon. *Min. stay: 2 nights at weekends & in high season.*

La Closerie Saint Martin

Katharina, Marcel and Fado the dog offer a tranquil retreat in their historic home, once part of the local monastery. In a wine-growing hamlet, five peaceful rooms from classic to contemporary, four-poster to panelled chalet-style, all mellow colours and white linen, period pieces and cosy fabrics. Bathrooms are fresh and modern. Bountiful breakfasts with home-made cake, yoghurt and fresh fruit are taken at one table in the airy dining room. Markets and châteaux are nearby; rent a bike or walk the Nature Park; read a book, visit the vegetable garden. Eat out or in: dinners start with a drink in the impressive wine cellar.

Rooms	2 doubles: €105-€115. 1 suite for 4: €165-€180.
Meals	Dinner, 3 courses, €26. Wine list available. Restaurants 5km.
Closed	Rarely.

Rooms	4 doubles, 1 twin/double: €80-€100. Discount for stays of 2+ nights. Extra bed/sofabed €25 p.p. per night.
Meals	Dinner with wine, apéritif & coffee, €32. Restaurants 10km.
Closed	Rarely.

Tel	+33 (0)2 47 95 34 22
Email	lapenesais@orange.fr
Web	www.lapenesais.fr

Michèle et Jean-Jacques Lejeune
La Pénesais,
6 rue de la Maison de Pierre,
37420 Beaumont en Véron, Indre-et-Loire

Tel	+33 (0)2 47 58 17 24
Email	info@lacloseriesaintmartin.fr
Web	www.lacloseriesaintmartin.fr

Katharina Hirt
La Closerie Saint Martin,
6 rue du Prieure, Les Roches Saint Paul,
37500 Ligré, Indre-et-Loire

ENTRY 304 MAP 4

ENTRY 305 MAP 9

Le Clos de Ligré

This elegant country house sings in a subtle harmony of traditional charm and contemporary chic under Martine's modern touch. Sponged walls, creamy beams and eye-catching fabrics breathe new life into rooms with old tiled floors and stone fireplaces, and the bedrooms on the second floor are great, with views over the huge garden. Windows are flung open to let in the light and the stresses of city living are forgotten in cheerful, easy conversations with your hostess, who joins guests for candlelit dinners. Bookcases, baby grand, buffet breakfasts at individual tables, a pool for the energetic... delightful.

Château de la Celle Guenand

In the heart of an old Touraine village, four hectares of delightful walled park and a fairytale castle that dates from 1442. It's large but not palatial, grand but not ornate, and refreshingly unstuffy. Much is being updated, everything is charming, and Stephen is putting all his energies into his new project. You get top mattresses on king-size beds, bedrooms with beautifully proportioned windows (cool conservative shades for the newest) and delicious quince jams at breakfast. After dinner: brocade sofas in faded reds, books to browse and a piano to play. All this, châteaux by the hatful, and the Brenne National Park. *Children over 6 welcome. Pets by arrangement.*

Rooms	2 doubles: €110.
	1 family room for 3: €110-€145.
Meals	Dinner with wine, €35.
Closed	Rarely.

Rooms	4 doubles: €120-€190.
	1 family room for 5: €160-€190.
Meals	Hosted dinner, 4 courses with wine, €48; children over 16, €30; under 16, €20. Restaurant in village.
Closed	1 October – 1 May.

Tel	+33 (0)2 47 93 95 59
Email	descamps.ligre@gmail.com
Web	www.le-clos-de-ligre.com

Martine Descamps
Le Clos de Ligré,
Le Rouilly,
37500 Ligré, Indre-et-Loire

Tel	+33 (0)2 47 94 93 61
Email	stephane@chateaucelleguenand.com
Web	www.chateaucelleguenand.biz

Stephen Palluel
Château de la Celle Guenand,
14 rue du Château,
37350 La Celle Guenand, Indre-et-Loire

ENTRY 306 MAP 9

ENTRY 307 MAP 9

Saint Victor La Grand' Maison

The 16th-century château bursts into view from its wooded hilltop, tall turrets and ivy-clad façade towering over the river Anglin. You can saunter down here past the pool and picnic on organic pâté under a 400-year-old oak; just water, trees and birdsong. Inside, read by the fire, tinkle on the baby grand, retire to bed. Deeply comfortable rooms in warm reds, blues and pastels have museum-worthy antiques, plush fabrics, gilt portraits, book-lined walls. Hugely friendly, Madame offers tastings, courses and talks by local savants – and there are gîtes in the grounds. "Simply a delight" says our inspector, "for anybody at all." *Pets by arrangement.*

Domaine du Ris de Feu

No longer part of a defensive frontier of castles, this 15th-century manor and lake is a sanctuary swathed in lush forest. The domain is the pride and joy of Caroline, who runs it to the highest eco and ethical standards, and husband Luc. Artisan builders (still discreetly on site) have restored using natural materials and traditional craft. Your charming fruit loft, on two floors, has oval windows, oak fittings and a wood-burner; upstairs, drift off under organic linen. After breakfast in the old bakery, wander and enjoy, listen to the birdlife, bathe in the lake, hire canoes or bicycles... explore this enchanted kingdom!

Rooms	2 doubles: €135-€138; rooms interconnect to form a suite for 4: €200. 1 suite for 2: €150-€155. Tourist tax €0.60 p.p. per night (B&B only); €3-€4.50 per day per house depending on occupancy.
Meals	Dinner €20. Wine €8-€20. Restaurant 1.5km.
Closed	Christmas, 7 January – 31 March.

Rooms	1 suite for 2: €105-€125.
Meals	Dinner from €35 (not Saturdays). Restaurant 900m.
Closed	Rarely.

Tel	+33 (0)2 54 37 46 55
Email	marie@saintvictorlagrandmaison.fr
Web	www.saintvictorlagrandmaison.fr

Marie Rouet Grandclément
Saint Victor La Grand' Maison,
36300 Ingrandes,
Indre

Tel	+33 (0)2 54 37 87 73
Email	contact@lerisdefeu.fr
Web	www.lerisdefeu.fr

Luc & Caroline Fontaine
Domaine du Ris de Feu,
36370 Chalais,
Indre

ENTRY 308   MAP 9

ENTRY 309   MAP 9

Le Manoir du Menoux

La Croix Verte

In the heart of a quiet village, through a formal French garden, is a pretty half-timbered house with a Normandy air. Pleasant Marie-Estelle is a straightforward lady with a quiet smile, serving breakfast around a large oak table in the dining room, or outside in summer. Sit listening to the gurgling stream down by the charming summerhouse; in chillier weather, the salons' daybeds make a comfy spot. Up the winding oak staircase are the light and luminous suite 'Diane', southern-coloured 'Manon' gazing over romantic rooftops, and 50s-feel 'Amélie'. Visit snail and chestnut fêtes, and Lac d'Eguzon for nautical things. Lovely.

Vincent and Élisabeth's serene home lies plumb in the heart of George Sand country. Linger under lime trees in a secret courtyard garden while relishing a plentiful breakfast; enjoy a dinner of home-grown produce; get cosy in the family sitting room before an open fire. A staging post in the 12th century, La Croix Verte stands in the heart of the village but you won't hear a peep as you slumber under a hand-stitched bedcover; the three charming loft bedrooms in natural tones share sofas, books and games. Come for heaps of character, unspoilt countryside, and artist hosts (potter and painter) who are an absolute delight.

Rooms	2 doubles: €70-€80.
	1 suite for 4: €97-€134.
Meals	Restaurant within walking
	distance.
Closed	Christmas & New Year.

Rooms	2 doubles, 1 twin: €70.
	Singles €60. Extra bed/sofabed
	€30 p.p. per night.
Meals	Dinner with wine, €25.
	Restaurant 1.5km.
Closed	Rarely.

Tel	+33 (0)2 36 27 91 87
Email	rivesme@wanadoo.fr
Web	www.manoirdumenoux.com

Marie-Estelle Rives
Le Manoir du Menoux,
15 rue Haute,
36200 Le Menoux, Indre

Tel	+33 (0)2 54 31 02 71
Email	lacroixverte36400@gmail.com
Web	www.maisonlacroixverte.com

Élisabeth & Vincent Portier
La Croix Verte,
12 rue des Maîtres Sonneurs,
36400 St Chartier, Indre

ENTRY 310   MAP 9

ENTRY 311   MAP 10

Château de la Villette

More pretty 19th-century hunting lodge than grand château, la Villette sits in 40 idyllic acres of parkland, close to a huge spring-fed lake: borrow the row boat and potter. Capable, hospitable, generous Karin – dynamic gardener, fine cook – loves and cares for each inch of the place. A winding staircase leads to a beauty of a bedroom done in Biedermeier style, with a sloping ceiling and serene views; the second room too is seductive. Feather duvets will cosset you, elegant breakfasts and dinners at the convent table will delight you, and nothing is too much trouble for Karin. *Minimum stay: 2 nights.*

Le Petit Château De Sainte Colombe

Soak up gracious touches of old rural France in this 15th-century château. Bedrooms exude romance and are festooned with antiques, religious statues and huge oils – from modest 'Tour Carré', reached from the terrace, to 'Jeanne d'Arc' overlooking the pretty courtyard. Fashion designer Anastasia has a keen eye, and velvet throws, soft quilts and big pillows abound. Breakfast in a sunny room on a long table, and dine on regional specialities, or try a plate of charcuterie and cheeses. Masses to do in the Loire Valley: weekly markets, famous châteaux, hot air ballooning; return for sundowners and barbecues in the summer kitchen. *Pets by arrangement.*

Rooms	1 double; 1 double with separate bathroom: €95. Singles €65.
Meals	Dinner with wine, €25.
Closed	Rarely.

Rooms	4 doubles: €75-€95. 1 suite for 4: €160. Extra bed/sofabed €10 p.p. per night.
Meals	Dinner with wine, €25. Child €12. Restaurants 3.5km.
Closed	15 November – 15 March.

Tel	+33 (0)2 54 36 28 46
Mobile	+33 (0)6 23 67 39 78

Karin Verburgh
Château de la Villette,
St Août,
36120 Ardentes, Indre

Tel	+33 (0)2 54 35 88 33
Email	info@chateaustecolombe.com
Web	www.chateaustecolombe.com

Anastasia Backstrand
Le Petit Château De Sainte Colombe,
36110 Bouges Le Chateau,
Indre

ENTRY 312   MAP 10

ENTRY 313   MAP 10

La Trolière

The beautifully proportioned house in its big shady garden has been in the family for over 200 years. The sitting room is a cool blue-grey symphony, the dining room smart yellow-grey with a rare, remarkable maroon and grey marble table: breakfast is in here, dinner, sometimes en famille, always delicious, is in the big beamed kitchen. Each stylishly comfortable room has individual character and Madame has a fine eye for detail. She is charming, dynamic, casually elegant and has many cats. Visitors have poured praise: "quite the most beautiful house we've ever stayed in"; "the evening meals were superb".

Château de Preuil

This Napoleonic mansion feels friendly despite its imposing columns and ornate ceilings – Pierre will introduce you to his horses while Marie whips up rum cocktails and Creole samosas from her native Réunion. Big, airy bedrooms have oak floors and garden views across the 51 acres of wildflower-speckled meadows. Marie's 12 varieties of hens provide eggs for breakfast – served in the dining room under a Murano glass chandelier or out on the terrace. You can chat or read in the sitting room or whack a ball about on the tennis courts. Hop on the motorway to visit pretty, half-timbered Bourges or tour markets – both flea and food – in Saint-Amand-Montrond. Spend a day leisurely gliding the canals in an electric boat; dip a toe in the bassin on your return should you be inspired to swim.

Rooms	4 doubles: €65-€85. Singles €61-€81. Extra bed/sofabed €10 p.p. per night.		**Rooms**	4 doubles: €110-€130.	
Meals	Dinner with wine, minimum 4 guests, €27-€30. No table d'hôtes on Tuesdays.		**Meals**	Dinner €35, available by arrangement. Restaurants 6km.	
Closed	Rarely.		**Closed**	Rarely.	

Tel +33 (0)2 48 96 47 45
Email marie-claude.dussert@orange.fr
Web www.chambreshoteslatroliere.com

Marie-Claude Dussert
La Trolière,
18200 Orval,
Cher

Email preuil@orange.fr
Web www.chateaudepreuil.fr

Pierre & Marie Ducas
Château de Preuil,
18190 Vallenay,
Cher

ENTRY 314   MAP 10

ENTRY 315   MAP 10

Les Bonnets Rouges

Cross the garden courtyard to the ancient, peaceful coaching inn where Stendhal once laid his head. Beyond the breakfast room, where 15th-century timbers, wraparound oak panels and stone alcoves dance in mixed-up glory for breakfast amid Turkish rugs, is the staircase up. Three bedrooms, wonderfully quaint and nicely tatty, have antique beds (one a four-poster), new mattresses, hanging rails, perhaps a roll top bath. Up steeper, narrower stairs, a pretty attic double has festoons of beams and the loo behind a curtain. Your charming host, Olivier, lives just across the courtyard. Sleep among angels beneath Bourges' unsurpassed cathedral.
Pets by arrangement.

Les Aubuées

In a peaceful street overlooking lush meadows, sheltered by old walls and surrounded by trees, is an 1850s maison de maître, a Belle Epoque residence; the first view takes your breath away. Little Toto and Chopin wag their welcome, followed by smiling Pascale. In big bedrooms on the first floor, wood, linen, silk and cotton blend with antique pieces and a luxurious modern feel pervades. Borrow the bikes, visit Sancerre and the cathedral at Bourges, return to a secluded courtyard and a delicious pool. Breakfast, served under the Napoleonic chandelier, is divine: Pascale, warm hostess, is a skilled pastry chef.

Rooms	2 doubles: €76-€78. 2 suites for 4: €132. Singles €67-€85. Extra bed/sofabed €22 p.p. per night.	**Rooms**	1 suite for 2, 1 suite for 4: €93-€140.
Meals	Restaurants within walking distance.	**Meals**	Restaurant 5km.
Closed	Rarely.	**Closed**	Rarely.

Tel   +33 (0)2 48 65 79 92
Email   contact@bonnetsrouges-bourges.fr
Web   www.bonnetsrouges-bourges.fr

Olivier Llopis
Les Bonnets Rouges,
3 rue de la Thaumassière,
18000 Bourges, Cher

Tel   +33 (0)2 48 57 08 24
Email   les.aubuees@gmail.com
Web   www.lesaubuees.fr

Pascale & Benoît Portier
Les Aubuées,
51 route de Montcorneau,
18500 Mehun sur Yèvre, Cher

ENTRY 316   MAP 10

ENTRY 317   MAP 10

Domaine du Château de Moison

A creamy chateau set in lush lawns, shaded by tall trees and given a lavish renovation by the owner's talented designer daughter Adele de La Palme. In the dining room find a full size stag of reclaimed wood twinned with an 18th-century hunting tapestry. The bedrooms, boldly themed around the graphics of artist René Gruau, have generous beds and state of the art gleaming bathrooms. Breakfast on the terrace or in the airy conservatory. Feel at home in the elegant salons, play the concert piano, watch the giant TV or wander the acres of garden. Book a meal with Bruno and discover his fine wines. This gem deserves more than an overnight stay.

La Verrerie

Deep countryside, fine people, fantastic bedrooms. In a pretty outbuilding, the double, with a green iron bedhead, old tiled floor and Provençal quilt, looks onto the garden from the ground floor; the suite's twin has the same tiles underfoot, beams overhead and high wooden beds with an inviting mix of white covers and red quilts. The Count and Countess, who manage forests, farm and hunt, enjoy doing B&B, they are charming and thoroughly hospitable. If you would like to dine in, you will join them for dinner in the main house. Members of the family run a vineyard in Provence, so try their wine.
Minimum stay: 2 nights at weekends.

Rooms	4 doubles: €150-€225. 1 family room for 4: €230-€260.		**Rooms**	1 double: €80. 2 family rooms for 4: €102-€156. Extra bed/sofabed €27 p.p. per night.
Meals	Dinner with coffee, €30-€35. Child €10. Restaurants 18km.		**Meals**	Dinner with wine, €22-€32. Guest kitchen. Restaurants 10km.
Closed	Rarely.		**Closed**	Rarely.

Mobile	+33 (0)6 20 65 03 83		**Tel**	+33 (0)2 48 58 90 86
Email	bdelapalme@gmail.com		**Email**	m.desaporta@wanadoo.fr
			Web	www.laverreriedivoy.com

Bruno de La Palme
Domaine du Château de Moison,
18380 Ivoy le Pré,
Cher

Étienne & Marie de Saporta
La Verrerie,
18380 Ivoy le Pré,
Cher

Le Bouchot

Come not for luxury but for deep country authenticity – and to make friends with a generous, charming, free-thinking family who gave up Paris for this lush corner of France. They have restored, renovated and eco-converted a run-down farm, insulated it with hemp, wattle and daub, then added wood-burning stoves, organic breakfasts... and cats, dogs, horses, hens, donkeys. Family rooms in outbuildings round the courtyard are wood-clad with sloping ceilings, rudimentary furnishings, mix and match bed linen, the odd rug. Dinner is in the kitchen diner or in the conservatories. A place for new horizons.

Le Moutier

This fine traditional townhouse hides behind vast cedars on the edge of the village. Behind its walls lie warmth, exuberance, good humour, windows flung open to let in light and fresh air, and Jean-Lou's vibrant paintings. All feels friendly and unpretentious: a den-like sitting room, a comfy leather sofa, wonderful books, an open fire. Two bedrooms are in the main house, two are accessed via the studio, heaving with paintings and brushes. All this and a charming garden, throngs of fruit trees, a few loitering hens and, best of all, table d'hôtes at which food and wine flow. B&B at its best.

Rooms	2 family rooms for 3, 1 family room for 4, 1 family room for 5: €75-€135.	**Rooms**	4 doubles: €85. Singles €75. Dinner, B&B €30 p.p. Extra bed/sofabed €20 p.p. per night.
Meals	Dinner with wine, €25. Restaurant 2km.	**Meals**	Dinner with wine, €30.
Closed	Rarely.	**Closed**	Rarely.

Tel	+33 (0)2 54 88 01 00	**Tel**	+33 (0)2 54 75 20 48
Email	annebeaudubouchot@gmail.com	**Email**	lemoutier.coursaget@wanadoo.fr
Web	www.lebouchot.net	**Web**	www.chambresdhotesdumoutier.com

Anne & Jean-Philippe Beau-Douëzy
Le Bouchot,
Route de Chaon,
41300 Pierrefitte sur Sauldre, Loir-et-Cher

Martine & Jean-Lou Coursaget
Le Moutier,
13 rue de la République,
41110 Mareuil sur Cher, Loir-et-Cher

ENTRY 320 MAP 5

ENTRY 321 MAP 4

La Folie Saint Julien

The three buildings are classic Loire Valley; the well-tended garden, its pool-in-a-barn cleverly fitted into an 18th-century wine tank, and the soft new décor – lovely bedrooms and bathrooms – bring a sense of ease and elegance. And Madame is a wonderful hostess; add her culinary prowess and you have a travelling gourmet's treat. Breakfast is the freshest imaginable with marvellous pastries (Madame took a course...). Then walk it off exploring the glorious châteaux. You can book dinner, and they will love you if you drive a vintage car. For wine buffs, cyclists, château-lovers, here is a touch of luxury in a sea of vineyards. *Parking on-site.*

La Roseraie de Vrigny

White shutters, beams, old stones, comfortable bedrooms, organic potager, communal breakfasts and generous hosts – quintessential Sawday's. Rosalind, musician and philosopher, and John understand what B&B is all about and treat their guests as friends; sup with them on fine French food in the candlelit dining room and you will be charmed. The garden is entrancing too, all rambling roses, contemplative spots, even a little corner that is forever Scotland (like your hosts) and a Chinese bridge across a weeping-willow'd stream. Perfectly restful and welcoming after a day contemplating the glories of Chenonceau! *Minimum stay: 2 nights in high season.*

Rooms	3 doubles: €115-€130. 1 suite for 2, 1 suite for 4: €150-€235.
Meals	Dinner, 4 courses with apéritif & wine, €35, on request. Restaurants 2km.
Closed	Rarely.

Rooms	1 double; 1 double with separate bathroom: €76-€80. 1 family room for 4: €128-€154. Singles €70. Extra bed/sofabed €26.
Meals	Dinner €35. Restaurant 1km.
Closed	Rarely.

Tel	+33 (0)2 54 32 71 08
Email	contact@lafoliesaintjulien.com
Web	www.lafoliesaintjulien.com

Christine Sensenbrenner
La Folie Saint Julien,
8 route de La Vallée,
41400 Saint-Julien de Chédon, Loir-et-Cher

Mobile	+33 (0)7 60 45 99 14
Email	rosalind.rawnsley@gmail.com
Web	www.laroseraiedevrigny.com

Rosalind Rawnsley
La Roseraie de Vrigny,
3 rue du Ruisseau,
41400 St Georges sur Cher, Loir-et-Cher

ENTRY 322   MAP 4

ENTRY 323   MAP 4

Château de Nanteuil

Revered grand-mère's house has faded charm but no châteauesque style or opulence: a few crumbly bits outside, frescoes and trunks in the hall, antlers in the dining room, floral wallpapers, large wardrobes and marble fireplaces in the bedrooms. These are light-filled and unashamedly old-fashioned but there's soul; bathrooms are time-warp 70s; river-water murmurs below your window. Most of all, you'll enjoy Frédéric – he's refreshingly unfussy and occasionally mercurial. In summer sit on the terrace by the river. *Minimum stay: 2 nights.*

La Villa Médicis

Why the Italian name, the Italianate look? Queen Marie de Médicis used to take the waters here in the 17th century: the fine garden still has a hot spring and the Loire flows regally past behind the huge old trees. Muriel, a flower-loving perfectionist (artificial blooms as well as fresh), has let loose her decorative flair on the interior. It is unmistakably yet adventurously French in its splash of colours, lush fabrics and fine details. Fine antiques and brass beds grace some rooms, while the suite is a great 1930s surprise with a super-smart bathroom. You are wonderfully well looked after in this elegant and stylish house.

Rooms	2 doubles: €99-€110. 2 family rooms for 4: €99-€110. Extra person €20.
Meals	Restaurants within walking distance.
Closed	1 November – 1 April.

Rooms	2 twins: €72. 1 suite for 2: €99. 1 triple: €86.
Meals	Dinner with wine, €32.
Closed	In winter, except by arrangement.

Tel	+33 (0)2 54 42 61 98
Email	contact@chateau-nanteuil.com
Web	www.chateau-nanteuil.com

Frédéric Théry
Château de Nanteuil,
16 rue Nanteuil,
41350 Huisseau sur Cosson, Loir-et-Cher

ENTRY 324 MAP 4

Tel	+33 (0)2 54 74 46 38
Email	medicis.bienvenue@wanadoo.fr
Web	www.lavillamedicis.com

Muriel Cabin-Saint-Marcel
La Villa Médicis,
Macé, 41000 St Denis sur Loire,
Loir-et-Cher

ENTRY 325 MAP 4

Château de la Rue

This 1810 'Directoire' mansion, approached via a grand avenue of trees, is lived in and loved by adorable Madame, who has been doing B&B for years. The croissants are home baked, the fruits are from the orchard – a historic walled beauty – the bedrooms are handsome ('Mme de Segur' the smallest, 'Cassandre'; the most luxurious) and the furniture, all antique with the exception of some comfortable sofas, look as if it has been here forever. The Château de Chambord is close but best of all, you can cycle along the river to Blois (restaurants, market, château): the Loire flows at the end of the park.

La Cave Margot

The approach is pretty, along a green open valley, the family is charming, and the house is an immaculate longère. Bedrooms are large, inviting and contemporary, with original features and superb bathrooms. Two open to gardens and terrace, one is up an outside stair overlooking an ancient walnut tree, one overlooks the troglodyte caves and the last is a large wooden kota set among pine trees. For families, couples and seekers of peace: billiards, books, a warming wood-burner and communal kitchen. Table d'hôtes is great fun and dinners are delivered with enthusiasm and imagination; Nathalie grows organic vegetables for savoury crumbles and Nicolas loves his wines. *Minimum stay: 2 nights at weekends & in high season.*

Rooms	3 doubles: €120-€180. 2 suites for 4: €250. Cot €20.
Meals	Candlelit dinner with wine, €42; cold platter, €20 (without wine); possibility to prepare a picnic hamper or canapés and drinks. Restaurants 2km.
Closed	January – February.

Rooms	1 double: €92-€115. 2 suites for 4, 2 suites for 5: €115-€160. Extra bed/sofabed €15 p.p. per night.
Meals	Dinner with apéritif, €20-€30. Restaurant 12km.
Closed	1 November – 28 February.

Tel	+33 (0)2 54 46 82 47
Email	chateaudelarue@wanadoo.fr
Web	www.chateaudelarue.com

Véronique de Caix
Château de la Rue,
41500 Cour-sur-Loire,
Loir-et-Cher

Tel	+33 (0)2 54 72 09 53
Email	info@lacavemargot.fr
Web	www.lacavemargot.fr

Nathalie & Nicolas Leal
La Cave Margot,
41360 Lunay,
Loir-et-Cher

ENTRY 326 MAP 4

ENTRY 327 MAP 4

Le Clos de la Vigneronne

You're just a few minutes from the A10, on the edge of a small village and surrounded by open fields on one side, tall bushy trees on the other. The house, built in 1850, is made of beautiful old white stone and has red shutters to add Gallic charm. Béatrice and Regis give you rather sleek modern bedrooms, a continental breakfast at separate tables and a kitchen with a wood-burner for rainy days. There's a small lending library too. Sleep peacefully in the quiet then discover châteaux, museums, gardens, sporty stuff in spades, regional wines and farmers' markets for foodies, all from this unfussy family home.

Château La Touanne

Lush trees and elaborate gates frame the graceful façade. Nicolas and Christine's courteous informality permeates their peaceful 17th-century château. Downstairs, ancestral portraits survey antiques, gilt mirrors and fine porcelain in sitting room and salon. Breakfast in the stately dining room, where locally sourced table d'hôtes dinners are also held. Bedrooms are sumptuous: marble fireplaces, high ceilings, fine oak parquet. The terrace leads into parkland, farm, and an orchard hiding the heated pool. Stroll through meadows to explore bosky riverside paths, borrow a boat. An authentic family château, just 90 minutes from Paris.

Rooms	3 twin/doubles: €75-€115. 1 family room for 4: €125-€145. Extra bed/sofabed €25 p.p. per night.
Meals	Restaurants 5-minute drive.
Closed	Christmas, 3 January – 25 January.

Rooms	3 doubles, 1 twin/double: €130-€180. Singles €100-€150.
Meals	Dinner, homemade salad with wine, €25.
Closed	Rarely.

Mobile	+33 (0)6 87 04 65 46
Email	closdelavigneronne@gmail.com
Web	www.leclosdelavigneronne.com

Béatrice Ecosse
Le Clos de la Vigneronne,
19 rue de Villeneuve,
45190 Messas, Loiret

Tel	+33 (0)2 38 46 51 39
Email	nicolas.daboville@orange.fr
Web	www.chateau-latouanne.com

Nicolas & Christine d'Aboville
Château La Touanne,
45130 Baccon,
Loiret

La Feuillaie

Monsieur's 'light and aromatic' dinners are paired with Loire Valley wines and served at Madame's beautifully dressed table. Risen gloriously from ruin, your hosts' 18th-century home hides in rambling grounds amid a duck-filled lake and 40 species of trees. Eclectic objects catch the eye in soundproofed bedrooms: a sculpted elephant, grandma's lace, ornate wallpapers, claw-foot baths. After dinner, there's billiards or cards by the fire, a piano and literally hundreds of recipe and wine books. (Inspired? They run cooking courses.) Borrow a bike and follow the Loire from this charming village to châteaux, gardens and lakes.

Château de Denonville

In deep rural plains, beneath skyscapes to die for, two millennia of history are stacked up here and you sleep on 14th-century foundations. In their east wing the delightful, welcoming owners serve a superior continental breakfast by the stone fireplace; in the vaulted, tapestry-hung salon there are prints, clocks and collections to explore, myriad books and two pianos. Bedrooms, properly draped and swagged, have good modern bathrooms. The main 19th-century stately home and its great gardens are open to the public while you're out visiting Chartres, the Loire châteaux, even Paris – before coming back to this superb place. *Parking on-site.*

Rooms	4 doubles, 1 twin/double: €148-€180. Extra bed/sofabed €35 p.p. per night. Children under 2, €15. Cot available on request.	**Rooms**	2 doubles: €90. 1 suite for 2: €110-€140. 1 family room for 6: €110-€170. Extra bed €15.
Meals	Dinner, 3 courses with apéritif, wine & coffee, €55; children €17. Restaurants 2km.	**Meals**	Dinner, 4 courses with wine, €25; Sun only. Restaurants 10-minute drive.
Closed	Rarely.	**Closed**	Rarely.

Mobile	+33 (0)6 16 75 71 27	**Mobile**	+33 (0)6 73 18 77 37
Email	contact@lafeuillaie.com	**Email**	chateau.denonville@gmail.com
Web	www.lafeuillaie.com	**Web**	www.chateaudedenonville.fr

Véronique & Philippe Frenette
La Feuillaie,
4 rue Basse,
45130 Saint Ay, Loiret

Aurélie Capet-Pehuet
Château de Denonville,
28700 Denonville,
Eure-et-Loir

ENTRY 330   MAP 5

ENTRY 331   MAP 5

Maison JLN

Come to enjoy this gentle, charming family and the serene vibes of their old Chartrain house. Up two steep twisting spirals to the attic, through the family's little prayer room (a shell for each pilgrim who's stayed here), the sweet, peaceful bedroom feels like a chapel itself with its honey floorboards and small windows (no wardrobe). Lots of books: reminders of pilgrimage, just beneath the great cathedral. Madame artistic, friendly, offers artists a small studio to borrow; Monsieur speaks nine languages and is quietly amusing; both are interested in your travels. An unusual and special place, in a timeless town. .

La Ferme de Bouchemont

Peaceful and surrounded by gardens yet not far from Chartres and its massive cathedral, 40 minutes from Versailles and under an hour from Paris. You can walk into the ancient, pretty village of Bleury St Symphorien from this fine old stone farmhouse, which was once part of the domain of Château d'Esclimont. You stay in either end of Stephane and Soizic's home. There's a suite for four, and three more bedrooms to choose from – big, comfortable spaces with squashy sofas. Breakfast at a long table is stuffed with good coffee, bread and croissants, fruit salad and yogurts. Join others for convivial dinners, and then settle in the guest sitting room with music, books and magazines. There's a decked terrace for cocktail parties, and a beautifully restored barn is used for weddings and events.

Rooms	1 twin with separate shower & wc on floor below: €58. Singles €47. Extra bed/sofabed €14 p.p. per night.	**Rooms**	2 doubles, 1 twin/double: €120-€190. 1 suite for 4: €145-€260. Extra bed €30.
Meals	Restaurants nearby.	**Meals**	Dinner, 3 courses, €29. Restaurants 5km.
		Closed	Rarely.
Closed	Rarely.		

Tel +33 (0)2 37 21 98 36
Email chartres.maison.jln@gmail.com
Web www.chambre-hotes-chartres.com

Jean-Loup & Nathalie Cuisiniez
Maison JLN,
80 rue Muret,
28000 Chartres, Eure-et-Loir

Email lafermedebouchemont@gmail.com
Web www.la-ferme-de-bouchemont.com

Stephane & Soizic Chala
La Ferme de Bouchemont,
11 rue de la Remarde,
28700 Bleury St Symphorien, Eure-et-Loir

ENTRY 332 MAP 4

ENTRY 333 MAP 5

Poitou - Charentes

Château de Lerse, page 258

Le Relais du Lyon d'Or

The pretty little hotel-restaurant stands in one of Charente's most beautiful medieval villages. American Diana brings her professional experience; Dominique, a fully-fledged French wine expert and dealer, will suggest the perfect bottle be it for dinner or a big event, simple or organic, for connoisseurs or big budgets. The public rooms, rebuilt round old flagstones and beams, are decorated in warm natural colours to enhance the beauty of the original architecture. Bedrooms, some big, some smaller, have intriguing and individual details; rafters for those under the roof, high ceilings and beams or rough terracotta floors for others; none are overdone and all have sparkling bathrooms. The varied menu focuses on traditional dishes and local and seasonal produce, served when possible on the pretty terrace alive with wisteria and roses, hydrangea and geraniums… Masses to see and do: the Valley of the Frescoes including the Abbey at St Savin (UNESCO), the markets of medieval Chauvigny and Loches, the superb Parc de la Brenne for birds, turtles and orchids, Poitiers… or the quiet wonders of nature in the nearby valleys. *Pets by arrangement.*

Rooms	8 doubles: €89-€149. 1 suite for 4, 1 suite for 5: €149-€209. Singles €79-€139. Extra bed/sofabed €15-€20 p.p. per night.
Meals	Breakfast €13. Dinner €27-€40. Wine €22-€500. Lunch for groups by arrangement. Restaurant closed mid-November to mid-March.
Closed	Rarely.

Dominique Fuscien & Diana Hager
Le Relais du Lyon d'Or,
4 rue d'Enfer, 86260 Angles sur l'anglin,
Vienne

Tel	+33 (0)5 49 48 32 53
Email	contact@lyondor.com
Web	www.lyondor.com

Hôtel Les Orangeries

The long cool pool beneath the trees will convince you that these people have the finest sense of how to treat an old house and its surroundings. A deep wooden deck, rustic stone walls, giant flower baskets, orange trees, candles at night – all create tranquillity and harmony. The young owners (he an architect) fell in love with the place and have cleverly blended 18th-century elegance with contemporary charm. Oak doors, exposed stone walls, cool stone floors... everything glows with loving care, like valued old friends. Bedrooms are light and uncluttered, those facing the main road are double-glazed but get hot in summer (earplugs can come in handy, too), the split-level apartments are a delight. The Gautiers' passions include the old-fashioned games they have resuscitated for you: croquet and skittles under the trees, two kinds of billiards, backgammon and mahjong. Olivia speaks English and her enthusiasm for house, garden and guests is catching. Award-winning food (Sustainable International Restaurant of the Year) is delicious, local, organic; breakfast, in the garden in summer, is all you'd hope for the price. Exceptional. *Pets by arrangement.*

Rooms	11 doubles: €85-€175. 4 apartments for 5: €145-€220. Singles €75-€90. Dinner, B&B €43-€56 p.p. Extra bed/sofabed €12-€18 p.p. per night.
Meals	Breakfast from €12.50. Dinner from €28. Wine from €19.50.
Closed	Rarely.

Tel	+33 (0)5 49 84 07 07
Email	accueil.orangeries@orange.fr
Web	www.lesorangeries.fr

Olivia & Jean-Philippe Gautier
Hôtel Les Orangeries,
12 avenue du Docteur Dupont,
86320 Lussac les Châteaux, Vienne

ENTRY 335 MAP 9

Hotel Saint-Martin

Run with efficiency by Edouard Pellegrin, this 17th-century *gentilhommerie* offers that most attractive combination for travellers – solidly comfortable rooms and superb food. It is set conveniently on the outskirts of town, beyond suburbia, in a little wooded valley with a small stream running just outside. The bedrooms are mostly smallish, beamed, traditionally furnished and very comfortable; the bigger rooms, with lovely old rafters, are on the top floor. The tower has been converted into a charming suite with a sitting area downstairs and a smallish stone-walled bedroom up steepish stairs. Food is the thing here – regional, seasonal and served with panache in the colour-washed restaurant or the pleasantly shaded and tranquil garden. New chef Aline Jarriault has worked with the best and there is an innovative yet classic feel, matched by some tempting wines. Choose between the menu terroir and the menu gourmand – or pull out all the stops and work your way through the menu dégustation! As for Saint Maixent l'Ecole, it's a pretty market town not far from Poitiers and La Rochelle.

Rooms	9 doubles, 1 twin: €90-€175. 1 suite for 2: €144-€180. 1 family room for 3: €135-€170. Dinner, B&B €105-€151 p.p. Extra bed/sofabed €15 p.p. per night.
Meals	Breakfast €16. Lunch from €18. Dinner €32-€79. Restaurant closed Sat & Mon lunchtime.
Closed	Christmas, 2 January – 7 February.

La Réception
Hotel Saint-Martin,
Chemin de Pissot,
79400 Saint Maixent l'Ecole,
Deux Sèvres

Tel   +33 (0)5 49 05 58 68
Web www.logis-saint-martin.com

ENTRY 336 MAP 9

La Baronnie Hotel & Spa

A step away from the harbour, a listed monument and a beautiful manor are linked to make one special hotel. La Baronnie, the 'finest house on the island', is over 300 years old. Jasmine scents the air in the delicious cobbled courtyard, and a wooden structure houses a massage room, a jacuzzi, a sauna and small pool. Inside, a stunningly beautiful sideboard is laden with breakfast goodies, from just-squeezed juices to an array of coffees, while an ornate iron staircase sweeps you up to big light bedrooms exuding country chic, finely tuned in gorgeous colours. Imagine pale rugs, thick curtains, elegant cushions, and antiques picked up in brocantes over the years. Some rooms overlook a courtyard and the quietest face the gardens, which are magnificent. Adorable Florence, the ever-attentive owner, knows her island well, its nature and history, its beaches, cycle paths, sand dunes and pines: she helped lead the rise in St Martin's popularity. Perfect for a spoiling weekend – or more: the little town teems with chic shops, restaurants, bars and atmosphere.
Private parking, €20 per day.

Rooms	15 doubles: €169-€379. 1 suite for 2: €279-€445. 6 family rooms for 4: €214-€445. Extra bed/sofabed €25-€55 p.p. per night.
Meals	Breakfast €19. Restaurants nearby.
Closed	Bank Holidays, 26 November – 3 February, 6 March – 30 March.

Tel	+33 (0)5 46 09 21 29
Email	info@hotel-labaronnie.com
Web	www.hotel-labaronnie.com

Florence Pallardy
La Baronnie Hotel & Spa,
17-21 rue Baron de Chantal,
17410 Saint Martin de Ré (Ile de Ré),
Charente-Maritime

ENTRY 337   MAP 8

Hôtel de l'Océan

A hotel of contrasts: big yet small; hotel and restaurant; perspex by thick curtains; Mediterranean by the Atlantic. The new owners, the delightful Anne and Frédéric, her happy-chef husband, have been running the highly regarded restaurant at L'Océan for ten years. Having left Paris to bring their children up in cleaner air and live a less frenzied life, they now feel completely at home on Ile de Ré and love pointing guests towards its treasures. Set back from the street in a quiet little town, the Océan has 29 bedrooms in sixes and sevens, each cluster with individual flavour, some round a courtyard pungent with rosemary and lavender, some tiny cottages among the hollyhocks. Children love the curtained cabin bed set in a buttercup-yellow alcove. Two new rooms in a wing are large and colonial looking, with super bathrooms (not all with showers) and a calm cool feel. Floors are covered in matting; ships, lighthouses and shells are dotted around against soothing colours. The dining room is another success in cream and palest green-grey. After your apéritif, dinner will involve fresh fish and herbs. *Beach 15-minute walk.*

Rooms	22 doubles, 4 twins: €85-€180. 2 triples: €137-€152. 1 quadruple: €199-€244.
Meals	Breakfast €10. Lunch & dinner €24-€50. Wine €14-€40. Restaurant closed Weds October to March.
Closed	January.

Anne & Frédéric Latour
Hôtel de l'Océan,
172 rue Saint Martin,
17580 Le Bois Plage en Ré (Ile de Ré),
Charente-Maritime

Tel	+33 (0)5 46 09 23 07
Email	info@re-hotel-ocean.com
Web	www.re-hotel-ocean.com

ENTRY 338   MAP 8

Jardins Aliénor

A short stroll from Chateau d'Oléron's tree-lined market square is an elegant hotel that first welcomed guests in the 17th century. Charming owners Laetitia and Marc bought and renovated the original hotel in 2004, extending into adjoining properties to create eight stylish en-suite rooms. Window boxes and pale blue shutters add a flash of colour to the fresh, whitewashed façade, while striking work by local artists is displayed in the salon and the bedrooms. Tranquillity reigns here – sleep deeply in wonderfully comfortable beds and pamper yourself with delicious Keiji products... Oléron is famous for seafood, particularly oysters and mussels; gourmands can indulge in regional specialities in the intimate dining room or eat al fresco in the luscious plant-filled courtyard. If you can bear to leave Jardins Aliénor, the island is crisscrossed with footpaths and cycleways, and framed by sandy beaches where you can take to the water on a surfboard, sailing boat or canoe. Back on the mainland, admire Royan's Belle Époque villas or take a day-trip to La Rochelle.

Rooms	7 doubles: €99-€204.
	1 family room for 3: €193-€275.
	Dinner, B&B €52 p.p.
	Extra bed/sofabed at no charge.
Meals	Dinner €26-€49.
Closed	Never.

Tel	+33 (0)5 46 76 48 30
Email	lesjardinsdalienor@wanadoo.fr
Web	www.lesjardinsdalienor.com/en/home

Laetitia Le Reun
Jardins Aliénor,
7-11 rue Maréchal Foch,
17480 Le Château d'Oléron,
Charente-Maritime

ENTRY 339   MAP 8

La Villa Ouest

The Atlantic coast where discreet upper-class French families stay generation after generation in elegant Belle Époque villas is safe, fashionable and wonderfully French. Alexandre, who used to work in fine old luxury hotels, bought this famous Art Deco establishment in 2015 and has renovated it for the 21st century. He's created a beautiful salon de thé – a light, modern space where his favourite colours, coral and turquoise, shine out from furnishings, artworks and objets, and where a sumptuous buffet awaits you each morning. Huge windows between the original columns give views of the sky and the luxuriant surrounding vegetation. The place is a combination of curiosity cabinet and family home. The bedrooms have excellent linen and will soon be as design-perfect as the common areas. The region offers family activities galore. You can ride on the beach (just 50 metres away), walk the coastal path, explore rock pools at low tide, visit Palmyre's open zoo, the aquarium in fine old La Rochelle, and see the chapel and royal bedchamber in France's last inhabited lighthouse at Cordouan.
Minimum stay: 2 nights in high season.

Rooms	18 doubles: €70-€190. 6 triples: €120-€190. 2 quadruples: €145-€220. Animals allowed upon request, only for garden level rooms €10 per night. Cot bed €15 per night. Tourist tax €1.65 p.p. per night.
Meals	Breakfast buffet €12; children 3-10 €8; children 0-3 free. Restaurants 1-minute walk.
Closed	Never.

Alexandre Rieunier
La Villa Ouest,
13 avenue de Pontaillac,
17420 Saint-Palais-sur-Mer,
Charente-Maritime

Tel	+33 (0)5 46 23 11 19
Email	contact@lavillaouest.com
Web	www.lavillaouest.com/en/ hotel-charente-maritime

ENTRY 340   MAP 8

Le Bourg

Stone cottages, nodding hollyhocks, ducks in the lane: Mareuil epitomises rural France, and the house sits in its heart. Arrive to a sweeping drive, an immaculate pool, a grand façade and Vanessa, who has travelled the world. After a final posting in Paris she landed in sunny Charente, and is very happy. Bedrooms are bright, airy and comfortable, with cosy bathrooms; dinners, in the ample dining room, are gastronomic, cosmopolitan, entertaining and preceded by pineau de Charente. You are surrounded by sunflowers and vines and Cognac is close. Friendly, interesting, great fun.

Rooms	3 twin/doubles: €95.
Meals	Dinner with wine, from €32.
Closed	Rarely.

Tel	+33 (0)5 45 66 29 75
Email	lebourg-charente@wanadoo.fr
Web	www.lebourg-charente.com

Vanessa Bennett-Dixon
Le Bourg,
9 rue des Ecoles,
16170 Mareuil, Charente

ENTRY 341 MAP 9

Maison de Maître Private Suite

You're in the sticks here, surrounded by deer, boar and birds, with fires to warm in winter and wine tasting tours on hot summer days. Stop off on the drive south to spend a few days among Madeleine's mannequins and china dolls; just you and the huddle of Viking sheep and the Norwegian forest cats. Climb up a winding wooden staircase to your suite with Gustavian furniture and French market finds. A Scandi palette of serene greys and white is a soothing backdrop to your little nook and the bath has field views. Breakfast is taken outside on the terrace in the freshest air – local croissants, homemade jam, cheeses and meat. Stroll around the greenest of gardens with ancient trees, cycle for miles along the quietest roads, find your own bargains in the brocante markets of Charente.

Château de Lerse

Brave the swing over the lake or stroll the lawns and admire the herd: Roel and Mic are proud owners of 40 Belted Galloways. This 12th-century stronghold in old Poitou sits in 105 hectares of woods and fields; that's what you see when you open your shutters. Medieval doors and carved archways remain but the feel is fairly minimalist. A vast awning over the courtyard extends eating hours, three sitting rooms mean you can spread out and there's a sunken (small) pool if you don't fancy the lake. Breakfast is a gourmet affair with ham, cheese, eggs, fruits and pastries. Dinner is cooked by chef Joss using seasonal ingredients plus veg from their patch and sometimes meat from their cattle. Pop into Montmoreau St Cybard (8km) for its market; sample Napoleon's favourite cognac in Jarnac (40km).

Rooms	1 suite for 2: €120. Extra bed/sofabed €75 p.p. per night.
Meals	Restaurants 2km.
Closed	Never.

Rooms	5 doubles: €140-€235. Extra bed €50, cot available at no charge. Tourist tax €0.30 per night per adult. 50% deposit on booking, the remainder within 4 weeks of arrival.
Meals	Dinner €50.
Closed	15 November – 5 January.

Tel	+33 (0)5 45 64 99 93
Email	montaurand@gmail.com
Web	www.montaurand.com

Jo Lee
Maison de Maître Private Suite,
Montaurand,
16320 Rougnac, Charente

Tel	+33 (0)5 45 25 95 90
Email	contact@chateaudelerse.com
Web	chateaudelerse.com

Roel & Mic
Château de Lerse,
16250 Pérignac,
Charente

ENTRY 342   MAP 9

ENTRY 343   MAP 9

Chariaud

Guests have the run of upstairs, where two airy rooms for couples have homely touches and low beams. One is en-suite, the other with a private bathroom adjacent. They share an open plan space with games and home cinema, a gift for a rainy day. Eat breakfast on the terrace above the flowery garden, or cosily in the family kitchen. The pigeonnier next to the house is a beauty, walking tracks lead to nearby villages and Aubeterre-sur-Dronne, full of alleyways and arty workshops, is delightful. Take time to chat with your music aficionado hosts Alex and Joy; they have dogs, cats and chickens too – it's informal and fun.

Le Logis du Paradis

Mellow stones, chunky beams, sensuous fabrics... there's a timeless feel to the Logis, with 18th-century buildings embracing a magnificent oval courtyard. In big luxurious bedrooms you snuggle down in superbly comfortable king-size beds under white linen... and wake in anticipation of a delicious breakfast. There's a pool in the aromatic garden, books on the landings, a tea and coffee kitchen, a bar in the former distillery. Pootle down delightfully empty country roads, discover the finest vineyards for a bit of wine tasting, take a picnic to a stunning beach. Return to a stroll round the walled *parc* by the pretty river Né before a four-course dinner. Sally's generous table features market-fresh local produce, fine wines, and a glass of the neighbour's superb XO Cognac to finish with. Highly professional.

Rooms	1 double; 1 double with separate bathroom: €75.
Meals	Dinner by arrangement. Restaurants 3km.
Closed	Rarely.

Rooms	5 doubles: €90-€150.
Meals	Lunch €19. Dinner €39, on request. Wine from €12.50. Restaurant 4km.
Closed	Mid-January to end February.

Tel	+33 (0)5 45 98 10 88
Email	joycalling0503@gmail.com

Tel	+33 (0)5 45 35 39 43
Email	info@logisduparadis.com
Web	www.logisduparadis.com

Joy Collett
Chariaud,
16210 Saint-Romain,
Charente

Sally Brimblecombe
Le Logis du Paradis,
La Magdeleine,
16300 Criteuil la Magdeleine, Charente

ENTRY 344 MAP 9

ENTRY 345 MAP 9

Domaine du Meunier

A lovely, friendly house built in 1893 and renovated perfectly. Find a living room with a library and a piano, a dining room and a games room. Bedrooms are calm and serene, breakfast is a feast with coddled eggs from the family's hens; dinner (twice a week in high season) is lively! The outbuildings have become gîtes, the 'Pinball Hall' hosts events, and the family live in the old mill. Stroll through the walled garden, let the children splash in the pool, doze in an antique deckchair; at high tide you can swim or sail. Views are gentle, while the nearby harbour, pretty with sailing boats, joins the port to the Gironde. Culture abounds with jazz nights and an outdoor film festival. This is a fascinating area... stay a while. *Pets by arrangement.*

La Porte Rouge

Central, cobbled, car-free Saintes – perfect for Francophile lovers. Do arrange a meal here at one big table (herbs from the walled garden). Cooking comes high on well-travelled (American) Jim and Monique's list of passions; history and art too – their relaxed, typically French home (a hotel since the 16th-century) is full to bursting with beautiful antiques from different countries. Quiet, comfortable bedrooms on the second floor have linen from Italy, beams, white stone walls, original wood and parquet floors, and modern bathrooms with antique tubs. Take a trip on the Charente which runs through this fine town. *Cot available.*

Rooms	3 doubles, 2 twins: €70-€80. Singles €70-€80. Extra bed/sofabed €10-€20 p.p. per night.	**Rooms**	2 doubles; 1 twin sharing bathroom with suite: €85-€110. 1 suite for 4: €125-€175. Extra bed/sofabed €15 p.p. per night.
Meals	Dinner €25, twice weekly in high season; book ahead. Restaurants 50m.	**Meals**	Dinner, 4 courses with wine & apéritif, €28, on request. Child €15. Restaurant 2-minute walk.
Closed	Rarely.	**Closed**	Rarely.

Tel	+33 (0)5 46 97 75 10	**Tel**	+33 (0)5 46 90 46 71
Email	info@domainedumeunier.com	**Email**	monique.potel@la-porte-rouge.com
Web	www.domainedumeunier.com	**Web**	www.la-porte-rouge.com

Ariane & Coen Ter Kuile
Domaine du Meunier,
36, quai de L'Estuaire, 17120 Mortagne sur Gironde, Charente-Maritime

Monique Potel
La Porte Rouge,
15 rue des Jacobins,
17100 Saintes, Charente-Maritime

Logis de l'Astrée

Along the rustic track to a long, low nobleman's house walled behind vines, and sweet Sophie to welcome you with a glass of their wine. All is beautiful inside and flooded with light: lofty ceiling beams painted white, 17th-century terracotta looking like new. Elegant beds are topped with blankets and sheets; two rooms have kitchenettes, one opens to the garden. A stone fireplace stacked with logs dominates the irresistible salon, and home-grown grape juices join homemade jams at the table. Explore the pretty Coran valley and the river on foot or by bike, and visit historic Saintes with its amphitheatre and cathedrals. *Minimum stay: 2 nights at weekends & in high season.*

La Tillaie

Renovated with great care by Olivier and Christophe, this three-storey maison is filled with special touches; furniture old and new, family heirlooms, an open fire, even a Jacuzzi and sauna. Spacious bedrooms have garden views and are thoughtfully decorated with interesting wallpaper and rugs; sparkling en suites are equally snazzy. Start your day with a breakfast of fresh pastries, cakes and jams – in the dining room or outside on the decking – before heading out to visit a nearby chateau or seaside town. Stroll to a nearby restaurant for dinner, or ask charming Olivier – a former chef – to cook you something special. *Parking on-site.*

Rooms	2 doubles with separate wc: €110-€130. 1 suite for 4: €125-€215. 1 studio for 2 with separate wc: €125-€145. Singles €105-€120. Extra bed/sofabed €29 p.p. per night.
Meals	Occasional dinner with wine, €35. Restaurants 5-minute walk.
Closed	Rarely.

Rooms	4 doubles: €85-€119. Extra bed/sofabed €15.
Meals	Dinner with wine, €25. Restaurants 2-minute walk.
Closed	Rarely.

Tel	+33 (0)5 46 93 44 07
Email	smangeart@terre-net.fr
Web	www.logis-astree.fr

Sophie Boutinet Mangeart
Logis de l'Astrée,
Le Logis, 17770 Saint Bris de Bois,
Charente-Maritime

Mobile	+33 (0)6 15 24 71 03
Email	latillaie@gmail.com
Web	www.latillaie.com

Olivier Rotensztajn
La Tillaie,
28 rue du Vieux Pont, 17250 Pont l'Abbé
d'Arnoult, Charente-Maritime

ENTRY 348 MAP 8

ENTRY 349 MAP 8

Chambres d'hôtes l'Ombrière

The former farm hunkers between tall walls and electric gates. Low windows peer over a beautifully maintained garden and one room has outdoor steps to the terrace. Vines and trees envelop the house, with patios front and back for sundowners accompanied by wide, farmland views and a pool for cooling off. You'll be well looked after by Françoise and Alain – she's the chef, he plays sommelier. Sip an aperitif of pineau made from their vines before four fabulous courses. Breakfast is served by the pool in summer, or on the big table in the dining room: pastries, breads, homemade jams, fromage blanc, eggs on request. Everything is organic, homegrown or very local. The velvety pastures of Charentes spill out around you in a patchwork quilt; the coast is 40 minutes with the isles of Oléron and Ré to discover.

Rooms	2 doubles: €99-€110. Singles €90-€100.
Meals	Dinner, 4 courses with wine, available on request. Restaurants 4km.
Closed	Rarely.

Tel +33 (0)6 80 14 71 82
Email af.bry@orange.fr

Alain & Françoise Bry
Chambres d'hôtes l'Ombrière,
9 rue du bois des froger,
17250 Geay, Charente-Maritime

ENTRY 350   MAP 8

Les Hortensias

Behind its modest, wisteria-covered mask, this 17th-century former wine-grower's house hides a charming interior – and a magnificent garden that flows through orchard to topiary, a delight in every season. Soft duck-egg colours and rich trimmings make this a warm and safe haven, light airy bedrooms are immaculate and unpretentious (one with its original stone sink, another with a pretty French pink décor), the bathrooms are luxurious, the walls burst with art and the welcome is gracious, warm and friendly. Superb value with goods restaurants a few miles away. It's a treat to stay here.

Rooms	2 doubles: €65. 1 triple: €72. Extra bed €20.
Meals	Summer kitchen. Restaurant 8km.
Closed	Rarely.

Tel +33 (0)5 46 97 85 70
Email jpmt.jacques@wanadoo.fr
Web www.chambres-hotes-hortensias.com

Marie-Thérèse Jacques
Les Hortensias,
16 rue des Sablières,
17380 Archingeay, Charente-Maritime

ENTRY 351   MAP 8

La Grande Barbotière

Eden Ouest

Between the fruit trees a hammock sways, breakfast is served next to a sparkling pool and sculpted chickens peck. Tucked behind gates (child-safe) in the heart of a busy village is a maison de maître of elegance and charm. Your hosts (she half Belgian, he from Yorkshire) have a wicked sense of humour and have created a luxurious and eclectic décor – gazelle antlers, pebbled showers, delicious French linen – for suites with private terraces. Table tennis, croquet, bicycles, toys, jasmine and, everywhere, that spirit-lifting light that you find on this cherished stretch of coastline. *Minimum stay: 2 nights. Children under 4 welcome; cot available.*

This fabulous building, built in 1745, stands in the old heart of La Rochelle. An immense amount of thought has gone into its renovation, and manager Lise is brimming with ideas as to how they can go the extra mile. Sweep up grand stairs to a marble fireplace and muted grey walls, a long polished dining table and a rococo-esque chandelier. Bedrooms are colour coordinated right down to the paintings; the suites have sofabeds for children, and large bathrooms with their own hammam and bath tubs crafted from wood; one bathroom's doors open to a patio and salty sea air. Treat yourself to a professional massage in your room or step out to tread the ancient cobbles and sample the local aperitifs. Catch a boat to the marvellous Ile de Ré. *Cot & high chair available.*

Rooms	1 studio for 3, 1 studio for 5: €80–€300. Can also be booked as self-catering for groups of 4-7.
Meals	Restaurants 4km.
Closed	Rarely.

Rooms	1 double: €125–€255. 4 suites for 3: €170–€255. Extra bed €25.
Meals	Restaurants within walking distance.
Closed	Never.

Tel +33 (0)5 46 43 76 14
Email maraisdoux@gmail.com
Web www.lagrandebarbotiere.com

Christopher & Jacqui McLean May
La Grande Barbotière,
10 rue du Marais Doux,
17220 St Vivien, Charente-Maritime

Tel +33 (0)6 82 62 68 97
Email contact@edenouest.com
Web edenouest.com

Bertrand Patoureau & Lise Humeau
Eden Ouest,
33 rue Thiers, 17000 La Rochelle,
Charente-Maritime

ENTRY 352 MAP 8	ENTRY 353 MAP 8

Entre Hôtes

A ten-minute walk from the charming, bustling harbour of La Rochelle is an 18th-century merchant's house with an immaculate décor and a secret garden. Olivier and Sabine live on the top floor and look after you exceedingly well. Bedrooms and bathrooms are large and luxurious – polished floors, perfect beds, a pleasing, neutral palette. We particularly liked the wine 'cave' bedroom at the end of the garden: secluded, vaulted, lit with a warm glow and blessed with a sun terrace. Breakfast, served at small tables in an L-shaped living space, is a treat, and if the sun shines, you spill into the garden.

Maison des Algues

In a residential area, behind private gates on the outskirts of Rivedoux Plage, is a single-storey hotel, whitewashed, shuttered and impeccably maintained. Nothing is too much trouble for Christian and Jocelyne, who will pick you up from the airport and insist on giving you the best: white towels for the bathroom, coloured towels for the pool, pâtisseries for tea. Bedrooms open to a wicker-chaired terrace and are roomy, restful and flooded with light. Spin off on a bike (there are ten, all free) and acquaint yourself with the island – the whitewashed houses of La Flotte, the fabulous white sands, the chic shops of St Martin.
Minimum stay: 2 nights in high season.

Rooms	5 doubles: €108-€180. Extra bed €25.
Meals	Restaurants 5-minute walk.
Closed	Rarely.

Rooms	3 doubles; 2 interconnect: €115-€185. 2 suites for 2: €115-€220.
Meals	Restaurants within walking distance. Guest kitchen.
Closed	Never.

Tel	+33 (0)5 16 85 93 33
Email	contact@entre-hotes.com
Web	www.entre-hotes.com

Sabine & Olivier Durand-Robaux
Entre Hôtes,
8 rue Réaumur, 17000 La Rochelle,
Charente-Maritime

Tel	+33 (0)5 46 68 01 23
Email	information@maison-des-algues.com
Web	www.maison-des-algues.com

Christian & Jocelyne Gatta-Boucard
Maison des Algues,
147 rue des Algues,
17940 Rivedoux (Ile de Ré), Charente-Maritime

Un Banc Au Soleil

Only birds and bells break the bubble around this handsome B&B, set in quiet gardens near Marsilly port. The old stables of Stéphane's family home are transformed: soaring beams, elegant stone, huge terrace doors, a window to the cellar... You can slip into the pool after a day on the beach or brew a coffee and sit by the wood-burner flipping through magazines. At night, find snowy linen, original art, perhaps an antique desk or African carving. And in the morning, a homemade feast with traditional breads, tarts and more; nothing is any trouble for sweet Corinne. Hike or cycle coastal paths, golf, sail, visit historic Rochefort or La Rochelle... *Minimum stay: 2 nights July-October.*

Le Clos de la Garenne

Charming owners and animals everywhere, from boxer dog to donkey to hens! Brigitte and Patrick gave up telecommunications for their dream of the country and the result is this heart-warming, small-village B&B. Avid collectors, they have decorated their roomy 16th-century house with eclectic flair, and old and new rub shoulders merrily; discover doll's house furniture and French cartoon characters, old armoires and antique treasures. Harmony breathes from walls and woodwork, your hosts are endlessly thoughtful, food is slow, exotic, organic (and delicious), and families are truly welcome. *Minimum stay: 2 nights in high season.*

Rooms	5 doubles: €85-€118. Extra bed €28.
Meals	Restaurants within walking distance.
Closed	Rarely.

Rooms	1 double: €79. 1 suite for 5: €169. 1 cottage for 3: €99. Extra bed/sofabed €20 p.p. per night. Tourist tax €0.60 per night.
Meals	Dinner with wine, €27; children over 12, €22; under 12, €12.
Closed	January/February.

Tel	+33 (0)6 24 96 82 70
Email	contact@unbancausoleil.com
Web	www.unbancausoleil.com

Stéphane & Corinne Lassegue
Un Banc Au Soleil,
25 Quater Rue du Port,
17137 Marsilly, Charente-Maritime

Tel	+33 (0)5 46 35 47 71
Email	info@closdelagarenne.com
Web	www.closdelagarenne.com

Brigitte & Patrick François
Le Clos de la Garenne,
9 rue de la Garenne,
17700 Puyravault, Charente-Maritime

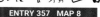

Manoir de Plaisance

There's airy grandeur in this former hunting lodge, where tall windows let light flood in and Juliette balconies add romance. For a grown-up house party there are guest sitting rooms for gatherings and 12 acres of grounds to roam. Ask for a picnic, find a peaceful spot by a lake and borrow a blanket for a shady siesta. The pool, tennis and fishing are right here and you can eat or shop in local market towns. The Marais Poitevin regional park is a green and watery wonderland of small canals and marshes ripe for exploring by punt, bike or on foot. For harbours and beaches, La Rochelle and the Ile de Ré are half an hour's drive; exceptional 12th century churches and the ruined abbey of Mazières are on hand too.

Chat Noir Chambre d'Hôtes

On the edge of a hamlet amidst rolling valleys, well travelled Chris and Michelle's eclectically furnished home oozes character from every stone and quirky corner, from the burgeoning library with log stove to the exposed stone walls, timber beams and elegant French beds in the bedrooms. One of the bathrooms is a few steps along the hall. Tuck into omelettes for breakfast at the kitchen table, snooze in a hammock in the tiered garden, take a dip in the pool or a soak in the hot tub. Markets, shops and restaurants are 10 minutes drive away, and Montmorillon, Poitiers and Limoges are all within striking distance.

Rooms	2 doubles: €138-€195. 2 suites for 2: €165-€245.
Meals	Dinner €36.
Closed	Christmas.

Rooms	1 double; 1 double with separate bathroom: €55-€60.
Meals	Dinner, 3-4 courses with wine, €25. Restaurants 15-minute drive.
Closed	End of October to beginning April.

Tel +33 (0)5 46 35 59 50
Email contact@manoirdeplaisance.com
Web www.manoirdeplaisance.com
Michael & Benjamin Hudson-Hamilton
Manoir de Plaisance,
Plaisance, 17170 Benon,
Charente-Maritime

Mobile +44 (0)7714 980001
Email chatnoir86250@gmail.com
Web www.chatnoir86.com
Chris & Michelle Burns
Chat Noir Chambre d'Hôtes,
Les Rechers,
86250 Genouille, Vienne

ENTRY 358   MAP 8

ENTRY 359   MAP 9

La Roseraie

You're tucked into a quiet, unassuming backstreet and hidden behind imposing walls. The big house presides over all: five bedrooms with modern walk-in showers in a white stone annex, a cobbled courtyard, a pool and parkland to stroll around. Breakfast is served in a little poolside bistro just for you – homemade jams, cakes, honey from the hives and eggs or charcuterie on request. Julie can make you dinners of her husband's beef and local cheese, or lunch baskets for exploring the marshes of the Vienne. When it pours, stoke the fires and borrow books and games. Families will love the two upstairs bedrooms and Julie's three young children are happy to make friends. Visit vineyards, walnut presses, hire punts to glide along the rivers or bikes for leisurely pedalling.

Château de Labarom

A great couple in their genuine family château of fading grandeur; mainly 17th century, it has a properly aged face. From the dramatic hall up the superbly bannistered staircase, you reach the salon gallery that runs majestically through the house. Here you may sit, read, dream of benevolent ghosts. Bedrooms burst with personality and wonderful old beds. Madame's hand-painted tiles adorn a shower, her laughter accompanies your breakfast (organic garden fruits and four sorts of jam); Monsieur tends his trees – he's a fount of local wisdom. A warm, wonderful and authentic place.

Rooms	4 doubles: €75-€95. 1 family room for 4: €75-€90
Meals	Dinner €27; €10 for children under 10. Wine from €15.
Closed	Never.

Rooms	2 doubles, 1 twin: €85-€95. Child's bed €25 per night.
Meals	Auberge nearby; restaurants 3-8km.
Closed	Rarely.

Tel	+33 (0)6 86 56 54 63
Email	info@laroseraiefrance.fr
Web	www.laroseraiefrance.fr

Julie Lembeye
La Roseraie,
78 rue Armand Caillard,
86170 Neuville de Poitou, Vienne

Tel	+33 (0)5 49 51 24 22
Email	labarom@labarom.com
Web	www.labarom.com

Éric & Henriette Le Gallais
Château de Labarom,
Route de Thurageau,
86380 Cheneché, Vienne

Aquitaine

Manoir Laurette B&B, page 285

Les Jardins de Brantôme

This is a grown up sort of place and Florence and Christophe give you a special stay. Christophe likes variety, no two breakfasts are the same. One day, ris au lait; the next crème aux oeufs, but always jam, bread, biscotti, yogurt – all homemade of course and delivered to your room if you want. Bedrooms are a study in serenity, with beds layered in Caravane linens, antique chairs and most with a private balcony or patio with front-row seats to the dawn chorus; just add an infusion from the tea tray and slip on the linen bathrobe and felt slippers for the perfect start. A cool courtyard garden and pool are shaded by trees; take a dip then find a spot to sip a glass of Périgord Bergerac and reflect on life in the slow lane. Pick up truffles and confit at the Friday market in Brantôme, visit châteaux and gardens, canoe on the river.

Rooms	6 doubles: €115-€195. 1 suite for 5: €155-€185. Extra bed/sofabed €25 p.p. per night.
Meals	Breakfast €14. Restaurants 10-minutes' walk.
Closed	Rarely.

Tel	+33 (0)5 53 05 88 16
Email	lesjardinsdebrantome@gmail.com
Web	www.lesjardinsdebrantome.com

Christophe & Florence Dupuy
Les Jardins de Brantôme,
33 rue Pierre de Mareuil,
24310 Brantôme, Dordogne

ENTRY 362 MAP 9

Château de la Côte

This spectacular 15th-century château has been owned and run by the same charming family since the last century. Travel past golden sunflower fields and the château emerges regally through a forested hilltop. The interior oozes aged grandeur – original stonewalls, wood panelling, a suit of armour in the hall, and huge fireplaces in almost all the rooms. Bedrooms are old-fashioned but impressive with antiques and numerous four-posters to choose from; bathrooms reflect the age of the building (sometimes slightly eccentric but always spotless). Ask for a room in the tower if you don't mind stairs; one has a fabulous private roof terrace-leading up from the bathroom! Views are panoramic. Dinner is a fixed simple menu of local specialities (quite expensive), and a continental breakfast can be taken in the 'tower room' or on the front lawn. Enjoy an aperitif or local wine under an ancient tree and admire the rolling countryside. There's also a pool, children's play area and a secret arbor within the twenty acres of grounds. A wonderful retreat full of character – come for history, romancing, rambling and exploring the Dordogne. *Minimum stay: 2 nights on weekdays; 3 at weekends & in high season.*

Rooms	10 doubles: €108-€136. 7 suites for 2: €154-€225. Singles €80-€90. Extra bed/sofabed €17-€25 p.p. per night.
Meals	Breakfast €14-€19. Dinner €29-€59; children €12-€25. Restaurants 3-minute drive.
Closed	15 November – 25 December, 5 January – 15 March.

Michel & Olivier Guillaume
Château de la Côte,
Lieu dit La Côte, 24310 Biras,
Dordogne

Tel	+33 (0)5 53 03 70 11
Email	contact@chateaudelacote.com
Web	www.chateau-hotel-dordogne.com

La Commanderie

The setting is special indeed, off a medieval street in a charming hamlet. Go through a stone archway, across generous parkland, beneath majestic trees into the steep-roofed *commanderie*. Here, the Knights of the Order of Malta put up 700 years ago en route to Santiago de Compostela and a low curved toll passage still forms part of the house. It is not so much a hotel as a houseful of guests overseen by diminutive Madame Roux, a considerate, welcoming hostess. An uncontrived collection of antiques warms the friendly bedrooms, each with its own personality on a blue and white theme punctuated by touches of dark blue; ceilings soar, floors of varying ages and diverse patterns are softened by Indian rugs. Downstairs, guests gather at round tables set with antique cane chairs, flowery curtains hang at tall windows, marble busts abound and you get two choices per gastronomic course – just right for this unassuming and atmospheric place. A delightful stone rill snakes through the grass to the pond and the Lascaux Caves are a mile down the road. Great value for what you get, and that includes very good, classic French food.

Rooms	5 doubles, 2 twins: €95.
Meals	Breakfast €10. Lunch €22. Dinner €25-€48. Restaurant closed Mondays.
Closed	Rarely.

Tel	+33 (0)5 53 51 26 49
Email	hotellacommanderie@wanadoo.fr
Web	www.hotel-lacommanderie.com

Madame Annick Roux
La Commanderie,
1 place du Verdier,
24570 Condat sur Vézère, Dordogne

ENTRY 364   MAP 9

La Métairie

If you love horses you'll be in your element: you can relax on the terrace and watch them in the next field. You can also ride close by. La Métairie was built as a farm at the beginning of the last century and converted into a 'boutique' hotel some 40 years ago, a U-shaped building smothered in wisteria and Virginia creeper. There's no road in sight and you really do feel away from it all – yet the Dordogne and its clifftop villages are minutes away. Borrow bikes if you're feeling energetic! Bedrooms are charming, cheerful and full of sunshiney yellows and huge beds. They have room for a couple of comfy chairs, too. Bathrooms match – big and bright – and three ground-floor rooms have French doors and a semi-private patio. The pool is big enough for a proper swim and when you come out you can read under the trees that waits for you by the pool. In summer you can eat out here, or on the flowery terrace. The dining room has black and white floors, washed stone walls and well-spaced tables. Go ahead, indulge, order the four-course *menu Périgourdin*. You can swim it off later. Delightful staff, too.

Rooms	9 doubles: €135-€195. 1 suite for 2: €195-€330. Dinner, B&B €55 extra p.p. Extra bed/sofabed €35 p.p. per night.
Meals	Breakfast €18. Lunch €18-€50. Dinner €43-€58; Périgourdine menu €55. Wine €25-€100.
Closed	November to March.

R. & H. Johner
La Métairie,
24150 Mauzac & Grand Castang,
Dordogne

Tel	+33 (0)5 53 22 50 47
Email	info@la-metairie.com
Web	www.la-metairie.com

Hôtel Edward 1er

Some people lounge beside the pool on their honeymoon; Arjan and Marije, your delightful, hands-on hosts, went hotel hunting on theirs. And they found one: a handsome 19th-century turreted townhouse on the edge of a miraculously preserved 13th-century village, voted one of the most beautiful in France. Now they are well established and have seamlessly extended into an adjoining building. Herbs are from the garden, vegetables and fruit are local, fish hails from Bordeaux and Arcachon; everything is made here except bread and ice cream, supplied by artisans. After you have explored the fortified village – four sides set round the huge central square, the surrounding houses corbelled out with arches – further medieval bastides beckon: there are a dozen or so. Arjan has prepared bicycle itineraries and can point out the best place to paddle a canoe. Or you may just want to lounge by the deep-blue pool, honeymoon-style! Lushly comfortable rooms await.

Rooms	11 doubles, 6 twins: €67-€210. Singles €65-€118. Extra bed/sofabed €22-€29 p.p. per night.
Meals	Breakfast €12. Dinner €29.50-€39.50. Wine €19-€50.
Closed	11 November – 29 March.

Tel	+33 (0)5 53 22 44 00
Email	info@hoteledward1er.com
Web	www.hoteledward1er.com

Arjan & Marije Capelle
Hôtel Edward 1er,
5 rue Saint Pierre,
24540 Monpazier, Dordogne

ENTRY 366 MAP 9

Villa la Tosca

Less than an hour from Bordeaux, on the edge of pretty seaside Taussat is this stunning villa. Luckily the owners snapped it up before developers got to it, they then spent three years whipping it into shape and the result is magnificent. You'll be blown away by the first glimpse, through tall palm trees, of this columned villa, towering over everything in sight, wrapped in a huge wooden veranda with views jutting out to Arcachon Bay. Pop through a gate in the garden (they've installed a natural pool – plants rather than chemicals filter out all the yucky stuff) and you're on the beach; fall asleep to the sound of lapping waves. Inside original details have been restored but the décor is contemporary with a smart, Eastern-vibe, modern art and sculptures. The reception rooms are on the ground floor, bedrooms on the three above. There's a huge comfy living room, a library and bar area. You eat (breakfasts, dinners, snacks during the day) in the dining room or out on the veranda seated on cool chairs. The suite at the top of the tower, with its wraparound sea views, will be the one you argue over. *Parking on-site.*

Rooms	6 doubles: €159-€449.
	2 suites for 2: €309-€599.
Meals	Breakfast €15-€25.
	Dinner, 3-courses, €49.
	Restaurants 10-minute walk.
Closed	Never.

Aurelien Roux
Villa la Tosca,
10 allée Du Bassin, 33138 Lanton,
Bordeaux, Gironde

Tel	+33 (0)5 56 60 29 86
Email	enquiries@villalatosca.com
Web	www.villalatosca.com

Hôtel Laminak

You are well looked after here. Cheerful new owners Pascale and Martial have devoted their careers to hospitality and are well-travelled. They've kept the enchanting feel of a simple little hotel (intimate, friendly) and redecorated the bedrooms (not vast but very attractive). Find pale beige and blue fabrics with flashes of red-striped Basque, maritime or bull-fighting themed artwork, lovely views over to green hills and crisp bathrooms with shining tiles. Unbend on a comfy sofa in the sitting room – it's cosy in here and there's lots of work by local artists; on balmy days discover plenty of boltholes in the garden, on the terrace or by the super swimming pool. All is relaxed and you can make yourself at home. Breakfasts are generous affairs with homemade jams and cakes, delicious local farm produce (cheese, ham, saucisson). You are on a quiet road outside the village of Arbonne with a few discreetly screened neighbours, it's a ten-minute hop to the best surfing coast in Europe and the heady charm of Biarritz, or the antiques fair at Ahetze, or a championship golf course – and the mountains are worth a week's effort in themselves. *Pool heated March – November, weather dependant.*

Rooms	12 twin/doubles: €75-€169. Extra bed/sofabed €17 p.p. per night. Children under 2 free.
Meals	Breakfast €12.
Closed	Rarely.

Tel	+33 (0)5 59 41 95 40
Email	info@hotel-laminak.com
Web	www.hotel-laminak.com

Pascale & Martial Mazabraud
Hôtel Laminak,
Route de Saint Pée, 64210 Arbonne,
Pyrénées-Atlantiques

ENTRY 368   MAP 13

Hotel Harretchea

Could anything be more Basque? Whitewashed walls and bulls-blood red shutters, lush rolling sheep pastures, the Atlantic to the west and the emblematic La Rhune to the east; take the little train up and spot wild Pottok ponies on the way. Sophie converted the 300-year-old village farmhouse to village hotel in 2014. A white bright breakfast room now leads out to a sun terrace and a small flowery garden. Her touch is light and elegant, she welcomes all with vivacious energy, even for a chat in her kitchen, and keeps toys in the sitting room as well as a piano. Her taste is clean-cut contemporary and she loves space so not even the jacuzzi is cramped. Wake up in a lovely bedroom where muted meets bright, tear yourself off your superb mattress, enjoy the big white-and-chrome shower, then head for the luscious breakfast buffet. It's all locally sourced: bread and pastries from the village baker, jam from nearby Lahonce, yogurt from St Jean Pied de Port, the gateway to Compostela. The Basque country has stupendous walks and endless treasures: stay a while and be pampered. Dinner is two minutes' walk.

Rooms	8 doubles: €85-€160. 1 suite for 2, 2 suites for 4: €115-€210. Extra bed in suites, €25 per night.
Meals	Restaurants 2-minute walk.
Closed	November, Christmas & January.

Sophie Mora
Hotel Harretchea,
20 chemin d'Harretchea,
64210 Ahetze, Pyrénées-Atlantiques

Tel   +33 (0)5 59 22 25 59
Email   contact@hotel-harretchea.com
Web   www.hotel-harretchea.com

ENTRY 369   MAP 13

Château d'Urtubie

Urtubie is old, very old: built in 1341 with permission from Edward III. The keep is still intact, though the roof was changed in 1654 to resemble Versailles. Your host Laurent, generous, charming, passionate about the place, is a direct descendant of Martin de Tartas who built it. Inside, all is elegant and inviting, and that includes the bedrooms, reached by a stair (or discreet lift). The first-floor 'prestige' rooms are light, airy, classical, imposing, and the 'charm' bedrooms on the second-floor are smaller. All are air-conditioned and are beautifully maintained, while bathrooms stock the family's new range of soaps and creams made from shea butter and verbena. On the outskirts of this pretty little Basque town, a hop from the motorway (you barely hear it) and five minutes from the beach, Urtubie is a sweet retreat in fine gardens with an elegantly decked pool. Don't imagine it's stuffy: Laurent couldn't be easier or more welcoming. Just walk 500m to the farm next door to eat at its Michelin-approved restaurant with views.

Rooms	1 double, 8 twin/doubles: €90-€175.
Meals	Breakfast €12. Restaurant 500m.
Closed	1 November – 30 April.

Tel	+33 (0)5 59 54 31 15
Email	info@chateaudurtubie.fr
Web	www.chateaudurtubie.fr

Laurent de Coral
Château d'Urtubie,
Urrugne, 64122 Saint Jean de Luz,
Pyrénées-Atlantiques

ENTRY 370 MAP 13

Hôtel Arraya

The drive to the village of Sare is breathtaking: winding road, red and white farmhouses, rolling hills. The hotel, which dominates Sare's square, has been in the family for three generations; it was a salon de thé after the war (and the 'gâteau Basque' is still delectable). Lawned terraces are the new gardens, a lap pool is planned, and the views of La Rhune tempt you to catch the mountain train. Pass the dappled dining terrace and the little shop (Basque linen, Basque pottery, homemade jam) to enter a double-glazed haven, overseen by smiling Madame. Two salons greet you – charming furniture, overstuffed sofas, a bar full of armagnacs, flowers from the garden. Upstairs, across two floors, with fire doors encased in handsome oak, are 16 bedrooms, sumptuous and serene, the quietest facing the garden. We loved the chests of drawers topped with old jugs and basins, the impeccable beds, the hand-sewn soft furnishings. Splash out on a 'prestige' suite if you can: the bathrooms are magnificent. Lovely Saint-Jean-de-Luz and its harbour are 12km, the hiking is marvellous, the beaches are close. *Parking on-site.*

Rooms	14 twin/doubles: €96-€195. 1 family room for 3, 1 family room for 4: €190-€245. Dinner, B&B €40 extra p.p.
Meals	Breakfast €12.50. Dinner €27-€50.
Closed	1 November – 31 March.

Laurence & Jean Baptiste Fagoaga
Hôtel Arraya,
Place Centrale, 64310 Sare
,Pyrénées-Atlantiques

Tel	+33 (0)5 59 54 20 46
Email	hotel@arraya.com
Web	www.arraya.com

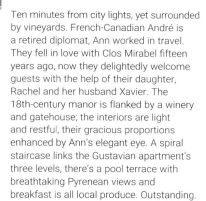

Clos Mirabel

La Bastide Estratte

Ten minutes from city lights, yet surrounded by vineyards. French-Canadian André is a retired diplomat, Ann worked in travel. They fell in love with Clos Mirabel fifteen years ago, now they delightedly welcome guests with the help of their daughter, Rachel and her husband Xavier. The 18th-century manor is flanked by a winery and gatehouse; the interiors are light and restful, their gracious proportions enhanced by Ann's elegant eye. A spiral staircase links the Gustavian apartment's three levels, there's a pool terrace with breathtaking Pyrenean views and breakfast is all local produce. Outstanding..

In six remote hectares of woodland with Pyrenean peaks beyond, a solid slate-roofed farmhouse. Enter the wide stone arch into a beautiful balcony-fringed, flagstoned courtyard: sip a cappuccino among ornamental acers, japonicas, box hedges as Virginia creeper winds its way over the walls. Inside, a patina of olives, pale greys and ecru provides a studied canvas for polished floors, white sofas, porcelain in bookcases, fine fittings and herbal prints. Lovely Chantale, at ease in six languages, helps with Jurançon wine routes, restaurants (a new one close by) and walks. If it's all too cool, bask in the jacuzzi. *Minimum stay: 2 nights. Children over 7 welcome.*

Rooms	4 doubles: €115-€159. 1 apartment for 6 with kitchen: €159-€259. Extra bed/sofabed €39 p.p. per night. Dogs welcome in apartment:€5 per day; max 2.
Meals	Dinner from €28.50; available 3-4 times per week. Restaurants 3km.
Closed	Rarely.

Rooms	3 doubles: €89-€99. Singles €80. Extra bed €35. Pets €5-€10. Hot tub €10 for stays less than 3 nights.
Meals	Brunch €10. Restaurant 1km.
Closed	Rarely.

Tel	+33 (0)5 59 06 32 83
Email	info@closmirabel.com
Web	www.closmirabel.com

Ann Kenny & André Péloquin
Clos Mirabel,
276 av des Frères Barthélémy, Jurançon,
64110 Pau, Pyrénées-Atlantiques

Tel	+33 (0)5 59 34 32 45
Email	chantale.albert@nordnet.fr
Web	www.labastide-estratte.com

Chantale Albert
La Bastide Estratte,
Quartier St Michel, Chemin de Bas Afittes,
64360 Lucq de Béarn, Pyrénées-Atlantiques

ENTRY 372 MAP 13

ENTRY 373 MAP 13

La Bergerie

Through ancient woods and unspoilt farmland you wind your way up to little Montestrucq, to a farm half a mile from the church, steeped in ancient character. Now, in the former bergerie, are sheepskin-strewn sofas, standing timbers, a huge open fire and, upstairs, bedrooms charming and cosy... Irish bed linen, pure wool carpets, Italian walk-in showers. Cassoulets, piperades, fondues, wild boar: Didier loves his 'cuisine gourmande' and sources with gusto; Sabine is full of smiles. The house faces south, the pool is inviting with a sauna too, and views soar over the hills to the majestic Pyrénées. *Heated pool.*

Dominxenea

You're well looked after here by bubbly Madame, steeped as she is in the Basque tradition of hospitality. The house is listed: find ox-blood red shutters and door, a courtyard garden and wide views of the mountains. You breakfast in the dining room or on the terrace; what could be nicer than a just-baked croissant and a fresh fruit salad surrounded only by views and birdsong. This is a gentle, quiet place – not for those seeking thrills. Bedrooms are old-fashioned and flowery with balconies; beds have thick mattresses and embroidered pillow cases, bathrooms are clean and comfortable. Hop on the petit train for even more views.

Rooms	2 doubles: €98-€138. 1 double, 1 twin, sharing bathroom; let to same party only: €98-€138. Extra bed/sofabed €20 p.p. per night.	
Meals	Lunch €20. Dinner €30. Gastronomic dinner €42. Non-alcoholic drinks complimentary. Restaurants 10km.	
Closed	Rarely.	

Rooms	3 twin/doubles: €55-€75. Extra bed €15. Sofabeds available.
Meals	Restaurants 10-minute walk.
Closed	1 November – 31 March.

Tel	+33 (0)5 59 38 63 76
Email	sabine.meyer3@orange.fr
Web	www.labergeriebearn.com

Sabine & Didier Meyer
La Bergerie,
2 chemin de Lhostebielh,
64300 Montestrucq, Pyrénées-Atlantiques

Tel	+33 (0)5 59 54 20 46
Email	hotel@arraya.com
Web	www.dominxenea.fr

Laurence & Jean Baptiste Fagoaga
Dominxenea,
Quartier Ihalar, 64310 Sare,
Pyrénées-Atlantiques

ENTRY 374   MAP 13

ENTRY 375   MAP 13

Bidachuna

The electronic gate clicks behind you and 29 hectares of forested peacefulness are yours – with wildlife. Open wide your beautiful curtains next morning and you may see deer feeding; lift your eyes to feast on long vistas to the Pyrenean foothills; trot downstairs to the earthly feast that is Basque breakfast; fall asleep to the hoot of the owl. Shyly attentive, Isabelle manages all this impeccably and keeps a refined house where everything gleams; floors are chestnut, bathrooms are marble, family antiques are perfect. Pop off to lovely St Jean de Luz for lunch or dinner, return to this manicured haven and blissful cossetting.

Ferme Elhorga

Unwind here with truly gracious hosts, a beautiful house with spoiling bedrooms and bathrooms, delightful views, a drinks menu (with little apero plates) and lawns which swoop down to a sparkling pool. Plenty of space and lots of hidden seating areas give you privacy – sneak off with your breakfast if you want: a gourmand affair with local charcuterie, brebis cheese, eggs to boil, a patisserie of the day and as much coffee and tea as you want – all day! A little kitchen is yours, there's a large living room filled with quirky brocantes, comfy sofas and leather armchairs, bikes are yours to borrow and the area has much to explore. Restful.

Rooms	2 doubles, 1 twin: €125. Singles €115.
Meals	Restaurant 6km.
Closed	Mid-November to mid-March.

Rooms	4 doubles: €120-€190. 1 suite for 2: €150-€220. Extra bed/sofabed €40-€50 p.p. per night.
Meals	Dinner €19. Guest kitchen and BBQ. Restaurants 1km.
Closed	Rarely.

Tel	+33 (0)5 59 54 56 22
Email	isabelleormazabal@gmail.com
Web	www.bidachuna.fr

Isabelle Ormazabal
Bidachuna,
Route D3, Lieu dit Otsanz,
64310 St Pée sur Nivelle, Pyrénées-Atlantiques

Mobile	+33 (0)6 08 68 13 30
Email	contact@elhorga.com
Web	www.elhorga.com

Julie Despons
Ferme Elhorga,
Chemin d'Elhorga, 64310 Saint Pée sur Nivelle,
Pyrénées-Atlantiques

Villa etcheBri

A tee's throw from surfing beaches, fringed by pines in the smart enclave of Chiberta, is a serene, secluded, 1960s villa. Here live Brigitte and her adorable bulldog Icare, happily sharing their home with guests. The setting is lovely: bamboos and palms on lawns, exotic plants in pots, and two ground-floor suites opening to a decked terrace and a fabulous pool. There are three bedrooms in all: clean, contemporary, restful in white, with splashes of sunshine from fabrics and towels. Bathrooms are... flawless! Walk to bars, restaurants, beaches, golf; set off for the lovely towns of Biarritz and Bayonne. *Parking on-site.*

Domaine de Sengresse

In the undiscovered Landes, two hours from Spain, a remote and ravishing 17th-century domaine. A solid stone house, a cathedral-like barn, an elegant pool, red squirrels in luscious acres and a 'petite maison' whose bread oven served the area's farms: such are the riches in store. A Godin stove and six-oven Aga feed today's guests in gourmet style from a wonderful array of homemade produce, the rooms are bathed in light and everything sparkles, from the luxurious bedrooms with their calming colours to the library brimful of books. More country hotel than B&B, run by the loveliest people. *Pets by arrangement.*

Rooms	3 doubles: €110-€195.
	2 suites for 4: €190-€350.
	Extra bed available.
Meals	Dinner €40; by arrangement.
	Restaurants 5-minute drive.
Closed	Rarely.

Rooms	3 doubles, 2 twin/doubles:
	€130-€150. Singles €115-€140.
Meals	Dinner with wine, from €35.
Closed	Rarely.

Mobile	+33 (0)6 73 53 36 48
Email	etchebri@gmail.com
Web	www.etchebri.fr

Brigitte Wallon – Van de Velde
Villa etcheBri,
9 avenue de la Forêt, 64600 Anglet,
Pyrénées-Atlantiques

Tel	+33 (0)5 58 97 78 34
Email	sengresse@hotmail.fr
Web	www.sengresse.com

Michèle & Rob McLusky & Sasha Ibbotson
Domaine de Sengresse,
Route de Gouts,
40250 Souprosse, Landes

Manoir le Bigourda

At the end of a long ridge, views of farms and valleys all around, this stone house has been rooted here for the past 400 years. The Italianate loggia overlooks the garden and is the setting for breakfasts of patisserie, homemade jam, eggs on toast. Book in advance for Carol Ann's very reasonable dinners, or head to Puymirol for Michelin-starred restaurants. There are lots of spaces to relax, in the guest wing or the family part of the house: a cushion-strewn drawing room with games and a roaring fire, big bedrooms with windows over the courtyard, plush en suite bathrooms, a heated pool. Warm and generous hosts lend bicycles and wellies for exploring towns, farms and vineyards, the bastide villages of Lauzerte and Tournon-d'Agenais. Summer brings night markets and châteaux concerts. .

Rooms	5 doubles: €95. Extra bed €30.
Meals	Dinner with wine, coffee & apéritif, €65 per couple. Children €10.
Closed	Never.

Tel	+33 (0)5 53 98 23 47
Email	info@lebigourda.com
Web	lebigourda.com

Carol Ann & Robert Wheeler
Manoir le Bigourda,
Le Bigourda, 47470 Engayrac,
Lot-et-Garonne

ENTRY 380   MAP 14

Domaine de Pine

Hidden among sunflower fields is a well-proportioned and delightful hotel, an intimate haven run by charming English hosts. Convivial meals are served on fine white linen on a summer terrace with stunning panoramic views, beamy bedrooms are large, light and elegant in whites and creams, and bathrooms sport fluffy robes. Springtime calls for lazing on loungers by the walled pool, happy hour is between 5pm and 6pm. For winter: a fitness room, snooker table, a roaring fire, a candlelit supper in a blue and white dining room. Step out for music festivals and markets – or stay put and explore. Brilliant.

Rooms	3 doubles: €125-€195. 1 family suite: €250-€395. Extra bed for child under 12 €17.50 per night. Cots available. Dogs welcome: €5 per day; max 2 per booking.
Meals	Breakfast from €17. Dinner from €38. Wine from €22. Restaurants 2-minute drive.
Closed	Rarely.

Tel	+33 (0)5 53 66 44 93
Email	email@ddpine.com
Web	www.domainedepine.com

Marcus & Cathy Becker
Domaine de Pine,
47470 Blaymont,
Lot-et-Garonne

ENTRY 381   MAP 14

Manoir Beaujoly

The medieval manor surveys fertile land rich in tales of knights and kings: a stunning hilltop setting. Horses graze, quails potter and guests gather by the pool in a ruined granary to barbecue trout from the river or duck from the market. The cool, thick-walled building wears its no-frills minimalism well: rough stone, hefty beams, a roll top bath, canvas wardrobes, ancient bullet holes... and 'open' bathrooms behind screens. There's a great fire in the monastic sitting room where delightful Dutch-German host serves breakfasts of cheese and charcuterie. Rampage, like those medieval Templars, across glorious 'French Tuscany'. *Minimum stay: 3 nights.*

Domaine de Rambeau

Handsome and enticing, this 18th-century manor house is perched on a hillside with views of silken wheat fields and distant valleys. But feast your eyes on the star of the show: an all-bells-and-whistles pool. Inside: an air of decadent splendour – even a knight in armour – where all is tasteful, relaxed and spacious in sitting, dining and bedrooms – just watch out for some low beams (and ask for an extra single if you need one). There's lovely artisan bread and homemade jams for breakfast, scrumptious dinners from generous owners and acres of parkland to mosey around – home to a huge and friendly black pig. *Pets by arrangement.*

Rooms	5 doubles: €120.		**Rooms**	4 doubles: €120-€130.
Meals	Restaurants 4km.			Extra bed €20.
Closed	Rarely.		**Meals**	Breakfast included.
				Dinner, 3 courses with wine, €32.
				Restaurant 4km.
			Closed	Rarely.

Tel	+33 (0)5 53 01 52 51	**Tel**	+33 (0)5 53 79 38 43
Email	be@beaujoly.com	**Email**	reeves.kim@hotmail.fr
Web	www.beaujoly.com	**Web**	www.domainederambeau.com

Lana Elise Siebelink
Manoir Beaujoly,
47340 Hautefage la Tour,
Lot-et-Garonne

Kim Reeves
Domaine de Rambeau,
lieu dit Rambeau, 47260 Castelmoron sur Lot,
Lot-et-Garonne

Domaine du Moulin de Labique

Modernity has been comfortably kept at bay here – a warm, easy-going atmosphere, shutters, tiles, retro wallpaper conserved and a lovely, child-safe pool in the gardens, with rambling old roses, a stream and a duck pond. You can chat about which village market, castle, or vineyard to visit over continental (with local honey, and eggs if you like) breakfast. Maybe head straight off from Le Moulin on foot or on horseback – there are stables at the end of the drive; or take the kids canoeing on the Lot, or zip-wiring at the tree-top adventure park. Christine is an excellent cook so do arrange dinner here (and ask about her cookery courses); she and Patrick know all the good places to eat nearby and La Table de Sens in Lougratte serves fresh, regional food that you can take away too.

Manoir Laurette B&B

Lora has filled her light-drenched 200-year old home with curios, artwork and furniture collected on her travels and it all works magically. Bedrooms are large and bright and have antique furniture; bathrooms are brand spanking new, two have roll tops. You can breakfast in bed or in the garden underneath the shade of the walnut tree: smoothies, granola, local honey, bacon sarnies, delicious buttermilk pancakes, proper coffee... You're slap bang in the middle of wine-tasting country, the steepled church in Lorette is a two-minute walk and for trips out sup champagne and oysters in Arcachon or hang out in trendy Cap Ferret. *Pets by arrangement.*

Rooms	3 doubles, 2 twins: €110-€140.
	1 suite for 4: €199.
	Dinner, B&B €83-€99 p.p.
Meals	Dinner €31. Wine €16-€30.
Closed	Rarely.

Rooms	3 doubles: €120-€140.
Meals	Restaurants 3km.
Closed	Rarely.

Tel	+33 (0)5 53 01 63 90
Email	moulin-de-labique@wanadoo.fr
Web	www.moulin-de-labique.net

Patrick & Christine Hendricx
Domaine du Moulin de Labique,
Saint Vivien, 47210 Villeréal,
Lot-et-Garonne

Mobile	+44 (0)7957 662008
Email	hello@manoirlaurette.com
Web	www.manoirlaurette.com

Lora Munro
Manoir Laurette B&B,
Lorette Ouest, 47180 St Martin Petit,
Lot-et-Garonne

ENTRY 384   MAP 9

ENTRY 385   MAP 9

Chambres d'Hôtes Janoutic

Charming Jean-Pierre finds the finest organic produce for his table. From croissants to charcuterie, 'poulets fermier' to orchard jams (apricot, blackcurrant, redcurrant, fig), it sounds delicious. This is a well-restored old farmhouse in the hamlet of Janoutic, two miles from the motorway, a great little stopover between Bordeaux and Toulouse. We like the two bright, carpeted bedrooms upstairs best, their rustic rafters hung with tobacco leaves in memory of old farming days; all have big walk-in showers. There's more: leather sofas and a great log fire; a wild garden with an aviary and a pool for newts and birds.

Préchac park

Anne and Allan love to entertain their guests so do book in for a delicious home-cooked supper with paired wines and good conversation. Afterwards retire to the billiard room for a game or a nightcap (from the honesty bar) in front of the fire. You're in the middle of a small village (bar, grocers, bakery) overlooking the church but it feels light and spacious – there are two huge bedrooms, one with a claw foot tub, and a third smaller bedroom. Behind the house is a hectare of parkland to wander. It's a 15-minute drive, or slightly longer bike ride to the renowned Château d'Yquem vineyard. Anne and Allan can supply picnics and bikes so saddle up for a ride along the easy-going cycle paths that criss-cross through the local pine forests. *Over 15s welcome.*

Rooms	2 doubles: €70.
	1 family room for 3: €70-€90.
	Singles €60. Extra bed €20.
	Cot available.
Meals	Dinner €28; children under 12,
	€19; 48 hours advanced booking
	required.
Closed	Rarely.

Rooms	3 suites for 2: €90-€95.
	Extra bed €22, with breakfast.
Meals	Dinner, 3 courses with wine, €29.
	Restaurants 7km.
Closed	Never.

Mobile	+33 (0)6 81 97 02 92
Email	jpdoebel@club-internet.fr
Web	www.chambresdhotesjanoutic.com

Jean-Pierre Doebele
Chambres d'Hôtes Janoutic,
2 Le Tach,
33124 Aillas, Gironde

Email	contact@prechac-park.com
Web	prechac-park.com

Anne & Allan Sanders
Préchac park,
2 avenue de la République,
33730 Préchac, Gironde

ENTRY 386   MAP 9

ENTRY 387   MAP 9

La Sauternaise

You stay in the very heart of the village of Sauternes, next door to the church in a smartly converted wine tasting building. The area is renowned for its sweet dessert wine – sit in the jasmine-covered courtyard sipping a cold glass and watch village life slip by. Pascale and Didier, your hosts, live a few hundred meters away in the vineyard. They settle you in, give you a set of keys, and each morning one of them pops over to prepare breakfast: pastries, crusty bread, cheese, fruit, ham and eggs. Eat in the dining room, or the courtyard on fine days. Walk to two vineyards – Château Guiraud (behind the house) and Château d'Yquem – or for lunch at one of the village restaurants (there are four). Hire bikes in the village; get in the car for trips to Bastide towns and chateau. Pascale and Didier can advise.

Domaine de l'Espelette

Take a picnic to the stream, stroll down the avenue into the village, let the children frolic, swim in the shaded pool. This long house, tucked into the hillside and overlooking the Romanesque church, dates from the 15th century. Unearth a treasure or two in the sitting room and library shared with the owners: books, magazines, paintings. Bedrooms are reassuringly chintzy, bathrooms generously marble. Madame is happy to serve breakfast until two o'clock; in such a haven she's used to guests oversleeping and the thick walls will ensure you won't hear a murmur from the grandchildren playing upstairs. *Minimum stay: 2 nights. Children over 12 welcome.*

Rooms	4 doubles: €115-€128.
Meals	Restaurants within walking distance.
Closed	Rarely.

Rooms	2 twin/doubles: €150-€200.
Meals	Welcome dinner by arrangement, €15. Wine from €15. Restaurant 1.5km.
Closed	Rarely.

Email	pascale@lasauternaise.com
Web	www.chambres-sauternes.com

Pascale & Didier Galhaud
La Sauternaise,
22 rue principale,
33210 Sauternes, Gironde

Mobile	+33 (0)6 63 82 01 78
Email	contact@domainedelespelette.com
Web	www.domainedelespelette.com

Silvia Prevost
Domaine de l'Espelette,
Route de Chaumont,
33550 Haux, Gironde

Château de Castelneau

A heavenly 14th-century château with Provençal towers. Behind: a shuttered 17th-century façade, a courtyard with outbuildings and an avenue lined with young trees. All around: hectares of vines. The de Roquefeuils are a warm, intelligent, enthusiastic couple, working their socks off to make the estate pay (and oh! the claret is delicious). Bedrooms are simple, comfortable, traditional – and there's a landing with videos for early risers. Downstairs: stone flags, rugs, books, paintings, eclectic aristocratic furnishings, and breakfasts generous and delicious. Enjoy the sunny pool and take a tour of the cellars. Outstanding.

Domaine de la Freynelle

Tranquillity on offer at a traditional Girondine manor on the edge of a hamlet, with airy rooms and quaint bric a brac. Multilingual host Sacha has worked as a journalist all over the world and loves cooking. She's passionate about caviar and has written a recipe book; much of what she serves is homegrown with eco-friendly pesticides like garlic! Discover every spot in the gardens – follow a herb trail, smell the roses, swim in the heated pool, play pétanque, tennis or get a hole in one on the par 3! Head off and pick fruit in the orchard or take a stroll for a café lunch. Saint-Émilion and Pomerol in easy reach. Enchanting. *Minimum stay: 2 nights July & Aug. Over 14s welcome.*

Rooms	2 twin/doubles: €130-€210. 1 annexe for 2: €130-€210.
Meals	Restaurants 2km.
Closed	1 November – 28 February.

Rooms	1 double, 1 twin sharing bathroom; let to same party only: €110-€125. 1 suite for 2 with kitchen, 1 suite for 2 with sitting room and gym: €110-€125.
Meals	Dinner, 3 courses with wine, €40; by arrangement. Restaurants 15-minute drive.
Closed	October – end of April.

Tel	+33 (0)5 56 23 47 01
Email	dianederoquefeuil@gmail.com
Web	www.chateaudecastelneau.com

Loïc & Diane de Roquefeuil
Château de Castelneau,
8 route de Breuil, Lieu-dit Châteauneuf,
33670 Saint Léon, Gironde

Mobile	+33 (0)5 57 24 97 42
Email	sachitza@yahoo.com
Web	www.brunchcaviar.com

Sacha de Frisching
Domaine de la Freynelle,
Plantey d'Oline,
33420 Espiet, Gironde

Ecolodge des Chartrons

La Suite

Feel inspired by this wonderful 18th-century house showcasing modern sustainable living ideals. Up the steep stone staircase are bedrooms with soft colours, organic linen and cheerful rugs; solar panels and sun pipes heat the water for splendid shower rooms, insulation is all natural wool and cork. Owners Muriel and Arnaud, artists and photographers in their spare time, mix their own black and white images with art and objects on the walls. Eat fabulous all organic breakfasts in the dining area or airy courtyard with glass roof. Nearby flows the Garonne, where converted riverside warehouses host cafés, shops and galleries. *Minimum stay: 2 nights.*

Sleep like kings in the heart of lovely Bordeaux. Climb the monumental staircase to your suite in a private mansion. It's a festival of pictures, colours and textures. There's so much to look at that it's hard to close your eyes. Vibrant Emmanuelle lives on the same floor, loves her city and will tell you all about its treasures and stories when she brings copious breakfast to your baroque-modern sitting room. Enjoy the high ceilings, original panelling and antiques, the superb bedding and fabrics. The bigger bedroom is exquisite but the elegant tall windows are single-glazed... A rare treat of a B&B. *Over 12s welcome.*

Rooms 3 doubles: €115-€149. 1 triple: €188. Extra bed/sofabed €32 p.p. per night.	**Rooms** 1 suite for 4: €190-€220.
Meals Restaurants within walking distance.	**Meals** Restaurants 2-minute walk.
Closed Rarely.	**Closed** 1 November – 31 March.

Tel +33 (0)5 56 81 49 13
Email veronique@ecolodgedeschartrons.com
Web www.ecolodgedeschartrons.com

Arnaud & Muriel Roudsovsky
Ecolodge des Chartrons,
23 rue Raze,
33000 Bordeaux, Gironde

Tel +33 (0)6 08 73 28 59
Email touna33@gmail.com

Emmanuelle Robine
La Suite,
15 Cours de Verdun,
33000 Bordeaux, Gironde

Casa Blanca

This chic, understated B&B is next to a leafy park in a quiet part of Bordeaux. Gildas lives on-site with his wife and is genuinely friendly; he'll tell you all about the house and area and give you a bottle of his family's claret to try – you can visit their vineyard too. Breakfast is a la carte and includes fruit, cheese, avocado toast, organic yoghurt and granola, plus eggs however you like them and pastries, bread and jams. Stay in and relax in the sitting area in your room, or the ground floor living area which has a bar and courtyard garden. You're minutes from dozens of good restaurants and the trendy Chartrons quarter, as well as the main town centre for art museums and the river. Rent bikes to explore, take a picnic to the park, ask Gildas about dinners using seasonal produce from the market.

L'Esprit des Chartrons

A delicious vintage townhouse in chic Chartrons, metres from the Garonne quays where Bordeaux's bourgeoisie once traded: 21st-century design blends with wine-soaked history. Playful bedrooms are named after famous local writers: glamorous Montaigne with bubble tub; red-brick, industrial-style Montesquieu; light-filled Mauriac. There are private terraces for tête-à-têtes, swish Italian bathrooms for pampering, a leafy sun terrace and a stylish stove-warmed salon for breakfast (crisp pastries, real hot chocolate). On a quiet lane, with covered parking, yet a stroll from restaurant-lined streets and World Heritage sites.

Rooms	5 doubles: €135-€195. Extra bed available in 2 rooms, €50.
Meals	Restaurants within walking distance.
Closed	Rarely.

Rooms	2 doubles, 1 twin/double: €115-€155. Singles €105-€135.
Meals	Restaurants nearby.
Closed	Rarely.

Tel	+33 (0)6 85 72 76 11
Email	booking@casablanca-bordeaux.com
Web	www.casablanca-bordeaux.com/en/

Gildas Quellien
Casa Blanca,
39 rue de la Course,
33000 Bordeaux, Gironde

Tel	+33 (0)5 56 51 65 87
Email	brigitte.gourlat@gmail.com
Web	www.lespritdeschartrons.fr

Brigitte Gourlat
L'Esprit des Chartrons,
17 bis rue Borie,
33300 Bordeaux, Gironde

Manoir d'Astrée

In the gentle folds of Bordeaux sits this 1766 house half way up a hill, with views across vineyards – swoop through electronic gates to find owner Béatrice who gives you a comfortable shared sitting room and four private-feeling bedrooms. There are three on the ground floor and one upstairs, all with a Gustavian flavour and extremely plush; sleep peacefully in beautifully dressed beds, pad around serious bathrooms with soft robes and pebble flooring. Breakfast (outside on balmy days) on local jams, honey and fresh pastries from the village baker. Splash in the pool, wander the grounds, visit vineyards, discover Perigueux. Restful.
Minimum stay: 2 nights; 3 in high season.

Clos Marcamps

A super-stylish makeover by the de Gamas who moved here from Paris with their young children. All is pale and lovely, clear and uncluttered – designed to enhance the elegant proportions of this handsome Chartreuse house. You eat – superbly and seasonally – in the main house. You sleep in beautifully compact rooms in the converted barns. Each has it's own entrance and is on two levels with beds upstairs. Bathrooms are sleek, with walk-in showers; one a spa bath. Roam the grounds; there's a wow of a pool, swings and table tennis; stroll through the vines; book beauty treatments, or baby-sitting, and head for Bordeaux. Smart.

Rooms	3 twin/doubles: €120-€160. 1 suite for 2: €145-€200. Extra bed/sofabed €40-€70 p.p. per night.
Meals	Restaurant 2km.
Closed	23 November – 31 March.

Rooms	2 doubles: €95-€250. 3 suites for 2: €110-€170.
Meals	Dinner €35. Restaurant 7km.
Closed	Rarely.

Tel	+33 (0)5 57 25 24 25
Email	contact@manoirdastree-bordeaux.com
Web	www.manoirdastree-bordeaux.com

Béatrice Rengner
Manoir d'Astrée,
Lieu dit Pelet, 33240 Lugon et l'Ile du Carnay,
Gironde

Tel	+33 (0)5 57 58 57 09
Email	contact@closmarcamps.fr
Web	www.closmarcamps.fr

Alexandre da Gama
Clos Marcamps,
2 chemin des Carièrres,
33710 Prignac et Marcamps, Gironde

ENTRY 396 MAP 9   ENTRY 397 MAP 8

Château l'Hospital

Vineyards surround the Duhamels' restored 15th-century Girondine home and Bruno is keen to show you around and share his passion for their organically produced Côtes de Bourg wines. He's also in charge of breakfasts – honey, fresh orange juice, homemade brioche and jams – served indoors or on the terrace, with uninterrupted views. Dinner, with terroir wine of course, can be arranged; perhaps after visiting Bordeaux, 30 minutes south. Bedrooms are spotless and spacious – no frills, no surprises! – with gleaming new floors and windows, and modern bathrooms. It's peaceful here, with lovely walks through the vines.

La Girarde

In gentle countryside of wooded valleys near pretty Ste Foy la Grande, this smartly renovated farmhouse has its origins in the wine industry; St Émilion lives and breathes wine. You will be impeccably looked after by lovely, relaxed, fuss-free owners Trish and Mark, who give you serene rooms in classical-chic style – heated stone floors, designer fabrics, African art, touches of tartan from home. All the bedrooms, upstairs and down, have big beds and super bathrooms, and dinners are delicious. Outside: a lovely terrace, a park-like garden edged with cedars and weeping willows, a heated saltwater pool. Gorgeous!

Rooms	1 double, 1 suite for 2: €79-€89. Singles €69-€72. Extra person €10.	**Rooms**	2 doubles, 2 twin/doubles: €115-€130. Extra bed/sofabed €30 p.p. per night.
Meals	Dinner with wine, €25-€35, on request. Children's meal available.	**Meals**	Dinner €27; children over 7, €15; under 7, €7. Wine €15-€45.
Closed	15 September – 15 October.	**Closed**	Rarely.

Tel	+33 (0)5 57 64 33 60	**Tel**	+33 (0)5 57 41 02 68
Email	alvitis@wanadoo.fr	**Email**	bienvenue@lagirarde.com
Web	www.alvitis.fr	**Web**	www.lagirarde.com

Christine & Bruno Duhamel
Château l'Hospital,
33710 Saint Trojan,
Gironde

Trish Tyler
La Girarde,
33220 St Quentin de Caplong,
Gironde

Château Gauthié

Outside a perfect bastide village, here is a château B&B run with warmth and energy. Stéphane cooks brilliantly and loves wine; Florence is enormous fun, a breath of fresh air. Restful, light-filled, traditional bedrooms have white bathrooms. An infinity pool overlooks the lake below, above it perches the rustic-modern treehouse, its balcony gazing over meadows and cows, its mother tree thrusting two branches through the floor. Solar-lit paths lead you down through the trees at night, a breakfast basket is winched up in the morning. Later... play badminton, fish in the lake, spin off on a bike, bask in the hot tub. *Min. stay: 2 nights; 7 nights in treehouses in summer.*

La Gentilhommière-Etincelles

This stone manor house is on a picturesque square in a village deep in the countryside, but well-placed for exploring the Dordogne and Périgord. Vincent has an infectious sense of humour and that happy knack of making you feel at home. Find big, comfy rooms with armchairs and a guest salon/library; wander past the veg patch to find the pool at the end of the garden. He's passionate about his B&B and good food. His restaurant, Etincelles, is open for dinner most evenings and for lunch on weekends and in the high season. It has a friendly, informal feel and there's just one menu - the five courses are an adventurous surprise, based on what's best on the day. Ask about markets, food producers, vineyards – Vincent has lots of tips - visit bastide towns, châteaux and ancient cave paintings.

Rooms	3 doubles, 1 twin: €90-€115. 1 treehouse for 2: €133-€175. 1 self-catering treehouse for 5: €1050-€1540 per week.
Meals	Dinner, 4 courses with wine €40. Wine €15-€50.
Closed	Mid-November to March.

Rooms	3 doubles: €115. Tourist Tax €0.75 p.p. per day. Enjoy two glasses of Mauzac de Plageoles and organic macaroons for €34 on arrival.
Meals	Restaurant Etincelles: dinner €59.
Closed	Christmas, Easter, Bank Holidays.

Tel	+33 (0)5 53 27 30 33
Email	chateau.gauthie@laposte.net
Web	www.chateaugauthie.com

Florence & Stéphane Desmette
Château Gauthié,
24560 Issigeac Monmarvès,
Dordogne

Tel	+33 (0)5 53 74 08 79
Email	accueil@gentilhommiere-etincelles.com
Web	www.gentilhommiere-etincelles.com

Vincent Lucas
La Gentilhommière-Etincelles,
Le bourg, 24440 Ste Sabine Born,
Dordogne

ENTRY 400   MAP 9

ENTRY 401   MAP 9

Le Bourdil Blanc

Jane is a perfectionist, and that extends to her chef's 'îles flottantes', should you be inspired to book dinner one night. She also spoils you with luscious fresh fruit at breakfast – and interesting, compelling conversation. Her beloved house is glorious with soft spaces, antiques and fine fabrics, modern shower rooms and old beams, kilims on parquet floors and open log fires. The super great garden has tennis, a big heated pool and all the secret corners you could wish for. Come for a week to ride horses, learn French or trawl the wonders of the Dordogne. Or just for a night before flying from nearby Bergerac.

Manoir de Beauregard

Charlotte and Thierry welcome you to their new family project: a 17th-century house set in 40 acres of gardens with grass paths and wide views. Inside is filled with taste and passion: discover antiques, French and Italian painted furniture, bedrooms with hand carved four-poster beds, embroidered sheets and limewashed beams. Splash in the pool in summer, warm yourself by a big log fire on chilly days with tea and homemade cakes. Cooking is a passion so you'll be well fed on the best local ingredients with vegetables and fruits from their garden. Charlotte also offers arts and crafts courses.

Rooms	3 doubles, 3 twins: €70-€90. Singles €70. Extra bed/sofabed at no charge.		**Rooms**	3 doubles: €145-€160. Extra bed/sofabed €35 p.p. per night. Cot and high chair €25.
Meals	Dinner €20, by arrangement.		**Meals**	Breakfast €8. Afternoon tea €5. Dinner, 4 courses, with wine, from €35. Restaurant 1.5km.
Closed	July & August (the house becomes self-catering accommodation)		**Closed**	20 November – 15 March.

Tel	+33 (0)6 32 62 43 15		**Email**	th.landron@gmail.com
Email	jhanslip@aol.com		**Web**	manoirbeauregarddordogne.com
Web	www.bourdilblanc.com			

Jane Hanslip
Le Bourdil Blanc,
24520 Saint Sauveur de Bergerac,
Dordogne

Thierry & Charlotte Landron
Manoir de Beauregard,
Le Grand But,
24140 Clermont de Beauregard, Dordogne

ENTRY 402 MAP 9 ENTRY 403 MAP 9

The Old Bakery

A place of rest for weary travellers in the Dordogne, simple and green with a wood stove in the snug and full English or continental breakfast each morning. Owner Louis has opened up this old baker's building, so that the sitting room and kitchen flow into one – and out through terrace doors to the lush garden. You can wander among the fruit trees or lie in the shade of an old pine, soaking up the peace of this hamlet near the market town of Montpon Ménestérol. Artworks, vintage furniture and objets will keep you intrigued, and you wake on a handmade mattress to see the sun rise over the vegetable patch.
Minimum stay: 2 nights at weekends.

Dolce Vita en Dordogne

You could sit under the trees with Alexandra and chat all day: she is the calmest and the loveliest of hosts. She and her soon-to-retire husband live in a handsome hunting lodge built by a Bordeaux wine producer, sharing the central courtyard with two large, luminous, ground-floor suites with private entrances, a fridge and impeccable décor. If the 'parc' is a joy – all hidden corners, luxurious pool, shaded lawns meandering down to the river – breakfast is a marvel. There are seasonal fruits and homemade everything: croque monsieur, clafoutis, brioches and wild plum jam, all beautifully presented in the long library, or outside in summer.
Parking on-site.

Rooms	1 double: €65-€75.		**Rooms**	2 suites for 2: €120-€140.
Meals	Dinner & picnics available.		**Meals**	Restaurants 10-minute drive.
Closed	Rarely.		**Closed**	January/February.

Tel	+33 (0)5 53 82 34 59		**Mobile**	+33 (0)6 70 72 88 78
Email	louoldbakery@icloud.com		**Email**	alexandra.hudson@ymail.com
Web	www.oldbakeryfrance.co.uk			

Lou O'Leary
The Old Bakery,
29 rue Jean Monnet,
24700 Montpon Ménestérol, Dordogne

Alexandra Hudson
Dolce Vita en Dordogne,
20 rue de la République,
24700 Moulin-Neuf, Dordogne

ENTRY 404   MAP 9

ENTRY 405   MAP 9

Le Moulin Neuf

Robert's greeting is the first line of an ode to hospitality written in warm stone in breathtaking gardens, set to the tune of the mill stream. Immaculate rooms in the guest barn are comfortingly filled with good beds and fresh flowers, bathrooms are sheer luxury, and views sweep over the lawns. Wake up to a royal breakfast of breads, croissants, pâtisseries, jams, fruits and tiny cheeses served on white tablecloths on the vine-shaded veranda or on the terrace overlooking the garden. All is beautifully, lovingly tended by Robert. His two happy rescue dogs will make friends with yours; find your own special spot in the gardens. *Children over 10 welcome. Minimum stay: 3 nights in winter. Pets by arrangement.*

Maison Oléa

High in the hills, on the rustic-suburban outskirts of Le Bugue, is a hospitable house, designed and built expressly for B&B. Roses billow around the infinity pool, views pour over the valley, and children are free to roam. The house hums with people, the owners are delightful and the bedrooms, four with terraces and one on the ground floor, are filled with light and decorated with flair; big bathrooms have a Mediterranean theme. This is the Dordogne, and hosted dinners – fun affairs – flourish truffles, duck and Perigordian treats, as well as fruit and veg from the great gardens. *Minimum stay: 4 nights in high season.*

Rooms	2 doubles, 2 twin/doubles: €94-€98. 1 family room for 5: €124-€218. Singles €82.60-€86.60.		**Rooms**	2 twin/doubles: €75-€105. 1 family room for 3, 2 family rooms for 4: €85-€105.
Meals	Restaurant in Paunat, 1km.		**Meals**	Dinner with wine, €25-€35. Restaurants 3km.
Closed	Rarely.		**Closed**	15 December – 15 January.

Tel	+33 (0)5 53 63 30 18		**Tel**	+33 (0)5 53 08 48 93
Email	moulin-neuf@usa.net		**Email**	maison.olea.dordogne@gmail.com
Web	www.the-moulin-neuf.com		**Web**	www.olea-dordogne.com

Robert Chappell
Le Moulin Neuf,
Paunat, 24510 Ste Alvère,
Dordogne

Murielle Nardou
Maison Oléa,
La Combe de Leygue,
24260 Le Bugue, Dordogne

ENTRY 406   MAP 9

ENTRY 407   MAP 9

Manoir de la Brunie

An elegant village manor in a glorious setting: the views are stupendous. The owners live in Paris but the genial manager will introduce you to a fine living room full of warm bright colours overlooking a sweeping lawn (play the piano, browse the books) and excellent bedrooms. The tower suite and small double have a modern feel, the other rooms, huge and high-ceilinged, are more classical; all have subtle colours, new wood floors, space for armchairs and sofas, and good lighting. Breakfasts are fresh, bathrooms delightful... there's a heated pool shared with gîte guests, a river beach nearby, riding next door.

Domaine la Fagette

This 17th-century stone farmhouse is one of only three in a hamlet hidden in a hilly woodland of truffle oaks but is only five minutes to the nearest village. Christophe puts creative energy into everything he does, including breakfasts of homemade bread, jams using fruit from the orchard and a different cake every day. Enjoy hearty dinners featuring classic Périgord fare – cassoulet, confit de canard, truffles – all seasonal and sourced within a 10km radius of the house, and served in the dining room or on the terrace. Spend lazy days at the swimming pool overlooking the valley and forest beyond while you help yourself to drinks from the honesty bar. Walks leave from the house, or there are plenty of villages, gardens and chateaux to explore. *Minimum stay: 4 nights in high season. Over 15s welcome..*

Rooms	3 doubles, 1 twin/double: €75-€110. 1 suite for 4: €125-€140. Extra bed €17.	**Rooms**	2 doubles: €75-€150. 2 suites for 4: €170. Tourist tax: €1 p.p. per night.
Meals	Dinner with wine, €27.	**Meals**	Dinner €25-€35.
Closed	November – March.	**Closed**	2 November – 28 March.

Tel	+33 (0)5 53 31 95 62
Email	manoirdelabrunie@wanadoo.fr
Web	www.manoirdelabrunie.com

Jacqueline Bazire
Manoir de la Brunie,
La Brunie, 24220 Le Coux & Bigaroque,
Dordogne

Tel	+33 (0)5 53 30 32 39
Email	domainelafagette@gmail.com
Web	www.lafagette.com

Christophe & Magaly Breuil
Domaine la Fagette,
La Basse Fagette,
24220 Castels, Dordogne

Les Hauts de Saint Vincent

La Maison d'Alice

Your delightful hosts have combined the best of modern design with old French charm and travellers' treasures to create a thoughtful elegance and different moods in each room. Fabulous Dordogne views top it all off and help to make this handsome 17th-century house special. Bedrooms full of light, originality and comfort lead to excellent newly-done bathrooms; the living and dining rooms breathe the simplicity and warmth of glowing wood against old stone; breakfast is on the terrace where eyes sweep out to the river and Josephine Baker's château. Take the children to see Castelnaud's giant catapults and improbable armour; book early for Lascaux.

You're close to the main road to Sarlat and the Dordogne's attractions yet it's very tranquil. Alice has her own quarters so you'll feel quite private, the garden is pretty and there are views over low wooded hills and the river. Choose between breakfast on your private terrace or sit with other guests round the kitchen table for homemade jams, local yogurt, three types of bread, fresh pastries and fruit salad. If the weather is bad there's a comfy sitting room with a big TV and loads of channels. There's much watery fun to be had on the river just a stroll away, or you can walk its banks for miles. Riding, fishing and cycling are easily organised and if you don't want to go out for dinner Alice (a private chef in Paris for many years) can offer you beautiful home cooking with much from her garden or local producers. *Min. stay: 2 nights.*

Rooms	4 doubles: €115-€140. 1 triple: €130-€160. Singles €110-€130.
Meals	Dinner, 4 courses with wine, €35. Restaurants 2km.
Closed	1 February – 15 March.

Rooms	2 doubles: €120.
Meals	Dinner €30, by arrangement (24h prior notice).
Closed	Never.

Mobile	+33 (0)6 08 21 19 10
Email	contact@leshautsdesaintvincent.com
Web	leshautsdesaintvincent.com

Fabrice & Stephanie Berbessou
Les Hauts de Saint Vincent,
Le Pech, 24220 Saint-Vincent-de-Cosse,
Dordogne

Tel	+33 (0)6 81 40 32 97
Email	lamaisondalice24@orange.fr
Web	lamaisondalice.com/en/home/

Alice Della Monta
La Maison d'Alice,
Serneix Le Trel,
24220 Vezac, Dordogne

ENTRY 410   MAP 9

ENTRY 411   MAP 9

Manoir de la Malartrie

On the banks of the Dordogne river, a beautifully restored 19th-century manor house with luxurious rooms and a cosy, beamed gîte. Surrounded by fragrant Mediterranean gardens planted with lavender and rosemary, this is an idyllic retreat for sybarites. Inside, charming Ouafaa has blended Moroccan style with Edwardian elegance. Sleep in sumptuous bedrooms furnished with antiques; eat Franco-Moroccan meals made with fresh veg from the potager in the magnificent salon. There's a sleek pool and you can watch boats sail by as you picnic in the grounds. Explore grand châteaux or stroll to pretty La Roque-Gageac for shops and restaurants. *Minimum stay: 3 nights. Heated pool available May-Oct.*

La Guérinière

Once a charterhouse in private parkland, this big, good-looking Périgord house, on a hill facing Domme, is a tribute to the rich sober taste of the area. Inside reflects outside: the same dark timbers against pale stone. The feel is warmly authentic and the owners have redecorated the bedrooms most charmingly, gradually replacing the modern furniture with country antiques. They used to run a restaurant; now there's a big candlelit table for guests and you may find more gourmets in the beamed dining room (outsiders are occasionally allowed in). Outside: palm trees and pool. A gem.

Rooms	4 doubles; 1 with terrace: €120-€220. 1 suite for 4: €200-€310. 1 apartment for 2: €175-€290. Sofabeds available €30 per night.	**Rooms**	2 doubles, 2 twin/doubles: €90-€105. 2 triples: €130-€160.
Meals	Dinner with wine & appetizer, €50. Available for groups of 8 or more. Restaurants 5-minute walk.	**Meals**	Dinner €30. Wine from €20.
		Closed	Never.
Closed	Mid-Dec to mid-March (except pre-booked Christmas parties).		

Tel	+33 (0)5 53 29 03 51	**Tel**	+33 (0)5 53 29 91 97
Email	lamalartrie@orange.fr	**Email**	contact@la-gueriniere-dordogne.com
Web	www.manoir-lamalartrie.com	**Web**	www.la-gueriniere-dordogne.com

Ouafaa Diebolt-Balbal
Manoir de la Malartrie,
La Malartrie,
24220 Vezac, Dordogne

Brigitte & Christophe Demassougne
La Guérinière,
Baccas,
24250 Cénac & St Julien, Dordogne

ENTRY 412 MAP 9   ENTRY 413 MAP 9

Les Chambres de la Voie Verte

Steps curl up and around the old stone walls and lead to four delightful rooms, each with its own outside entrance. Find soft colours, comfortable beds and state-of-the-art bathrooms with walk-in showers. From the top floor, views stretch over the town to Montfort château beyond. Enjoy breakfast off white Limoges china at the long table in the house next door, and on the terrace on warm days. Extrovert Madame was born in this house and knows the village and everyone in it very well; she's passionate about the history, hiking, bike rides, gastronomy... and happy to advise. The old railway track for cycling to Sarlat and Souillac is near. *Minimum stay: 2 nights in high season.*

La Roche d'Esteil

Another haven of peace in the bustling Dordogne – this time with a marvellous chef. Four miles from Sarlat, on the edge of the village, is a Perigourdine farmstead in lovely lawned grounds, with a pool hiding behind a walled garden. Maarten and Karen, serious but fun, loving their new life, left stressful jobs in Belgium (she ex lawyer, he ex sommelier) to bring up their young son in the country. They have four country comfortable bedrooms in two restored barns, and one in the house. Get cosy in the sitting rooms, laze by the pool, linger over dinner in the rustic-chic dining room. Maarten's twice-weekly 'cuisine du terroir' will enchant you. *Minimum stay: 4 nights in high season.*

Rooms	2 doubles, 2 twin/doubles: €72-€87. Extra bed/sofabed €22 p.p. per night.	**Rooms**	3 doubles: €95-€135. 1 suite for 3, 1 suite for 4: €95-€180. Singles €85-€92. Extra bed/sofabed €28 p.p. per night.
Meals	Restaurants 100m. Caterer available.	**Meals**	Dinner, 3 courses, €38. Child under 10 €15.
Closed	Rarely.	**Closed**	1 December – 16 March.

Mobile	+33 (0)6 70 09 38 95	**Tel**	+33 (0)5 53 29 14 42
Email	annie.boyer43@orange.fr	**Email**	contact@larochedesteil.com
Web	www.leschambresdelavoieverte.com	**Web**	www.larochedesteil.com

Annie Boyer
Les Chambres de la Voie Verte,
24200 Carsac Aillac,
Dordogne

Karen & Maarten Ilegems
La Roche d'Esteil,
Lieu dit La Croix d'Esteil,
24200 Sainte-Nathalène, Dordogne

ENTRY 414   MAP 9

ENTRY 415   MAP 9

Les Charmes de Carlucet

A sense of calm luxury hangs over this fine old house in the Dordogne's golden triangle where prehistoric men made their stunning cave paintings. Your young Anglo-Swedish hosts, well-travelled, enterprising and attentive to detail, serve perfectly soft-boiled eggs for breakfast. Calm-coloured sitting and dining rooms are huge, furnished with a relaxed mix of period and comfortable contemporary pieces; upstairs, the super bedding is brand new and the best room has a terrace. There's a lovely garden to relax in and a huge pool but you're near Sarlat la Canéda and only 15 minutes from Lascaux caves – do book your visit well ahead.

Auberge de Castel-Merle

High above the valley of the Vézère is an atmospheric inn where a Templar castle once stood; terrace views are peerless. It's been in Anita's family for generations, she and Christopher lovingly renovated the buildings with great care, keeping the traditional look, and using walnut wood from the land to restore bed heads and doors. Pastel, pelmets and painted flowers on the walls clothe the dining room where you breakfast on truffle omelettes; modest bedrooms, overlooking courtyard or woods, have beams, stone walls and wooden floors; shower rooms are compact. Walk to the hamlet, hike through the forests. Great value.

Rooms	5 doubles: €95-€145. Extra bed/sofabed €25 p.p. per night.
Meals	Restaurants 10-minute walk.
Closed	23 June – 7 September (operates as a self-catering house for 12)

Rooms	7 doubles, 1 twin: €82-€88. Singles €69-€79.
Meals	Wine €9-€28. Picnics and light snacks available on request. Restaurants 10-minute walk.
Closed	2 October – 1 April.

Mobile	+33 (0)6 84 22 79 86
Email	contact@carlucet.com
Web	www.carlucet.com

Kerry Flaherty-Rask
Les Charmes de Carlucet,
24590 St Crépin & Carlucet,
Dordogne

Tel	+33 (0)5 53 50 70 08
Email	hotelcastelmerle@yahoo.fr
Web	www.hotelcastelmerle.com

Anita Castanet & Christopher Millinship
Auberge de Castel-Merle,
24290 Sergeac,
Dordogne

ENTRY 416   MAP 9

ENTRY 417   MAP 9

La Boissière

In a bucolic valley in the Périgord Vert, a stately B&B bordering village and fields. Built in the 18th-century, the beautiful house sits in immaculate lawns shaded by lime trees; the silence is blissful. Delightful Caroline and Dominique have expertly converted an annexe to create three elegant, spacious rooms. Finely-dressed beds, antiques and contemporary bathrooms add charm and comfort. Terracotta-floored Agapanthe opens onto the garden, while Escallonia has extra space for a child or two. Breakfast on brioche and home-made jam in the soothing dining room, take a dip in the pool, or hire kayaks to paddle down the Dronne.

Le Logis La Montagne

What an idyllic spot from which to explore Lusignac, St Severin and Ribérac. Le Logis is set in a 17-acre park and St Emilion vineyards are only 40km away. Welcoming Cornelia will quickly make you at home; monsieur is a wine dealer. Their 1700s Chartreuse house has been beautifully restored with an eye to its former glory; four bedrooms and a suite lead off a long corridor (on the first floor) where coffee machine and comfy chairs wait, and light pours in. Outside, one of the loveliest pools we've seen: sloping down from a sandy 'beach', shared with the gîte. Ideal for groups, so gather your best friends for an enchanting escape.

Rooms	1 double, 1 twin/double: €95-€105. 1 suite for 3: €105. Extra bed €30.
Meals	Restaurants 3km.
Closed	1 November – 28 February.

Rooms	4 doubles: €125-€175. 1 suite for 2: €195-€210. Extra bed €10 per night + €12 for breakfast.
Meals	Please enquire with owner. Restaurants 2km.
Closed	November – Easter.

Tel	+33 (0)5 53 91 14 51
Email	ddemercey@hotmail.fr
Web	www.laboissiere-grandbrassac.com

Caroline de Mercey
La Boissière,
Le Bourg, 24350 Grand Brassac,
Dordogne

Tel	+33 (0)5 53 91 51 87
Email	lelogislachartreuse@gmail.com
Web	www.lelogis-lamontagne.fr

Cornelia Dumoncel d'Argence
Le Logis La Montagne,
La Montagne, 24600 Allemans,
Dordogne

ENTRY 418 MAP 9

ENTRY 419 MAP 9

Le Chatenet

Brantôme has layers of history. The grand Benedictine abbey, carved out at the bottom of the cliffs, overlooks the river Dronne, and just up the road, a perfect distance from hustle and bustle, is this Périgord-style stone house built at the end of the 17th century. Jane and William are super hosts and give you big rooms with stunning fabric on the walls, billiards in the games room, swimming pool, breakfast eggs and milk from the nearby farm. Canoe the rivers, explore grottoes, sit on the veranda and follow the sun as it sets over walnut trees and green valleys. The town is a ten-minute stroll – don't miss the Friday market.

Château de Clauzuroux

An archway and grand courtyard greet your arrival at the 17th-century country chateau. Proud owners Patrick and multilingual Séverine are friendly hosts – it's been in the family since 1825. Roam bewitching gardens, breathe in lavender and rose amongst manicured topiary, admire the old mill race staircase and pretty pigeonnier, swim in the heated pool. Take your pick of terraces for lazy afternoons (chambre 'Jaune' and 'Coco' have their own delightful roof spaces too). Angoulême and Périgueux are in reach for days out, Brantôme for canoeing on the Drôme, and pretty Villebois-Lavalette is a short drive for shops and restaurants.

Rooms	3 twin/doubles: €135-€160. 2 suites for 2: €175-€220. Extra bed €25.
Meals	Dinner from €30. Wine from €25. Restaurant 1km.
Closed	Mid-October to mid-April.

Rooms	2 doubles, 2 twin/doubles: €100-€150. 1 family room for 3: €150.
Meals	Restaurants 3km.
Closed	Mid-October to April.

Tel	+33 (0)5 53 05 81 08
Email	lechatenet@gmail.com
Web	www.lechatenet.com

Jane & William Laxton
Le Chatenet,
Lieu-dit Le Chatenet,
24310 Brantôme, Dordogne

Tel	+33 (0)6 09 41 24 19
Email	sdereixdelaplane@yahoo.fr
Web	www.clauzuroux.com

Séverine & Patrick Dereix de Laplane
Château de Clauzuroux,
24320 Champagne et Fontaine,
Dordogne

ENTRY 420   MAP 9

ENTRY 421   MAP 9

Limousin

Le Jardin des Lys, page 308

La Maison des Chanoines

Built for the canons (*chanoines*) of Turenne, this ancient hotel-restaurant has been in Claude's family for 300 years. No wonder the family held on to it: the 16th-century, mellow-stoned house with its steep slate roof is one of the loveliest in a very lovely village. Chantal, charming and gracious, takes care of guests from dawn to dusk, always with a smile. The pretty bedrooms, freshly decorated, are scattered among outbuildings, two of them approached via a little bridge from the garden. Well lit, they have parquet floors and white walls; bathrooms ooze fluffy towels. The stone-flagged breakfast room feels ancient and airy. Dining takes place in the cosy old cellar whose ceiling vaults over just six white-clothed tables – nicely intimate – or under a fairy-lit pergola in the garden amid honeysuckle and roses where you are asked to 'pour your ice-bucket water onto the tomatoes'. The food is a delight; Claude is the chef and will use only the freshest, most local produce for his much-praised regional dishes. Ask about their three-day gourmet stay. Great value. *Private parking available.*

Rooms	2 doubles , 1 twin/double: €90-€140. 2 suites for 3: €105-€140. 1 family room for 4: €115-€155.
Meals	Breakfast €11. Dinner €41-€59.
Closed	Never.

Tel	+33 (0)5 55 85 93 43
Email	maisondeschanoines@wanadoo.fr
Web	www.maison-des-chanoines.com

Chantal & Claude Cheyroux
La Maison des Chanoines,
Rue Joseph Rouveyrol,
19500 Turenne, Corrèze

ENTRY 422   MAP 9

Maison Grandchamp

In an historic town, be welcomed by a charming, cultured couple to a 400-year-old house of fascinating origins. Thrill to Marielle's tales: her ancestors built and extended the house, their portraits hang in the panelled drawing room; find time for François' knowledge of history, geography and the environment. Up the elegant spiral stairs, bedrooms are in proper but unpompous château style, big, soft and quiet. Breakfast is in the beamy 16th-century dining room, or by the kitchen fire, or in the terraced garden overlooking jumbled rooftops, or on the luminous veranda. Explore Treignac – you're right next to the church and the town is filled with medieval and renaissance buildings. Hike or bike through beautiful parkland at the foot of the mountains. Foodies will flock to the local markets which pay homage to the farmers and growers of the area: wild mushrooms and chestnuts in autumn, Limousin beef, black pork, truffles and wine made with grapes rested on straw. There are lots of watery activities you can take part in too in the rivers, lakes and canyons; try canoeing, kayaking and sailing.

Rooms	2 twin/doubles; 1 twin/double with separate bathroom: €80-€94. Extra bed €25. Overflow room for 2 available. €5 discount per night if you book 3+ nights.
Meals	Dinner with apéritif & wine, €29-€32, on request. Restaurants within walking distance.
Closed	6 November – 1 April.

Marielle & François Teyssier
Maison Grandchamp,
9 place des Pénitents,
19260 Treignac, Corrèze

Tel	+33 (0)5 55 98 10 69
Mobile	+33 (0)6 59 05 09 46
Email	teyssier.marielle@wanadoo.fr
Web	www.hotesgrandchamp.com

ENTRY 423   MAP 10

Moulin de Marsaguet

The nicest people, they have done just enough to this proud old building so it looks as it did 200 years ago when it forged cannon balls. The farm is relaxed and natural, the bedrooms quaint, they have ducks and animals (including Lusitanian horses), three teenagers and a super potager, and make pâtés and 'confits' by the great mill pond, hanging the hams over the magnificent hearth in their big stone sitting room with its old-fashioned sofa. Relish the drive up past tree-framed lake (boating possible) and stone outbuildings and the prospect of breakfasting on home-grown ingredients. *Pets by arrangement.*

Les Hauts Prés de Fressanges

Getting here is half the fun. Narrow twisting roads lead you up to the ancient house with views across the Limousin landscape dotted with châteaux and pretty villages. You stay in the main house where breakfasts of fresh pastries and homemade jams are served in the dining room at one big table, or out in the sunny courtyard. If you prefer independence choose the separate studio (not July or August) which has its own little kitchen but you can have breakfast brought to you. There are miles of unspoilt country to walk, cycle, canoe, or ride. The village of Magnac-Bourg is a ten-minute drive and has good restaurants and shops; Limoges is 25 minutes, and one of the most beautiful villages in France, Collonges-la-Rouge, just an hour.

Rooms	3 twin/doubles: €62.
Meals	Dinner with wine, €25. Restaurant 3km.
Closed	November to mid-April.

Rooms	1 family room for 3: €110-€135. 1 studio for 4: €110-€155. Tourist tax €0.40 p.p. per night. Extra bed €25 p.p. per night.
Meals	Restaurants 7km.
Closed	15 December – 31 January.

Tel +33 (0)5 55 75 28 29
Email renaud.gizardin@sfr.fr
Web www.moulin-marsaguet.com

Valérie & Renaud Gizardin
Moulin de Marsaguet,
87500 Coussac Bonneval,
Haute-Vienne

Email leshautspresdefressanges87@orange.fr
Web www.leshautspresdefressanges87.fr

Claire Fournerie
Les Hauts Prés de Fressanges,
Lieu-dit Fressanges,
87260 Vicq-sur-Breuilh, Haute-Vienne

ENTRY 424 MAP 9

ENTRY 425 MAP 9

Les Jardins de Lily

Le Jardin des Lys

St Leonard de Noblat lies on an ancient pilgrim route and this B&B would have suited weary travellers: light rooms, a colourful garden with shady spots, a heated pool and a cosy fire in the lounge which you share with the owners. The feel is very tranquil and relaxed. Breakfast on fresh pastries and homemade strawberry jam on the sunny patio or at the communal table in the lounge before exploring. Wander through medieval streets, visit historic museums and churches or while away the afternoon with a picnic by the river Vienne. Return for a dip in the pool before heading out for a clutch of good places to eat close by. This is great walking, cycling and kayaking countryside and Limoges and Lake Vassivière are near.

Follow the brass shells in the cobbles to find Carole's elegant stone town-house opposite the soaring Collégiale. Peace reigns, apart from the tolling of bells and the whistling of swallows. Inside, all is light and airy with tall windows looking on to village views or the little walled garden. Carole's enthusiasm for Limousin is evident – local modern art, recipes researched from Limousin's rich gastronomic past and ingredients sourced from local farmers. Hand-made chocolates and *massepain* pillow-treats are from the local shops where you can get small gifts as B&B guests. There's much to keep you in the village including guided historic tours, walks around the lake (you can fish with a permit) and an amazing patisserie. Join walking paths through the woods 5km away or drive to Limoges (half an hour) for museums.

Rooms	3 doubles: €80-€85. 1 family room for 4: €110-€115. Extra bed/cot €15 per night. Singles from €60.
Meals	Restaurants 5 minute's walk.
Closed	30 November – 15 February.

Rooms	4 doubles: €99-€129. 1 family room for 5: €218-€233.
Meals	Dinner with wine, coffee & apéritif, €35; by arrangement. Child, €15. Restaurants 1-minute walk.
Closed	Rarely.

Email	surroca@wanadoo.fr
Web	www.lesjardinsdelily.fr

Email	le-jardin-des-lys@orange.fr
Web	www.le-jardin-des-lys.com

Lily Surroca
Les Jardins de Lily,
10 rue de Strasbourg,
87400 Saint Leonard de Noblat, Haute-Vienne

Carole Pagès
Le Jardin des Lys,
3 place de la Collégiale,
87400 Saint Léonard de Noblat, Haute-Vienne

Château Ribagnac

Guests will gently unwind here in Patrick and Colette's generous spirited, fuss-free care. Good food and wine, roaring fires, the offer of an early supper for children and no pesky rules. There's plenty of space, inside and out. Children can bound off to find the playground and jump in a lake while you laze beside the heated open-air pool. Breakfasts are sociable affairs with homemade jam and honey from their bees, dinners of local seasonal and home grown produce are candle-lit and outdoors whenever possible. Wild swimmers, walkers and wildlife lovers will adore this pretty, lake-filled, part of France. Roam through woods spotting deer, wild boar and birds of prey or hop in the car to lovely St Leonard de Noblat (15 minutes). It brims with medieval history and is on the Compostela route. *Min. stay: 2 nights in high season.*

Rooms	4 suites for 2: €120-€170.
Meals	Dinner with wine, €45.
Closed	Christmas.

Tel +33 (0)5 55 39 77 91
Email reservations@chateauribagnac.com
Web www.chateauribagnac.com

Patrick & Colette Bergot
Château Ribagnac,
87400 St Martin Terressus,
Haute-Vienne

ENTRY 428 MAP 9

Château du Fraisse

After 800 years of family and estate symbiosis, Le Fraisse is a living history book, mainly a rustic-grand Renaissance gem by the great Serlio – pale limestone, discreetly elegant portico, Henry II staircase and an astonishing fireplace in the vast drawing room. Your cultured hosts, two generations now, will greet you with warmth, happily tell you about house and history and show you to your room: fine furniture, paintings and prints, traditional furnishings; one bathroom has a fragment of a 16th-century fresco. If you return late at night you must climb the steep old spiral stair to your room as the main door is locked.

Rooms	1 double, 1 twin: €90-€100. 1 suite for 3, 1 suite for 4: €135-€150.
Meals	Restaurants 6km.
Closed	Mid-December to mid-January.

Tel +33 (0)5 55 68 32 68
Email infos@chateau-du-fraisse.com
Web www.chateau-du-fraisse.com

Marquis & Marquise des Monstiers Mérinville
Château du Fraisse,
Le Fraisse,
87330 Nouic, Haute-Vienne

ENTRY 429 MAP 9

La Pissarelle

In a green and lovely corner of France, discover the wee hamlet where Annie's family have always farmed. Here she and Wolfgang, (he worked with NATO and speaks impeccable English), have returned to renovate a highly personal, treasure-filled farmhouse with a cosily simple Petite Maison for guests just across the patio. Having lived all over the world, they adore having visitors at their table in the former cattle byre or in the new veranda – and hope you might park your horses in their field. Before the vast ex-château fireplace, you will be regaled with tales of local life and exotic lands. A fascinating couple.

Maison Numéro Neuf

Lisa and Duncan from England have embraced life in southern La Souterraine. She is the least ruffled, most contented of chefs; he serves wines with finesse; both love house, children, guests, and their secret garden with hens. Now, at last, the renovation of the former residence of the Marquis de Valady is complete. So much to enjoy: the fine proportions, the sweeping balustrade, the antique mirrors, the crystal-drop chandeliers, the pale walls, the glowing parquet... and superb breakfasts and dinners. If Lisa pops a hot water bottle into your bed it will be encased in white linen: the hospitality here is exceptional.

Rooms	1 cottage for 4: €80-€200. Children under 3 free. Extra single available.	**Rooms**	2 doubles; 1 twin sharing shower: €65-€115. Singles €45-€85. Dinner, B&B €57-€109 p.p. Extra bed/sofabed €25-€35 p.p. per night. Extra 2 rooms available.
Meals	Dinner, 3 courses, €28. Child €12.50. Brunch €5. Lunch, 2 courses with wine, €18. Picnic €10. Restaurant 7km.	**Meals**	Dinner €22-€45. Wine €18.
Closed	Rarely.	**Closed**	Rarely.

Tel	+33 (0)5 55 64 30 58	**Tel**	+33 (0)5 55 63 43 35
Email	lapissarelle@gmail.com	**Email**	reservations@maisonnumeroneuf.com
Web	www.lapissarelle.com	**Web**	www.maisonnumeroneuf.com

Wolfgang & Annie Oelsner
La Pissarelle,
La Clupte,
23430 Châtelus le Marcheix, Creuse

Duncan & Lisa Rowney
Maison Numéro Neuf,
Rue Serpente,
23300 La Souterraine, Creuse

ENTRY 430 MAP 9

ENTRY 431 MAP 9

Auvergne

Gîte du Tapissier, page 313

Auberge de Chassignolles

The 1930s inn sits opposite the medieval church and next to the ruins of a 13th-century castle, its bar happily occupied by friendly locals. At 950 metres, the village has lovely views over fields and forests, stretching to the peaks of the Auvergne and Mont Dore. You'll find pure mountain air, a slow pace, and a place to stay with a slice of pizzazz thanks to new owner Peter, fresh from his restaurant success in Bristol. It hums with unpretentious good looks, young staff and seriously delicious, locally-sourced food. Upstairs, tall windows light old parquet, white walls and warm old furniture in plain simple rooms – a 1930s inlaid bedroom suite dressed in pure white linen, a deep and friendly armchair. One room above the restaurant is a library/sitting room and there's a meadow with farmyard animals, veg plot and fruit trees over the road. The pretty, old-style restaurant – country furniture, check cloths, crinkly lamps, a fascinating mixture of old crockery – is the place for *cuisine du terroir*, all freshness and taste. It's a perfect focus for revived community life and a boon for travellers.

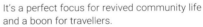

Rooms	6 doubles, 1 twin: €45-€75. 2 family rooms for 4: €75-€105. Singles €50-€55. Extra bed/sofabed €15 p.p. per night. Dinner, B&B €62-€68 p.p.
Meals	Breakfast €8.50. Sunday lunch, 4-5 courses, €25-€28, other days on request. Dinner, 4-5 courses, €27-€30 (not Mon). Wine €10-€80.
Closed	Christmas.

Peter Taylor
Auberge de Chassignolles,
Le Bourg, 43440 Chassignolles,
Haute-Loire

Tel   +33 (0)4 71 76 32 36
Email   aubergedechassignolles@gmail.com
Web   www.aubergedechassignolles.com

Gîte du Tapissier

At the top of a twisty mineral village, the big black farmhouse is dated 1490-1575. Sensitively renovated by this welcoming, dynamic family (she does yoga, he does upholstery – superbly), any gloom wafting from the great stones vanishes before Sylvie's use of colour. The Blue room is... streaky blue, its floor like roiling magma, its superb shower done in multi-hued volcanic stone from Brazil, its big balcony a treat; the more traditional Gîte room has a kitchen/diner and a terrace onto fields and volcanoes – whence the black stone; breakfast in the family kitchen showcases local produce. Then visit spectacular Polignac – and more.

Château de Lescure

At the head of a long shapely valley stands this 18th-century château guarded by an atmospheric 11th-century keep where bedrooms are steeply, sensationally 'gothic' or French château in style. In the big inglenook dining hall, eco-committed Sophie – she's a carriage driver too – serves home-smoked ham, her own organic veg and fruit. Michel's passions are heritage conservation and blazing trails across the hills straight from the door. They are bilingual hosts who may invite you to join in bread-making, cooking, wide-ranging conversation and visiting their medieval garden... Stunning views, absolute peace, an inimitable welcome.

Rooms	1 double, 1 twin/double: €77-€87. 1 family room for 3 with separate wc: €107-€127. Extra bed/sofabed €15-€20 p.p. per night.	**Rooms**	1 twin; 1 double with separate shower room downstairs; 1 double with separate shower: €90. Extra bed €30.
Meals	Auberge 15 mins walk; choice in Le Puy 7 mins drive.	**Meals**	Dinner with wine, €28; children under 14, €15; under 5 free.
Closed	Rarely.	**Closed**	15 November – 31 March.

Tel	+33 (0)4 71 02 56 42	**Tel**	+33 (0)4 71 73 40 91
Email	pubellier@orange.fr	**Email**	michel.couillaud@orange.fr
Web	www.pubellierphilippe.fr	**Web**	www.chateaudelescure.com

Philippe & Sylvie Pubellier
Gîte du Tapissier,
Cheyrac,
43000 Polignac, Haute-Loire

Michel Couillaud & Phoebe Sophie Verhulst
Château de Lescure,
15230 St Martin Sous Vigouroux,
Cantal

Les Maisons de Concasty

Half a mile high lies the river-ploughed plateau: fresh air, wild country, vast space. Built 300 years ago, the family mansion has been brought up to date by clever, delightful Martine: Jacuzzi, hammam, yoga – and organic food and veg from her permaculture garden to keep you blooming. Locally sourced produce, plates of foie gras, asparagus and more... are served on the covered patio that overlooks the pool and the view. Martine chats happily while cooking, pairing her dishes with an impressive choice of organic wines; she does great breakfasts, too. Each of the six rooms has a fabulous bathroom, with Italian-style showers and roll top bath, and cosy beds to retire to after long walks over the granite plateaux of the Auvergne, canoeing on the river Lot or day tripping around medieval villages. *Min. stay: 2 nights; 3 in high season.*

Maison d'Hôtes de Charme La Fournio

The approach is mysterious and magical, the views to the Auvergne are spectacular, and your host likes nothing better than to share with you his enchanting home. Cherrywood glows with beeswax, copper pots shine, 18th-century floor boards creak and gorgeous old roses grow around the door. Albert is also a passionate cook, of local sausages and Cantal cheeses, homemade jams and tasty fruit purées. Listen to birds – and cow bells – from the garden, discover lovely Argentat on the Dordogne, settle in with cards by the wood-burner, retire to delicious beds dressed in hand-embroidered linen. Exquisite! *Minimum stay: 2 nights in high season.*

Rooms	4 doubles: €124-€138.1 suite for 4 with private terrace, 1 suite for 2 with private living room area: €142-€292. Extra person €18-€35. Pets €10, by arrangement.
Meals	Dinner €35, by arrangement.
Closed	December-March.

Rooms	1 double: €90-€95. 1 family room for 3: €80-€110. 1 cottage for 3: €90-€145. Singles €75-€90. Extra bed/sofabed €20 p.p. per night. Cot available.
Meals	Dinner €23. Restaurants 2km & 7km.
Closed	Never.

Tel	+33 (0)4 71 62 21 16
Email	maisons-concasty@orange.fr
Web	maisons-concasty.fr

Tel	+33 (0)4 71 69 02 68
Email	albert.charles@wanadoo.fr
Web	www.lafournio.fr

Martine Causse
Les Maisons de Concasty,
Auberge de Concasty,
15600 Boisset, Cantal

Albert Marc Charles
Maison d'Hôtes de Charme La Fournio,
18 Lieu dit Escladines,
15700 Chaussenac, Cantal

ENTRY 435 MAP 10

ENTRY 436 MAP 10

Domaine la Reveille

Find peace here on the edge of a village in the Livradois-Forez regional park. The house is up at 600m, with woods, pond and pool inside its high-walled grounds. Dutch owners Charles and Tarcies speak excellent English and love sharing their home with guests, advising on walks, bike rides, car tours and local sites. Breakfast is served individually, while home-cooked dinners are sociable affairs around a large table. Living room and corridors have modern paintings and quirky touches; bedrooms on three floors have lovely views, good mattresses, simple shower rooms (one also has an elegant bath) and calming colours.

Le Manoir d'Alice

Just a whisker off the A75, plunge into lush central France and a resplendent manor house built by the former Marquis de Lastic's mother in a fit of pique – the original family château can be visited in nearby Parentignat. Wrought iron gates swing open to turrets, pointy roofs and creamy stone. There's room for the whole family or a group of friends in airy bedrooms named after notable women in French history. There's much history in the wood-panelled corridors and a private, still-consecrated chapel on the first floor with the family coat of arms and papal bulls. Breakfast on croissants and homemade jams in the dining room, where dinners of local produce are also served. On sunny days the outdoor pool is a pleasant spot for a dip, while the hiking and biking are excellent whatever the weather.

Rooms	5 doubles: €89-€108. Extra bed/sofabed €30 p.p. per night.
Meals	Dinner, 4 courses, €26. Child €10.
Closed	Rarely.

Rooms	1 twin: €95-€115. 1 family room for 3, 2 family rooms for 4: €95-€185. Extra bed €40 p.p.
Meals	Dinner with wine €39; children €15; by arrangement. Restaurants 4km.
Closed	January – February.

Tel	+33 (0)4 73 72 32 29
Email	info@domainelareveille.com
Web	www.domainelareveille.com

Charles Engelen
Domaine la Reveille,
3 Rue du Compart,
63220 Dore l'Eglise, Puy-de-Dôme

Email	lamaisondalice@laposte.net
Web	www.lemanoirdalice.com

Isabelle Morel
Le Manoir d'Alice,
29 route des Pradeaux,
63500 Parentignat, Puy-de-Dôme

ENTRY 437 MAP 10

ENTRY 438 MAP 10

Les Frênes

Perched above Saint Nectaire, the old farmhouse has stupendous views from its hillside garden of the romanesque jewel below and woods and mountains soaring beyond. Monique, chatty and knowledgeable, enthuses her guests with descriptions of the Auvergne in perfect English. She doesn't pretend to offer luxury, just the cosy comfort of a real home. You stay in an attached one-bedroom cottage with a shower and kitchen area downstairs. Breakfast is in Monique and Daniel's vaulted dining room, full of exposed beams and stone; eat copiously and enjoy the humour, zest and kindness of a couple who were born to hospitality. Astonishing value.

Chez Helen

Montpeyroux is a beautifully revived medieval hilltop village and the Pittmans' house, full of quirks, brocante and family warmth, has a bowl-over view. Sun floods the taupe-cosy bedroom; your sitting room lies cool and restful in the vaulted former wine store. Helen happily shares her knowledge of her adopted region with you over breakfast here or on the terrace; Kevin works in town and is here in the evenings. Charming and relaxed, they love life here. You have a little terrace and private entrance. The village has excellent eateries, from crêpes to creative gourmet. Do stay, there's masses to see and do. *Minimum stay: 2 nights in high season.*

Rooms	1 cottage for 2: €60.
Meals	Restaurants in St Nectaire, 2km.
Closed	Rarely.

Rooms	1 suite for 2: €90-€100.
Meals	Restaurants 3-minute walk.
Closed	Rarely.

Tel	+33 (0)4 73 88 40 08
Email	daniel.deforge@orange.fr
Web	deforgef.wixsite.com/lesfrenes

Monique Deforge
Les Frênes,
Sailles, 63710 St Nectaire,
Puy-de-Dôme

Tel	+33 (0)4 73 89 93 28
Email	helen.t.pittman@gmail.com
Web	www.chezhelen63.com

Helen Pittman
Chez Helen,
Montée du Guetteur,
63114 Montpeyroux, Puy-de-Dôme

Château Royal de Saint-Saturnin

A volcanic region is the perfect cradle for this magnificently turreted and castellated fortress, high on the forested fringes of one of France's most beautiful villages. A stone spiral, worn with age and history, leads to five swish bedrooms in the oldest wing. The Louis XIII suite, its bathroom tucked into a tower, spans the castle's width; views are to tumbling rooftops and gardens and parkland behind. The vaulted dining room, decked with gleaming coppers, is the background for relaxed breakfast spreads, and your hosts are friendly and well-travelled. Once owned by Catherine de Médici, now open to the public.

Château de Vaulx

A jewel in the forest, a fairytale haven. Creak along the parquet, swan around the salon... sleep in one tower, wash in another. It's been in the family for 800 years, and traditional rooms have furnishings worthy of the troubadours who sang here. It's an adorable chateau owned by an adorable pair who welcome you like long lost friends. Philippe and Martine are nurturing the castle as their parents did, with joy – and updating a bit. Breakfast on brioche, yogurt, eggs, cheese, and honey from their hives, stroll from peaceful lawn to sweeping view, settle in to sociable dinners at the delicious, candlelit table. *Arrival from 5pm.*

Rooms	2 doubles: €221-€286. 3 suites for 2: €256-€296. Extra bed/sofabed €20 p.p. per night.		**Rooms**	2 doubles: €80-€100. 1 family room for 3: €100-€130. Extra bed/sofabed €30 p.p. per night.
Meals	Breakfast €18, €12 per child under 13. Restaurant 0.5km.		**Meals**	Dinner with wine, €30.
Closed	12 November – 28 March.		**Closed**	November – April.

Tel	+33 (0)4 73 39 39 64		**Tel**	+33 (0)4 73 51 50 55
Email	contact@chateaudesaintsaturnin.com		**Email**	ph.vast@orange.fr
Web	www.chateaudesaintsaturnin.com		**Web**	www.chateaudevaulx.net

Emmanuel & Christine Pénicaud
Château Royal de Saint-Saturnin,
Place de l'Ormeau,
63450 Saint Saturnin, Puy-de-Dôme

Guy & Régine Dumas de Vaulx, Philippe & Martine Vast
Château de Vaulx,
63120 Ste Agathe, Puy-de-Dôme

Manoir de la Manantie

Passionate about regional gastronomy – do eat with them, it's a real treat – Véronique and Guillaume quit Paris to pour their talents into this fine neoclassical manor. They've done it up to the nines, from the grand entrance with its volcanic stone stair, smart in crisp red, to the big, super-modern bathrooms. Grand, high-ceilinged bedrooms (the suite is vast), are full of light and antique furniture. The woodwork alone is worth a visit, so too is the English gentleman's room, with its head-high hog-roasting fireplace. Walk into Lezoux, stroll in the park and enjoy the Auvergne's fabulous National Parks – and cheese. *Minimum stay: 2 nights; 3 nights in high season.*

Suites de Campagne Les Eydieux

At the northern tip of the Auvergne Volcanoes Regional Park are these two guest suites, perfect for a total escape – it's around 7 miles to shops and restaurants (and 15 miles out of season). Artistic and chatty Marie-Claire and her husband Cyr have painstakingly renovated their old farm buildings: exposed stone walls, ceilings open to the rafters and hand-picked furniture set the tone, complemented by modern bathrooms. Breakfast of fresh fruit, jams and bread sets you up for walking, swimming or visiting châteaux. Return to a jacuzzi bath and a vegetarian dinner, or rustle up supper in the communal kitchen. Rural bliss! *Parking on-site.*

Rooms	3 suites for 2: €145-€240. 1 single: €115-€150. Extra bed/sofabed €50-€70 p.p. per night.	**Rooms**	1 suite for 4, 1 suite for 5: €145-€250.
Meals	Breakfast served in bedroom, €10. Cheese & charcuterie platter €35-€45; pre-booking only. Wines €15-€35. Restaurants 15km.	**Meals**	Restaurants 10km. Guest kitchen.
Closed	Rarely.	**Closed**	Rarely.

Tel	+33 (0)4 44 05 21 46	**Tel**	+33 (0)4 73 86 91 95
Email	veronique@manoir-manantie.fr	**Email**	leseydieux@orange.fr
Web	www.manoir-manantie.fr	**Web**	www.leseydieux.com

Veronique Vernat-Rossi
Manoir de la Manantie,
Rue Georges Clémenceau,
63190 Lezoux, Puy-de-Dôme

Marie-Claire Mercier
Suites de Campagne Les Eydieux,
Les Eydieux,
63410 Saint Angel, Puy-de-Dôme

ENTRY 443   MAP 10   ENTRY 444   MAP 10

Le cuisinier en Combraille

This beautifully restored old farmhouse is surrounded by meadows, forest and peaceful gardens. Cees and Jakob, who used to run a cookery school, live on site and are warm and convivial hosts. Breakfast is a buffet of fruit salad, homemade jams, cheese, bread and eggs, and you can dine at separate tables in the dining room, on the veranda or in the garden. Jakob will also produce dinner by request using home-grown fruit and veg and wine from their extensive cellar; they'll happily ply you with drinks and snacks too. Find your own space in the garden to read or doze, walk to the village (20 minutes) for a spot of not-very-many-people watching or order a picnic hamper and head off on marked trails. You need to drive to good restaurants, weekly markets and medieval villages. *Children over 8 welcome.*

Rooms	2 doubles, 1 twin/double, 1 twin: €68-€98. 1 family room for 3: €96-€106. Extra bed/sofabed €20 p.p. per night. Pets by arrangement: €6 per pet per night.
Meals	Dinner €28.
Closed	1 November – 29 March, 19 June – 24 June.

Tel +33 (0)4 73 52 19 54
Email info@sejour-culinair.fr
Web www.sejour-culinair.fr

Jakob Scheper
Le cuisinier en Combraille,
Lieu-dit Vivier,
63330 Verghéas, Puy-de-Dôme

Manoir du Mortier

Head down the long drive to the Manoir... surrounded by 50 hectares of oak forest, this is about as remote as it gets. Sumptuously restored by vivacious Catherine, the rooms are straight out of an interior design book. Her inherited antiques, fabrics and vintage finds make every corner a treat for the eye. The round tower room opens to the pool terrace, the square tower suite is perfect for a family. Find white-hung beds, traditional toile de Jouy and bathrooms, down winding staircases, with big walk-in showers. Enjoy the pure air rambling on forest paths or exploring bridleways on horseback – Catherine has horses for accomplished riders (and stabling for yours). The lofty breakfast room with its large table is an inviting place to eat, relax, play mini billiards and chat to other guests. *Min. stay: 2 nights.*

Rooms	1 double, 2 twin/doubles: €75-€140. 1 suite for 5: €200-€220. Extra bed/sofabed €25 p.p. per night. Cots available.
Meals	Dinner, 3 courses with wine & coffee, €32. Restaurants 5-10km.
Closed	8 January – end of March.

Mobile +33 (0)6 30 34 06 40
Email manoirdumortier@yahoo.fr
Web manoir-du-mortier.fr

Catherine Greninger
Manoir du Mortier,
Le Mortier,
03360 Meaulne, Allier

ENTRY 445 MAP 10

ENTRY 446 MAP 10

Château de Clusors

Atop a hill, this small château has gazed on untouched countryside since the 14th century. Steeped in history (Henri is full of stories; Madame de Montespan once stayed here), the place is still a working farm: friendly and down-to-earth, Madame manages a herd of Charolais cows. Up the spiral stone stair are big bedrooms with fine furniture and excellent modern bathrooms; breakfast is set before family portraits and a bookcase stocked with leather-bound tomes. Outside: a large garden with orchard and pool; rest in the shade of a lime tree and admire the magnificent view. Wonderfully, authentically French.

Rooms	2 triples: €105. Extra bed €20.
Meals	Restaurants nearby.
Closed	Rarely.

Christine & Henri Thieulin
Château de Clusors,
03210 St Menoux,
Allier

Tel	+33 (0)4 70 43 94 69
Mobile	+33 (0)6 70 79 27 75
Email	henri.thieulin@orange.fr
Web	www.chateaudeclusors.com

ENTRY 447   MAP 10

Midi - Pyrénées

Château de Canac, page 329

Château de Projan

The interiors are remarkable and the proportions grandiose, a pleasure to stride. And the history of the 18th-century château is fascinating: ask Richard and Christine to tell you the stories. Eclectic, quirky and entertaining is the mix of antiques with paintings, tapestries and sculpture from the Art Nouveau, Cubist and Art Deco periods; equally special, the inlaid marble floor at the foot of the staircase. First-floor bedrooms have wide oak boards, tomette tiles, antique writing desks; one great room has a 15m ceiling with original mouldings, others still have their timber frames. Most astonishing are the recent panelled bathrooms, gleaming with massive mirrors and huge showers. There are two dining terraces with views across to the Pyrénées, a hall-cum-piano room, fireplaces for chilly evenings... make yourselves at home in grand fashion, book in for cookery courses, Armagnac tastings, fabulous sejours. The kitchen opens to the ground-floor hall so you can watch chef/patron Richard prepare his Gascon specialities, which you can then savour accompanied by local wines. Welcoming, and perfect for the jazz festival in Marciac.

Rooms	6 doubles, 1 family room for 4: €130-€200. Singles €100-€130. Dinner, B&B €115-€140 p.p. Extra bed/sofabed €15 p.p. per night.
Meals	Breakfast €14. Dinner €38-€60.
Closed	February; week before All Saints' Day; 21-28 December.

Christine & Richard Poullain	**Tel**	+33 (0)5 62 09 46 21
Château de Projan,	**Email**	chateaudeprojan@gmail.com
32400 Projan, Gers	**Web**	www.chateau-de-projan.com

Château de Labro

In a large park with vast pastures, woods and every imaginable tree, this fine 16th-century château has all the ingredients for a magical stay. A drive leads to an old gated entrance beyond which a walled vineyard hides a huge pool and a lawn. Nearly all the bedrooms are large, with fine parquet floors and views to slate roofs, the garden or the foothills of the Massif Central. Those in the main house are dedicated to local artists, others, off a stone-flagged courtyard, have four-posters and a delectable treehouse, complete with chandelier, sits in the branches of an ancient oak tree. A generous breakfast is laid on elegantly dressed tables in a delightful room complete with stag's head; the restaurant is in a separate building and has a large salon. Check out the magnificent wine rack (sample their 'Marcillac'); indulge in special food in a gorgeous setting. New manager Matheiu Muratet looks after it all with ease and charm, owner Monsieur Rouquet pops in from time to time. Take a trip to the Gorges du Tarn or the Roquefort cheese caves, hike or bike in the wonderful l'Aubrac. Enchanting.

Rooms	12 doubles, 1 twin: €90-€179.
	1 suite for 2: €290-€390.
	3 triples: €159-€199.
	1 apartment for 4: €250-€280.
	1 treehouse for 2: €250.
Meals	Breakfast €15. Dinner €29-€45.
	Wine €14-€79.
Closed	Rarely.

Tel	+33 (0)5 65 67 90 62
Email	chateau.labro@wanadoo.fr
Web	www.chateaulabro.fr

Jean & Nizou Rouquet
Château de Labro,
Labro, 12850 Onet-le-Château,
Aveyron

ENTRY 449   MAP 15

Le Mûrier de Viels

You won't meet a soul on the drive to get here, except possibly a wild deer. This intimate hotel, made up of a sprinkling of 18th-century buildings on several lush levels, hides among the oak woods and gazes down on the river with beautiful views of the valley. Come for a smiling welcome and an atmosphere of relaxed comfort: Joséphine and Oz left stressful lives in Britain to realise their dream of owning a small hotel and bringing up a family in France. The layout is charming, with reception, restaurant and guest rooms scattered among terraces and secret corners. The pool area has a great view, as do most of the rooms; there's space and blissful tranquillity. In the bedrooms where rustic stone walls rub shoulders with white plaster you'll find stylish modern French furniture and soothing colours, big walk-in showers, good reading lamps and fat pillows. The suite has a fitted wardrobe with antique doors, a comfy raffia sofa and a stunning view through a huge window. Every room is pristine. Treat yourself to Oz's beautiful cooking on the terrace or in a dining room bright with yellow leather chairs.

Rooms	3 doubles, 1 twin: €80-€110.
	1 suite for 3: €110-€140.
	2 family rooms for 3: €100-€150.
	1 cottage for 4: €450-€750.
Meals	Breakfast €10. Picnic on request.
	Dinner €25-€30. Wine €10-€27.
Closed	13 November – 28 February.

Joséphine & Oz
Le Mûrier de Viels,
12700 Causse & Diège,
Aveyron

Tel   +33 (0)5 65 80 89 82
Email mail@le-murier.com
Web   www.le-murier.com

Hôtel Relais Sainte Anne

In the centre of beautifully preserved Martel, step in from the quiet street, take a deep breath, feel the still magic of the place. The fabulous garden has endless secret corners and pathways running through high box-edged lanes. The several buildings that house the bedrooms were once a girls' school, the delightful covered terrace was their playground, the old school house is now an oriental suite exuding opulence and space. Warm old stones and terracotta, fine fabrics and heavy rugs abound. We loved the lighter rooms, too, and the three simpler yet pretty rooms for smaller budgets: such a friendly touch. Bathrooms are original and fun: black and terracotta, a bit of gilt or candy stripe, a flowery frieze. All this, a perfectly lovely family (Madame still says "I'm so happy here" and gets a kick out of each new decorative idea) and innovative cuisine, served on the terrace or in the intimate dining room by a big open fire. A 'lovers' table' dressed with roses and candles can be set under the porch of the little chapel. Sophistication without self-consciousness – a rare treat.

Rooms	7 doubles, 4 twins: €85-€185. 4 suites for 2: €155-€275.
Meals	Breakfast €13-20. Dinner, market menu, €30. Wine €19-€90. Restaurant open for dinner every day except Tuesdays, open for lunch on Sunday and Bank Holidays only.
Closed	4 November – 18 April.

Tel	+33 (0)5 65 37 40 56
Email	relais.sainteanne@wanadoo.fr
Web	www.relais-sainte-anne.com

Ghislaine Rimet-Mignon
Hôtel Relais Sainte Anne,
Rue du Pourtanel,
46600 Martel, Lot

ENTRY 451   MAP 9

La Bruyle

Charming and stylish – Franck and Pascale were born to run a B&B. On hand with creative apéritifs and inspired ideas for exploring the Dordogne, they make their home a pleasure to visit. Local artisans helped them transform the 18th-century house into a chic retreat, restoring ancient beams and flagstones. Outside, sage green shutters add a cheery flash of colour to the mellow stone façade and there's a fruit tree filled garden with a pool. Inside, country décor reigns; four immaculate en suite rooms have pretty linen, oak floors and bucolic views. Locally sourced breakfasts of farm eggs, homemade cake and jams are superb. *Meet & Cook: Cookery classes available; enquire with owners.*

Moulin du Goth

The 13th-century mill – imaginatively restored by its Australian owner – guards a garden of rare peace and beauty. Find a mill pond, home to wildlife and flashing kingfishers, willows, lawns, garden sculptures and masses of colour. Coral is full of fun, and a kind, dedicated host. She gives you big, dramatically raftered rooms with decorative iron beds and touches of old-world charm. Delicious dinners are occasionally served – you eat in the stunning vaulted dining room (its arrow slit intact) or out in the garden, on the terrace, within sound of the tinkling stream. Guests adore this friendly place. *Children over 5 welcome. Pets by arrangement.*

Rooms	4 doubles: €85-€120. Extra bed €15, under 5s only.
Meals	Dinner with wine, €30. Restaurants 4km.
Closed	Rarely.

Rooms	1 double: €90-€95. 1 suite for 5: €90-€185. Singles €75. Extra bed/sofabed €30 p.p. per night.
Meals	Dinner with wine, €27-€31. Restaurants 3km.
Closed	Rarely.

Tel	+33 (0)5 65 37 48 03
Email	contact@labruyle.com
Web	www.labruyle.com

Pascale Brunet & Franck Leroy
La Bruyle,
Lieu-dit Colonjac,
46110 Saint-Michel-de-Bannières, Lot

Tel	+33 (0)5 65 32 26 04
Email	coral.heath@orange.fr
Web	www.moulindugoth.com

Coral Heath-Kauffman
Moulin du Goth,
46600 Creysse,
Lot

ENTRY 452 MAP 9

ENTRY 453 MAP 9

Les Hauts des Magrières

Nathalie is justifiably proud of the house her architect husband designed and built – an ultra-modern glass box attached to a barn conversion that stands alone on a hilltop with distant views down to the Dordogne. Bedrooms are in the original barn and have thick stone walls and plenty of privacy. They're linked by a glass passageway to the welcoming salon and dining room, complete with a fireplace and grand piano and designed to bring the outdoors in. Breakfast includes homemade jams and yogurts, eggs and cheese; ask Nathalie about dinner or drive five minutes into Martel for a choice of restaurants. Explore Lot's glorious treasures, which include ancient clifftop villages and underground caves, or just relax on the terrace or by the swimming pool. *Minimum stay: 2 nights.*

Domaine de Labarthe

These vital, welcoming, interesting people, who are in the wine trade and grow walnuts, have turned one wing of the handsome old family house into elegant B&B rooms, three in subtle designer colours, two in traditional cosy French style; and the two-storey pigeonnier would be perfect for a couple or small family. Laurence's dinners alone are worth the visit, then there's the fine heated pool on the olive-studded terrace, the rose garden and Italianate formality rolling past walnut groves to the Lot countryside, gastronomy and wine, old villages and unmissable Cahors. Such wealth. *Pets by arrangement.*

Rooms	2 doubles: €135. Singles €120.
Meals	Restaurants 4km.
Closed	30 November – 15 January.

Rooms	2 doubles, 3 twin/doubles: €145-€155. Extra bed €30 per child; under 13s only. 2 self-catering suites available (one with disabled access).
Meals	Occasional dinner, 3 courses, €36.
Closed	Rarely.

Tel	+33 (0)6 76 74 25 03
Email	lesmagrieres46@yahoo.com
Web	www.lesmagrieres.fr

Nathalie Gineste
Les Hauts des Magrières,
46600 Martel,
Lot

Tel	+33 (0)5 65 30 92 34
Email	contact@domaine-de-labarthe.com
Web	www.domainedelabarthe.com

Laurence & Guillaume Bardin
Domaine de Labarthe,
46090 Espère,
Lot

Pella Roca, Cabane & Spa en Quercy

In peaceful woodland, near the charming Sanchez's stone Quercy house, these two rustic cabins are simply delightful. Each has lovely wide views, a comfy double-bedded room in white and wood: candles, rattan blinds, corner kitchen, mini-bar and bathroom. Glass doors fold back to bring the outdoors in. A breakfast basket comes each morning, and you can order dinners. Each cabin has a jacuzzi and sauna (convertible into bunk beds); the heated pool and playground are shared. The Lot is great for cycling, walking, climbing, caving and canoeing; gorgeous villages and markets too - a neighbouring farm makes beer and wine. Toulouse 90 minutes. *Parking on-site.*

Rooms	1 cabin for 2, 1 cabin for 4: €200-€360. Children €50. Cot bed €15. Short breaks €550-€994.
Meals	Restaurants 8-minute drive.
Closed	Rarely.

Tel	+33 (0)5 63 02 85 14
Email	contact@pella-roca.com
Web	www.pella-roca.com

Isabel Sanchez
Pella Roca, Cabane & Spa en Quercy,
Lieu dit Limougne, 82240 Labastide de Penne,
Tarn-et-Garonne

Chambres d'Hôtes Les Brunes

Swish through large wooden gates into a central courtyard and garden filled with birdsong to find lovely Monique and her 18th-century family home, complete with tower. Bedrooms are up the spiral stone tower staircase which oozes atmosphere; all are a good size ('Le Clos' is enormous) and filled with beautiful things. Antiques, beams, rugs, gilt mirrors and soft colours give an uncluttered, elegant feel; bathrooms are luxurious, views from all are lovely. You breakfast on homemade cake, farm butter and fruit salad in the handsome farmhouse kitchen. *Minimum stay: 2 nights in high season.*

Rooms	2 doubles, 2 twins: €93-€158. Extra bed/sofabed €30 p.p. per night.
Meals	Guest kitchenette. Restaurant 5km.
Closed	Rarely.

Tel	+33 (0)5 65 48 50 11
Email	lesbrunes@wanadoo.fr
Web	www.lesbrunes.com

Monique Philipponnat-David
Chambres d'Hôtes Les Brunes,
Hameau les Brunes,
12340 Bozouls, Aveyron

Château de Canac

This turreted chateau, dressed in red stone, has been given new life and lavish interiors by the Busset family. It has a regal air – grand but not stuffy with chevron parquet floors, chalky heritage colours, heavy tapestries and huge romantic bedrooms. Bathrooms beckon with roll top baths, drenching showers and Murano glass chandeliers. Table d'hôte dinners will be a treat as Michelin-starred Hervé oversees the menu, although son Henri is usually your host. A plush guest salon is shared with grandmère Busset. There's noise and bustle from the city outskirts but it's well-placed for exploring Rodez's medieval centre. *Parking on-site.*

Le Couvent

Louise couldn't be kinder and there's a mellow, bohemian feel to her former convent home. She's carefully mixed finds from her global travels with antiques, brocante and modern pieces and the result is charming. Peaceful, comfortable bedrooms have practical showers and lovely valley views over the pretty village. Breakfast under the pergola, in the nooked and crannied garden, or in the sunny salon. And do arrange to have homemade dinner too. Wander down for a dip in the river, the dogs may come with you; visit Lautrec's magical Château du Bosc, Albi and Cordes; relax – to birdsong or to the crackling logs of a winter fire. *Parking on-site.*

Rooms	3 doubles: €150-€270.	**Rooms**	1 double, 1 twin: €85-€100.
Meals	Dinner, 3 courses, €40.		1 family room for 4: €85-€110.
	Restaurants 10-minute drive.		Extra bed/sofabed at no charge.
Closed	Rarely.	**Meals**	Dinner, 2-4 courses with wine,
			€18-€25. Restaurants 10km.
		Closed	Rarely.

Tel	+33 (0)5 31 97 10 50	**Tel**	+33 (0)5 65 72 06 00
Email	reservation@chateaudecanac.com	**Email**	louise@lecouventfrance.com
Web	www.chateaudecanac.com	**Web**	lecouventfrance.com

Henri Busset
Château de Canac,
Impasse de Canac,
12000 Rodez, Aveyron

Louise Flynn
Le Couvent,
12800 St Just sur Viaur,
Aveyron

Le Gouty

A lovely old farmhouse on two levels, a terrace at the back for meals (lots of produce from sweet neighbours) and the dreamiest sunsets and views – Phillipe and Lynda, embarking on a new life in France, love the house, the community and the region. Guest bedrooms, each in a renovated farm building, have chestnut floors and reclaimed beams, the showers are super-large, and one bedroom has its own terrace – raise a glass to the view. You are in heart of the sparsely populated Aveyron – 'la France profonde.' Homemade yogurt and fig jam at breakfast, apple juice from the village and wonderful walks from the door.

Nichoir

A pastoral paradise that your hosts share by setting up night cameras and bat detectors – great for children. They've restored their rambling farmhouse for family-friendly living with lots of books, games and space, comfortable and super adaptable sleeping arrangements. And moreover... an old bread oven (now used for pizzas) and forge untouched since its last use, a well that still provides water for the lovely garden, good dinners in the guest living room and Oska the softie Newfoundland dog. Views are magnificent, the loudest noise is the frogs on the pond, Simon and Noella, endlessly thoughtful, will give you a memorable time.
Pets by arrangement.

Rooms	2 doubles: €60. Singles €58.
Meals	Dinner €25. Restaurant 10km.
Closed	Rarely.

Rooms	1 double: €75-€105.
	1 apartment for 3: €75-€115.
	Singles €75. Dinner, B&B €100 p.p.
	Extra bed/sofabed €15 p.p. per
	night.
Meals	Dinner with wine, coffee & apéritif,
	€25. Light supper €12.50
	Vegetarian dishes on request.
Closed	Rarely.

Tel +33 (0)5 65 49 40 31
Email le.gouty@nordnet.fr
Web legouty.webplus.net

Phillipe & Lynda Denny
Le Gouty,
12380 Pousthomy,
Aveyron

Tel +33 (0)5 63 54 31 75
Email simon.mauger@sho-shin.net
Web www.lebruel.net

Simon & Noella Mauger
Nichoir,
Le Bruel,
81340 Lacapelle Pinet, Tarn

Maison des Oiseaux

Your own little apartment in a medieval village house with a garden at the back and miles of views. The Australian owner has transformed two stone barns into an elegant bolthole for two: one your living space, the other... your library! It's a haven of comfort and peace, with cool terracotta floors, a kitchenette in a cupboard, a fine sleigh bed and French windows opening to those spectacular views. Shutters give privacy from the street, and Ruth lives discreetly upstairs. She brings you a continental breakfast and has created a great info pack too. After a day of spectacular gorges and historic places (don't miss Albi) take a drink and book to the lower garden: enchanting, with nooks and exotic planting. Cordes is car-free and beautiful; boutiques, restaurants and market lie down the steep cobbled hill. *Minimum stay: 3 nights.*

Les Vents Bleus

Gaillac vineyards surround this old wine master's house – the definition of relaxed French country chic, with a decorative smattering of foreign pieces. Florence and Olivier are delightfully attentive and want you to love this rich, rural area as much as they do. Calm rooms charm with church views, high, beamed ceilings, stone and light-painted walls, linen cushions and canopies. Breakfasts – dinners too in summer – are memorable, out under the rambling vine shelters. And it's simply lovely, after a spin on a bike, to plunge into the sparkling pool to gentle cooing from the pigeonnier. Cordes is close.

Rooms	1 double: €120.
Meals	Continental breakfast left by owner on arrival. Restaurants 5-minute walk.
Closed	Never.

Rooms	3 doubles: €100-€110. 1 family room for 5: €130-€160. 1 triple: €120-€130.
Meals	Dinner €30; children under 12, €15; July & August twice a week only. Platter €18. Restaurants 5km.
Closed	End December to end March.

Mobile	+44 (0)7810 081429
Email	ruth.e.bird@gmail.com
Web	www.maisondesoiseaux.net

Ruth Bird
Maison des Oiseaux,
20 rue de la Boucarie,
81170 Cordes sur Ciel, Tarn

Tel	+33 (0)5 63 56 86 11
Email	contact@lesventsbleus.com
Web	www.lesventsbleus.com

Florence & Olivier Tracou
Les Vents Bleus,
Route de Caussade,
81170 Donnazac, Tarn

ENTRY 462 MAP 15

ENTRY 463 MAP 15

Pechauzi

Le Domaine de Perches

Follow meandering lanes to peaceful Pechauzi, at the foot of a hill below the beautiful village of Castelnau de Montmiral. There's a relaxed atmosphere in the stone farmhouse, and a gleeful welcome from the family labradors. Sleep in spacious double rooms or cosier twins tucked under the eaves, which share a bathroom. Your hosts bring a love of food, baking and ecology to their new life in France, so there'll be delicious breakfasts and four course dinners with regional specialities. Stay home to bake bread with Elizabeth or spot wildlife with ecological consultant Jonathan. Watersports, wine tours and markets nearby too. *Parking on-site.*

Sheltered below the country lane, the 17th-century pale-stone building faces south, revelling in its fruitful valley. Inside: a club-like morning room, a library with a classical fireplace, a white-furnished salon in the old winery. Dip into the pool hiding below the terrace; dream under a willow by the lily pond. Bedroom moods vary: mushroom shades here, ivories and greys there; a draped bed head, a claw foot tub, immaculate lighting. Monsieur is passionate about architecture and design and his lovingly collected paintings and antiques add sparkle to the sobriety. A very beautiful place. The table d'hôtes looks outstanding. *Minimum stay: 2 nights in high season. Pets by arrangement €15 per night.*

Rooms	5 twin/doubles: €90-€95. Singles €80. Extra bed/sofabed €30 p.p. per night. 2 studio apartments available for overflow B&B accommodation.	**Rooms**	1 double, 1 twin/double: €155-€175. 1 suite for 2: €195-€215.
Meals	Dinner, 4 courses with wine, €30. Restaurants 5-minute drive.	**Meals**	Dinner with wine, €50. Restaurants nearby.
Closed	Rarely.	**Closed**	Christmas, 15 January – 3 March.

Mobile +33 (0)6 47 81 87 23
Email enquiries@pechauzi.com
Web www.pechauzi.com

Jonathan & Elizabeth Adey
Pechauzi,
Lieu-dit Pechauzi,
81140 Castelnau de Montmiral, Tarn

Tel +33 (0)5 63 56 58 24
Email domainedeperches@orange.fr
Web www.domainedeperches.com

M. Guyomarch
Le Domaine de Perches,
Perches, 2083 Route de Laborie,
81600 Gaillac, Tarn

ENTRY 464 MAP 14

ENTRY 465 MAP 15

Domaine du Buc

Bright, smiling Brigitte is proud of her lovely 17th-century domaine, in the family for 100 years. An imposing stone staircase leads to wonderful big bedrooms with original parquet and grand mirrors, period beds, subtle paint finishes and 19th-century papers, and quirky treasures discovered in the attic: sepia photographs, antique bonnets, vintage suitcases. Showers are top-range Italian and the old arched billiards room makes a perfect salon. It's unusually, richly authentic, the breakfasts are locally sourced and delicious and you are eight miles from Albi, World Heritage Site. A huge treat. *Minimum stay: 2 nights July & August.*

Mas de Sudre

George and Pippa are ideal B&B folk – relaxed, good-natured, enthusiastic about their corner of France, generous-spirited and adding lots of extras to make you comfortable. Set in rolling vineyards and farmland, Sudre is a warm friendly house with beautiful furniture, shelves full of books, big inviting bedrooms and a very lovely garden full of sunny/shady fragrant corners in which you can sleep off delicious breakfast. The more energetic may leap to the pool, boules, bikes or several sorts of tennis and you are genuinely encouraged to treat the house as your own. French guests adore this very British B&B.

Rooms	3 twin/doubles: €110-€150. Extra rooms available.
Meals	Restaurant 1.5km. Guest kitchen.
Closed	December to mid-March.

Rooms	2 doubles, 1 twin: €80.
Meals	Restaurants nearby.
Closed	Rarely.

Tel	+33 (0)5 63 55 40 06
Email	contact@domainedubuc.com
Web	www.domainedubuc.com

Brigitte Lesage
Domaine du Buc,
Route de Lagrave,
81150 Marssac sur Tarn, Tarn

Tel	+33 (0)5 63 41 01 32
Email	masdesudre@gmail.com
Web	www.masdesudre.fr

Pippa & George Richmond-Brown
Mas de Sudre,
81600 Gaillac, Tarn

ENTRY 466   MAP 15

ENTRY 467   MAP 15

Combettes

Come for an absolutely fabulous French bourgeois experience: a wide 16th century stone staircase, deeply worn, high ceilings, southern colours, loads of stairs, interesting objets at every turn. Add the owners' passion for Napoleon III furniture, oil paintings and ornate mirrors and the mood, more formal than family, is unmistakably French. Bedrooms, some with rooftop views, are traditional and very comfortable; breakfast is served overlooking the old part of Gaillac. A treat to be in the heart of town, with utterly French people. Madame is a darling and it's excellent value for money.

Clos Saint Blaise

Magali and Guilhem now call this noble abode home – a charming pair of Anglophiles with a young family and two friendly dogs. Expect a very warm welcome. Inside, ancestral furniture is laced with brocante treasures, and the two doubles, both en suite, have high ceilings, big windows and a quirky, nautical theme inspired by Lapérouse (ask Guilhem!) A comfortable lounge has leather couches and glass tables. Breakfast is a feast of handpicked local goodies served under the giant wisteria, or in the glass veranda. Wander under ancient oaks in the grounds, float in the pool, and discover historic Albi, home to Toulouse-Lautrec. *Parking on-site.*

Rooms	3 doubles, 1 twin: €50-€65. 1 suite for 2: €80. Singles €50. Extra bed/sofabed €10 p.p. per night.
Meals	Restaurants 30m.
Closed	Rarely.

Rooms	2 doubles: €90-€100. Extra bed €10 per child per night.
Meals	Restaurants 7km.
Closed	Rarely.

Tel	+33 (0)5 63 57 61 48
Email	contact@combettesgaillac.com
Web	www.combettesgaillac.com

Lucile & Marie-Pierre Pinon
Combettes,
8 place St Michel,
81600 Gaillac, Tarn

Mobile	+33 (0)6 80 00 50 07
Email	clossaintblaise@orange.fr
Web	www.clossaintblaise.fr

Magali & Guilhem Bertrand
Clos Saint Blaise,
Chemin de Saint Blaise,
81000 Albi, Tarn

Hôtel Cuq en Terrasses

Philippe and Andonis gave up good jobs in Paris to buy this 18th-century presbytery after falling in love with the region. Perched in mouthwatering gardens on the side of a hill, the multi-level mellow stone edifice looks – and is – utterly inviting. All the rooms have original terracotta floors, hand-finished plaster, exposed beams. Evening meals, on the terrace in summer, are a delight for eye and palate: something different each day, fresh from the market, beautifully balanced by wines from the region. Guests are full of praise, for the food and the gardens, the pool and waterfall, the blissful views, the wonderful hosts. *Children over 10 welcome.*

La Villa de Mazamet & Le Petit Spa

A 'coup de foudre' caused Mark and Peter to buy this grand 1930s house in walled gardens, a few minutes' walk from the market town of Mazamet. Renovation revealed large light interiors of wood-panelled walls, parquet floors and sweeping windows. Furnished with modern elegance, the ground floor invites relaxation in comfy sofas or quiet corners. Bedrooms, with sumptuous beds and fine linen, are calmly luxurious; bathrooms are Art Deco gems. Your hosts are interesting, relaxed and well-travelled, meals in the restaurant are gastronomic. Ideal for Carcassonne, Albi and all those medieval villages. *Minimum stay: 2 nights. Over 14s welcome. Public transport 200m.*

Rooms	3 doubles, 2 twin/doubles: €85-€165. Extra bed/sofabed €20 p.p. per night. Dinner, B&B €92-€128 p.p.	
Meals	Snacks available. Hosted dinner €38; book ahead. Wine €16-€25.	
Closed	28 October – 27 April.	

Rooms	3 doubles, 2 twin/doubles: €120-€200. Whole property available for exclusive use.
Meals	Dinner €35. Wines from €14.
Closed	November – March.

Tel	+33 (0)5 63 82 54 00
Email	cuq-en-terrasses@wanadoo.fr
Web	www.cuqenterrasses.com

Philippe Gallice & Andonis Vassalos
Hôtel Cuq en Terrasses,
Cuq le Château,
81470 Cuq Toulza, Tarn

Tel	+33 (0)5 63 97 90 33
Email	info@villademazamet.com
Web	www.villademazamet.com

Peter Friend & Mark Barber
La Villa de Mazamet & Le Petit Spa,
4 rue Pasteur,
81200 Mazamet, Tarn

ENTRY 470 MAP 15

ENTRY 471 MAP 15

La Lumiane

Step off the narrow street to discover a delightful sweet-smelling garden and its pool. Friendly, vivacious Mireille and charming English Stuart run this gracious house with enthusiasm for their new life and the guests it brings. Up the stunning stone staircase, bedrooms breathe tradition old fireplaces and antiques; rooms in big the garden wing are less grand, more contemporary. All have an uncluttered mix of florals and stripes (due to put on modern style very soon). In winter, eat well in the formal dining room or on the terrace by candlelight, wake to the sound of the church bells. Much authenticity and charm.

Lexis

Your charming, artistic hosts spent years resuscitating the elegant 200-year-old Gascon house, doing it all themselves, with love and taste. Gorgeous floors and fireplaces have been preserved, subtle personal touches added and the result is utterly relaxing. Antony is a keen vegetarian cook, a sculptor and a musician; Camilla went from theatre design to interior design. But it's more than personality. Bedrooms have big new beds, armchairs, paintings and new walk-in showers, communal rooms have a myriad of beautiful things. Outside are quiet places, a pool and boules, croquet, badminton and ping-pong, and lovely Gascony to explore. *Parking on-site.*

Rooms	5 doubles: €62-€79.
Meals	Dinner with wine, €25-€30, on request. Restaurant 50m.
Closed	Rarely.

Rooms	1 double; 1 double with separate shower room: €70. Extra bed €20.
Meals	Dinner with wine, €30. Child €15. Restaurants 10-minute drive.
Closed	Rarely.

Tel	+33 (0)5 62 28 95 95
Email	info@lalumiane.com
Web	www.lalumiane.com

Mireille Mabilat & Stuart Simkins
La Lumiane,
Grande Rue,
32310 St Puy, Gers

Tel	+33 (0)5 62 08 18 67
Email	gogascony@gmail.com
Web	www.gogascony.com

Camilla Bates & Antony Holloway
Lexis,
lieu dit Bailliargue,
32150 Cazaubon, Gers

Laouarde

In rolling Armagnac country: a former wine estate, an 1823 house with watchtower views. Simon and Catherine swapped London for warm limestone and blue shutters, beautiful sash windows and oak parquet, and 25 acres of meadows, orchards and peace. Wonderful breakfasts (compotes from the garden, delectable croissants) are taken by the open fire or on the pool terrace, and Simon's dinners are mouthwatering. Up the beeswax-polished stair are delicious bedrooms full of personality, from country-pretty to elegant Bourbon. Read, listen to music, take an aperitif in the walled courtyard, explore this amazing region. *Minimum stay: 2 nights.*

La Raillère

It's deeply peaceful here among vines in rolling Gers countryside – great for walking and cycling. Charming owners Amanda and Colin have breathed new life into the stone farmhouse. The feel is homely and elegant with some grand family château pieces, friendly dogs and cats, a horse and pony in the fields. Roomy bedrooms have rugs on wooden floors, smart wallpapers and super-comfy big beds: one four-poster, one with wrought iron bedstead. Light bathrooms are impressive. They've also created a pretty courtyard and garden, shaded by ancient oaks. Breakfasts are delicious – try the peach jam and house honey, and dine on wild boar or local duck for supper. *Minimum stay: 2 nights in high season.*

Rooms	1 twin: €95-€120. 2 suites for 2: €105-€130. 1 single: €65-€70.	**Rooms**	2 doubles: €85-€120. Child's bed €20.
Meals	Dinner €35 (Sunday-Wednesday). Restaurants 1km.	**Meals**	Dinner with wine, €30. Restaurants 10-minute drive.
Closed	Rarely.	**Closed**	Rarely.

Tel	+33 (0)5 62 63 13 44	**Tel**	+33 (0)5 62 58 33 54
Email	info@laouarde.co.uk	**Email**	french.forsythe@btconnect.com
Web	www.laouarde.com		

Simon & Catherine Butterworth
Laouarde,
32190 Vic Fezensac,
Gers

Amanda Soden
La Raillère,
32360 Jegun,
Gers

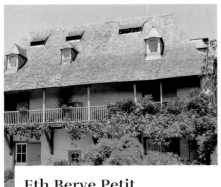

Eth Berye Petit

Beauty, harmony, tranquillity... all who stay, long to return. The grand old village maison de maître, in Henri's family for centuries, opens to soft green rolling meadows and the majestic Pyrénées – the finest view in all France! Basque-born Ione, graceful and gracious mother of two, ushers you up the venerable stair to wonderful warm bedrooms in pastel hues – one with a balcony – and luscious beds wrapped in antique linen. The living room, where a fire roars and a fine dinner is served on winter weekends, is a delight to come home to after a day's skiing or hiking. For summer? A dreamy garden. Exceptional.

Chateau de La Lanette

Delightful, energetic hosts have put their hearts into bringing La Lanette back to its 1870s glory. Find polished parquet floors, carved doors, opulent marble fireplaces; sleep in a vast bedroom or suite, sweep down gorgeous stairs to breakfast on pancakes or muffins in the splendid dining room. Heather and Russell have created a holiday haven for all – walkers, cyclists, couples and families. Spend the morning in the pool or borrow picnic things and explore the Pyrénées; return to early children's supper, then park them in the playroom while you relax in the sitting room before your own delicious adult dinner in peace. *Parking on-site.*

Rooms	3 twin/doubles: €75.	**Rooms**	1 double: €120.	
Meals	Dinner with wine, €25. Auberge 100m.		2 suites for 5: €160-€200. 2 family rooms for 4: €140-€160. Extra bed/cot available at no charge.	
Closed	24 December – 2 January.	**Meals**	Dinner, 3 courses with wine, €30. Children under 12, €12. Restaurants 10-minute drive.	
		Closed	Rarely.	

Tel	+33 (0)5 62 97 90 02	**Tel**	+33 (0)5 62 99 20 31
Email	contact@beryepetit.com	**Email**	info@lalanette.com
Web	www.beryepetit.com	**Web**	www.lalanette.com

Henri & Ione Vielle
Eth Berye Petit,
15 route de Vielle,
65400 Beaucens, Hautes-Pyrénées

Heather Mumby
Chateau de La Lanette,
Route Nationale,
65370 Salechan, Hautes-Pyrénées

Les Pesques

Surrounded by rolling farmland, at the end of a quiet lane, a gorgeous old manor house in a luxuriant garden – a happy place and home. Brigitte has decorated in peaceful good taste and all is charmingly cluttered, each country antique the right one. Now the stable has been transformed into the prettiest, airiest country bedroom you have ever seen, all soft grey-blues with white linens and touches of red, and a window onto the field where the hens and horse run. It's a joyful house where Brigitte concocts delicious dinners with vegetables from the potager and has a brocante shop in the garden. All the bedrooms are dreamy.

Chaumarty

Head up, up to a hilltop farmhouse with panoramic views to the Pyrénées and a lovely family who've spent 12 years fixing up their eco-friendly home. It's all hemp, lime, wood and terracotta, solar energy, a natural swimming 'bassin', horses, a donkey, a sand pit and a swing for your kids to share with theirs... such fun. Inside are two big, beamed guest rooms with country antiques, good beds and walk-in ochre showers. Sink into an easy chair by the wood-burner and browse books that reveal a passion for all things bio... as do family dinners with Italian-Swiss Stefano and Violaine from Bordeaux. Great value, too.

Rooms	1 double, 1 twin: €70. 1 family room for 3: €70-€85.
Meals	Dinner with wine, €22.
Closed	Rarely.

Rooms	1 double: €65-€75. 1 family room for 4: €105-€115. Singles €60-€70. Dinner, B&B €55-€60 p.p.
Meals	Dinner with wine, €22. Restaurant 5km.
Closed	Rarely.

Tel	+33 (0)5 61 97 59 28
Email	reserve@les-pesques.com
Web	www.les-pesques.com

Brigitte & Bruno Lebris
Les Pesques,
31220 Palaminy,
Haute-Garonne

Tel	+33 (0)5 61 08 68 64
Email	chaumarty@free.fr
Web	www.chaumarty.com

Violaine & Stefano Comolli
Chaumarty,
31550 Gaillac-Toulza,
Haute-Garonne

Domaine de Terrac

A spacious luminous house: this 200-year-old barn with wooden chalet extension in the foothills of the Pyrénées feels restorative. Your Canadian and Welsh hosts settle you in to one of five large restful rooms, two have their own verandas, all have huge windows so you can drink in the magical hilltop views. Each bedroom has a neat en suite, big TV, and goose feather duvets on smart mattresses. Breakfast, full English or continental style, and dinner are locally sourced and served on the terrace or in the airy dining room. The large gardens – fruit trees, veg patch, woods – are beautiful. Look out for a wood fired hot tub and sauna; massages and facial treatments available too. *Minimum stay: 2 nights in high season. Parking on-site. Over 14s welcome in high season.*

Rooms	4 doubles, 1 twin: €90-€125.
Meals	Dinner, 4 courses, €35. Wine available, €10-€40. Restaurants 3km.
Closed	Rarely.

Tel +33 (0)5 61 96 39 60
Email domainedeterrac@wanadoo.fr
Web domainedeterrac.com

Barry Judson
Domaine de Terrac,
Lieu-dit Terrac,
09420 Rimont, Ariège

Impasse du Temple

Breakfast among the remains of a Protestant chapel, sleep in a townhouse, one of a terrace built in 1758; John and Lee-Anne are its second owners. Delightful, humorous Australians, they have restored their elegant mansion and are very much part of the community. Graciously high ceilings, a sweeping spiral staircase, lovely great windows in an oasis of ancient, stream-kissed oaks... arrive as strangers, leave as friends. The food is fantastic and the pastel-shaded bedrooms are generous, with just enough antiques; one even has the vast original claw-footed bath. The attention to detail is exceptional and readers sing their praises.

Rooms	2 doubles: €82. 1 suite for 4: €129-€136. 2 triples: €104-€109. Extra bed/sofabed €27 p.p. per night.
Meals	Dinner €25. Wine €9-€20. Restaurant nearby.
Closed	Rarely.

Tel +33 (0)5 61 01 50 02
Email john.furness@wanadoo.fr
Web www.chezfurness.com

John & Lee-Anne Furness
Impasse du Temple,
09600 Léran,
Ariège

La Genade

Up in her beloved mountains with the wild streams splashing and an unbroken view of 13th-century Lordat, Meredith loves sharing her heaven. A passionate climber, skier and cyclist, she rebuilt a ruined auberge; old stones and new wood, craggy beams, precious furniture and a cheery fire make it rustic, warm and elegant. Under truly American care, rooms have fine linens, oriental rugs and books. The welcome is genuine, breakfast is fresh and generous, dinners are animated and delicious. Walkers and cyclists should stay a week: you're at 900m on the south side of St Barthoelemy Peak and there's a repair room specially for bikes – excellent value. The village has a 12th-century church to explore and there are many chapels and Romanesque churches within an hour's drive. Nature lovers will be happy too with wildlife all around you and more wild orchid varieties than in any other area of France. Return to comfortable bedrooms with fine linen, a hot shower or a soak, a drink by the fire and home-cooked dinner. You'll feel relaxed here. *Minimum stay: 2 nights; 1 for cyclists.*

Rooms	2 doubles, 1 twin: €65-€70. Extra bed €10.
Meals	Dinner with wine, €23-€26; please enquire for Christmas & New Year.
Closed	Never.

Tel	+33 (0)5 61 05 51 54
Mobile	+33 (0)7 87 45 33 26
Email	meredith.dickinson@orange.fr
Web	www.chambre-dhote-pyrenees-lagenade.com

Meredith Dickinson
La Genade,
La route des Corniches,
09250 Axiat, Ariège

ENTRY 482 MAP 14

Languedoc - Roussillon

Le Mas Trilles

Stéphane and Amparo have taken over the family's rambling, honey-coloured 17th-century farmhouse; some old-fashioned touches, and their personal welcome makes it feel more like home than hotel. First to greet you are the sounds of birdsong and rushing water, then, perhaps the head-spinning scent of orange or cherry blossom from the lovely redolent garden. There are two comfortable sitting rooms, one with its original beams, both with paintings, cool terracotta tiles and places to read and relax. Many bedrooms, larger in the main house, are reached by unexpected ups and downs; all have shower-in-bath systems. There are some fine antiques, a few little terraces, and woods and mountains beyond. The largest room has magnificent views of the Canigou mountain, the spiritual home of the Catalan nation; cheaper rooms are quite small. Breakfast on the sweet terrace with homemade fig or apricot jam or in front of a crackling fire on chilly days. Down by the river there are fine views of the mountains and an intoxicating feeling of space.
Pets by arrangement.

Rooms	11 doubles: €85-€229. Pets €13 p.n. Cots €12 per night. 3rd person €29; 4th person €15; 5th person €15.
Meals	Breakfast €13.50; €10 for children under 12. Restaurant 200m.
Closed	Early October to late April.

Tel	+33 (0)4 68 87 38 37
Email	info@le-mas-trilles.com
Web	www.le-mas-trilles.com

Stéphane & Amparo Bukk
Le Mas Trilles,
Le Pont de Reynès, 66400 Céret,
Pyrénées-Orientales

ENTRY 483   MAP 15

Relais des Chartreuses

Come for the exceptional food. A breakfast buffet is laid out on the terrace; evening meals are a culinary adventure of seasonal dishes matched with a list of local wines. Friendly staff look after you well up in the wooded hills above Le Boulou. Tuck yourself away in the pretty gardens with your book – you can chase the sun (or the shade) all day. Loll about on a lounger, plunge in the pool, take a siesta in your elegant bedroom – some are bigger than others, one has a private terrace. This is a brilliant place for forays to Spain and the south coast; Collioure, beloved of Matisse, is 20 minutes away, Céret, Picasso's favourite, is even closer. Seek out the Musée d'Art Moderne, and the huge Saturday market – it stretches over several streets and sells everything.

Rooms	9 doubles, 3 twin/doubles: €66-€172. 1 suite for 4: €180-€310. 1 family room for 5: €220-€320. Singles €55-€80. Extra bed/sofabed €10-€25 p.p. per night.
Meals	Buffet breakfast €15; under 12s €10. Dinner, 4 courses, €38; under 12s €25. Wine €16-€76. Restaurant 5km.
Closed	15 November – 4 March.

Pierrette Blocklet
Relais des Chartreuses,
106 avenue d'en Carbonner,
66160 Le Boulou, Pyrénées-Orientales

Tel	+33 (0)4 68 83 15 88
Email	relaisdeschartreuses@gmail.com
Web	www.relais-des-chartreuses.fr

ENTRY 484   MAP 15

Domaine de la Fauvelle

A tree-lined avenue leads to La Fauvelle – an impressive building, built as a ceramic factory in 1850 and bought by the present Norwegian owners in 2001. They've restored everything stylishly and created a comfortable, relaxed and welcoming place to stay. A vast entrance hall leads to a dining and lounge area with high ceilings, modern art and grand arched windows. Enjoy breakfast here or under the grape vines on the terrace overlooking lawn, palm trees and a large saltwater pool – lots of choices including bacon, omelettes, cheese, croissants, fruit, jams and juices; an enormous antique cupboard serves as a bar. The big ground floor bedrooms all have French windows and views on to the bird-filled garden or patio; find fresh, clean lines with splashes of Catalan colours, polished terracotta floors and mosaic-walled en suites. Walk into lively Thuir for supper (10 minutes); visit local vineyards; take a peek at Spain from Canigou – one of the highest mountains in the Pyrénées. Pretty village Castelnou with its château on the hilltop is festooned with small shops and restaurants and sandy beaches are a 30-minute drive. *Parking on-site.*

Rooms	14 twin/doubles: €100-€130. Extra bed €15.
Meals	Restaurants 10-minute walk.
Closed	Christmas.

Tel	+33 (0)4 68 50 50 50
Mobile	+47 952 18 441
Email	reception@lafauvelle.com
Web	lafauvelle.com

Morten Norli
Domaine de la Fauvelle,
60 avenue Fauvelle, 66300 Thuir,
Pyrénées-Orientales

ENTRY 485   MAP 15

Château des Ducs de Joyeuse

The drive up is impressive, the castle even more so: 1500s and fortified, part Gothic, part Renaissance, standing in its own patch of land on the banks of the Aude. A large rectangular courtyard is jolly with summer tables and parasols, the stately dining room has snowy linen cloths and flowers, the staff are truly charming and helpful, and the menu changes daily depending what is fresh. Vaulted ceilings and well-trodden stone spiral stairs lead to formal bedrooms with heavy wooden furniture, some beamed and with stone fireplaces; there's a heraldic feel with narrow high windows, studded doors and smart bedspreads in navy blue and bright red. Ask for a room with a watery view. Bathrooms glow with tiled floors, bright lights and stone walls – some up to two metres thick: perfect sound insulation. Historical information about the building is on display everywhere, owners Isabelle and Vincent are full of ideas and can help you plan your trips out. Hearty souls can knock a ball around the tennis court then cool off in the outdoor pool – or brave that lovely river. Good value.

Rooms	10 doubles, 11 twins: €121-€161. 2 family rooms for 4: €222-€245. 12 triples: €198-€283. Singles €118-€150. Tourist tax €1.45 per night p.p.
Meals	Breakfast and dinner, 3 courses, €49. Children €27. Wine €21-€125.
Closed	Early November to early April.

Isabelle & Vincent Nourrisson
Château des Ducs de Joyeuse,
1 allée Gorges Roux,
11190 Couiza, Aude

Tel	+33 (0)4 68 74 23 50
Email	reception@chateau-des-ducs.com
Web	www.chateau-des-ducs.com/en/

ENTRY 486   MAP 15

L'Auberge du Cèdre

Here, on the edge of the wild, wooded Cévennes, you can link up with the Robert Louis Stevenson Trail – and you don't have to hire a donkey! The majestic Pic Saint Loup towers over the vineyards that surround this old, rambling, maze-like hotel. It's a popular destination for get-up-and-go types, including families, and those who love to eat well. The lush garden setting feels just wild enough for the magnificent sculptural cedar tree to stand free above it, branches spread. Laze in the deckchairs, splash in the pool, play boules under the chestnut trees. This big, bustling, ethically run house could hardly be more friendly or laid-back. If you tire of mountain biking, climbing and wild-river swimming, head south for the fountains and dappled squares of Montpellier. You can be there in an hour, and still find time for Roman Provence... Arles, Nîmes and the Pont du Gard.

Rooms	11 twin/doubles; 4 twin/doubles with separate shower & shared wc: €72-€112. 1 triple with separate shower & shared wc: €72-€117. 4 suites for 4: €114-€216. 1 apartment for 6: €120-€220. Dinner, B&B €50-€93 p.p.
Meals	Breakfast included. Light lunch €15. À la carte €29-€45 (weekends). Wine €9-€98.
Closed	Mid-November to mid-March.

Tel	+33 (0)4 67 59 02 02
Email	welcome@auberge-du-cedre.com
Web	www.auberge-du-cedre.com

Françoise Antonin & Lutz Engelmann
L'Auberge du Cèdre,
Domaine de Cazeneuve,
34270 Lauret, Hérault

ENTRY 487 MAP 15

L'Enclos des Lauriers Roses

The tiny reception gives no clue as to what lies beyond; a hamlet within a village. Step across a sunny dining room, through French windows – and blink. Scattered around three swimming pools is a cluster of cottage rooms. Newly built of pantile and stone recovered from old village houses, most have a private terrace or garden. Large, airy and prettily furnished with painted Provençal pieces and fabulous mattresses, each has a different charm – 'Mimosa' has a finely upholstered yellow bed, 'Amarilys' has big chunky terracotta tiles. Walls are white, ceilings neatly beamed, there might be a bed tucked under a stone arch or extra beds for children on the mezzanine. Bathrooms are modern and marbled and a fridge keeps drinks chilled. Madame supervises the excellent restaurant, Monsieur does the wine – 500 bottles in the cellar – and their sons take care of the buildings and garden. Eat on the terrace or in the dining room; the locals love the cooking, too. Nîmes, Avignon and beaches are less than an hour, swim in the Gorges du Gardon, walk among the pines. As for the village, it's charming.

Rooms	11 twin/doubles: €80-€190.
	10 family rooms for 4: €120-€290.
	2 triples: €95-€130.
	Dinner, B&B €80-€130 p.p.
	Extra bed/sofabed €15 p.p. per night.
Meals	Breakfast €15.
	Lunch & dinner €26-€45.
Closed	2 November – 16 March.

Bargeton Family
L'Enclos des Lauriers Roses,
71 rue du 14 Juillet,
30210 Cabrières, Gard

Tel +33 (0)4 66 75 25 42
Email contact@hotel-lauriersroses.com
Web www.hotel-lauriersroses.com

Domaine des Escaunes

A big old house beautifully converted into a hotel by Patricia and Marc. It's a family-friendly space with some downstairs bedrooms in a modern annexe and plenty of sitting/dining rooms to be sociable in, or to escape to. The 1535 building has seen many incarnations since it was built, but lots of its ancient features remain: an enormous stone fireplace in the old kitchen where you breakfast in winter, stone flagged floors, high ceilings, thick walls, a maze of corridors and staircases. You'll find terraces for resting on, a mulberry tree for shade, walled gardens and a very beautiful pool. Children will discover a treehouse and a safe garden for running free. There's a restaurant which is also open to the public for French gastronomic food; the amiable head chef offers cooking classes for all – children included. *Minimum stay: 5 nights in high season.*

Rooms	17 doubles: €120-€190. 4 suites for 2, 1 suite for 4: €210-€340. Extra bed €30 per night.
Meals	Dinner, 3 courses, €38. Cheese board, €8. Restaurants 5km.
Closed	Never.

Tel	+33 (0)4 66 37 49 44
Email	info@escaunes.com
Web	www.escaunes.com

Marc Vermeulen
Domaine des Escaunes,
5 rue des Bourgades,
30210 Sernhac, Gard

ENTRY 489   MAP 16

Hôtel de l'Atelier

On a narrow street in the historical centre of Villeneuve lès Avignons is this ivy-clad, former cardinal's palace with tall windows and pale shutters. Now kindly Stephane looks after you impeccably in elegant rooms with beamed ceilings, stone arches, antique furniture and plenty of private places to sit inside or out. Inner courtyards have tables and chairs for alfresco breakfasts under vine-covered pergolas, there's a roof terrace with loungers for a chilled glass of rosé and a garden with a smooth lawn. Bedrooms (over three floors and no lift) are light and airy with brand new everything – some with a balcony or terrace, all with soft colours and spotlessly clean bathrooms. Wake (no hurry) to breakfasts of local cheeses, eggs, homemade jams and pastries before heading off to explore. Stephane encourages guests to write about their days out on a large blackboard – a great conversation starter. A bus stop just down the road will whisk you to the centre of town for museums, history, cafés and river boat trips. If you're

sporty speak to Stephane who is too – but there's no need to do anything if you just want to rest.

Rooms	7 doubles, 10 twin/doubles: €75-€169.
	3 family rooms for 3: €115-€169.
	2 singles: €75-€109.
	Extra bed/sofabed €18 p.p. per night.
Meals	Breakfast €9.50; children €6.
	Restaurants 10-minute walk.
Closed	Rarely.

Stephane Lenny
Hôtel de l'Atelier,
5 rue de la Foire,
30400 Villeneuve lès Avignon, Gard

Tel   +33 (0)4 90 25 01 84
Email   contact@hoteldelatelier.com
Web   www.hoteldelatelier.com

La Lozerette

In September 1878, Robert Louis Stevenson set off from Le Monastier, with Modestine the donkey, to walk the 220 kilometres to St Jean du Gard. Towards the end of his journey he stopped off at the Cévennes village of Cocurès, on the river Tarn, just above the National Park. Here, Pierrette runs the country inn started by her grandmother and passed on to her by her parents. Laid-back staff, warm and friendly, handle all comers to this busy hotel. Pierrette herself is hands-on, running the reception, taking orders in the (excellent) restaurant, managing the wine cellar: a trained sommelier, she will pick you out just the right bottle; her cheeseboard is to die for. Bedrooms, mostly a good size, colour coordinated but not twee, have wooden floors, oh-so-comfortable beds and stripey, checked or flowery décor. The small bar with its cheerful bucket chairs is charming, the gardens pretty, the balconies bright with flowers. The whole hotel shines. Take a drink into the garden or play boules, walk in the National Park, follow Stevenson's trail – on foot, donkey or horseback. Good value, one of the best.

Rooms	12 twin/doubles: €69-€108.
	8 family rooms for 4: €105-€112.
	Dinner, B&B €65-€86 p.p..
Meals	Breakfast €9-€15.
	Lunch & dinner €18-€50.
	Children's meals €11.50.
Closed	Christmas, New Year.

Tel	+33 (0)4 66 45 06 04
Email	lalozerette@wanadoo.fr
Web	www.lalozerette.com

Pierrette Agulhon
La Lozerette,
Cocurès, 48400 Florac,
Lozère

ENTRY 491   MAP 15

Transgardon en Cévennes

Sentiers Perdus

A light-filled valley and utter solitude. Eco-minded Pascal and Frédérique fell in love with this remote hamlet, then restored the main house and a pretty stone cottage with three, very private, bedrooms, all with their own entrance. Find gorgeous linen, gleaming antique furniture, good bathrooms. Wander up the path and over a bridge to the welcoming main house for a hunker by the stove, breakfasts of homemade brioches and honey from their bees, or a divine supper of local meat and home grown veg. Swim in the stream under the old bridge (catch a trout in the rockpool?). Hike, cycle, explore... or do nothing.

Brave the steep winding road to reach this astonishing place. All alone, half way up a six-hectare hillside is the 400-year-old stone farmhouse that the Goughs have rebuilt outside and redesigned inside. Each of the four floors opens directly onto one of those terraces, the views across the deep narrow gorge are pine-green, the only sounds the wind and the odd wild-boar rustle. Big stone bedrooms have great white beds, industrial-style furniture, a restful lack of clutter, and splendid new bathrooms. Kevin and Michèle are resourceful, interesting and love having guests. They keep chickens for breakfast eggs and collect rainwater to protect the house from landslides. Walk to your heart's content, along the valley and over the hill to deserted hamlets. Take gorgeous labra-springer Barney, he loves to lead the way.

Rooms	3 twin/doubles; 1 with extra bed on mezzanine: €83-€110. Singles €90. Extra bed €25. Discounts for 4+ nights (June-August) & 5+ nights (September-December).
Meals	Dinner with wine, €28. Restaurants 6km.
Closed	Rarely.

Rooms	2 doubles: €110-€145.
Meals	Dinner €35 with wine; available by arrangement. Picnics available. Restaurants 10-minute drive.
Closed	1 November – 28 February.

Tel	+33 (0)4 34 25 90 23
Email	transgardon@transgardon.fr
Web	www.transgardon.fr

Frédérique & Pascal Mathis
Transgardon en Cévennes,
Transgardon,
48240 St Privat de Vallongue, Lozère

Tel	+33 (0)6 59 69 38 74
Email	info@sentiersperdus.com
Web	www.sentiersperdus.com

Kevin & Michele Gough
Sentiers Perdus,
La Melarede,
30110 Sainte-Cécile-d'Andorge, Gard

ENTRY 492 MAP 15

ENTRY 493 MAP 16

La Maison Papillons

Overlooking a hamlet on the borders of the Gard and the Ardèche is a hillside farmhouse, a heavenly B&B with a self-catering barn too. Welcome to hand-woven rugs on polished concrete floors, upcycled rustic doors and Italian walk-in showers. Not only is the house beautiful, it is run by Caroline and Olivier, warm, delightful hosts, passionate about art, sustainability and nature. The suite, beneath the family house, comes with its own patio, so start the day in the sun and feast on fruits, pancakes and homemade granola. Discover the Pont d'Arc, laze by the pool, hike or bike through lavender fields with Oliver – your enthusiastic guide. *Minimum stay: 2 nights.*

Pont d'Ardèche

An ancestor built this fine fortified farmhouse 220 years ago; it stands by the Ardèche with its own small beach. Inside: a cavernous hall, a stone stair lined with portraits, and fresh simple bedrooms above, saved from austerity by Ghislaine's painted furniture and friezes. The glorious park – old plane trees, hidden deckchairs – invites lingerers, there's a lovely pool shared with gîte guests, and summer dinners can be enjoyed the other side of the river at their son's 'guinguette' (grilled meats, delicious salads). Pierre can accompany you on canoe trips: your sociable hosts enjoy all their guests.

Rooms	3 doubles: €100-€150. 2 triples: €130-€170.
Meals	Restaurants 10-minute drive.
Closed	Rarely.

Rooms	1 double: €80. 2 family rooms for 4: €80-€110. 1 triple: €80-€95. Child under 10, €10. Extra bed €15 per person per night.
Meals	Guest kitchen available.
Closed	Rarely.

Mobile	+33 (0)6 20 46 80 05
Email	contact@lamaisonpapillons.fr
Web	www.lamaisonpapillons.fr

Caroline Girault de Burlet
La Maison Papillons,
Hameau de Monteil,
30620 Montclus, Gard

Tel	+33 (0)4 66 39 29 80
Email	pontdardeche@orange.fr
Web	www.pont-dardeche.com

Ghislaine & Pierre de Verduzan
Pont d'Ardèche,
30130 Pont St Esprit,
Gard

ENTRY 494 MAP 16

ENTRY 495 MAP 16

Maison Orsini

This medieval house, overlooking the walled City of Avignon (splash out on a terrace room with a view) is the former palace of Cardinal Orsini. Rich in decorative tiles, steep narrow stairs and 14th-century timbers, it has been in the family for three generations. Today the owners live over the road but are hugely helpful and on the spot for breakfast, served in an atmospheric, vaulted chapter house at one big table; all is delicious. Xavier is an artist who runs workshops on site; splendid suites combine modern art with country antiques and chandeliers. The grassed grounds are beautiful – there's even a pool.

La Claire Demeure

Surrounded by great plane trees that have never been pruned, a charming southern home. The stone vaulted salon bears witness to the days of the Knights Templar; the sofas are comfy, the fireplace glows in winter, the piano (not grand) is ready to play. Kind Claire, friendly and refined, gives you elegant bedrooms with flagged floors and high windows, fine linen, fresh flowers, a sprinkling of antiques. Her husband knows all about Gigondas and Châteauneuf-du-Pape so don't miss the vineyards. This is a wonderful area where markets, cafés and galleries abound.

Rooms	1 double: €130-€170. 2 suites for 4: €150-€310. Extra beds available.		**Rooms**	2 doubles: €70-€93. Singles €65-€88. Extra bed/sofabed €15-€20 p.p. per night.
Meals	Restaurants 3km.		**Meals**	Restaurants 10km.
Closed	Rarely.		**Closed**	1 November – 1 April

Mobile	+33 (0)6 82 27 65 94		**Tel**	+33 (0)4 66 37 72 48
Email	maisonorsini@gmail.com		**Email**	claire.tytgat@wanadoo.fr
Web	www.maisonorsini.com		**Web**	www.laclairedemeure.fr

Anne-Marie & Xavier Peltier
Maison Orsini,
Montée de la Tour,
30400 Villeneuve-les-Avignon, Gard

Claire Granier
La Claire Demeure,
1424 route de Jonquières,
30490 Montfrin, Gard

Habanera

The owners – artists, perfectionists – love nothing more than to share with guests their passion for the Camargue, and the treasures of Arles and Nîmes. Birdwatching, riding, fishing, archaeology... they can recommend the best tours and the best people. As for the house, its sleepy village façade is deceptive: in reality it is immense, with high ceilings, tall windows and a stunning courtyard garden. Walls are subtly limewashed, linen is hand monogrammed, toiletries are très chic, and the suite, spacious and serene, has its own boudoir. For breakfast? Fruit smoothies, Fougasse d'Aigues-Mortes pastries, homemade crème caramels. *Minimum stay: 2 nights.*

Bien Loin d'Ici

In the wild Provençal garrigue... pines, olive trees, aromatic shrubs, a beautiful dark lap pool, an eco-house built of chunks of local pine, street art hiding in the garden: sustainability partnering with sleek design. Each of the three lodges has a jacuzzi and sauna on a private terrace, a guitar in the big room, and lots of glamour among the 20th-century musical references. Manuel and Elodie care for the details – designer lighting, classic modern furniture, high-quality bedding – and bring an organic breakfast hamper to your door each day. Lounge on the muslin-draped sofas by pool, barbecue in the summer kitchen; set off for cultural hub Nîmes; explore the Cévennes or the Camargue wildlife reserve on Manuel's bikes. Then order hot or cold platters, for supper by the pool or in your own space.

	Habanera		Bien Loin d'Ici
Rooms	3 doubles: €110. 1 suite for 2: €145.	**Rooms**	3 doubles: €240.
Meals	Restaurant in village, 200m.	**Meals**	Platters for two, €50. Wine €10-€30. Restaurants 10-minute drive.
Closed	Rarely.	**Closed**	October to March.

Tel	+33 (0)4 66 57 58 46	**Mobile**	+33 (0)6 86 76 14 30
Email	reservation@habanera.fr	**Email**	manuelmamane@gmail.com
Web	www.habanera.fr	**Web**	www.bienloindici.com/en/

Michel Joassard
Habanera,
65 rue de la Poste,
30640 Beauvoisin, Gard

Manuel Mamane
Bien Loin d'Ici,
386 Traverse d'Engance,
30000 Nîmes, Gard

ENTRY 498   MAP 16   **ENTRY 499   MAP 16**

La Maison du Vilain Petit Canard

Be greeted by big smiles from Andy and Lyn, as they welcome you into their home. You'll find much beauty within; the beams, shutters and 'veneto cotta' floors are all new, and French windows open to garden and pool. Start your day with a bountiful breakfast: croissants, cheeses, charcuterie, jams; end it in a beautiful sleigh bed. The sunny bedrooms upstairs are for one party only, with a lovely furnished loggia (and a fridge) between them, overlooking the garden. Medieval Uzès has its own Duc and Duchesse – visit the Ducal Palace. Sip home-grown tisanes in the Jardin Medieval; set off for Roman antiquities. Orange, Nîmes and Arles are an easy drive, as are the glorious vineyards of Châteauneuf-du-Pape. Return to the peaceful garden, shrouded from the neighbours by leafy trees.
Min. stay: 3 nights. Children over 10 welcome.

Rooms	2 doubles: €100.
Meals	Restaurants 5-minute walk.
Closed	Christmas, 1 July – 31 August.

Mobile	+44 (0)7900 014122
Email	challands3kids@gmail.com

Lyn Challands
La Maison du Vilain Petit Canard,
46 rue de la Tour du Roi,
30700 Uzès, Gard

ENTRY 500 MAP 16

Demeure Monte Arena

Towering over the village, by the castle, this handsome 17th-century townhouse mixes history and modernity with panache. Vaulted ceilings and flagged floors sit with modern art and black leather. Bedrooms are huge, spread between the two towers. Colours are soft, bedlinens crisp, fine antiques nudge funky lights, bold rugs are spread on ancient tiles. Two rooms are duplex with stunning staircases. All have views over the courtyard garden. Breakfast – organic and homemade – is here or in the vaulted dining hall; dinners, too. Nîmes and Avignon are close or relax in the garden with its scents, secluded corners, and secret jacuzzi.

Rooms	2 doubles: €102-€165. 2 suites for 3, 1 suite for 5: €156-€300. Extra bed/sofabed €27 p.p. per night.
Meals	Dinner, 3-4 courses, €35-€55. Restaurants 10-minute walk.
Closed	Rarely.

Tel	+33 (0)4 66 03 25 24
Email	info@monte-arena.com
Web	www.monte-arena.com

Martine Sanchez
Demeure Monte Arena,
6 place de la Plaine, Montaren & St Médiers,
30700 Uzès, Gard

ENTRY 501 MAP 16

Villa de Labruguière Lacoste

Enjoy the company of Sinsay and his guests on the sun-dappled breakfast terrace. Fruits from the garden, eggs from the hens and views stretching to the Cévennes. This 18th-century mansion, its south wing a former coach house, sits on the main street of a wine-growing village. Behind its gates lies another world. Three generations live here, in luminous rooms filled with personal touches: grandfather's paintings, grandmother's quilts, a young child's decorations. In the part-wild garden, find a secret corner, laze beneath the cedar, dip into the pool. Nearby, discover Sauve, an unspoiled medieval town beside the river Vidourle, and Anduze, where you can buy garlanded garden pots and see the famed bamboo forest. Then it's back to a (pre-booked) dinner: vegetarian with an oriental touch. *Minimum stay: 2 nights.*

Château Massal

Sit down to a welcoming cup of tea with Françoise; she is one of a French silk family that has lived here for generations. She speaks good English and delights in meeting her guests, as does her daughter who visits at weekends. They share a passion for the region, the Cévennes: its gorges, valleys and paths, and the villages of Bez and Esparon that lie on the other side of the river. This 19th-century château flanks the road, as its terraced gardens ramble behind. Inside: an elegant dining table for breakfasts, and, up a spiral stone stair, light-filled bedrooms with a château feel. One has a bathroom in the tower, another an old grand piano too large to move! After an adventurous day out – riding in Causses, braving rapids in St Bauzille de Putois – you can recover at La Merlanson up the hill, where the chef specialises in 'cuisine du terroir'.

Rooms	3 doubles: €65-€90. 1 family room for 4: €80-€110. Extra bed/sofabed €15 p.p. per night.
Meals	Dinner, 3 courses: vegetarian €20; gourmet €30; by arrangement.
Closed	15 November – 31 March

Rooms	4 doubles: €68-€98. Child's bed available.
Meals	Restaurant within walking distance.
Closed	Mid-November to March.

Tel	+33 (0)6 68 81 77 84
Email	welcome@villa-de-lablac.com
Web	www.villa-de-lablac.com

Sinsay Phothirath
Villa de Labruguière Lacoste,
372 route de Lézan,
30350 Canaules, Gard

Tel	+33 (0)4 67 81 07 60
Email	francoiseduluc@gmail.com
Web	www.cevennes-massal.com

Françoise & Marie-Emmanuelle du Luc
Château Massal,
Bez & Esparon,
30120 Le Vigan, Gard

ENTRY 502 MAP 16

ENTRY 503 MAP 15

Castle Cottage

On the edge of unspoilt woodland, in a garden full of trees and colour where 23 tortoises roam (no touching please)... it's hard to believe you're only a tram ride from Montpellier. The house is recent, the vegetation lush, the tempting pool (mind the alarm) set among atmospheric stone 'ruins'. In the house are small but comfortable beds in pretty rooms (shuttered in summer) full of family pieces and colour, a good shower room and doors to the terrace. Outside is a sweet little independent 'studio' for two. Your exuberant, dynamic hostess loves this place passionately, her garden is an oasis even in winter and the beach is nearby.
Minimum stay: 2 nights at weekends.

Domaine de Pélican

In summer, vignerons drop by for Monday tastings – followed by a special dinner: book to join in. This eco-leaning wine estate has a mulberry-lined drive and a real family atmosphere: he is quiet and gentle, she energetic and charming. In the old barn, bedrooms have soft-coloured walls, some beds on mezzanines (no windows but glazed doors), pretty shower rooms. Old honey-coloured beams protect the dining room – a dream that gives onto the terrace and rows of vines beyond. Cool off in the saltwater pool, or wild-swim in the river Hérault. Ideal for those interested in good wine, peacefulness and proper French country cuisine.

Rooms	1 double: €128. 1 suite for 4: €186-€216. Children under 5 free. Extra bed €32. Suite also available for 2-3 guests.	**Rooms**	2 doubles, 1 twin: €80-€90. 1 suite for 4: €80-€90
Meals	Breakfast on request (studio only). Restaurants in Montpellier, 3km.	**Meals**	Dinner with wine, €28. Restaurant in village.
Closed	Rarely.	**Closed**	Rarely.

Tel	+33 (0)4 67 72 63 08	**Tel**	+33 (0)4 67 57 68 92
Email	castlecottage@free.fr	**Email**	domaine-de-pelican@wanadoo.fr
Web	www.castlecottage-chambresdhotes.com	**Web**	www.domainedepelican.fr

Dominique Cailleau
Castle Cottage,
289 chemin de la Rocheuse,
34170 Castelnau le Lez, Hérault

Isabelle & Baudouin Thillaye du Boullay
Domaine de Pélican,
34150 Gignac,
Hérault

ENTRY 504 MAP 15

ENTRY 505 MAP 15

Sanssoucis

Near the centre of a small but busy wine-making village and tucked behind a high wall, find a serene 17th-century house that was once a church and convent. Gerad and Johnny, who live in another part of the house with their two gentle dogs, are warm and friendly. You'll feel very private in the garden with the only sound from the fountain. Chill out on sofas in the shaded Moroccan-style cabana, cool off in the swimming pool on hot days and help yourself to a drink from the summer kitchen. Continental breakfast is served on refectory tables in the farmhouse-style breakfast room or separately in the garden. Explore the village, visit vineyards, spend long days on sandy beaches. Return to an evening aperitif with your hosts in the wood-panelled salon and sociable dinners prepared by a local chef once or twice a week. *Min. stay: 2 nights.*

La Bergerie de Laval

Keen cyclists and walkers, your kind hosts, Sonia and John, make unwinding easy at their traditionally dressed villa in vineyards two minutes from Pézenas. The pool, jacuzzi, lingering breakfasts (homemade jams, excellent pastries); the smell of Mediterranean plants and a hammock hung between mature pines – all help! As do the quietly decorated ground-floor rooms that come with super bedding, refreshed brocante furniture, parquet floors, good bathrooms and towels. Dine in the village or simply picnic if you've had a big day out: being sporty on Lake Salagou, eating from the Étang de Thau or marketing in medieval St Guilhem. *Minimum stay: 2 nights.*

Rooms	5 twin/doubles: €130-€160.
Meals	Dinner available by arrangement. Restaurants 5-minute walk.
Closed	1 April – 10 June, 12 September – 31 December.

Rooms	1 double; 2 doubles with separate wc: €65-€105.
Meals	Restaurant within walking distance.
Closed	1 December – 28 February.

Email gerad@geradkite.com
Web www.sanssoucis.co

Gerad & Johnny
Sanssoucis,
6 rue de l'Eglise,
34320 Roujan, Hérault

Tel +33 (0)4 67 90 77 86
Email jwh.sj.potts@gmail.com
Web www.la-bergerie-de-laval.com

Sonia & John Potts
La Bergerie de Laval,
21 chemin de Laval,
34120 Tourbes, Hérault

ENTRY 506 MAP 15

ENTRY 507 MAP 15

Meze Maison

The welcoming aperitif sets the tone. Rob left a demanding job to turn this graceful 19th-century merchant's house into an elegant, relaxed home. Stone stairs curve to two floors of bedrooms, soft with silvery colours, chandeliers and chic bathrooms. Balconies with French windows look over the town or gardens of the nearby château. Painted in the subtle hues of Farrow & Ball and beautifully beamed, the open-plan living space is coolly stylish: antique mirrors, books, oversize table lamps. Breakfasts are served at the white dining table. Explore harbours, beaches and Meze's fish restaurants. Gentle hosts, serene surroundings.

La Casa Occitane

A fine old townhouse right in the heart of this bustling fishing port, famous for its seafood. Step straight in to a large hallway with a beautiful stone staircase and iron banisters, high limewashed walls hung with large oils of nymphs and shepherds, vibrant colours. Roberto, a charming Italian, and his French wife Peggy can organise wine tastings or visits to local markets and lend you bikes. Sleep well on thick mattresses with snowy linen (two rooms are big enough for a sofabed), wander the pretty garden with pool, take a book to the vast sitting room, eat hearty breakfasts (bacon, eggs, cheese) with freshly-baked bread on the terrace. *Minimum stay: 2 nights in high season.*

Rooms	3 doubles, 1 twin/double: €120-€195. Singles €105. Extra bed/sofabed €30 p.p. per night.
Meals	Restaurants within walking distance.
Closed	Rarely.

Rooms	3 doubles: €100-€160. 1 cottage for 2: €100-€170. Extra bed/sofabed €25 p.p. per night.
Meals	Restaurants 5-min walk.
Closed	Rarely.

Mobile	+33 (0)6 21 16 43 42
Email	rob@mezemaison.com
Web	www.mezemaison.com

Rob Budden
Meze Maison,
34140 Meze,
Hérault

Tel	+33 (0)4 67 90 51 09
Email	contact@lacasaoccitane.com
Web	www.lacasaoccitane.com/en/

Roberto Aiello
La Casa Occitane,
23 boulevard Lamartine,
34340 Marseillan, Hérault

La Maison des Rossignols

The village is known for its wine and Romanesque church; get up early on a clear day and you're rewarded with a Pyrenean view. This is an elegant, fresh-painted maison de maitre whose warm, kind owners prepare for you a generous English breakfast (or a French one should you prefer) in a big friendly kitchen with a bright red wall. Immaculate and uncluttered bedrooms off a wide landing have sweeping wooden floors, handsome old pine doors, and space for button-back sofas. After a day out in idyllic Lagrasse or splendid Carcassonne, prepare to be spoiled by Marco's fabulous dinners.

Le Jardin d'Homps

Dutch charm now fills this handsome old townhouse with its impressive panelling and Art Nouveau windows. Gerda and Thomas have made the street-side theirs so you have lofty, uncluttered bedrooms overlooking the informal garden; parquet floors and beautiful large beds. Yours too: the sparkling pool and gentle hammock swinging from a pair of pine trees; the large sitting room – shelves of crime novels, doors onto the terrace; buffet breakfast feasts and friendly, French and Italian-style dinners. Rent bikes or a Canal du Midi barge for the day, sample Minervois wines, delve into things Cathar, return to restful, historic Homps. *Minimum stay: 2 nights in high season.*

Rooms	3 doubles, 1 twin: €80-€85. Singles €75.		**Rooms**	3 twin/doubles: €80-€110. 2 suites for 4: €130-€160.
Meals	Dinner with wine, €35, by arrangement. Restaurants 4km.		**Meals**	Dinner €20-€30. Restaurants 5-minute walk.
Closed	1 December – 1 March.		**Closed**	1 November – 31 March.

Mobile	+33 (0)6 32 16 43 13		**Mobile**	+33 (0)6 71 89 15 70
Email	maison.rossignols@gmail.com		**Email**	contact@jardinhomps.fr
Web	www.chambres-hotes-rossignols.com		**Web**	www.jardinhomps.fr

Marco Raumann
La Maison des Rossignols,
7 traverse du Mourel,
11120 Pouzols-Minervois, Aude

Gerda & Thomas Wijnands
Le Jardin d'Homps,
21 grand rue,
11200 Homps, Aude

ENTRY 510   MAP 15   **ENTRY 511   MAP 15**

Château de Puichéric

There's a thousand years of history steeped in the tower and walls of this château but much has been altered and rebuilt since: a spectacular 17th-century stone staircase, 18th-century frescoes, Art Deco wallpaper and tiles. When Dominica and Philippe arrived in 2010 they installed a modern heating system with lashings of hot water so now you get deep comfort in an ancient castle. View-filled bedrooms (one looks over the Corbières) are simply but well furnished with original furniture, new mattresses, modern bathrooms. Your generous hosts feed you well: continental breakfast on the terrace, join them for a barbecue supper. *Minimum stay: 2 nights in high season. Children under 2 free.*

Les Chambres d'Aimé

Come by train. This large stone house dates from 1860 and is on a quiet row of terraced houses leading down to the main square of La Bastide St-Louis, the 13th-century 'new town' below the medieval Cité of Carcassonne. At the back, a garden with a shaded terrace and a small swimming pool are perfect for lounging about. You'll feel quite independent in bedrooms with seating areas, and you can help yourself to tea and coffee on the landing. Breakfast is at separate tables in the dining room or on the terrace: croissants, breads, home-made yoghurt and jams, fruit and ham. It's a five-minute walk to shops and restaurants and a lively Saturday morning market. Amble along the scenic Canal du Midi or take a boat trip, explore the magnificent medieval fortress, soak in the very French atmosphere.

Rooms	3 twin/doubles: €80-€100.
	2 family rooms for 4: €120.
	Extra beds/sofabed €15.
Meals	Dinner €25; children €12.
	Wine €10.
Closed	Rarely.

Rooms	5 doubles: €70-€130.
Meals	Restaurants within walking distance.
Closed	Rarely.

Tel	+33 (0)4 68 75 40 95
Email	contact@chateaudepuicheric.fr
Web	www.chateaudepuicheric.fr

Dominica Teuschl
Château de Puichéric,
2 Rue de l'Église,
11700 Puichéric, Aude

Tel	+33 (0)9 69 80 98 52
Email	info@leschambresdaime.com
Web	delruearnaud.wixsite.com/lcda-eng

Arnaud & Véronique Delrue-Marty
Les Chambres d'Aimé,
69 rue aimé ramond,
11000 Carcassonne, Aude

ENTRY 512   MAP 15

ENTRY 513   MAP 15

La Forge de Montolieu

Napoleonic cannonballs were once fashioned in this striking country forge, in a secluded valley where flowers and bird-filled forests give way to waterfalls and trout-rich pools. Later, textiles emerged from its creamy walls... Now home to a charming Franco-American family, it's a wonderful renovation project with four country-pretty bedrooms, new Italian showers and a kitchenette in the guest wing. Charles' photos hint at their passion for the place, and you'll learn more over a lazy brunch, a family supper or five-course dinner – organic with seasonal veg. Walk the dogs through a pocket of woods to book-happy Montolieu.

Villelongue Côté Jardins

Painters, poets, nature-lovers love this place, where history and romance combine. Dark 16th-century passages and uneven stone floors open into heavily beamed rooms sympathetically revived. Big, simple bedrooms, authentic in their white cotton and old armoires, the more recent on the ground floor, look out to the ancient trees of the park or the great courtyard and ruined Cistercian abbey. Sisters Renée and Claude, warm, knowledgeable, generous, were born here and provide convivial breakfasts and dinners. Wild gardens and duck ponds, lazy cats and lovely walks into the landscape.

Rooms	2 doubles, 1 twin: €88-€100. 1 triple: €100-€120. Extra bed/sofabed €22 p.p. per night. Two self-catering properties for 4-6.
Meals	Cooked breakfast €5. Dinner €18-€30. Wine from €4-€25. Guest kitchenette. Restaurant 2km.
Closed	Rarely.

Rooms	1 double, 1 twin: €70-€80. 1 family room for 3: €70-€83.
Meals	Dinner with wine, €25.
Closed	Christmas.

Tel	+33 (0)4 68 76 60 53
Email	info@forgedemontolieu.com
Web	www.forgedemontolieu.com/en/

Charles Cowen
La Forge de Montolieu,
Hameau de Franc,
11170 Montolieu, Aude

Tel	+33 (0)4 68 76 09 03
Email	villelonguecotejardins@gmail.com
Web	www.villelongue-cote-jardin.com

Claude Antoine & Renée Marcoul
Villelongue Côté Jardins,
Lieu-dit Villelongue,
11170 St Martin le Vieil, Aude

ENTRY 514 MAP 15

ENTRY 515 MAP 15

La Rougeanne

Monique and Paul-André bought this old wine-grower's estate on the edge of town and carefully restored it inside and out. They look after you beautifully – she has endless energy and adores people, he is quiet and charming. Find an airy guest sitting room, gardens with views to the Pyrenees and luxurious bedrooms. Breakfast in the orangery, or under the pomegranate trees in summer: pastries, bread, fruit, cheese, homemade cake, jam made by a neighbour. It's a few minutes' walk to Moussoulens village for places to eat – there's a bakery and store too. Discover hilltop bastides and castles of the Cathars. Carcassonne, nearby, has lively Thursday and Sunday markets. Montolieu, a five-minute drive, has tons of bookshops to browse – the French version of Hay. Cyclists love the Canal du Midi routes.

Domaine Michaud

The Danen family happily welcome you into their home, an 18th-century former winemaker's house in an unspoilt area of France. The views here are spectacular: over rolling countryside and woods with the Pyrenees and Corbières mountains in the distance. The big living room has a fireplace, tapestries on the walls, antique furniture and a terrace for breakfast. Dinner is so good locals come to join in: veg from the garden, everything locally sourced, no menu – just what's fresh and tasty in the market that day, accompanied by Malepère wines. Take a dip in the pool or jacuzzi and play tennis or billiards; settle into an armchair and read next to the fireplace. Ask about hiking, cycling or riding in the area; Carcassonne and the Canal du Midi are just 15 minutes' drive. *Min. stay: 2 nights. Over 13s welcome.*

Rooms	3 doubles, 1 twin: €110-€130. 1 family room for 4: €110-€210. Extra bed/sofabed €30 p.p. per night.
Meals	Restaurants within walking distance.
Closed	1 November – 31 March.

Rooms	4 twin/doubles: €130-€190. 1 suite for 2: €155. Extra bed €45 per night.
Meals	Dinner, 3 courses, €40. Restaurant 4km.
Closed	Rarely.

Tel	+33 (0)4 68 24 46 30
Email	info@larougeanne.com
Web	www.larougeanne.com

Monique & Paul-André Glorieux
La Rougeanne,
8 allée du Parc,
11170 Moussoulens, Aude

Mobile	+33 (0)6 44 29 42 30
Email	info@domainemichaud.eu
Web	www.domainemichaud.eu

The Danen Family
Domaine Michaud,
Route de la Malepère, Roullens,
11290 Carcassonne, Aude

ENTRY 516 MAP 15   ENTRY 517 MAP 15

Château Haute-Fontaine

Vineyards crossed with wild walks circle this unpretentious, sea-breezy château, home to sociable British hosts beyond a mighty pine-flanked drive... it's a stunning approach. Paul and Penny have a small local team and you can explore their garrigue-rich estate, tour the cellars, hear their story. Mingle with guests from the three gîtes – and some snoozing cats; breakfast in a courtyard with clambering jasmine. You sleep in the former grape-pickers' house, up steepish stairs: terracotta tiles, ochre walls and a simple, family feel. Beds are wicker or wrought-iron, shower rooms large and shared; there's a kitchen for twilight feasts and communal sitting room. Walk into the village for dinner; the coast is close.

Castell Rose

A beautiful, pink marble gentleman's house in its own parkland on the edge of a very pretty town between the sea and the mountains; the views are superb. Evelyne and Alex are both charming and give you large graceful bedrooms with calm colour schemes, good linen, tip-top bathrooms and elegant antiques. After a good breakfast, wander through the flourishing garden with its ancient olive trees to find a spot beside the lily pond, or just float in the pool. It's a five-minute stroll to village life, or take the yellow train up the mountain from Villefranche for more amazing views.

Rooms	2 doubles, sharing 2 bathrooms & wcs with all: €60-€70. 1 single, sharing 2 bathrooms & wcs with all: €50. 1 triple, sharing 2 bathrooms & wcs with all: €75.
Meals	Breakfast €6. Guest kitchen. Restaurant 1km.
Closed	1 September to Easter.

Rooms	3 doubles, 1 twin: €85-€99. 1 family room for 4: €119-€139.
Meals	Restaurant 500m.
Closed	Rarely.

Tel	+33 (0)4 68 41 03 73
Email	haute-fontaine@wanadoo.fr
Web	www.chateauhautefontaine.com

Paul & Penelope Dudson
Château Haute-Fontaine,
11100 Bages,
Aude

Tel	+33 (0)4 68 96 07 57
Email	castellroseprades@gmail.com
Web	www.castellrose-prades.com

Evelyne & Alex Waldvogel
Castell Rose,
Chemin de la Litera,
66500 Prades, Pyrénées-Orientales

ENTRY 518 MAP 15

ENTRY 519 MAP 15

Château d'Ortaffa

Medieval Ortaffa sits in a pocket of sunshine between the Pyrénées and the lively port of Collioure, and this big old winemaker's château – once the Episcopal palace of the bishops, adjoined to historic residential buildings – perches on its ancient fortified walls. Large French windows open to the terrace, where breakfast comes with a stunning tableau of mountains and sea with village rooftops tumbling below. Slip into a beautifully restored house, luxurious and with a relaxed holiday feel, whose elegant, pastel-shaded library and guest rooms display your hosts' love of antiques and fine art. Your room may have Picasso prints, bookshelves, an antique child's bed, or quirky graffiti in the loo; one beauty, in pale greys and blues, reveals remnants of the former chapel. Alain (once in advertising) and Michelle (in antiques) are friendly, articulate and know their patch well. Roll down to the port for seafood, slide south along the coast to Spain... for Cadaques, Figueras, Girona. A special spot, away from the bustle of Collioure.

Minimum stay: 2 nights on weekdays. .

Rooms	2 doubles: €110-€130. 2 suites for 2: €110-€130. Extra bed/sofabed €30 p.p. per night.
Meals	Restaurant in village.
Closed	Rarely.

Michelle & Alain Batard
Château d'Ortaffa,
8 rue du Château, 66560 Ortaffa,
Pyrénées-Orientales

Tel	+33 (0)6 64 14 53 42
Mobile	+33 (0)6 64 14 53 42
Email	chateau.ortaffa@gmail.com
Web	www.chateau-ortaffa.com

ENTRY 520   MAP 15

Rhône Valley - Alps

La Ferme du Chozal, page 371

Le Clair de la Plume

Set in a sea of lavender, laden with literature, history and flowers, Grignan is a treat of a little town. So is this welcoming hotel within its sheltering walls (some rooms are in another charming house 100m away). Push the heavy gates of the pink *maison de maître* onto a special place. Jean-Luc Valadeau has created a warm hospitable 'home with all the comforts of a hotel'. He and his staff are a community, ushering you through deliciously elegant rooms where antique pieces catch your eye, and the small terraced garden has a natural pool and a lovely view over the town. Peaceful bedrooms are divided between the main and the second house. A combination of great taste and authenticity mixes Louis Philippe wardrobes, country-style wicker, luxurious bathrooms, washed or ragged walls, original tiles and shining oak planks. After a generous breakfast, walk into town or borrow bikes and explore the picture-perfect villages. Then return to the organic garden restaurant for exotic selections of teas and mouthwatering pâtisseries among the roses or a delectable dinner in one of the restaurants. *Pets by arrangement.*

Rooms	2 doubles, 10 twin/doubles: €129-€395. 3 suites for 4: €395-€495. Extra bed/sofabed €45 p.p. per night.
Meals	Breakfast €24. Bistro menu from €26.50. Gastronomic menu from €75.
Closed	Rarely.

Jean-Luc Valadeau
Le Clair de la Plume,
2 Place de Mail,
26230 Grignan, Drôme

Tel	+33 (0)4 75 91 81 30
Email	info@clairplume.com
Web	www.clairplume.com

Château les Oliviers de Salettes

After three years of renovations and meticulous attention to detail from gentle owners Robin and Dominique, the hotel runs like clockwork. The building that exists today, a three-storey house of impressive proportions with a turret at each end, was part of a much larger château, the centre of a vast vineyard. Now it lords it over five hectares of finely landscaped parkland, with dining terraces, boules pitch and infinity pool, and panoramas that reach to the Alps. Honeymooners, families, the lazy and the lively: all will love it here. Apart from cookery lessons, wine tastings and electric-bike rentals, there's tree climbing and paragliding, canoeing and windsurfing, riding and golf. And a sweet spa to recover in: how about a bamboo massage? Uncluttered bedrooms are full of lofty splendour and furnished in classic French style, their stone walls and great beams intact; bathrooms (one in the dovecote) are state of the art. But dinner is the highlight of the stay: beautiful food from beautiful produce accompanied by heavenly views. The 'menu du midi' is great value.

Rooms	13 doubles: €99-€190. 8 suites for 2, 1 suite for 4 with private terrace: €169-€445. Dinner, B&B €54-€56 p.p.
Meals	Breakfast €16. Lunch €15-€29. Dinner, 4-5 courses, €43-€65. Wine €26-€60. Restaurants 1km.
Closed	Rarely.

Tel	+33 (0)4 75 00 19 30
Email	contact@chateau-lesoliviers.com
Web	www.chateau-lesoliviers.com

Robin Leyssens & Dominique Berger
Château les Oliviers de Salettes,
1205 route du Château,
26450 Charols, Drôme

ENTRY 522 MAP 11

Château de la Commanderie

Grand it appears, and some of the makers of that grandeur – Knights Templar, princes and prime ministers – gaze down on you in the dining room, a favourite restaurant for the discerning palates of Grenoble. Yet the atmosphere is of an intimate family hotel. The whole place is awash with antiques and heirlooms, breakfast is delicious, good taste prevails and flowers add that touch of life and genuine attention. And there are massages galore in the sumptuous spa. Bedrooms are in four buildings, old and new, adding to the sense of intimacy. Rooms in château and chalet are traditional with carved wooden beds and gilt-framed mirrors, though some of them give onto a small road. The Orangerie's rooms (as you'll discover once you have negotiated the rather plain corridors) look out over fine parkland, and are deliciously peaceful. The least expensive rooms are in the Petit Pavillon, on the roadside. But whichever you choose, you will be beautifully looked after by the Beaumont brothers – they grew up here – in this smart suburb of Grenoble. *Signs for 'La Commanderie' indicate an area of town, not the château.*

Rooms	42 twin/doubles: €102-€190. Singles €102-€180. Dinner, B&B €107-€123 p.p..
Meals	Buffet breakfast €16.50. Lunch & dinner €30-€84. Wine €30-€50. Restaurant closed Mondays, Saturday lunch & Sundays, & 1-15 August lunch.
Closed	20 December – 3 January.

Monsieur de Beaumont
Château de la Commanderie,
17 avenue d'Echirolles, Eybens,
38320 Grenoble, Isère

Tel   +33 (0)4 76 25 34 58
Email resa@commanderie.fr
Web   www.commanderie.fr

La Ferme du Chozal

Meals with family and friends taste best in the mountain air. From the suntrap terrace of this small hotel you can try fish from the lakes, meat from the pastures, and edible flowers from the garden. Ferme du Chozal has some of the best views in the village; on a clear day you can see Mont Blanc. Frédéric and Anne-Christine offer you home-baked bread for breakfast, homemade yogurts and jams, Beaufort butter and cheeses, eggs, ham and fruit salads, and their staff, young and multi-lingual, are charming. Wake to green fields, birdsong and cowbells, hike to the Cormet de Roseland's glorious lake, and return to new pine, old beams, soft beds and deep baths. Cosy up in a little library filled with magazines, board games and books (and DVDs for the mini cinema), laze by the heated pool, soak in the jacuzzi with an aperitif. In the second chalet (connected by a tunnel) is that wonderful restaurant and its excellent cellar. Some bedrooms have low beams, others have balconies.

Rooms	6 doubles: €130-€195. 1 suite for 4: €225-€340. 3 family rooms for 2: €170-€255. 1 chalet for 2: €265-€380. Singles €130. Extra bed/sofabed available.
Meals	Breakfast buffet €19. Dinner from €32.
Closed	1 November – 20 December.

Tel	+33 (0)4 79 38 18 18
Email	informations@lafermeduchozal.com
Web	www.lafermeduchozal.com

Anne-Christine & Frédéric Boulanger
La Ferme du Chozal,
73620 Hauteluce,
Savoie

ENTRY 524   MAP 12

Hôtel Le Cottage Bise

Not many hotels are blessed with such an eye-capturing lakeside position; gazing from the terrace at the sun setting over the Roc de Chère, you could be in a Wagner opera. The three buildings that make up this supremely well-run hotel resemble – quelle surprise! – Alpine chalets; what's more, they are set in well-planted gardens with a classy pool and perfectly gravelled pathways. Jean-Claude and Christine run their relaxed and not-so-small hotel with quiet Savoyard efficiency and a proper concern for your comfort. Rooms, each one different, come in two styles: traditional, with floral papers and antique paintings, and contemporary, with paler walls and modern art; all are big with swish bathrooms and the balconied suites have splendid views to the lake and mountains. The food – served in the restaurant or on the lake-view terrace – is first class (note, half-boarders have less choice). You are away from the bustle of Annecy but close enough to dabble if you wish... the old quarter is a delight. Sail, windsurf, waterski, pedalo – the lake laps at your feet.

Rooms	25 twin/doubles: €150-€320. 6 suites for 4: €300-€500. Extra bed/sofabed €10-€15 p.p. per night.
Meals	Breakfast €21. Lunch €30-€75. Dinner €47-€75. Wine €25-€70. Restaurants within walking distance.
Closed	October to April.

Jean-Claude & Christine Bise
Hôtel Le Cottage Bise,
Au Bord du Lac, 74290 Talloires,
Haute-Savoie

Tel	+33 (0)4 50 60 71 10
Email	cottagebise@wanadoo.fr
Web	www.cottagebise.com

The Farmhouse

The day starts with a breakfast spread in the cattle shed – now a deeply atmospheric dining room – and ends with a slap-up dinner hosted by Dorrien. Many years ago he gave up England for the oldest farmhouse in Morzine – the lovely, steeply pitched Mas de la Coutettaz at the peaceful end of town. Push open the mellow carved door to find a 1771 interior of dark chunky beams, huge Morzine slate flags and patina'd pine doors with original mouldings. Big, characterful, comfortable bedrooms, whose bathrooms promise white robes and lavish lotions, are reached via a central stone stair; some have mountain views. At the end of the garden is an exquisite little mazot, its bedroom up a steep outside stair. Morzine is the perfect staging post for Avoriaz and the Portes du Soleil, so come for hiking, biking, swimming in the lakes followed by lively dinners. Return to a hot toddy in the bar and a crackling log fire, lit at the merest hint of chill, even in summer – final proof (as if you needed it) that you will adore The Farmhouse and long to return. *Please refer to website for winter prices. Short breaks available, please enquire with owner.*

Rooms	3 doubles, 2 suites for 2, 3 cottages for 2: €160-€260. 1 family room for 3, 2 family rooms for 4: €160-€312. Singles from €80.
Meals	Dinner, 4 courses with wine, €50.
Closed	7 April – 15 June, 17 September – 15 December.

Tel	+33 (0)4 50 79 08 26
Mobile	+33 (0)6 83 86 55 49
Email	info@thefarmhouse.co.uk
Web	www.thefarmhouse.co.uk

James Wakelin
The Farmhouse,
429 chemin de la Coutettaz,
74110 Morzine, Haute-Savoie

ENTRY 526   MAP 12

Au Coin du Feu-Chilly Powder

The homeward piste takes you to the door; the cable car, opposite, sweeps you to the peaks. The chalet is named after its magnificent central fireplace... on one side gleaming leather sofas, on the other, red dining chairs at a long table. Everything feels generous here: great beams span the chalet's length, windows look up to the cliffs of the Hauts Forts, high ceilings give a sense of space. There's a reading room on the mezzanine above the living area with books, internet, antique globe and worn leather armchairs, and a small bar made of English oak by a carpenter friend. Bedrooms are Alpine-swish and themed: there's the 'Toy Room' for families, the 'English Room' that sports a bowler hat. The carpets are sisal, one room's four-poster is veiled in muslin and the bathrooms have luxury bathrobes and shower heads as big as plates. The chef produces the best of country cooking, and Paul and Francesca can organise everything, including torchlight descents. There's massage, a sauna, a hot tub outside, DVDs to cheer wet days – even an in-house crèche. A great spot for families.

Rooms	9 twin/doubles: €100.
	8 family rooms for 4: €120-€150.
	Dinner, B&B €895-€1,425 p.p. per week in winter.
Meals	Picnic lunch €10.
	Dinner with wine, €45.
Closed	Rarely.

Paul & Francesca Eyre
Au Coin du Feu-Chilly Powder,
2740 rue des Ardoisières,
74110 Morzine, Haute-Savoie

Tel	+33 (0)4 50 74 75 21
Email	paul@chillypowder.com
Web	www.chillypowder.com

La Ferme de Margot

A real old farmhouse on the south-facing flank of Morzine with original slates, knobbly beams, and heaps of space. Everything has been beautifully considered by generous English owners (who live downstairs), from the study/snug with its wood-burner to the fabulous living area on the top floor to the media room in between. Imagine silver reindeer heads, a sweeping crushed-velvet sofa, a long matt-white dining table, cowhide wallpaper a wooden 'sun-beam' ceiling and tartan flourishes. Step out for beautiful mountain and lakeside walks; there's a good golf course ten minutes' away. Return to fabulous food, beers and wines. *Minimum stay: 2 nights in summer.*

The White Valley

This spanking new chalet, a minute's car-hop from the summer gondola to Avoriaz, is a pretty stroll from the centre of Morzine. The views are stupendous, the luxuries fabulous and the breakfasts are the best. Imagine decked wraparound balconies large enough for yoga and pilates (just ask) and soaks in the hot tub as you gaze on the peaks. On the first floor are statement chandeliers, big sofas, sophisticated colours. Bedrooms, immaculate in new pine, are above and below, compact but with plenty of storage. Bathrooms are handsome, with rainfall showers and delicious treats... owners Andrew and Nancy know how to spoil! *Parking on-site.*

Rooms	4 twin/doubles: £140. 1 suite for 4: £150-£200. Winter: from £795 p.p. per week.
Meals	Dinner with wine, £40. Restaurants within walking distance.
Closed	Rarely.

Rooms	4 twin/doubles: £125. 1 family room for 4: £200.
Meals	Restaurants 700m.
Closed	Rarely.

Tel	+33 (0)9 67 01 12 68
Email	hello@grandcruski.com
Web	www.grandcruski.com

Jane & Stephen Fenlon
La Ferme de Margot,
332 chemin Martenant,
74110 Morzine, Haute-Savoie

Tel	+33 (0)7 60 71 11 27
Email	enquiries@thewhitevalleycompany.com
Web	www.thewhitevalleycompany.com

The White Valley Company
The White Valley,
74110 Morzine,
Haute-Savoie

ENTRY 528   MAP 12   **ENTRY 529   MAP 12**

Chalet Châtelet

The cow-belled Vallée d'Abondance envelops this pretty pine chalet, the result of years of your hosts' creative energy. Oak floors, soft shapes and high ceilings hug reclaimed furniture and works by other members of this arty family. Warmth comes from a Finnish stove and solar panels – an eco-lover's dream and you still find bliss in the hot tub (along with spectacular views). Expect cultured chat in the intimate dining room and Suzie's range-cooked local and organic food. Bedrooms have stunning views too, and dreamy bathrooms; gaze to mountains you climbed, snow-shoed or skied that day. Heavenly. *Minimum stay: 3 nights in high season.*

Chalet Cannelle

The diffuse light of a contemporary chandelier spills onto the white walls of this stylish chalet. Circled by wintry snows or June's wild flowers, in a hamlet just outside Chatel, the lovely old farmhouse has balconies for big windows and stunning views, pine-cosy sleeping quarters, a kids' toy-filled den with its own TV. Delicious treats (eggs from the hens, truffled pecorino, Lake Geneva trout) flow from the kitchen or the terrace's wood-fired oven. Gather for log fires and nightcaps around the three-beam coffee table as you discuss the exploits of the day. Once in you won't want to leave. *Minimum stay: 2 nights at weekends.*

Rooms	2 doubles, 1 twin/double: €120-€150. Winter: €560-€770 p.p. per week.
Meals	Dinner with wine, €35. Children under 12, €15.
Closed	Rarely.

Rooms	1 double, 4 twin/doubles: €110-€150. 1 family room for 4: €140-€160. Winter: €990-€1290 p.p. per week.
Meals	Catered in winter, on request in summer.
Closed	Rarely.

Tel	+33 (0)4 50 73 69 48
Email	info@chalet-chatelet.com
Web	www.chalet-chatelet.com

Pascal & Suzie Immediato
Chalet Châtelet,
353 Route de l'Envers,
74360 Bonnevaux, Haute-Savoie

Tel	+33 (0)4 50 73 30 97
Email	info@chaletcannelle.co.uk
Web	www.chaletcannelle.co.uk

Lorraine McDermott
Chalet Cannelle,
Suvay,
74360 Chatel, Haute-Savoie

ENTRY 530 MAP 12

ENTRY 531 MAP 12

Entre Lac et Montagne

Come to explore gracious, sporty, lakeside Evian – minutes' away. Or head for the mountains – the nearest ski resorts of Bernex and Thollon are a 15-minute drive. And footpaths take off from the door of this well-planned, modernised home above the charming old village of Neuvecelle. The guest wing has a comfortable, lake-view sitting room and each bright bedroom a private balcony or terrace (where you can breakfast): one gazes to Lake Léman, the other is in the pretty garden near the heated pool. The Burtons are keen to share their enthusiasm for this rich area, and to cook – do arrange dinner with them and learn more. *Children over 12 welcome.*

Chalet Miller

Up from the mountain village (2km) the road winds steeply to three chalets. The first is Chalet Miller, a converted cowshed in three luscious acres with a lawn, wildflower meadow, fabulous woodland behind, hanging tree tents and a summer pool. Inside you're steeped in alpine comfort: pine-clad walls, air-sprung mattresses, woody bathrooms, monogrammed towels. The bedrooms, sitting room and balcony are up, while one bathroom is downstairs, reached via the kitchen. Lisa, a professional masseuse, treats you to dinners with local produce in the conservatory, and an excellent continental breakfast. A tranquil place, only 30 minutes from Geneva. *Minimum stay: 2 nights.*

Rooms	2 doubles: €95. Extra sofabed in guest sitting room €45; available when both rooms booked by same party.	**Rooms**	1 double, 1 twin/double, sharing separate bathroom; let to same party only: £89.
Meals	Dinner with wine, €33. Restaurants 5-minute walk.	**Meals**	Dinner with wine, £25. Restaurants 2km.
Closed	Rarely.	**Closed**	Rarely.

Tel	+33 (0)4 50 84 98 34	**Mobile**	+44 (0)7921 214528
Email	oldgranarychrism@aol.com	**Email**	chaletmillergeneva@gmail.com
Web	www.evianchambredhote.com		

Christopher & Christine Burton
Entre Lac et Montagne,
Avenue de Verlagny,
74500 Neuvecelle, Haute-Savoie

Lisa Miller
Chalet Miller,
74380 Lucinges,
Haute-Savoie

ENTRY 532 MAP 12

ENTRY 533 MAP 12

Maison La Cerisaie

This lovely green-shuttered 1830s chalet has been part of the community for years; today it shines. No short cuts have been taken by generous hosts Sally-Anne and Simon (ex-Navy) who delight in providing the best. Start the day with breakfast at a time to suit you (fresh croissants, local jams, Nespresso coffee, Pukka teas), plunge into mountain adventures, return to a hot tub in the garden and supper at the auberge. Or eat in: the food is varied and delicious. Warm, woody, clean-cut bedrooms wait on the first floor, one with an extra sofabed, two with the views, all with bathrobes and toasty bathroom floors. *Minimum stay: 2 nights.*

Les Racines

Screened by trees, with the lake in front and mountains rearing beyond, this house is in a silent green world. Unexpectedly modern – dramatic sloping roofs, large windows – inside all is light and uncluttered. A large living area is coolly furnished with leather sofas on tiled floors; glass-encased stove for chillier days. Bedrooms are stylishly simple with polished wood floors, white walls and balconies. Anglo-Russian couple, Stanley and Vera – early rat-race retirees – love sharing their peaceful spot: go cycling, swimming, or take the lakeside path to Annecy. Return to drinks on the terrace, and the sound of birdsong.

Rooms	1 double, 2 twin/doubles, 1 family room for 3: €120-€140.
Meals	Dinner, 3 courses, with wine, €40; by arrangement.
Closed	Rarely.

Rooms	1 double; 1 double with separate bathroom): €120-€160. Whole villa for 7 available €3500-€5250 per week.
Meals	Restaurants 15-minute walk.
Closed	Rarely.

Tel	+33 (0)4 50 89 94 78
Email	contact@maisonlacerisaie.com
Web	www.maisonlacerisaie.com

Simon & Sally-Anne Airey
Maison La Cerisaie,
Salvagny, 74740 Sixt Fer à Cheval,
Haute-Savoie

Tel	+33 (0)9 87 40 19 97
Email	chezlesracines@gmail.com
Web	www.chezlesracines.com

Vera Root
Les Racines,
567 Allée le Beau,
74410 Saint-Jorioz, Haute-Savoie

Château des Allues

A breathtaking setting for an atmospheric château, 13th century and facing the mountains. There's an incredible feeling of openness and space, and a house party feel if you stay. Stéphane's warm personality gives the place soul; Didier is charming; dinners are innovative and delicious and vegetables are from the potager – a glory. Inside: flowers, paintings, sculptures, quirky-chic antiques, music classical and modern, and comforting old-style suites with huge walk-in wardrobes and tip-top bathrooms. Climb snow-topped peaks, collapse by the pool, visit the Château de Miolans. Breakfast will set you up for a hearty day out. *Cot available. Dogs welcome.*

Chalet Colinn

Mylène and Elizabeth love the outdoors, hence their five-year fight to reincarnate a fallen ruin as a luxury mountain retreat. Join them for gourmet dinner under soaring, raftered ceilings in the grand living space which hovers above Tignes dam. Or soak in the terrace hot tub under the stars; there's a sauna too. Urban rusticity, mountain chic: the place reeks Italian style yet is impossibly hidden in this tiny hamlet. For daytime adventure: the slopes at Val d'Isère, or Tignes, or the Vanoise park. Just ask Elizabeth, off-piste skier extraordinaire.

Rooms	2 doubles: €155-€165.
	1 suite for 2, 2 suites for 4: €165-€255.
Meals	Dinner with wine, €48; book in advance. Restaurants 5-min. drive.
Closed	Rarely.

Rooms	3 twin/doubles: €120.
	2 triples: €180.
	Dinner, B&B €110-€300 p.p.
Meals	Dinner €35. Wine from €13.
Closed	Rarely.

Mobile	+33 (0)6 75 38 61 56
Email	info@chateaudesallues.com
Web	www.chateaudesallues.com

Stéphane Vandeville
Château des Allues,
335 rue Audibert,
73250 Saint Pierre D'Albigny, Savoie

Tel	+33 (0)4 79 06 26 99
Email	contact@chaletcolinn.com
Web	www.chaletcolinn.com

Elizabeth Chabert & Mylène Charrière
Chalet Colinn,
Le Franchet de Tignes, BP 125,
73150 Val d'Isère, Savoie

ENTRY 536   MAP 12

ENTRY 537   MAP 12

Les Marais

Opt for the simple country life at this friendly farm, which has been in the family for over 100 years and has returned to organic methods. A couple of horses, a few hens, and a reminder of a gentler, slower pace of life. Madame, although busy, always finds time for a chat. The bedrooms are in a separate wing with varnished ceilings, antique beds, some florals; baths are old-fashioned pink, new showers delight Americans. At the foot of the Vercors range, French charm, utter peace.

Les Péris

Here is the B&B we all dream of (and a real slice of proper France). You're well looked after: Élisabeth cossets her guests, puts flowers and sweets in the bedrooms and sends you off with walnuts from the farm. In the family for ten generations, the old stone house facing the mountains is happy and delightful. Join family, friends and guests round the long kitchen table for walnut cakes at breakfast and Élisabeth's delicious menu curieux that uses forgotten vegetables. Roomy, old-fashioned bedrooms with armoires breathe a comfortable, informal air. Great for kids: a garden for wild flowers and a duck pond for splashing in. *Parking on-site.*

Rooms	1 twin: €57. 1 triple: €73. Tourist tax €0.75 p.p. per night.	**Rooms**	1 double, 2 twins: €50-€60. 1 family room for 4: €50-€120.
Meals	Restaurants 3km.	**Meals**	Dinner with wine, €23.
Closed	Rarely.	**Closed**	21 December – 2 January.

Tel	+33 (0)4 75 47 03 50	**Tel**	+33 (0)4 75 59 41 94
Email	imbert.jean-pierre@wanadoo.fr	**Mobile**	+33 (0)6 43 30 79 73
Web	pagesperso-orange.fr/les-marais	**Email**	chambresperis@gmail.com

Christiane & Jean-Pierre Imbert
Les Marais,
285 route des Massouillards,
26300 Charpey, Drôme

Élisabeth Berger
Les Péris,
205 chemin des Péris,
26120 Châteaudouble, Drôme

La Moutière

Surrounded by gorgeous gardens, the bastide sits large and square amid old outbuildings concealing perfectly converted gîtes. Bare stone façades and limestone trims under a Provençal roof set the tone for simple, fresh, uncluttered interiors: new limestone floors, white furniture, neutral tones and flashes of unexpected colour. Bedding is sumptuous, bathrooms fashionably funky, views from the beautiful pale blue pool glide pleasingly over rows of poplars and fields of lavender. Your wonderfully exuberant Belgian hostess gives convivial weekly dinner parties under the chestnut trees during high season. Divine. *Pets by arrangement.*

L'Évidence

Amid the terraced hills and chestnut forests of the Ardèche is a rambling multi-levelled farmhouse squirrelled away on the village edge, with mountains beyond. A pleasure to step inside and find three fresh bedrooms: Zanzibar, reached through a slick jacuzzi'd bathroom, is big and Africa-infused; Oslo, up top, is all cool blues; cosy Jaïpur (once a goat cellar) is womb-like and intimate, ideal for romancers. Breakfast in bed, or take bread and brioche to the kitchen. Suppers of seasonal bounty can be booked too, saving a drive to a restaurant – and there's a little pool. Smiley Christine, new to B&B, is a delight.

Rooms	4 twin/doubles: €130-€140. Singles €120-€130. Extra bed/sofabed €30 p.p. per night.	
Meals	Dinner €40. Guest kitchen. Restaurant 3km.	
Closed	Rarely.	

Rooms	3 doubles: €90-€120. Extra bed/sofabed €25 p.p. per night.
Meals	Lunch or picnic €15. Dinner with wine, €30. Restaurant 10km.
Closed	Rarely.

Tel	+33 (0)4 75 46 26 88
Email	lamoutiere@gmail.com
Web	www.lamoutiere.com

Françoise Lefebvre
La Moutière,
Quartier Moutière,
26230 Colonzelle, Drôme

Tel	+33 (0)4 75 94 15 89
Email	christine.moser@l-evidence.com
Web	www.l-evidence.com

Christine Moser
L'Évidence,
145 impasse de Peyreplane,
07380 Prades, Ardèche

Château Clément

On a wooded hill this ornate 19th-century
château is both luxurious eco-hotel and
family home. An extraordinary wooden
staircase sweeps you up to airy bedrooms
of understated elegance with original
glowing parquet, antiques, tall views to
gardens and the undulating Ardèche.
The apartment is a must for families.
Magnificent new garden-level rooms in
exciting contemporary style have private
terraces. Marie-Antoinette, her family and
her team are as welcoming as can be,
grow their own fruit and veg and give you
fabulous breakfasts. Wander the rose-
strewn garden to find a shady spot, drift in
the south-facing pool. *Minimum stay: 2
nights in high season.*

Château de Fontblachère

Framed by a forested valley and
mountainous horizons, this 17th-century
château marries Provençal peace with
deep comfort and style. Eric greets you in a
courtyard whose manicured hedges and
white roses dissolve into parkland: a
panoramic pool, Japanese fish pond, an old
tennis court... Under vaulted ceilings are
more treats: a log fire, piano, candles, art,
and Turkish cushions in the orangery
where you may dine on iced melon soup
and quail. Sprightly Eric pours and chats all
the while. Immaculate rooms have space
for families and the valley cries out for
walking, riding and fishing in the Rhône.

Rooms	2 doubles: €180-€250. 2 suites for 2, 1 suite for 6: €230-€600. Singles €150-€250. Extra bed/sofabed €80 p.p. per night.
Meals	Restaurants 5-minute walk.
Closed	4 November – 12 April.

Rooms	2 doubles: €100-€115. 1 family room for 3, 1 family room for 4, 1 family room for 5: €150-€255. Extra bed/sofabed €30 p.p. per night.
Meals	Dinner with wine, €35; by arrangement. Restaurants 3km.
Closed	October to March.

Tel	+33 (0)4 75 88 33 53
Email	contact@auchateauclement.com
Web	www.auchateauclement.com

Marie-Antoinette Rojon
Château Clément,
La Châtaigneraie,
07600 Vals les Bains, Ardèche

Tel	+33 (0)4 75 65 15 02
Email	chateau@fontblachere.com
Web	www.chateau-fontblachere.com

Bernard Liaudois & Eric Dussiot
Château de Fontblachère,
07210 St Lager Bressac,
Ardèche

Château de Pâquier

Old, mighty, atmospheric – yet so homely. Enormous rooms, high heavy-beamed ceilings, large windows with sensational valley views; terraced gardens and animals; impressive bedrooms up an ancient spiral staircase that sets the imagination reeling; with their handsome wardrobes, polished beds and heated terracotta floors. Twice a week Hélène prepares dinner for guests in her modernised 17th-century tower kitchen (wood-fired range, stone sink, cobbled floor). She makes her own bread, honey, jams and walnut aperitif, and the wines come from their Montpellier vineyard. Stay one night and you'll wish you'd stayed more.

Longeville

There is a gentle elegance about this house and the people who live in it, including three sleek cats and two friendly dogs. Of Scots and Irish origin, the Barrs also give you run of the pretty garden with swimming pool. Their love for this 1750s farmhouse shows in their artistic touch with decorating, their mix of old and modern furniture, their gorgeous big bedrooms done in soft pale colours that leave space for the views that rush in from the hills. A high place of comfort and civilised contact where dinner in the airy white living room is a chance to get to know your kind, laid-back hosts more fully.

Rooms	3 twin/doubles: €88-€98. 2 family rooms for 5: €92-€102. Extra bed/sofabed €20 p.p. per night.
Meals	Dinner with wine, €16-€27; by arrangement.
Closed	Rarely.

Rooms	2 twin/doubles: €90. Singles €60.
Meals	Dinner with wine, €25.
Closed	Rarely.

Tel	+33 (0)4 76 72 77 33
Email	chateau.de.paquier@free.fr
Web	www.chateaudepaquier.fr

Jacques & Hélène Rossi
Château de Pâquier,
Chemin du Château,
38650 St Martin de la Cluze, Isère

Tel	+33 (0)4 74 27 94 07
Mobile	+33 (0)6 87 47 59 46
Email	mary.barr@wanadoo.fr

Mary & Greig Barr
Longeville,
5 Longeville,
38300 Succieu, Isère

ENTRY 544   MAP 11   ENTRY 545   MAP 11

Le Traversoud

Rooms are named after painters; lovely 'Cézanne' lies under the eaves on the top floor. Nathalie, warm, bright and amusing, and attentive Pascal welcome you to their farmhouse, guide you up the outside stairs to colourful, comfortable bedrooms and spotless shower rooms and treat you to some of the best home cooking in France, served at a long table; even the brioche is homemade. The garden overflows with grass and trees, crickets chirrup, the Bernese Mountain dog bounds, the donkeys graze and the exuberant courtyard is a safe space for your children to join theirs. Wonderful, informal B&B.

Domaine de Boiron

An eccentric sort of place with interiors that add to the theatre. Arrive to an impressive courtyard, pass under the atmospheric 'plafonds a la Française' ceiling, up a dramatic staircase to eight big bedrooms with delightfully dated bathrooms. Spread out in the large sitting rooms, gather for breakfast around the family dining table, allow a chef to cook for you in the evenings if you don't want to go out. You're on the edge of the Dombes region, a vast area of small freshwater lakes. Visit gastronomic capital Lyon by train from local St André (20 minutes). Return to country silence – just the odd honk of the resident goose. Roam the 40 pretty hectares, swim in the pool, see horses, deer and a goat or two. The owners have grand plans: cultivating the gardens, more rooms, polo, cookery courses.

Rooms	1 twin: €60.1 family room for 3, 1 family room for 4: €76-€92. Children under 10, €10.	**Rooms**	7 doubles: €100-€150. 3 suites for 4: €100-€180. Extra beds available.
Meals	Dinner with wine, €25.	**Meals**	Dinner €35-€45, by arrangement.
Closed	Rarely.	**Closed**	Never.

Tel	+33 (0)4 74 83 90 40	**Email**	info@chateaudescreusettes.fr
Email	deroi.traversoud@orange.fr		
Web	garnier.traversoud.free.fr/index.htm		

Nathalie & Pascal Deroi
Le Traversoud,
484 chemin Sous l'École,
38110 Faverges de la Tour, Isère

Antoine Prost
Domaine de Boiron,
650 chemin de Boiron,
01120 Cordieux, Ain

ENTRY 546 MAP 11

ENTRY 547 MAP 11

Château de Tanay

Surrounded by flat lands, a magnificent château in acres of parkland with pool. Inside is equally splendid. A sleek modern décor illuminates fine stonework and medieval beams, there's a games room for children, a grand piano for musicians and a convivial dining table; in summer, take breakfast by the moat beneath the willow. Spend the day in charming old Lyon or treat the family to the Parc des Oiseaux... return for a château tour with your hosts, pick up dinner at the local takeaway pizzeria. Big tasteful bedrooms lie in the courtyard stables but the family room is in the château itself – with an amazing massage bath.

Château de Marmont

An amazing avenue of plane trees delivers you to an authentic 'time warp' château experience – and private access directly onto the second hole: bring the golf clubs! Madame, a classical historian, is a joy, and her house as colourful as she. Find polished family heirlooms, original wallpapers, a billiard room you can use. Up the grand stairs is a bedroom with books and fresh flowers, and a bathroom with a claw foot bath and trompe-l'œil walls. Breakfasts are in the orangery or by the fire: classical music plays, the candle is lit, the coffee is hot, the oranges and the squeezer are to hand and the homemade jam is delicious.

Rooms	4 twin/doubles: €95-€130. 1 suite for 4: €160-€200. Extra bed available. Not all rooms suitable for babies and children – please ask beforehand.
Meals	Restaurant 100m.
Closed	October – April.

Rooms	1 double: €95. 1 suite for 3-5: €160.
Meals	Restaurant 3km.
Closed	November 1 – February 2.

Mobile +33 (0)9 53 36 87 42
Email info@chateau-tanay.com
Web www.chateau-tanay.com

Benoît Haym
Château de Tanay,
Chemin de Tanay,
01600 St Didier de Formans, Ain

Tel +33 (0)4 74 52 79 74
Web www.chateau-marmont.info

Geneviève Guido-Alhéritière
Château de Marmont,
2043 route de Condeissiat,
01960 St André sur Vieux Jonc, Ain

ENTRY 548 MAP 11

ENTRY 549 MAP 11

Ferme de Perignat

Kind and enthusiastic Parisians, Caroline and Jean-Robert, have done a grand job restoring this characterful 15th-century farm. The timbered stone and brick walls of the farmhouse peep out from a terracotta-tiled roof topped by a rare minaret-shaped Saracen chimney. Two comfortable beamed bedrooms, each with their own stylish modern bathroom, are prettily furnished with brocante bits and bobs. Breakfast in the stately hall or outside where tumbling rose bushes surround the fish-filled pond. There's a gentle Yorkie in residence and it's very dog friendly here. Foodies will head for gastronomic bliss in La Bresse.

Domaine de la Chapelle de Vâtre

The Wilson's estate centres on the 17th-century Romanesque chapel, whose bell is rung once a year to mark the end of the harvest. Beamed, terracotta tiled, simply stylish twin rooms are in two separate, stone buildings. Ground floor Fleurie, the lightest, has a walk-in shower. Brightly painted St Veran, the biggest with light airy bathroom, and smaller St Amour, with mini shower room, have hill views. Across the way the breakfast/tasting room has separate tables and Christine is flexible over times. Drink in views of the Haut Beaujolais from the lovely infinity pool, tour the winery and sample the produce. *Cot available. Parking on-site.*

Rooms	1 double: €115-€125. 1 suite for 2: €100-€135.
Meals	Dinner, 4 courses with apéritif, €30; wine not included. Children €15-€20. Wine list available.
Closed	Rarely.

Rooms	3 twin/doubles: €70-€115. Extra bed/sofabed €20 p.p. per night.
Meals	Restaurants 5-minute drive.
Closed	Rarely.

Mobile	+33 (0)6 33 01 30 69
Email	cf01190@gmail.com
Web	www.fermedeperignat.fr

Caroline Fabre
Ferme de Perignat,
Hameau de Perignat,
01190 St Etienne sur Reyssouze, Ain

Tel	+33 (0)4 74 04 43 57
Email	vatre@wanadoo.fr
Web	www.vatre.com

Christine Wilson
Domaine de la Chapelle de Vâtre,
Lieu Dit Les Bourbons,
69840 Jullié, Rhône

ENTRY 550   MAP 11

ENTRY 551   MAP 11

Maison d'hôtes de La Verrière

Hugging the edge of a beautiful valley in Beaujolais, the high views from nearly every room of this serenely secluded family home are magnificent. Whether waking in your quirky country bedroom, meeting guests at the breakfast table (sampling yogurt cake and nine homemade jams) or swimming in the natural salt pool among wild mountain flowers, the valley is always there – particularly beautiful in autumn. Grégoire's guided walks start from the house. Both he and Christine love having guests to stay, and their French cuisine is so good (never the same dish twice) there's no reason to dine anywhere else.

Les Pasquiers

Come to meet Marie and Guillaume in their beautiful home in a wine-country village. Oriental rugs and fine antiques rub shoulders with contemporary art, and gorgeous books lie around for everyone to peruse. There's a grand piano in the drawing room, heaps of CDs, bedrooms are sunny, beds have beautiful linen, new bathrooms are on their way and the garden is divine – languid terraces, organic potager, summerhouse, pool. Marie loves to cook, and great dinners are shared 'en famille' while the owners' children play with your own. One of the best – and surprisingly close to the autoroute.

Rooms	3 twin/doubles: €82-€92. 1 triple: €100-€110. 1 quadruple: €118-€128. Extra bed/sofabed €18 p.p. per night.	**Rooms**	1 twin/double, can interconnect with family room: €90. 1 suite for 4: €90-€150. 1 family room for 5: €90-€165. Extra bed €25, with breakfast.
Meals	Dinner with wine, €32; child €4-€21. Picnic by arrangement. Restaurant 15km.	**Meals**	Dinner with wine & apéritif €35; children under 14 €12. Restaurants 6km.
Closed	Rarely.	**Closed**	Never.

Tel	+33 (0)4 74 04 71 46	**Tel**	+33 (0)4 74 69 86 33
Email	christine.gesse@orange.fr	**Email**	lespasquiers@orange.fr
Web	a.la.verriere.pagesperso-orange.fr	**Web**	www.lespasquiers.com

Christine Gesse & Grégoire Lamy
Maison d'hôtes de La Verrière,
69430 Les Ardillats,
Rhône

Marie & Guillaume Peyraverney
Les Pasquiers,
69220 Lancié,
Rhône

La Croix de Saburin

Close to the autoroute, yet with to-die-for views – they soar over vineyards to Mounts Brouilly and Blanc. Built in regional style against the hillside is this very French, contemporary-smart house. Sociable and perfectionist, Monique and Jean-Michel began B&B when they retired; small pretty bedrooms have chalky mango-wood tables, sparkling bathrooms, glorious views. Guests are spoilt with the salon: tea-making kit and plenty of books. Rare birds, orchids and butterflies dwell in the valley below; cycling, wine tasting and Lyon are close by. Dine with the family on salade Lyonnaise and chicken in champagne. Intimate and stunning.

Les Hautes Bruyères

Once settled on this wooded hilltop in restfully subdued, country-smart comfort, you can't imagine that super-urban Lyon is only 10 minutes away. Karine's converted farm buildings are sophisticated yet simple – and so is she, with a genuine interest in other people and a flair for interiors. With 2000 years of European history in its bones and a solid reputation for good food, Lyon has myriad treasures to see and taste. After a day of discovery (or work) in the city or the countryside, relax in the green and birdsung garden. Tomorrow there will be delicious breakfast in the 'auberge' dayroom.

Rooms	1 double: €72. 1 family room for 3: €72-€90. Dinner, B&B €28 p.p.	**Rooms**	2 doubles: €145-€250. Extra bed €35.
Meals	Dinner with wine, €25.	**Meals**	Bocuse cookery school in village: weekday bookings. 6km Lyon centre. Guest kitchen for light preparations.
Closed	Rarely.	**Closed**	Rarely.

Tel	+33 (0)4 74 69 02 82
Email	jean-michel.legat@orange.fr
Web	lacroixdesaburin.free.fr

Jean-Michel & Monique Legat
La Croix de Saburin,
Saburin,
69430 Quincié en Beaujolais, Rhône

Tel	+33 (0)4 78 35 52 38
Email	contact@lhb-hote.fr
Web	www.lhb-hote.fr

Karine Laurent
Les Hautes Bruyères,
5 chemin des Hautes Bruyères,
Écully, 69130 Lyon, Rhône

ENTRY 554 MAP 11

ENTRY 555 MAP 11

Château d'Origny

Werner and Melinde's house has no bright lights outside to disturb the stars, no noise to pierce the quiet, just acres of tidy parkland to potter and restful suites – one with a library, another with a hammam and sauna. Pretty Roanne is a short drive away for markets. Breakfast on platters of fruit and endless varieties of local jam, spend the day exploring (and eating) and return to Werner's classic French cuisine in the cosy tiled kitchen – he changes the menu weekly, but there's always a cheese plate from nearby Mons. The fireplace roars in winter, and you can watch the chef at work. There are few châteaux that can claim one of the world's best restaurants as near neighbours, but Restaurant Troisgros is just around the corner and there's a car service to get you there. Loosen your belt for dinner at the original maison or follow the river north to La Colline du Colombier for a Troisgros taste of Burgundy.

Rooms	5 suites for 2: €170-€350
Meals	Dinner €49. Wine €25-€100. Restaurants 2km.
Closed	Rarely.

Email	werner.de-clippel@orange.fr
Web	www.chateaudorigny.com

Werner & Melinde De Clippel
Château d'Origny,
2210 Route de Roanne,
42155 Ouches, Loire

ENTRY 556 MAP 11

Provence - Alps - Riviera

Le Domaine des Tilleuls

Bowl down the plane-tree lined road into the touristy, buzzing atmosphere of the town with its shops and good places to eat. Then step through an ancient gate to find peace and calm in this stone house (a silk farm in the late 1700s) with its huge garden, cooling pool and shading lime trees. You will be greeted by Louis and Florence Saint Joire who live on site and are always handy. There's plenty of space, so even if the place is full you can feel private: take breakfast in the large dining room with tiled floor, or the greenhouse-like annexe, or in the garden when the sun is out. Sleep peacefully in bedrooms split between the main house (bright and airy, some with beams, all relaxing and comfortable) and more compact rooms in the annexe (painted pastel colours with antique furniture). Cyclists are very happy (they return again and again) with the start of the Mont Ventoux ascent on the doorstep, good hiking around the Dentelles de Montmirail is a 10-minute drive, Roman excavations are nearby and lavender fields are abundant. But you can just don a straw hat (hanging by the garden door) and hang around here happily doing not very much. *Minimum stay: 2 nights in high season.*

Rooms	10 doubles: €78-€115. 7 family rooms for 3, 2 family rooms for 4: €99-€135. Extra bed €12-€15.
Meals	Breakfast €10-€13. Restaurants 1-minute walk.
Closed	1 November – 25 March.

Tel	+33 (0)4 90 65 22 31
Email	info@hotel-domainedestilleuls.com
Web	www.hotel-domainedestilleuls.com

Louis & Florence Saint Joire
Le Domaine des Tilleuls,
Route de Mont Ventoux,
84340 Malaucène, Vaucluse

ENTRY 557 MAP 16

Les Florets

The setting is magical, the walks are outstanding, the greeting from the Bernard family, who bought Les Florets 60 years ago, is heartfelt. It sits at the foot of the majestic Dentelles de Montmirail, a small range crested with long, delicate stone fingers in the middle of Côtes du Rhône country. Over 40km of clearly marked paths call you, so appetites build for sublime food served beneath plane, chestnut and lime trees on the almost theatrical terrace; the low stone walls are bright with busy lizzies and the peonies were blooming in March. You'll also sample some of the wines that the family has been producing since the 1880s. Brightly-coloured corridors lead to simple but well-organised, well-renovated rooms, some with traditional florals, others in taupe and ivory, some housed in chalets above. Good bathrooms but no mozzie meshes or air con. We liked the quirky ceramic soup tureens in reception, the scintillating glass carafes in the warm red dining room and the beautiful new hillside pool. All this, and the wine list a work of art. Book well ahead, people return year after year.

Rooms	10 doubles, 4 twins: €105-€170. 1 suite for 2: €180. Dinner, B&B €130-€160 p.p.
Meals	Breakfast €17. Lunch & dinner from €40. Restaurant closed Wednesdays all day & Thursday for lunch.
Closed	January to mid-March.

Thierry & Dominique Bernard
Les Florets,
1243 route des Florêts,
84190 Gigondas, Vaucluse

Tel   +33 (0)4 90 65 85 01
Email   accueil@hotel-lesflorets.com
Web   www.hotel-lesflorets.com

ENTRY 558   MAP 16

Le Château de Mazan

The Marquis de Sade's father and uncle were born here, an unexpected connection, given the luminosity inside. Though the infamous Marquis preferred Paris, he often stayed at Mazan, organising France's first theatre festival here in 1772. The château sits in an appealing little town at the foot of Mont Ventoux. Floors are tiled in white-and-terracotta squares that would drown a smaller space, ceilings are lofty, windows are huge with the lightest curtains. This is a family hotel and Frédéric, who speaks good English, runs a smooth team while Mother does the fabulous décor, each room an ethereal delight: pale pink walls, a velvet sofa, a touch of apricot taffeta, a flash of red. Ground-floor bedrooms have French windows to a private sitting area; a couple of the rooms in the annexe across the road have their own terraces. There are frondy palms and secluded spots in the garden – doze in the shade of the mulberry trees – and a beautiful terrace for dinner; the chef has worked in starred restaurants and is keen to win his own. Stay on a Friday and catch Carpentras market. Altogether wonderful.
Car park down hill.

Rooms	12 doubles: €129-€315. 3 suites for 4: €335-€415. 14 family rooms for 4: €175-€345. Singles €129-€159. Extra bed/sofabed €30 p.p. per night.
Meals	Breakfast €18. Lunch from €16. Dinner from €39. Restaurant closed Tuesdays; Mondays out of season. Wine from €22.
Closed	Christmas, 1 January – 9 March.

Tel	+33 (0)4 90 69 62 61	**Danièle & Frédéric Lhermie**
Email	reservation@chateaudemazan.com	Le Château de Mazan,
Web	www.chateaudemazan.fr	Place Napoléon,
		84380 Mazan, Vaucluse

ENTRY 559   MAP 16

Le Mas des Grès

A party atmosphere reigns at this spotless roadside hotel that the attentive owners – German-Swiss Nina and Franco-Italian Thierry – run with clockwork precision and sustainability in mind. Nina looks after you and Thierry conjures up superb food: inspiration from his Italian grandmother. Join in the preparations or sit and enjoy it all in the big beamed dining room or, in summer, under the soaring plane trees on a terrace lit by twinkling lights and candles. Children eat and then potter to their hearts' content. Plainish bedrooms vary in size, with neat quilts on firm beds and views over fields; bathrooms, some with superb Italian showers, are tiled top to toe. Nina knows everyone and can rustle up almost any local delight, from Châteauneuf-du-Pape wine tastings to Lubéron bike trips, trout fishing with the family or golf at one of 15 courses. A favourite is a guided nature hike to gather culinary plants and herbs; for collectors of brocante, popular L'Isle sur la Sorgue is up the road. Return to a kids' playground and a family-happy roadside pool.

Rooms	10 doubles: €110-€270. 2 suites for 4: €200-€340. Price includes dinner, B&B.
Meals	Breakfast €12. Picnic lunch €15. Buffet lunch €20 (July & August only). Dinner €36. Wine €15-€100.
Closed	11 November – 28 March.

Nina & Thierry Crovara
Le Mas des Grès,
1651 route d'Apt,
84800 Lagnes, Vaucluse

Tel   +33 (0)4 90 20 32 85
Email info@masdesgres.com
Web   www.masdesgres.com

La Bastide de Voulonne

The utterly Provençal bastide sits in splendid isolation in lavender fields spread beneath the ancient hilltop villages of the Lubéron range. As you swing into the circular drive, there are ancient plane trees, wisps of tamarisk, tufts of lavender and blue shutters against golden ochre walls. Glorious – and a genuine family-friendly place, too: family suites, early children's suppers, DVDs galore, safe pool and lawn areas. The heart of this 18th-century farmhouse is a courtyard where you can breakfast to soft fountain music. Bedrooms (and beds) are huge, done in natural local colours, with tiled or parquet floors. The garden – it's more like a park – is vast, with a big pool not far from the house. The busy owners have refreshed the herb garden for the kitchen and menus focus on local food, while cherries, apricots, pears, figs and raspberries come from their orchards. After a convivial apéritif, with Julien if he's free, dinner is served at separate tables on the terrace or in a big dining hall whose centrepiece is the carefully restored bread oven.

Rooms	10 twin/doubles: €112-€159. 3 suites for 5: €180-€285.
Meals	Buffet breakfast €13. Dinner €36; €18 for children. Wine €30. Early supper for children.
Closed	1 November – 31 March.

Tel	+33 (0)4 90 76 77 55
Email	contact@bastide-voulonne.com
Web	www.bastide-voulonne.com

Penny & Julien Hemery
La Bastide de Voulonne,
Cabrières d'Avignon,
84220 Gordes, Vaucluse

ENTRY 561 MAP 16

La Bastide de Boulbon

It will fire your imagination. Leave the main road for a secret, dead-end village. There, on the hill, are windmills and a huge castle, old houses line the quaint narrow streets that climb to the summit. In the middle, is this impressive 200-year-old mansion. Jan and Marie-Claire came from Belgium three years ago and have already made their mark by combining proper professional skills with genuine pleasure in receiving guests. They have put their heart and soul into the renovation and decoration and have done a fabulous landscaping job on the garden. Four huge taupe parasols marry the dining patio to the elegant façade with its same-coloured shutters; the giant centuries-old plane trees and trickling stone fountain teach a gentler sense of time. Inside, elegant proportions, clean lines, modern simplicity and the subtlest palette of neutral and dusky tones, with the occasional bold piece of art, make for restful spaces. Be prepared to eat well: Marie-Claire grew up in one of Brussels' best restaurants and has taken on a new French chef. The scene is set for a luxurious, relaxing stay.

Rooms	2 doubles, 4 twin/doubles: €145-€180. 2 suites for 4: €205-€240.
Meals	Breakfast €17. Dinner €15-€20. Wine €22-€80.
Closed	November to March.

Jan De Mulder & Marie-Claire Callens
La Bastide de Boulbon,
Rue de l'Hôtel de Ville,
13150 Boulbon, Bouches-du-Rhône

Tel   +33 (0)4 90 93 11 11
Email contact@labastidedeboulbon.com
Web   www.labastidedeboulbon.com

Le Mas des Carassins

Walking distance from lovely St Rémy, the charming mas settles gently into its leafy
cocoon, a massive garden bursting with oleanders, lavender, lemons and fine pieces by
local designers and Balinese artists. After a swim – in one of two pools – you have
boules, badminton and bikes to hire. This is Van Gogh country and the hotel lies within
the conservation area of Roman Glanum. In the pretty dining room, oil paintings by a
friend add a splash to white walls and meals are a special feast of market produce
accompanied by excellent local wines. Air-conditioned bedrooms in the old mas are
dreamy, washed in smoky-blue or ochre shades; dark wrought-iron beds are dressed
in oatmeal linens and white quilts; ground-floor rooms open to small gardens or wooden
decks. In contrast, the newest rooms are done with contemporary furniture, Parisian
and Balinese art, pebble showers. All is spotless and every room is air-conditioned.
The young owners have thought of everything: pick-up from the airport or train, car
hire, tickets for local events – and there's
parking, a bonus so close to town.
Children over 12 welcome.

Rooms	19 twin/doubles: €112-€234.
	3 suites for 2: €215-€265.
Meals	Breakfast €16. Dinner €36.
	Half-board €31.50 extra p.p.
	Wine €18-€85.
	Restaurants 5-minute walk.
Closed	January to early March,
	2 weeks in December.

Tel	+33 (0)4 90 92 15 48	**Michel Dimeux & Pierre Ticot**
Email	info@masdescarassins.com	Le Mas des Carassins,
Web	www.masdescarassins.com	1 chemin Gaulois, 13210 Saint Rémy de
		Provence, Bouches-du-Rhône

ENTRY 563   MAP 16

Le Mas de Peint

In the heart of the Camargue, book in for an energetic, gastronomic short break and live as a 'cowboy'! Frédéric is proud of his beautiful family farm – 250 bulls, 15 horses and swathes of arable land. He looks after you well too; find an elegant French country-farmhouse feel – no flounces or flummery, just impeccable style. Bedrooms are deep green or old rose; generous curtains are checked dove-grey; floors come tiled or wool-carpeted. There are eye-catching interesting pieces everywhere – a collection of fine pencil sketches and some bold artworks, an antique commode, a carved bedhead – and some rooms with mezzanine bathrooms under old rafters. Breakfast royally in the big family kitchen or on the wisteria-draped terrace, then drift over the canal to the secluded pool, encircled by teak loungers, scented with jasmine. We recommend dinner: the fabulous, innovative chef delivers light, regional food under a muslin canopy at tables aglow with Moroccan lamps; follow with coffee and cognac in the clubby cigar room or the seductive salon. *Minimum stay: 3 nights in high season.*

Rooms	2 doubles, 6 twin/doubles: €250-€335. 4 suites for 2, 1 suite for 4: €395-€540. Extra bed/sofabed €35 p.p. per night.
Meals	Breakfast €12-€22. Lunch €29-€39. Dinner €41-€69. Restaurant closed on Thursdays.
Closed	Early January to mid-March; mid-November to mid-December.

Frédéric Bon
Le Mas de Peint,
Le Sambuc, 13200 Arles,
Bouches-du-Rhône

Tel   +33 (0)4 90 97 20 62
Email contact@masdepeint.com
Web   www.masdepeint.com

La Bastide de Moustiers

The views of the lovely village of Moustiers-Sainte-Marie, the estate with its family of deer and the mountains all around give a magical feel. The hotel, however, has its feet firmly on the ground. This beautifully restored bastide rests at the foot of the cliffs of Moustiers: a 17th-century house, a cluster of stone cottages, and 13 bedrooms between them. For breakfast, lunch and divine dinner (the owner is Alain Ducasse) tables topped with white parasols sit on shaded terraces, and all is impeccable yet rustic. If you don't want to dine in, then the village, bustling with shops and restaurants, is a sprint up the hill or a three-minute drive. Staff are here to satisfy every whim and the attention to detail is striking, from your flip-flops and towels for the delicious pool to the helipad for the wealthy. Paragliders, riders, canoeists and climbers find heaven in the Parc Naturel du Verdon, and mountain bikes are available on request. Dreamy bedrooms to come home to (two with beds on mezzanines, most with private patios) complete the five-star picture. *Cot available. Parking on-site.*

Rooms	7 doubles, 4 twin/doubles: €220-€420. 2 suites for 2: €380-€900. Extra bed/sofabed €50 p.p. per night.
Meals	Restaurant on-site: breakfast €24; lunch and dinner €60-€90. Restaurants within walking distance.
Closed	Rarely.

Tel	+33 (0)4 92 70 47 47
Email	contact@bastide-moustiers.com
Web	www.bastide-moustiers.com

Sarah Chailan
La Bastide de Moustiers,
Chemin de Quinson, 04360 Moustiers-
Sainte-Marie, Alpes-de-Haute-Provence

ENTRY 565   MAP 16

Le Moulin du Château

A sleepy place – come to doze, your silence broken only by the call of the sparrowhawk or the distant rumble of a car. This 17th-century olive mill once belonged to the château and stands at the foot of a venerable grove; the vast press is now a reception area where modern art hangs on ancient walls. The Moulin, a long, low, stone building with lavender-blue shutters and the odd climbing vine, stands in its own gardens surrounded by lavender and fruit trees. In the bedrooms light filters though voile curtains, shadows dance upon the walls. The feel is uncluttered, cool, breezy, with vibrant colours: turquoise, lilac, lime – luminous yet restful. This is an easy-going 'green' hotel where the emphasis is on the simple things of life. Edith and Nicolas use regional and organic food, boules is played under the cherry tree, poppies grow on an old crumbling stone staircase and views stretch across fields to village and château. There are great walks, bikes for gentle country excursions, a swimming and boating lake nearby, and further afield are the Cistercian abbey of Le Thoronet, the Gorges du Verdon and Digne les Bains.

Rooms	6 doubles, 4 twin/doubles: €104-€132. Extra bed/sofabed €16-€22 p.p. per night.
Meals	Breakfast €10. Picnic lunch €10. Dinner, 3 courses, €28; 4 courses, €32 (except Mon & Thurs). Wine €6-€40. Restaurants nearby.
Closed	November to March.

Edith & Nicolas Stämpfli-Faoro
Le Moulin du Château,
04500 Saint Laurent du Verdon,
Alpes-de-Haute-Provence

Tel	+33 (0)4 92 74 02 47
Email	info@moulin-du-chateau.com
Web	www.moulin-du-chateau.com

Mas du Brulat – Olives and Vines

Exit the busy A50 autoroute connecting Toulon to Marseilles and drive through well-tended vineyards towards a tiny hamlet near the medieval hilltop village of Le Castellet. The oldest house in the village – it dates from 1594 – retains a traditional warm Provençal façade but the interiors have been stylishly modernised. A big continental breakfast can be taken in the restaurant, on the terrace or in your room and includes hams, cheese, homemade fruit compote, bread, local honey and viennoiseries. Rooms have countryside views and swish touches: a Nespresso machine, bathrobes and slippers, a minibar. Eat at the restaurant here or walk two minutes to the local pizzeria; choose a book from the library shelves on the landing, laze by the pool or play petanque. You can walk to Le Castellet in 30 minutes or drive to the beach and local markets in 15 minutes.

Rooms	5 doubles: €138-€248. 1 suite for 2, 1 suite for 4: €215-€370. 1 annexe for 3: €250-€345.
Meals	Restaurants within walking distance.
Closed	6 January – 7 February.

Tel	+33 (0)4 79 05 06 00	**Mas du Brulat**
Email	reservations@olivesandvines.eu	Mas du Brulat – Olives and Vines,
Web	www.olivesandvines.eu/	47 route du Grand Vallat,
	mas-de-brulat-main/	Le Brulat, 83330 Le Castellet, Var

ENTRY 567 MAP 16

Hôtel Notre Dame

On the edge of cobbled Collobrières, with wonderful views of the Massif des Maures, is an 18th-century staging post, a delicious modern hotel. Its inspired creators, Olivier and his wife (chef) Nili, speak several languages, embrace all nationalities and love what they do. Each elegant, simple room is named after a precious stone – sapphire, jade, coral; pick the colour of your choice on booking. Imagine cool floor tiles, glowing paintings, thick cream curtains, repro Louis XIV tables, bright mosaic'd showers and beautiful stone ceilings washed in white. The Pearl Suite has three windows and is full of light, and some rooms have divans that double up as child beds (families are welcomed with open arms). Outside: a secret garden with an eco-friendly pool, fenced and safe for children, and pretty tables at which guests linger over dinner under the trees and listen to the flowing river. As for the food, there are four different kinds of breakfast – from Scandinavian to continental – served until late. Dinner too is delicious; the wines are from the bio vineyards of Correns. Beyond: the palms and sands of Le Lavandou.

Rooms	11 doubles: €89-€135.
	3 suites for 3: €119-€195.
	2 family rooms for 4: €209-€245.
Meals	Breakfast €12. Dinner, 2-3 courses, €22-€28 (book min 24 hours in advance, closed Thurs).
Closed	5 January to mid-March.

Olivier Faivre
Hôtel Notre Dame,
15 avenue de la Libération,
83610 Collobrières, Var

Tel   +33 (0)4 94 48 07 13
Email   hotelnotredame@gmail.com
Web   www.hotel-collobrieres.com

La Villa d'Andrea

You travel through peaceful Var countryside to reach these oh-so-stylish studio apartments. Sandra's deft handiwork immediately catches the eye – driftwood furnished into her own designs, including a striking table and chairs in the most sought-after apartment: the studio with the beautiful stone interior. Provençal in style, with pale walls, blue shutters and terracotta roofs, the whole pretty place is divided into two sections: the more traditional Sud whose apartments are typified by wood, wicker and wrought-iron furniture, and softened by pastoral scenes from local artists; and the much more exotic Zen whose quirky touches – to bedheads, lamps, tiling and intricate pebble framed mirrors – run throughout. All but four come with tasteful kitchenettes and private terraces. Open windows wide to take in the gardens and two lovely pools, complete with stone bars, lush plants and pine trees, and roof supports made from tree bark. No communal indoors here, but outside is ideal for relaxation after a day spent on Pampelonne's legendary beach – or in St Tropez.

Rooms	4 doubles: €100-€220. 19 studios for 2: €150-€340. Extra bed/sofabed €40-€70 p.p. per night.
Meals	Breakfast €17.
Closed	7 October – 18 April.

Tel	+33 (0)4 94 79 22 84
Email	contact@lavilladandrea.com
Web	www.lavilladandrea.com

The Owner
La Villa d'Andrea,
321 Chemin de la Pinède,
83350 Ramatuelle, Var

ENTRY 569 MAP 16

La Ferme d'Augustin

A 13th-century gateway heralds your arrival to the olive farm that opened to guests (just a few wanderers and celebrities) in the early days of Brigitte Bardot... she still lives nearby. Fifty years on: fabrics from Provence, tiles from Salernes and *objets* stylishly scattered by owner Ninette. The décor is wonderfully relaxed, the pool is discreet and the place is filled with garden roses. The farm rests in a relatively untouched spot of this legendary peninsula, a minute from Tahiti Beach and two miles from St Tropez, reached by a road known only to the locals, or a 15-mile coastal path: the position is among the best on the Riviera. Couples, families, foodies flock. Organic veg from the potager, wines from the vines, fruits from the orchard and their own olive oil structure a cuisine that is as authentic as it is simple; savour the flavours of Provence from the terrace or the pergola. Their very own bath soaps and gels express the same Provençal spirit; bedrooms in apartments are cosy and characterful, some with whirlpool baths and sea views. A rich, relaxed Riviera retreat.

Rooms	22 doubles: €255–€565. 24 suites for 2: €495–€1215. Extra bed/sofabed €50 p.p. per night.
Meals	Breakfast €20, served until 2pm. Lunch à la carte €15–€50. Dinner à la carte €30–€60.
Closed	5 November – 22 March.

Vallet Family
La Ferme d'Augustin,
Route de Tahiti, Saint Tropez,
83350 Ramatuelle, Var

Tel   +33 (0)4 94 55 97 00
Email info@fermeaugustin.com
Web   www.fermeaugustin.com

Hôtel Le Cavendish

Civilised and convivial, the Cavendish is a joy, offering a drink on arrival and a complimentary bar in the evening. Set back from the bustle of Cannes, this splendid rebirth of a Napoleon III mansion displays Madame Welter's talents. Subtle modern comforts and splendid rooms, some with balcony or terrace, are the frame. Sensuous, exuberant, almost edible choices of fabric and colour that are never overdone – crunchy raspberry taffeta, tasselled pistachio green, twilight mauve – clothe the frame. Quirky old-fashioned charm enfolds it all. It's like being a guest in the grand house of a *grand homme*, such as its namesake, Lord Cavendish. How attentive to offer leaf teas for breakfast, how attractive to dress the curvy Carrara marble staircase with candles at dusk, how delightful to slip between lavender-scented sheets at night. Freshly baked croissants, cakes and crumbles, homemade jams and cheerful staff make mornings easy, especially if you are attending one of the events at the Festival Hall, ten minutes away. Superb.
Minimum stay: 3 nights in high season.

Rooms	23 doubles, 12 twins: €125-€330. Singles €110-€250. Extra bed/sofabed €30 p.p. per night.
Meals	Breakfast €20 (included for Sawday guests). Complimentary bar 6pm-8.30pm.
Closed	15 December – 16 March.

Tel	+33 (0)4 97 06 26 00	**Christine & Guy Welter**
Email	reservation@cavendish-cannes.com	Hôtel Le Cavendish,
Web	www.cavendish-cannes.com	11 boulevard Carnot,
		06400 Cannes, Alpes-Maritimes

ENTRY 571   MAP 16

Villa Garbo

A sparrow's spit from the heart of Cannes, its railway station and myriad fleshpots, the elegant and evocatively re-named Villa Garbo brings you the luxury of a smart hotel and the practicality of a serviced apartment. Choose your breakfast from the buffet and have it on the terrace or in your room. Your suite or apartment, done in taupe and pink, has an immaculate stylish kitchen, good lighting, comfy beds and a contemporary marble bathroom with a striking black mirror. The whole place is carefully furnished and colour-coordinated in period and modern style – antique chandeliers and tonic lime green chairs, marble fireplaces and ethnic touches, 1890s candlesticks and leather sofas. The owners and staff are genuinely friendly, always ready to answer your questions round a (free) aperitif and expertly creating a convivial house-party atmosphere. The private beach is the height of indulgence in bustling, celeb-ridden Cannes. You will feel like a guest in a high-class mansion with impeccable servants at your beck and call.

The Penthouse is a wow with its own roof terrace. *Minimum stay: 2 nights.*

Rooms	2 suites for 4: €380-€800. 8 apartments for 2: €180-€330. Extra bed/sofabed at no charge.
Meals	Restaurants 2-minute walk. Complimentary bar 6pm-8.30pm.
Closed	8 December – 1 April.

Christine & Guy Welter
Villa Garbo,
62 boulevard d'Alsace,
06400 Cannes, Alpes-Maritimes

Tel	+33 (0)4 93 46 66 00
Email	reservation@villagarbo-cannes.com
Web	www.villagarbo-cannes.com/en/

Hôtel La Jabotte

What makes La Jabotte special? Is it the courtyard scented with oranges or the bedrooms the colours of jewels? Or is it Pierre and Nathalie, new owners of this delightful little hotel, an explosion of colour, beautifully clean and inviting? Enthusiastic and inspired, they are hard at work updating things (new bedding all round, air-conditioning too) while their three cool cats breathe that inimitable feline calm. Down a small side street, 60 metres from the beach, you will find polished stone floors, cherry-red walls and pots of roses. Pass the deep aubergine sofa, go through the gliding wall of glass and into the enchanting pebbled courtyard off which lie the bedrooms. Each has table and chairs outside the door and lovingly labelled plants; it feels more home than hotel and you get to know your neighbours (the family suites are sensibly separate in the villa). Bedrooms are small but charming, shower rooms have delicious lotions and fulsome towels. After fresh fruit and croissants, saunter into Old Antibes – or drift down to the free sandy beach and your own parasol. *Minimum stay: 3 nights in high season. Children over 8 welcome.*

Rooms	7 doubles: €84-€174. 1 suite for 2, 1 suite for 4: €124-€274.
Meals	Breakfast €12. Restaurants within walking distance.
Closed	Never.

Tel	+33 (0)4 93 61 45 89
Email	info@jabotte.com
Web	www.jabotte.com

Nathalie & Pierre Lesjean
Hôtel La Jabotte,
13 avenue Max Maurey,
06160 Cap d'Antibes, Alpes-Maritimes

Hôtel Windsor

A 1930s Riviera hotel with a pool in a palm grove and exotic birds in cages – a lush escape in the heart of Nice. Indoors, Hôtel Windsor has introduced the Thirties to the 21st century by asking contemporary artists to decorate some of the rooms. The result is gifts of wit, provocation, flights of fancy and minimalist sobriety: Joan Mas's *Cage à Mouches*, cosmopolitan Ben's writing on the walls, Antoine Beaudoin's frescoes of Venice, Egypt, India – and Tintin, all-time favourite. Plain white beds have contrasting cushions or quilts, furniture is minimal but interesting, little bathrooms are delightful and one room is painted in glimmering gold. Clear bright colours everywhere, including the richly exotic public areas; the charming Odile is passionate about contemporary art and chooses a different artist every year to reinvent the lobby. Outside, a tropical garden gives space for reflection among bamboo, fruiting trees and bougainvillea. Light filters through onto warmly smiling staff who prepare sumptuous buffet breakfasts under the palms in summer and run a superb spa, with gym, on the fifth floor.

Rooms	57 twin/doubles: €92-€215. Dinner, B&B €36 p.p. Extra bed/sofabed €20-€30 p.p. per night.
Meals	Breakfast €6-€14. Dinner à la carte €29-€40. Wine from €21. Restaurant closed Sundays.
Closed	Never.

Odile Redolfi-Payen
Hôtel Windsor,
11 rue Dalpozzo, 06000 Nice,
Alpes-Maritimes

Tel	+33 (0)4 93 88 59 35
Email	contact@hotelwindsornice.com
Web	www.hotelwindsornice.com

Villa L'Aimée

in the northern part of Nice, a short tram ride from the city's rich culture (buses also stop virtually at the gate), Villa L'Aimée was built in 1929 and is typical of its period – an elegant white villa. Toni's decoration has restored the villa to a modern opulence. Much-travelled – one of her lives was in the art world – Toni, who is English, has created delightful bedrooms in subtle colours with damasks and silks, fine linen, tulle canopies and elegant furnishings, exuding an air of luxury. The original parquet is breathtaking, the breakfasts excellent. A peaceful corner of Nice from which to invade the bubblier down-town and expore beaches, museums – particularly Marc Chagall – and culture in the castle and cathedral. This is the capital of the French Riviera so the people-watching down on the harbour is second to none and there are excellent restaurants to try. Walkers will be happy travelling to Parc du Mont Boron in the eastern part of the city with over seven miles of hiking trails to choose from. Return to much comfort. *Children over 12 welcome.*

Rooms	2 twin/doubles, 1 twin: €110-€145.
Meals	Restaurants within walking distance.
Closed	December-March.

Tel	+33 (0)4 93 52 34 13
Mobile	+33 (0)6 71 82 67 72
Email	bookings@villa-aimee.co.uk
Web	www.villa-aimee.co.uk

Toni Redding
Villa L'Aimée,
5 av Piatti, 06100 Nice,
Alpes-Maritimes

ENTRY 575   MAP 16

Villa Kilauea

A grand Mediterranean villa that looks so settled in Nice's lush western hills you'd never know it was a 21st-century creation. There are balustrade-edged terraces, panoramic views and a blissful pool. Bedrooms above the pool house have a zen-like calm: wrought-iron four-posters draped in muslin, teak floors, white walls; orchids and silks hint at the exotic. The Lavender Room in the main house opens to the garden and is as feminine as the rest. Nathalie, the perfect host, kind, gentle and generous to a tee, delights in juggling family life with her B&B. Nice is a ten-minute drive down the hill. *Minimum stay: 2 nights; 4 in high season. Over 14s welcome.*

Les Cyprès

Glorious views stretch over countryside and town from Frances's apricot-coloured villa. Its beautiful big garden bears olives, flowers and fruit in profusion – fig, cherry, strawberry... discover secret areas for dining or hiding away with a book. Bedrooms are traditional and minimalist with pretty bedspreads and smart bathrooms, and breakfast is scrumptious: bread, brioche, homemade jams galore. Explore the fascinating old town, tootle over to Nice, and get back in time truly delicious four-course dinners. Whet your whistle with an apéritif in the cosy-rustic sitting room... prepare to be spoiled. *Minimum stay: 2 nights in high season.*

Rooms	3 doubles: €145-€195. 1 suite for 2: €185-€235.
Meals	Restaurants in Nice.
Closed	30 November – 15 March.

Rooms	3 doubles: €85-€90. Extra bed €25.
Meals	Dinner, 4 courses, €25. Light dinner with wine, €18. Restaurant 1km.
Closed	Christmas.

Mobile	+33 (0)6 25 37 21 44
Email	nathalie@villakilauea.com
Web	www.villakilauea.com

Nathalie Graffagnino
Villa Kilauea,
6 chemin du Candeu,
06200 Nice, Alpes-Maritimes

Mobile	+33 (0)6 46 27 54 95
Email	contact@lescypres.fr
Web	www.lescypres.fr

Frances Thompson
Les Cyprès,
289 route de Châteauneuf,
06390 Contes, Alpes-Maritimes

La Parare

Cradled in summer by cicada chant and the gentle wind, cocooned in winter in a romantic log-warmed bedroom, you will be bewitched by the subtle mix of clean-cut modernity and fine oriental detail that your much-travelled polyglot hosts have achieved in this craggy old house with a beautiful garden. Karin from Sweden and French/Dutch Sydney love pampering people. The rough hills outside highlight the delicacy inside, the natural walled pool, the stunning bathrooms (one with a tub for two), the civilised conversation if you have dinner. You can drive up the road and catch the tram straight into Nice. Worth every centime. *Minimum stay: 2 nights at weekends; 4 in high season.*

Le Mas du Chanoine

Wake up and smell the roses from the patio (15 varieties share the garden, along with lavender bushes, bougainvillea, fig and citrus trees), where you breakfast on Mariage Frères tea and Pascale's homemade jams and cakes in front of a striking stained-glass window. Inside, a treasure trove: Louis XVI Provençal cabinetry and marvellous stone fireplaces; oak parquet floors and marble bedside tables; a natural stone basin and a sunken bath. Explore the cobbled streets of Saint Paul de Vence, then soak tired limbs in the security pool with Opiocolor mosaic tiling. After dusk... pastis and boules on the floodlit court. *Minimum stay: 2 nights; 3 in high season.*

Rooms	4 doubles: €155–€190.
Meals	Dinner with wine, €35–€50, by arrangement.
Closed	Rarely.

Rooms	3 suites for 2: €160–€250. Extra bed/sofabed €15–€50 p.p. per night.
Meals	Restaurants 2km.
Closed	15 December – 28 February.

Tel	+33 (0)4 93 79 22 62
Email	sydney@laparare.com
Web	www.laparare.com

Sydney van Volen
La Parare,
67 calade du Pastre, 06390 Châteauneuf
Villevieille, Alpes-Maritimes

Tel	+33 (0)6 27 27 16 49
Email	pascale@masduchanoine.com
Web	www.masduchanoine.com

Pascale Barissat
Le Mas du Chanoine,
831 chemin de la Bastide Rouge,
06570 St Paul de Vence, Alpes-Maritimes

ENTRY 578   MAP 16

ENTRY 579   MAP 16

Le Clos de Saint Paul

A young Provençal house on a lushly planted and screened piece of land where boundary hedging is high. In a guest wing, each pretty bedroom has its own patio, each bathroom is small and there's a summer kitchen for guests to share. Friendly energetic Madame has furnished in contemporary style – greys, yellows, painted chairs, the odd antique. She genuinely cares that you have the best, offers a welcome glass of rosé on her stunning shaded terrace and serves a very fresh breakfast in the garden. The large mosaic'd pool is a pleasure on a summer's day, and legendary St Paul de Vence is worth a trip. *Minimum stay: 2 nights.*

Bleu Azur

Breakfast, ferried to the friendly communal table (or the elegant terrace) is a feast of croissants, fruits, jams and Jean-Yves' speciality: Breton crêpes. Nothing is too much trouble for these humorous hosts who have followed a long-held dream, to create an exceptional B&B. Their chosen patch, on the edge of a cobbled village between mountains and sea, has sumptuous gardens and shimmering views that reach to the Bay of Antibes. All six suites (including those for families) are sophisticated, spacious and on the ground floor. After a glamorous day on the Riviera, come home to a dive in the pool. *Minimum stay: 2 nights in high season.*

Rooms	1 double, 2 twin/doubles: €75-€120. Singles €70-€85. Extra bed/sofabed €20 p.p. per night. Pets on request, €10 per night.	**Rooms**	3 twin/doubles: €145-€185. 3 apartments for 2: €185-€213. Extra bed/sofabed €32 p.p. per night.
Meals	Summer kitchen. Restaurant 1km.	**Meals**	Dinner, 3 courses with wine, €35-€45; by arrangement. Restaurants 800m. Kitchen available.
Closed	Rarely.	**Closed**	Rarely.

Tel	+33 (0)4 93 32 56 81	**Tel**	+33 (0)4 93 32 58 55
Email	leclossaintpaul@hotmail.com	**Email**	contact@maisondhotes-bleuazur.com
Web	www.leclossaintpaul.com	**Web**	www.maisondhotes-bleuazur.com

Béatrice Ronin Pillet
Le Clos de Saint Paul,
71 chemin de la Rouguière,
06480 La Colle sur Loup, Alpes-Maritimes

Nadine Barrandon
Bleu Azur,
674 route des Queinières,
06140 Tourrettes-sur-loup, Alpes-Maritimes

La Bastide du Bosquet

It's peaceful at this substantial stone
farmhouse and you're well away from
crowds. Smiling Anais will greet you and
delight in telling you about short cuts to the
nearby beach and the history of the house
– Guy de Maupassant wrote *Bel Ami* in one
of the bedrooms. Relax in big airy
bedrooms with antique furniture and hand
painted objects, enjoy a breakfast of fresh
bread and pastries with homemade jams
on the outdoor terrace – if you want
something different just ask Anais. Make a
snack for the beach in the small guest
kitchen, grab a couple of parasols and
follow the path through the glorious
gardens or take a short stroll to the sites of
Antibes and the sounds of Juan les Pin.

Villa du Roc Fleuri

You'll feel on top of the world in this square
villa overlooking rooftops all the way to
town – a labour of love for Fanny.
Breakfast on homemade jams and crêpes,
local pastries and plenty of teas in the
great glass veranda, or out on the terrace.
Do order dinner – your host's an inventive
cook, or head into town for restaurants.
Bedrooms are simple, light and airy with
French doors and tall windows, the two at
the front overlook a tropical garden across
the road – all have modern bathrooms with
waterfall showers. The suite is in a
separate building and has its own terrace.
Plenty to do from island hopping to
beaches and culture.

Rooms	4 doubles: €135-€200. 2 doubles can have adjoining rooms to make a suite for 4. Extra bed/sofabed €35 p.p. per night.
Meals	Restaurants 3-minute walk.
Closed	15 November – 1 March.

Rooms	4 doubles: €90-€140. 1 suite for 4: €140-€200.
Meals	Dinner with wine, €35. Restaurants 1km.
Closed	Rarely.

Email	bastidelebosquet@gmail.com
Web	www.lebosquet06.com

Anaïs Le Maire
La Bastide du Bosquet,
14 Chemin des sables,
06160 Antibes, Alpes-Maritimes

Mobile	+33 (0)6 30 20 82 41
Email	contact@villadurocfleuri.fr
Web	www.villadurocfleuri.fr

Fanny Larroze
Villa du Roc Fleuri,
11 rue du Rocher,
06400 Cannes, Alpes-Maritimes

ENTRY 582   MAP 16

ENTRY 583   MAP 16

L'Harmas

This rambling old house has all the charm of 18th-century Provence and is very much a family home. The vast garden has lovely vistas and secret corners and is surrounded by woodlands on a hill above a village on the main road to Grasse. Anders and Helen live in a separate apartment upstairs and enjoy having an aperitif with their guests. Breakfasts are a treat: everything organic, locally sourced or home-grown: fruit salad, pastries, hams and cheeses. Dine around a long table in the elegant dining room or out on the porch with views of the garden. There are several good restaurants within a ten-minute drive, including Michelin-star dining at La Bastide Saint Antoine in Grasse. Cannes, Antibes and Nice are all less than an hour away – or just stay at home and enjoy the garden, pool, summer kitchen and boule court. *Cot available.*

Rooms	3 doubles, 1 twin: €125-€170.
Meals	Breakfast €12.
Closed	Rarely.

Tel +33 (0)6 62 08 26 00
Email ripa.consult@gmail.com

Anders Ripa
L'Harmas,
26 Avenue du Docteur Belletrud,
06530 Peymeinade, Alpes-Maritimes

ENTRY 584   MAP 16

Maison du Bonheur

In the hilltop village of Montauroux is this whitewashed townhouse with orange shutters, both elegant and understated. Behind, a big surprise: palm trees, lawns, lavenders, and a veranda with a heaven-sent view. Austrian Elisabeth, warm and delightful, gives you two small elegant bedrooms upstairs, and a smart bathroom in contemporary style. Explore the caves of St Cezaire and the vineyards of Provence Verte, enjoy a pizza and a *pastis* on the village square. Then home to an open-plan dining room full of light, and a sitting room cosy and enticing: white walls, chunky beams, sofas, books and beautiful art, some of it Elisabeth's.

Rooms	1 double, 1 twin/double: €70-€95. Let to same party only.
Meals	Restaurants 2-minute walk.
Closed	Rarely.

Tel +33 (0)4 94 47 68 64
Email chuffart.elisabeth@gmail.com

Elisabeth Chuffart
Maison du Bonheur,
24 rue de l'Eglise,
83440 Montauroux, Var

ENTRY 585   MAP 16

Mas la Jaïna

A large new house with villa-like arches surrounded by quiet farmland. Your eco-friendly hosts Ingrid and Johan – and their golden retrievers – usher you enthusiastically into a large room with a dining table and sofas. Bedrooms are themed and vary wildly – each sponsor a different cause – but all have very comfortable mattresses and can be reached from the outside. Breakfasts of fresh fruit salad, local cheese and eggs from their hens set you up for a lazy day by the natural swimming pool, in sauna and hot tub, or wandering through the herb garden and rows of lavender. Plenty of activities and space for children too. *Minimum stay: 4 nights in high season. Pets by arrangement. Electric car charger available.*

La Maison du Prince

Wake to breakfast on the terrace, where potted palms create an exotic mood and church bells chime. With Patrice your host and Grimaud your backdrop, it's an idyllic way to start the day. This is a beautiful home in one of the best-kept 'villages perchés' of Provence. Set off for St Tropez's boutiques and bustle, or Pampelonne Plage where the beautiful people bask. Return to Grimaud, streets bright with bougainvillea, drink in breathtaking views from the castle ruin, have dinner out. The house is named after Prince Ranier of Monaco, once a frequent visitor. Find books, old prints and lithographs and distinctive Moroccan touches – from the vaulted cellars to the third-floor bedrooms. Each room is individual and each immaculate. Two have peaceful terraces; some have views of the Gulf of St Tropez. *Min. stay: 2 nights.*

Rooms	2 doubles: €80-€140. 2 suites for 2: €140-€235. Extra bed/sofabed €30 p.p. per night.	**Rooms**	5 doubles: €110-€150. Extra bed €20. Parking available nearby, €10 per day.
Meals	Dinner €15-€45. Restaurants nearby.	**Meals**	Restaurants 2-minute-walk.
Closed	Rarely.	**Closed**	1 November – 16 December, 7 January – 15 March.

Mobile	+33 (0)6 88 99 79 93	**Tel**	+33 (0)6 99 90 19 68
Email	maslajaina@me.com	**Email**	info@maisonduprince.com
Web	www.maslajaina.com	**Web**	www.maisonduprince.com

Ingrid & Johan Hombergen
Mas la Jaïna,
Les Espourounes,
83830 Bargemon, Var

Patrice Faviere
La Maison du Prince,
22 Rue des Templiers,
83310 Grimaud, Var

ENTRY 586   MAP 16

ENTRY 587   MAP 16

Bastide Avellanne

Château Nestuby

Vineyards and glorious views over the Var surround you at this peaceful 17th-century bastide. Linn and her friendly staff want you to enjoy the slow pace here. Bedrooms (some upstairs, some down) each bear a painter's name and have antique pieces, flowers and garden views; shower rooms have organic cotton towels and sprigs of lavender; gîte guests have an apartment and studio in the grounds. Eat in the huge living and dining area or out on the pretty front terrace; food is organic, vegetables are mostly from the garden. Plenty to do: explore the bougainvillea-bright grounds, swim, play petanque or tennis, book massage or yoga, get stuck into a game of chess – there's a giant set under the shade of a centuries-old oak tree. Bikes and tours can be arranged and the coast is 30 minutes away.

Bravo, Nathalie! – in calm, friendly control of this gorgeous, well-restored, 19th-century bastide. One whole wing is for guests with simple, light, vineyard-view bedrooms, pastel-painted and Provençal-furnished with a mix of old and new (including WiFi); a big bourgeois sitting room (little used: it's too lovely outside); a spa on the roof terrace; an excellent estate shop; and a great spring-fed tank for swims. Jean-François runs the vineyard, the tastings and the wine talk at dinner with sweet-natured ease. You're on a working farm (aspiring viticulturists will love it) but in the tranquil Provence Verte..

Rooms	3 doubles: €169-€229. 2 suites for 4: €199-€299. Extra bed/sofabed €15 p.p. per night.	**Rooms**	4 twin/doubles, 1 triple: €95. 1 suite for 2: €180. Extra bed/sofabed €20 p.p. per night.
Meals	Dinner €25-€34; children €15. Wine from €20. Restaurants 4km.	**Meals**	Restaurants 1km.
Closed	November – March.	**Closed**	Rarely.

Tel	+33 (0)4 94 69 89 91	**Tel**	+33 (0)4 94 04 60 02
Email	info@bastideavellanne.com	**Email**	nestuby@wanadoo.fr
Web	www.bastideavellanne.com	**Web**	en.nestuby.com

Linn Vislie
Bastide Avellanne,
83890 Besse sur Issole,
Var

Nathalie & Jean-François Roubaud
Château Nestuby,
4540 route de Montfort,
83570 Cotignac, Var

ENTRY 588 MAP 16

ENTRY 589 MAP 16

Une Campagne en Provence

In spring, water gushes through myriad irrigation channels dug by the Knights Templar! Martina and Claude, proud possessors of the European Ecolabel, have planted 3,750 trees on their vast estate. The bastide keeps its fortress-like proportions and, like its owners, has bags of charm. Simple furnishings are lit by huge windows, floors are terracotta, and breakfasts and dinners put the accent on Provençal produce and their own wine. A pool with a view, a sauna, a Turkish bath, a well-stocked library, a mini cinema in the cellar... an isolated paradise for all ages, overseen by a charming young family, two geese and one dog. *Pets by arrangement.*

Mas Sainte Anne

On its hilltop on the edge of pretty Peynier, the old *mas* stands in glory before Cézanne's Montagne Sainte Victoire: pull the cowbell, pass the wooden doors and the red-shuttered farmhouse rises from beds of roses. Beautifully restored, it once belonged to the painter Vincent Roux and memories of his life live on, thanks to your gracious and very helpful hostess. The Roux room is the nicest, all beams, terracotta tiles, fantastic ochre/green bathroom down the hall and delicious garden view. The house has a wonderful old-fashioned patina and the gardens are perfectly kept. *Minimum stay: 2 nights.*

Rooms	3 doubles: €104-€140. 1 suite for 2: €131-€154. 1 studio for 2 with kitchenette: €150-€200.
Meals	Hosted dinner with wine & apéritif, €40-€42 (Thurs-Sat). Restaurant 3km.
Closed	Mid-December to end of March.

Rooms	1 double; 1 double with separate bathroom: €95-€115.
Meals	Summer kitchen. Restaurants in village.
Closed	3 weeks in August.

Tel   +33 (0)4 98 05 10 20
Email   info@provence4u.com
Web   www.provence4u.com

Martina & Claude Fussler
Une Campagne en Provence,
Domaine le Peyrourier,
83149 Bras, Var

Tel   +33 (0)4 42 53 05 32
Email   stanpeynier@gmail.com
Web   www.massainteanne.com

Jacqueline Lambert
Mas Sainte Anne,
3 rue d'Auriol, 13790 Peynier,
Bouches-du-Rhône

ENTRY 590   MAP 16

ENTRY 591   MAP 16

Les Arnauds

Come for a lovely old laid-back stone house, with pretty views of fields and hills. Here lives Sheila, with cats and ducks! You can share the family's living space or retreat to the guest sitting room, but summer evenings are usually spent outside, drinking in the scents and peace. Breakfasts with delicious fig, cherry and apricot jams set you up for the festivals and flower markets of Aix (6km). Return to comfortable beds on carpeted floors and ceiling fans to keep you cool. Time it right (from May to October) and you can join in with the lavender and olive harvests: great fun. *Minimum stay: 2 nights.*

Le petit Figuier

In a Provençal village known for its international piano festival is a grand eighteenth-century house with two elegant rooms. Bubbly Lis welcomes you into a chequerboard-tiled hall where musical guests can try out the old family piano. Both rooms are on the second floor: the Rose room, a cosy twin room, has iron beds and garden views; the Tamara room, a chic country-style double, has a sunny balcony and a smart en-suite. Take breakfast on the terrace in the tranquil garden shaded with fig and olive trees. Take a dip in the pool, relax in the garden or hop in the car to find beautiful villages and the Silvacane Abbey. In the evening, stroll to good restaurants nearby. *Minimum stay: 2 nights.*

Rooms	2 doubles: €80-€120. 1 suite for 2: €115-€125.	**Rooms**	1 double, 1 twin: €110-€125. Extra bed/sofabed €35 p.p. per night.
Meals	Restaurant 3km.	**Meals**	Restaurants 2-5 minute walk.
Closed	Rarely.	**Closed**	Rarely.

Tel	+33 (0)4 42 20 17 96	**Mobile**	+33 (0)7 82 20 19 38
Email	shspencer@gmail.com	**Email**	lis.steeden@hotmail.com
Web	www.lesarnauds.com	**Web**	www.lepetitfiguier.com

Sheila Spencer
Les Arnauds,
1902 chemin du Pont Rout,
13090 Aix en Provence, Bouches-du-Rhône

Lis & Graham Steeden
Le petit Figuier,
23 rue du Poilu, 13640 La Roque d'Anthéron,
Bouches-du-Rhône

Mas de la Rabassière

Amazing views to the coast, fanfares of lilies at the door, Haydn inside and 'mine host' smiling in his 'Cordon Bleu' chef's apron. Vintage wines and a sculpted dancer grace the terrace table. Cookery classes with house olive oil and easy airport pick-up are all part of the elegant hospitality, aided by Thévi, Michael's serene assistant from Singapore. Big bedrooms and a drawing room with a roaring fire are comfortable in English country-house style: generous beds, erudite bookshelves, a tuned piano, Provençal antiques... and tennis, croquet, a pool. A little fading around some edges but stacks of character.

Le Mas Saint Florent

Lounge by the pool as classical music plays; sip wine under the plane trees. This 18th-century house of magnificent proportions, surrounded by green gardens and grounds, is a short drive from Arles. Interiors in reassuringly traditional style are personalised by objets from the owners' travels. Breakfast is a sumptuous affair at pretty tables; dinner comes with local wines. There are four drawing rooms where log fires smoulder, and a smoking room with a grand piano. Gilbert and Olivier want their guests to feel at home. Pop into Arles for shops, restaurants, museums... and the amphitheatre, a stunning venue for bull-running, bullfighting and concerts. Arles is also the gateway to the Camargue, whose marshy wind-blasted delta is home to bulls, flamingoes and wild horses. Set off on a safari.

Rooms	2 doubles: €95-€165.
Meals	Dinner with wine, €55. Vegetarian or vegan meals available on request.
Closed	Rarely.

Rooms	3 doubles: €195-€255. 1 suite for 4: €255-€355. 2 family rooms for 3: €255. Singles €145-€240. Extra bed/sofabed €10 p.p. per night.
Meals	Breakfast €16.50. Dinner €36. Wine €18-€38.
Closed	Never.

Tel	+33 (0)4 90 50 70 40
Email	michaelfrost@rabassiere.com
Web	www.rabassiere.com

Michael Frost
Mas de la Rabassière,
2137 chemin de la Rabassière,
13250 Saint Chamas, Bouches-du-Rhône

Tel	+33 (0)4 90 97 02 79
Email	massaintflorent@orange.fr
Web	www.le-mas-saint-florent.com

Gilbert Poirier
Le Mas Saint Florent,
Route de la Crau,
13280 Raphèle lès Arles, Bouches-du-Rhône

ENTRY 594 MAP 16

ENTRY 595 MAP 16

Le Mas Montredon

As a mountain and travel guide, Hervé is the ultimate host regaling you with travel stories or his guitar and songs. Isabelle, wonderfully warm and friendly too, adds her art, interior design and cooking talents. Their 15th-century Provençal mas incorporates all their passions and talents, especially 'travel'. Visiting the bedrooms is like taking a world tour from Bolivia and Peru to Vietnam and the Himalayas. Buddhas beneath giant old beams, handsome tribesmen by a superb fireplace, Isabelle's art, Hervé's travel photos... Discover atmospheric Camargue, its wild white horses, black bulls, myriad birds and salt pans; hike and climb with Hervé; borrow bikes, and don't miss Roman Arles. Return to plunge in the little pool, dine on Isabelle's delicious cooking and retire to a glorious big bedroom.

Rooms	4 doubles: €100-€150.
	1 family room for 4: €100-€140.
	Extra bed €30.
Meals	Dinner €29; child €9-€15,
	by arrangement.
	Restaurants 5-minute drive.
Closed	Never.

Tel	+33 (0)4 90 52 07 50
Email	lemasmontredon@gmail.com
Web	www.lemasmontredon.com

Hervé Pichoux & Isabelle Montégudet
Le Mas Montredon,
Chemin de Bouchaud à Gageron,
13200 Arles, Bouches-du-Rhône

ENTRY 596 MAP 16

Galerie Huit Arles

In the ancient heart of Arles, a fascinating 17th-century mansion. Warm vibrant Julia is curator of aesthetics, cultured conversation and a gallery that combines art with hospitality. Flagstones, fireplaces and original panelling abound, homemade jams at breakfast accompany a stylish tea selection and occasional dinners are paired with wine from friends' vineyards. And staircases wind past Chinese scrolls to your suite: exquisite tommette tiles, dreamy 'ciel de lit,' restored frescoes, marble touches and a small mosaic shower room with a gilded mirror. Explore Arles, a town ripe for discovery, enjoy the Camargue wilds! *Minimum stay: 2 nights.*

Rooms	1 suite for 2: €95-€130.
	Extra bed €30.
Meals	Occasional dinner with wine, €35.
	Restaurants nearby.
Closed	Rarely.

Mobile	+33 (0)6 82 04 39 60
Email	contact@galeriehuit.com
Web	www.galeriehuit.com

Julia de Bierre
Galerie Huit Arles,
8 rue de la Calade,
13200 Arles, Bouches-du-Rhône

ENTRY 597 MAP 16

Mas de la Croix d'Arles

La Ressence

St Rémy is Provence on a plate: the ancient streets, artists, restaurants, the colourful weekly market, lush valleys and clear light which inspired Van Gogh. A short walk down the canal, a properly Provençal farmhouse distils this peace in a bubble of olives, vines and fruit trees. Tucked away in a pale stone bungalow are two light-filled B&B rooms, whose slate tiles, painted beams and fiery red splashes give a chic twist to Provençal style. You share a plunge pool with gîte guests, and breakfast on the terrace with lovely Jordane, who'll spill the area's best-kept secrets from hilltop Les Baux to the ochre-tinged Lubéron.

Come for the wild setting, deep in a spectacular gorge – wooded slopes climb on either side and you can walk or cycle miles from the door. Rooms are in an old house attached to the owners' mill, all beautifully restored with double glazing and super showers. Eat plentiful breakfasts of fresh local produce, served at a large table inside or small tables in the garden in summer, with timings to suit you. Tasty suppers and simple lunch platters on request too, and hospitable Françoise leaves juice, coffee and cake in the guest kitchen for you to help yourselves. You're on one of the main routes through the Lubéron, so exploring is easy – head to the hills, stroll the beautiful villages of Bonnieux and Lourmarin, bring home market food for picnics in the garden.

Rooms	1 double, 1 twin: €75-€90.
Meals	Restaurants within 1km
Closed	Rarely.

Rooms	2 doubles, 2 twin/doubles: €150-€170. Singles €130-€150.
Meals	Dinner €20; available by arrangement. Restaurants 5km.
Closed	Rarely.

Tel	+33 (0)4 90 90 04 82
Email	masdelacroixdarles@sfr.fr
Web	www.masdelacroixdarles.com

Jordane Marsot
Mas de la Croix d'Arles,
Chemin des Servières, 13210 St Rémy de Provence, Bouches-du-Rhône

Tel	+33 (0)4 90 04 54 27
Email	welcome@laressence.fr
Web	www.laressence.fr

Thierry & Françoise Lecourt
La Ressence,
Route de Lourmarin – RD 943,
84480 Bonnieux, Vaucluse

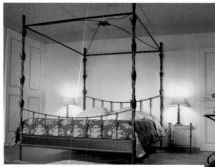

La Couleur des Vignes

There's a 5m-long table for breakfast, a sand pitch for boules, a 20m infinity pool for swims, beds brimful of lavender, and unsurpassable views. Marc and Berenice, warm, welcoming and well-travelled, took early retirement to follow a dream: a house in the sun in Provence. Built on a hillside, it has thick walls, ancient tiles, restored doors, masses of light. The entrance and bedrooms are on the first floor and the living areas (subtle lights, low sofas) are below, opening to delicious lawns and pergola. Imagine limestone floors, pure white bathrooms, neutral colours with accents of rust-red, and galleried suites for families. *Parking on-site.*

Sous L'Olivier

Old stonework rules the scene, big arched openings have become dining-room windows, a stone hearth burns immense logs in winter, and all is set round a pretty courtyard. Charming young bon viveur Julien cooks for you: breakfasts are sumptuous affairs and convivial dinners are worth a serious detour – in summer perhaps a generous BBQ. Gentle Carole is behind the very fresh, Frenchly decorated bedrooms. Agricultural land is all around, you are close to the Lubéron mountains, the big, child-friendly, saltwater pool is arched with canvas shading and surrounded by giant pots and plants. Lovely people, fabulous food. *Minimum stay: 2 nights. Pets by arrangement.*

Rooms	3 twin/doubles: €100-€150. 2 family rooms for 2: €120-€150. Extra bed €30; under 13s only.
Meals	Restaurants 6km.
Closed	16 December to mid-March.

Rooms	3 doubles: €100-€145. 2 suites for 4: €100-€145. Extra beds available.
Meals	Dinner with wine, €34.
Closed	31 October – 1 April.

Tel	+33 (0)6 77 85 97 92
Email	lacouleurdesvignes@gmail.com
Web	www.lacouleurdesvignes.com

Marc & Bérénice van der Elst
La Couleur des Vignes,
84480 Bonnieux,
Vaucluse

Tel	+33 (0)4 90 20 33 90
Email	souslolivier@orange.fr
Web	www.chambresdhotesprovence.com

Carole, Julien, Hugo & Clovis Gouin
Sous L'Olivier,
997BD 900, 84800 Lagnes,
Vaucluse

Maison Noel

Imagine a tiny Provençal village with a sun-dappled café-bar, an excellent auberge, a ruined castle, and a square off which lies Maison Noel. Enchanting, historic, and partially shaded by an old lime tree, it is the home of a charming and well-travelled hostess. The heart of the house is downstairs (open fireplace, country kitchen), the décor is stylish and soothing, and you can spill into a heavenly garden for supper (borrow the barbecue!). A perfect springboard for Provence, with a capacious bed to come home to and your own secluded patio. Artists and romantics will not want to stir. *Minimum stay: 2 nights in high season. Children over 8 welcome. Pets by arrangement.*

Le Domaine Saint Jean

With lovely Lubéron views over vineyards and distant hills, this sturdy farm centres on a courtyard and its quenching old trough and pump. Thea and Eric came south for warmth and their Provençal project celebrates their care and flair. Thea cooks up a local feast once a week and lays on fine outdoor breakfasts too. Antique dealer Eric's finds add intrigue to calm, clean-lined rooms: white linen and beams, bursts of vibrant fabrics, good new bathrooms. There's a shared pool to plunge in and lounge by, a bar/games/sitting room to retreat to, handy access to kitchens and such a rich area to visit; visual and cultural treats all around. *Smoking permitted in gardens.*

Rooms	1 double: €95-€130. Singles €75-€110.
Meals	Restaurant 2-minute walk.
Closed	1 November – 31 March.

Rooms	1 double, 1 twin/double: €75-€140. 1 family room for 3, 1 family room for 4: €110-€200.
Meals	Dinner, 3 courses with wine, €30; once a week. Tapas with wine, €15. Restaurants 2km.
Closed	1 November – 5 April.

Mobile	+33 (0)6 72 45 36 03
Email	trishmichie@gmail.com
Web	www.come2provence.com

Trish Michie
Maison Noel,
12 place du Bataillet,
84800 Lagnes, Vaucluse

Tel	+33 (0)4 32 50 10 77
Email	thea@ledomainesaintjean.com
Web	www.ledomainesaintjean.com

Thea Hemery
Le Domaine Saint Jean,
Saint Jean,
84490 Saint-Saturnin-lès-Apt, Vaucluse

ENTRY 602 MAP 16

ENTRY 603 MAP 16

Villa Vagabonde

The whole modern, minimalist place, grey and white inside and out, breathes peace and comfort. Relax into Veerle and Wim's dream house. They came from corporate Belgium for a new life, converted an old Provençal farmhouse in the Lubéron National Park to sleek purity and opened three fine, light rooms to guests. All is brand new, the stone-walled breakfast terrace, patios and pool are as quiet and delightful as the interior. Under your hosts' welcoming care come and enjoy a thoroughly grownup B&B. Twenty minutes' walk from Gordes and a hop from Aix, Avignon and Arles, Vagabonde is made for lovers of modern style and old Provence. *Minimum stay: 3 nights in high season. Over 16s welcome. Parking on-site.*

La Prévôté

You're on an island, tucked down a network of wiggly streets. Drop your luggage (park nearby), then walk through the ancient stone arch and into a courtyard with convivial tables and shady canopy. Inside, the bar has funky chairs and – quite a talking point – a tributary of the Sorgue running underneath. The hub of this bustling place though is its fabulous 'Maître Restaurateur' restaurant and charming owners Severine and Jean-Marie: locals flock here for their food. Up stone stairs to bedrooms on the first and second floors: colourful and airy, with brocante finds. Browse antique shops in town, and head off to Avignon or Orange.

Rooms	3 twin/doubles: €135-€165.
Meals	Restaurants 20-minutes walk.
Closed	1 November – 15 March.

Rooms	4 twin/doubles: €145-€195.
	1 suite for 2: €200-€225.
	Extra bed available.
Meals	Dinner, 3 courses, €41.
Closed	Rarely.

Mobile	+33 (0)6 42 99 80 32
Email	info@villavagabonde.com
Web	www.villavagabonde.com

Wim & Veerle
Villa Vagabonde,
Chemin des Escortiels,
84220 Gordes, Vaucluse

Tel	+33 (0)4 90 38 57 29
Email	contact@la-prevote.fr
Web	www.la-prevote.fr

Severine Alloin
La Prévôté,
4 rue Jean Jacques Rousseau,
84800 L'Isle sur la Sorgue, Vaucluse

ENTRY 604 MAP 16

ENTRY 605 MAP 16

L'Observance

You couldn't be better placed for ambling round historic Avignon than at this B&B within the city's old walls. The latest incarnation of a building that has in its lifetime been part of a monastery, a barracks and a factory, there are now five light, spacious en suite rooms in the main house and an annexe converted into a cosy apartment for four. Dutch hosts welcome you with a glass of wine and you start the day in the newly-glazed breakfast room with pastries, ham, cheese and eggs. Though the Palais des Papes and Pont D'Avignon are only a short stroll, it's blissfully calm. Cool off in the sparkling pool after a busy day sightseeing. *Minimum stay: 3 nights in high season.*

Aux Augustins

In the centre of Avignon, behind an unassuming shop front, a 14th-century convent lovingly renovated by owners Sabine and Patrick. No expense has been spared, from French linen to locally made wrought iron bedheads and sparkling new shower rooms. Exposed stone walls and archways lend character and all rooms have views into the peaceful inner courtyard, the perfect spot for a breakfast of croissants, fruit and hot chocolate. Park nearby for a price or further out for less, or leave the car at home: it's just five minutes' walk to shops and restaurants. Go boating on the Rhône, sample the local wines, walk the mountains. *Minimum stay: 2 nights; 7 nights during July festival.*

Rooms	4 doubles, 1 twin/double: €95-€175. 1 apartment for 4: €160-€220. Extra bed/sofabed €20 p.p. per night.		**Rooms**	2 doubles: €105-€130. 1 suite for 2: €135-€160. 2 studios for 2: €115-€145.
Meals	Restaurants 5-minute walk.		**Meals**	Restaurants 5-minute walk.
Closed	Rarely.		**Closed**	Never.

Tel	+33 (0)4 13 66 05 85		**Tel**	+33 (0)4 90 81 00 42
Email	info@lobservance.com		**Email**	contact@autourdupetitparadis.com
Web	www.lobservance.com		**Web**	www.autourdupetitparadis.com/fr

Jacqueline & Jeroen Tutein Nolthenius
L'Observance,
Rue de l'Observance,
84000 Avignon, Vaucluse

Sabine & Patrick Eouagnignon
Aux Augustins,
16 rue Carreterie,
84000 Avignon, Vaucluse

ENTRY 606   MAP 16   ENTRY 607   MAP 16

Château La Roque

Look an eagle in the eye, up here on the edge of the Lubéron; the glorious views still stretch over the tranquil valley. Kind and interesting, Jean can tell you about the golden ratio used to build the castle: bedrooms are huge and comfortable with carefully-chosen antiques, lovely bedding and designer fabrics. One has a deep-coral bed under vaulted ceilings and genuine 13th-century wardrobe doors. Each handsome, roomy bathroom is done with the best fittings. After visiting a pretty Provençal town or famous vineyard (Gigondas, Châteauneuf...), return to a delicious dinner on the vine-dappled terrace or in the garden.

La Nesquière

The gardens alone are worth the detour: trees and greenery galore, riots of roses, all flourishing in a huge many-terraced park by a river. The 18th-century farmhouse harbours a fine collection of antiques – one of Isabelle's passions – tastefully set off by lush indoor greenery and lovely old carpets on ancient tile floors. Softly old-elegant rooms have hand-embroidered fabrics and genuine old linens, including Provençal quilts – truly exquisite – with splashes of red, orange and beige against white backgrounds. Themed weekends, too (cookery, wine, embroidery), and a warm, gracious welcome from Isabelle and her family.

Rooms	2 doubles: €135-€220. 3 suites for 3: €240-€320. Extra bed/sofabed €35 p.p. per night.
Meals	Breakfast €20. Dinner, 4 courses, €46 Thurs-Sat; gourmet platter Tues & Weds; book ahead. Wine €22-€200.
Closed	Late November to early March. Open New Year.

Rooms	5 twin/doubles: €115-€170.
Meals	Platter available on request.
Closed	Rarely.

Tel	+33 (0)4 90 61 68 77
Email	chateaularoque@wanadoo.fr
Web	www.chateaularoque.com

Chantal & Jean Tomasino
Château La Roque,
263 chemin du Château,
84210 La Roque sur Pernes, Vaucluse

Tel	+33 (0)4 90 62 00 16
Email	lanesquiere@wanadoo.fr
Web	www.lanesquiere.com

Isabelle de Maintenant
La Nesquière,
5419 route d'Althen,
84210 Pernes les Fontaines, Vaucluse

ENTRY 608 MAP 16

ENTRY 609 MAP 16

Le Mas de la Pierre du Coq

What's especially nice about this 17th-century farmhouse is that it hasn't been over-prettified. Instead, it has the friendly, informal elegance of a house that's lived in and loved; grey-painted beams, soft stone walls, seductive bathrooms. The Lorenzes loved it the moment they saw it; it reminded gentle Stéphan of the house he grew up in. Bustling Martine starts your day with a terrific breakfast, Stéphan shows you the walks from the door. The gardens, sweet with roses, oleanders and lavender, are shaded by ancient trees and the pool and views are glorious. Stay for as long as you can; book excellent dinners in advance.

Château Eydoux

Down a long drive at the end of a country lane lies this handsome building. The home of friendly Guido and Ann, their young son and three dogs, it's peacefully set in 17 acres of gardens and woodland, and has superb views of Mont Ventoux. Oozing style and elegance, from shabby chic to pop art, expect parquet floors, a stone fireplace, light spacious bedrooms, a jacuzzi bath and smart bathrooms. Lavish breakfasts are served in the garden; fresh produce abounds. Wander the grounds, take a dip in the pool, hike the mountains, visit Orange and Avignon, or sample the local wines. It's just a ten-minute drive to shops and restaurants. *Minimum stay: 2 nights; 7 July/August (Fri-Fri). Parking on-site.*

Rooms	1 double, 2 twins: €135-€150. 1 suite for 4: €230.	**Rooms**	2 doubles: €115-€140. 1 family room for 4: €200-€225. 2 triples: €175-€200.
Meals	Dinner with wine, €40.	**Meals**	Occasional dinner, 3 courses with wine, €35. Restaurants 4km.
Closed	Rarely.	**Closed**	Rarely.

Tel +33 (0)4 90 67 31 64
Email lorenz.stephane@wanadoo.fr
Web www.masdelapierreducoq.com

Stéphan & Martine Lorenz
Le Mas de la Pierre du Coq,
434 chemin de Sauzette,
84810 Aubignan, Vaucluse

Mobile +33 (0)7 87 08 53 18
Email demetsann26@gmail.com
Web www.chateau-eydoux.com

Ann de Mets
Château Eydoux,
673 avenue Général Eydoux,
84870 Loriol Du Comtat, Vaucluse

Château Juvenal

The château is lived in and loved every day, thanks to Anne-Marie and Bernard, who also produce an award-winning wine and delicious olive oil from their 600 trees. They nurture some superb specimen trees, too, out in the park. The traditional bedrooms with high ceilings and tall windows are all on the first floor and range from cosy to spacious; the sitting and dining rooms sport chandeliers and exquisite furniture. Grab your shopping basket and visit the local market, for the summer kitchen next to the pool. There are wine visits, a hammam and two lovely apartments for longer stays. *Minimum stay: 4 nights.*

Atelier du Renard Argenté

Delightfully wiggly lanes through the Forêt d'Uchaux lead you to the old 'mas' with a gorgeous garden with pool. You enter into the conservatory and dining area to be greeted by charming Gail and Christian – when he's at home he'll take you truffle hunting, or you can sign up to a cookery course. It's all very plush, with pastel colours, exposed stone walls, tinkling music and candlelight. Sleep peacefully on thick mattresses with clouds of goose down; breakfast on local yogurts, homemade cakes; proper lunches (or picnics) can be rustled up effortlessly, and dinner is sublime. A right royal pampering to be had here. *Pets by arrangement.*

Rooms	1 double, 2 twin/doubles: €120-€135. 1 suite for 3: €128-€144. 2 apartments for 6: €860-€1660. Singles €100-€115.
Meals	Summer kitchen. Hosted dinner with wine, €45, once a week.
Closed	9 November – 9 March.

Rooms	5 doubles: €120-€245.
Meals	Gourmet dinner €55.
Closed	Rarely.

Tel	+33 (0)4 90 62 31 76
Email	chateau.juvenal@gmail.com
Web	www.chateaujuvenal.com

Anne-Marie & Bernard Forestier
Château Juvenal,
120 chemin du Long Serre,
84330 Saint Hippolyte le Graveyron, Vaucluse

Mobile	+33 (0)6 09 39 33 14
Email	contact@atelier-renard-argente.com
Web	www.renarda.com

Gail Bodiguel
Atelier du Renard Argenté,
90 chemin des Chevres,
84550 Mornas, Vaucluse

ENTRY 612 MAP 16

ENTRY 613 MAP 16

L'Évêché

Narrow, cobbled streets lead to this fascinating and beautifully furnished house that was once part of the 17th-century Bishop's Palace. The Verdiers are charming, relaxed, cultured hosts – she a teacher, he an architect/builder. The white walls of the guest sitting room-library are lined with modern art and framed posters, and the cosy, quilted bedrooms, all whitewashed beams and terracotta floors, have a serene Provençal feel. Views fly over beautiful terracotta rooftops from the balconied suite, and handsome breakfasts are served on the terrace, complete with exceptional views to the Roman bridge. *Pets by arrangement.*

Château MontPlaisir

On the outskirts of little Valréas is a 17th-century château immersed in a sea of vines. New to winemaking, Benoit and Eugenie are passionate about wines and guests, and will give you a chance to taste their award-winning vintage. Delicious breakfast (homemade cakes, jams, Bulgarian yogurt) is brought to a room with small tables and a stone fireplace with drawn angels. Bedrooms reveal the best of everything: round sinks, antique sofas, aged tommette floors; it is an exquisite restoration. Set off for the gourmet markets of Nyons and Vaison-la-Romaine, explore vineyards on château bikes, return to an octagonal pool set in a vast decked terrace. *EV charge point available.*

Rooms	3 twin/doubles: €90-€100. 2 suites for 2: €130-€160.
Meals	Restaurants nearby.
Closed	Christmas & New Year.

Rooms	2 doubles: €120-€150. 1 family room for 3: €120-€150.
Meals	Restaurants 1.5km.
Closed	Rarely.

Mobile	+33 (0)6 03 03 21 42/ (0)6 48 24 08 29
Email	eveche@aol.com
Web	www.eveche.com

Aude & Jean-Loup Verdier
L'Évêché,
14 rue de l'Evêché, Cité Médiévale,
84110 Vaison la Romaine, Vaucluse

Tel	+33 (0)6 73 65 55 38
Email	benoit@chateaumontplaisir.com
Web	www.chateaumontplaisir.com

Benoît Chaignon
Château MontPlaisir,
1 Chemin des Blagiers,
84600 Valréas, Vaucluse

ENTRY 614   MAP 16

ENTRY 615   MAP 16

Le Clos de Rohan

Cloaked in a remote valley sweet with lavender lies an 18th-century farmhouse with ingeniously restored barns – find lavender stalks in the plaster! Lovely generous rooms have classy bathrooms, iron beds, crisp linen, a patio and terrace each, and views over valley and hills fat with bees. The chic two-storey suite comes with a kitchenette, the other suite is more rustic, and there's a shared living room with a cosy wood-burner. In a courtyard garden heady with blooms breakfast on homemade honey, cherries, plums, and then daydream by the small pool. Provence at its bucolic best.

Le Jas du Bœuf

Arrive at this restored sheep barn (a jas) and immediately feel enveloped by calm. Jérôme (ex-Parisian) and Dana (he's Canadian) are delightful, their dachshunds equally as welcoming. Choose from rooms in the house or by the infinity pool, all with private entrances. Breakfast is original and varied: homemade yoghurt topped with fruit from the garden, sweet or savoury muffins beautifully presented, an elegant fried egg, always served with your choice of the best teas and coffees. There's a summer kitchen next to the pool for making light meals, or your hosts will direct you to good restaurants, the nearest only a five-minute drive away. Walk, hike or cycle the surrounding countryside, visit nearby hilltop villages or take a day trip to the coast; return to take a dip in the pool or relax in the garden with a book from the library.

Rooms	2 suites for 2: €120-€130. Extra bed/sofabed €20-€60 p.p. per night.	**Rooms**	4 doubles: €95-€140. Extra bed/sofabed €30 p.p. per night. Dogs €10 per day.
Meals	Dinner with wine, €30. Guest kitchen.	**Meals**	Summer kitchen. Restaurants 3-8km, please ask for recommendations.
Closed	Rarely.	**Closed**	Rarely.

Tel	+33 (0)4 92 74 49 42
Email	francoise04.cavallo@gmail.com
Web	www.le-clos-de-rohan.eu

Françoise Cavallo
Le Clos de Rohan,
04150 Simiane la Rotonde,
Alpes-de-Haute-Provence

Tel	+33 (0)4 92 79 01 05
Email	lejasduboeuf@orange.fr
Web	www.lejasduboeuf.fr

Jérôme Mantel & Dana Silk
Le Jas du Bœuf,
Lieu-dit Parrot, 04230 Cruis,
Alpes-de-Haute-Provence

ENTRY 616 MAP 16   ENTRY 617 MAP 16

La Maison du Guil

The 16th-century stone and timber priory, the oldest house in this remote narrow hamlet, has the same glorious views as ever, out over the rooftops to the surrounding peaks. Inside is all stone and timber, too, beautifully architect-renovated and furnished with a cleancut imaginative eye. The big living room has a stunning arched stone ceiling, the perfect foil for high-modern scarlet chairs and table cloths. Delighted with their Alpine venture, the charming new young owners will offer you a big traditional bedroom or a funkier cave-like room with stone nooks for lights and a sunken shower. Superb. *Minimum stay: 3 nights in high season.*

Chalet Le Pot de Miel

Rebecca and Michel run a charming B&B in the family resort of Montgenèvre, just 1km from Italy. Homemade breads, honey from their bees and croissants from the bakery are eaten round a communal table which has stunning mountain views. Dinner is served here too – regional French dishes with a twist. You can ski all day on the pistes (starting from the garden), nip over to Italy, visit the weekday market, cycle in summer. Return to an honesty bar, a very welcoming living room with a beautiful fireplace, TV and billiards in a separate room, indoor and outdoor hot tubs for weary limbs, very comfortable bedrooms with balconies. *Parking available.*

Rooms	2 doubles: €120-€130. 2 family rooms for 3: €120-€130. Child €45.
Meals	Dinner with apéritif & coffee, €36. Wine from €5. Restaurant 3km.
Closed	Rarely.

Rooms	4 doubles: €195-€225. 1 family room for 4: €235-€275. Singles €110-€195. Dinner, B&B €20-€37 p.p. Extra bed/sofabed €35 p.p. per night.
Meals	Dinner with wine, €37; children €20. Restaurants 5-minute walk.
Closed	Rarely.

Tel	+33 (0)4 92 50 16 20
Email	info@lamaisonduguil.com
Web	www.lamaisonduguil.com

Tom Van De Velde
La Maison du Guil,
Chemin de la Font, 05600 Eygliers,
Hautes-Alpes

Tel	+33 (0)4 92 21 93 55
Email	lepotdemiel@hotmail.fr
Web	www.lepotdemiel.com

Rebecca & Michel Coulliais
Chalet Le Pot de Miel,
Hameau de l'Obelisque,
05100 Montgenèvre, Hautes-Alpes

ENTRY 618 MAP 12

ENTRY 619 MAP 12

Corsica

Chambres d'Hôtes à Vallecalle, page 433

Chambres d'Hôtes à Vallecalle

Welcome to the master house in Vallecalle, on the village edge, an eagle's nest
with exquisite valley views. Here live Paul Henri and Myriam, warm, witty, welcoming,
living the dream, raising a family, happy to advise you on their beloved adopted land –
the food, the culture – or leave you in peace to explore their home, beautiful in its
simplicity. Bedrooms, two with 18th-century floorboards, are spacious and gracious.
The terraced gardens have oranges, olives, a hammock, corners for shade and sun, and,
below, a river to bathe in. Myriam's dishes, always delicious, can be delicate, intriguing or
hearty. Stay in!

Rooms	1 double: €66.1 suite for 5: €71-€135. 1 family room for 4: €71-€100.
Meals	Dinner with wine, €25. Restaurant 7km.
Closed	Rarely.

Tel	+33 (0)4 20 20 04 19
Email	phgaucher@sfr.fr
Web	www.chambresencorse.com

Myriam & Paul Henri Gaucher
Chambres d'Hôtes à Vallecalle,
Village de Vallecalle, 20232 Vallecalle,
Haute-Corse

ENTRY 620   MAP 16

Casa Blanca,
page 290

Index by property name

Index by property name

Index by property name

Index by property name

Château de la Resle, page 84

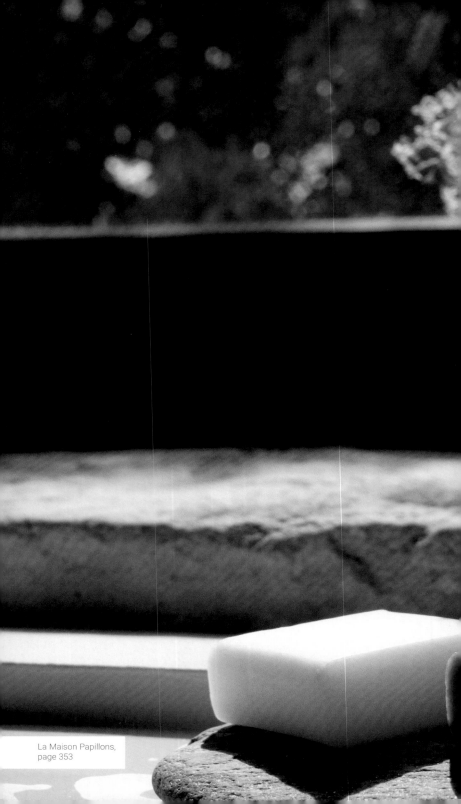

La Maison Papillons,
page 353

A beautiful
collection

Index by town

Index by town

Index by town